CAN NEWY.

YN RHODDI HANES AL
Y DDAMWAIN DRUENUS
A GYMERODD LE
NGWAITH MR. POWELL,
SEF
Pwll y Dyffryn, gerllaw Aberdar,
Ar ddydd Llun, Mai 10fed, 1852,

Pryd y taniodd y Damp, fel y lladdwyd tri a thri-
ugain o honynt yn feirwon yn y fan, bu farw tri eraill yr un dydd, a dau eraill trannoeth.

Enwau ac oedran y rhai a laddwyd:—

Edward Davis. 34 oed, David Davis, 14, Richard
Smith, 38, Richard Smith, 17, Richard Jonathan, 43,
David Rees, 52, Ebenezer Morris, 32. David Morris,
10, John Morris, 11, James Jones, 37, William
Jones, 12, Daniel Matthews, 18, Richard Richards,
55. Thos. Jenkin Rees, 29, Owen Jenkins, 27,
William Lewis. 23, Rees Hopkins, 50, John Hopkins,
15, William Marks, 15, Charles Marks, 11, Jenkin
Rosser. 22, John Thomas, 12, Jenkin Aubrey, 28,
David Lewis, 32, Thomos Williams. 28, John Rees,
36, William Ashton, 22, David Jenkins, 36, Edmund
Phillips 16, Charles Davis. 46, Evan Evans, 47,
Evan Evans. 21, Richard Evans, 11, Samuel Rees,
37, Charles White, 35, Thomas Pritchard, 36, William
Richards, 16, John Richards, 12, Thomas Rees, 23,
William Andrews, 29, James Griffiths, 20, Thomas
Rees, 13, John Jenkins. 12, Thomas Evans, 41,
Charles Thomas, 46, Evan Thomas, 19, David Thomas,
17, Charles Thomas, 11, Henry Davis, 26, Rosser
Thomas, 32, Rowland Rowlands, 43, David Jones,
38, Lewis Jones, 42, William Jones. 16, John Jones,
14, Owen Evans, 56, Thomas Morgan, 23, William
Samuel, 16, John Griffiths, 21, Daniel Deer, 26, David
John, 11, Levi Harris, 27, Thomas Phillips, 30,
David James, 36,

Cynon

Coal

"Then"

History of a mining valley

This painting in the National Museum of Wales is inscribed on the back "Elan Cottages, Aberdare" and is by W. H. Williams (1773-1829). It is not known where the cottages were situated. Williams was of Devonshire origin but settled in Edinburgh when young. He published engravings of Highland views and afterwards travelled much in Greece resulting in more publishing related to his travels and the acquisition of the nick-name "Grecian Williams".

NMGW

Cynon Coal

History of a Mining Valley

"Now"

Written and published by Cynon Valley History Society
2001

This book is dedicated to the miners of the
Cynon Valley, past and present

Contents

© Cynon Valley History Society, 2001

ISBN 0 95310 760 4

Printed in 11pt Baskerville MT by Gomer Press, Llandysul, Ceredigion SA44 4QL

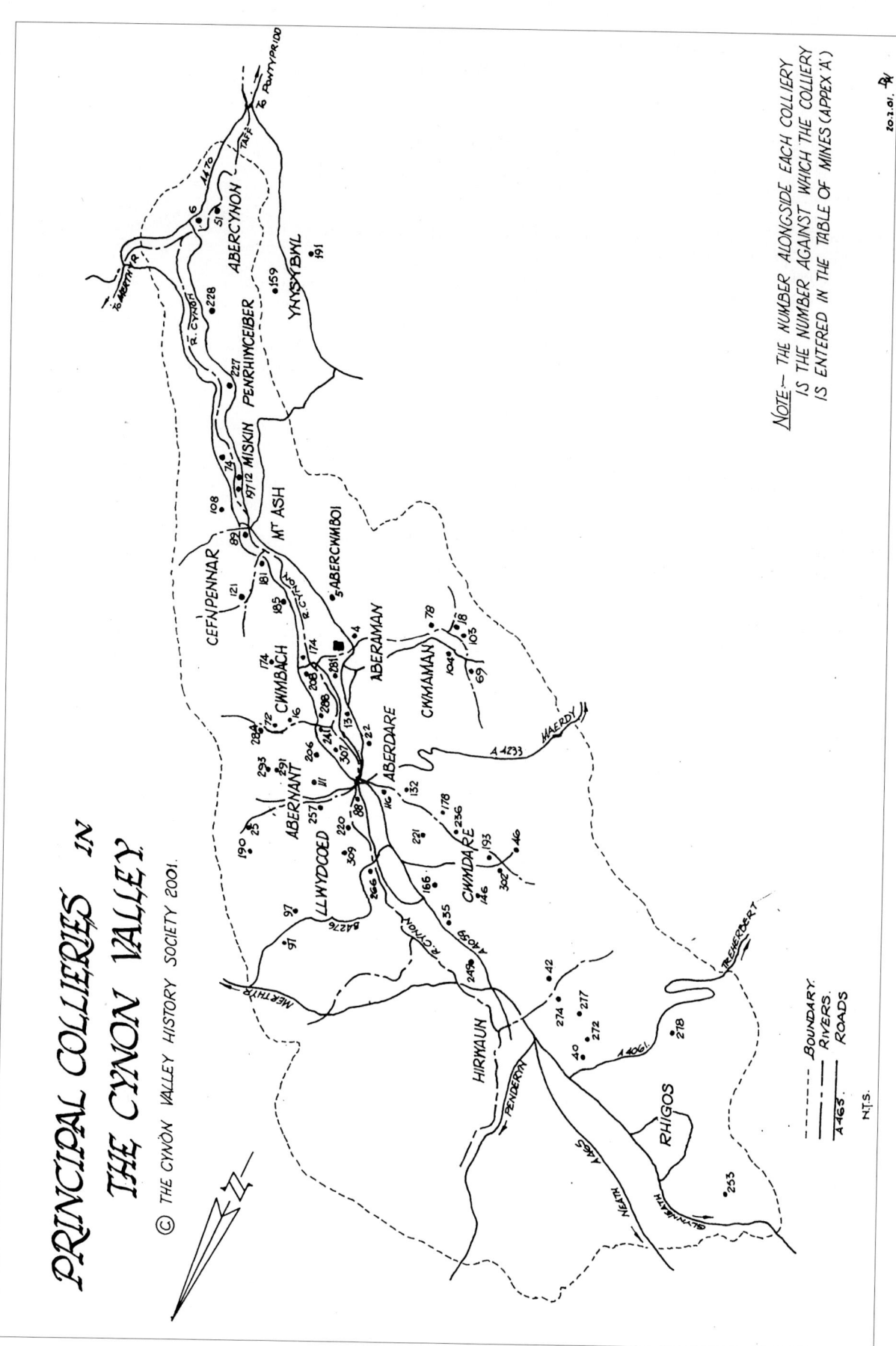

PRINCIPAL COLLIERIES IN THE CYNON VALLEY

© THE CYNON VALLEY HISTORY SOCIETY 2001.

NOTE:— THE NUMBER ALONGSIDE EACH COLLIERY IS THE NUMBER AGAINST WHICH THE COLLIERY IS ENTERED IN THE TABLE OF MINES (APPEX 'A')

----- BOUNDARY.
——— RIVERS.
A465 ROADS
N.T.S.

List of plates

Abbreviations: Colly = Colliery; OCS = Opencast Coal Site

Foreword

The importance of coal mining to the economy of the Cynon Valley and the way in which it created a community of many thousands with its own mythologies, traditions and customs is the subject of this book. All communities are special in their own way to the people that live in them, and it is not the purpose of this book to make a case that the Cynon Valley is more special than any other community, whether it be elsewhere in the coalfield or indeed anywhere else. It is our home, we have an affection for it and it is interesting. That is enough. Affected by those mysterious ties that bind us to the days of long ago, the writers of this book have been driven by a kind of duty to arrange where possible and set down not only those parts of our history which are accessible in books and archives but those records which exist in the minds of men and, of course, women. It was a difficult task, for the nineteenth century historians were not of great assistance to us, giving way on the one side to an urge to romanticise the past and on the other side a lofty disregard for dates which in their time would be easily ascertainable, but which are in most cases now beyond recovery.

Again, the question of mining records is a difficult problem. It seems that many small mines kept no records in the early days. Of those which did, some were destroyed and some are inaccessible. Of some of the smaller undertakings virtually nothing is known. In the case of the larger undertakings the Final Report of the South Wales Coalfield History Project has some sad comments to make. Speaking of the loss or destruction of incalculably valuable material over the years, partly due to the attitude of the Trade Union movement towards the preservation of their own records, it says: 'it cannot be doubted that there was . . . an ambivalent and apathetic attitude towards the the question of preservation at central, district and local level of many of [the records of] the organisations of the coalfield'. Regarding the attitude of the coalmasters the Report has this to say: 'The question of the existence of records of colliery companies and individual collieries seemed to be enshrouded in a cloak of mystery . . . the records of the South Wales and Monmouthshire Coalowners Association had been deposited, after nationalisation of the industry, at the National Library of Wales although not without, it appears, being extensively gutted first by the coalowners'. But this does not mean that we should not put on record what is known, nor does it mean that we should wait until more information (if any) comes to light, for we shall never know all we need to know, and what is difficult to write today will be more difficult in years to come, when memories will no longer be available to us, and when most remains of the industry will have disappeared.

The Society therefore, while regretting that so much was not put on record in years gone by, feels that this deserved tribute to our ancestors should be undertaken now rather than in years to come. It has a successful record of publishing local history, having produced some fourteen publications relating to local history in the twenty nine years of its existence, including two volumes of 'Pictures from the Past' and eight volumes of 'Old Aberdare'. Among its members are persons with a deep interest in and knowledge of mining history and geology. However the book will not solely be a technical history but will cover the way of life of the miners' families in days now past, and members with knowledge in this field will also contribute to the writing of this book, which will be illustrated with a photograph of every colliery of significant size (where such photograph survives), as well as photographs relating to the everyday life of the mining community. In some cases, due to the shortage of suitable photographs, it has been necessary to use photographs which have been used previously in books. Photographs not otherwise attributed are used by kind permission of Rhondda Cynon Taff Libraries.

The reader should note that the terms 'colliery' and 'mine' are virtually synonymous but the word 'pit' which usually means a shaft can sometimes mean a colliery. In this book, the term 'level' is used for all tunnels from the surface to a coal seam, except that where the name of a level etc includes another word such as 'drift', it remains unaltered. The imperial units of measurement have been retained when describing coal seams, etc. Apart from the authoritative list of all local mines which is found in appendix A, the book includes a list of sources for the information in appendix A, a glossary of mining terms which, it is hoped, will be interesting and useful, a bibliography and short biographies of prominent coalmasters.

The book has been written by members of a working group of the Cynon Valley History Society consisting of Elfed Bowen, Ken Collins, Huw Davies, Bryn Davies, Tom Evans, John Mear and Doug Williams. The co-ordinating editor was John Mear, who wishes to put on record the boundless patience of the Society's secretary, Eric Rose, when dealing with apparently endless requests for chapter drafts from the computer. The Society records with deep regret that three other members of the working group died during the duration of the project. Mel Godsall was an experienced mining engineer who made a valuable contribution to the list of mines which comprises Appendix A. Elwyn Evans's knowledge of local geology obtained in the course of his professional duties was always at the disposal of the working group. The sudden and unexpected death of the Society's much-liked Chairman, Norman Price, in February 2000 came as a great shock not only to our members but to his many other friends.

We hope that the book will satisfy a need for those who are interested in the history of this valley, and act as a spur to future generations to extend this knowledge.

Acknowledgements

The History Society is grateful to the Tower Colliery for their generous sponsorship and to the following persons and institutions who assisted in the making of this book:

Brian Davies, Harry Rogers, Walter Rees, Carwyn Powell, Gerwyn Jones, Tom A. Jones, Phill Jenkins (Celtic Energy), Colin Morris, Denzil Hamlin, Howell Rowlands (former farrier at Tower Colliery), Geraint Hodder (Ventilation Officer at Tower Colliery), Ken Davies (company secretary and director at Tower Colliery), Surveying staff at Tower Colliery, Martin Evans (former surveyor of mines), The late Will Jones (former master haulier at Tower Colliery), John Murray (publishers) Ltd and Michael Llewellyn, author of 'The sand in the glass'. We are also indebted to Roger Tiley of Ystradgynlais for letting us use some of their excellent Tower Colliery photographs.

Thanks are also due to the staff at Aberdare Central Library (especially Alan Prescott), also Mountain Ash Library, Cardiff Central Library, The Glamorgan Record Office, Anita Parry, Alan Vernon Jones, Ivor Morgan, The Rev. Roger L. Brown, Douglas Williams, Geoffrey Evans, Marian Morgan, Simon Blinkhorne, Brian Messer and Desmond Edwards (former Bevin boy).

CHAPTER ONE

The end of the eighteenth century witnessed the beginning of great changes in the Cynon Valley which included the transformation of the insignificant village of Aberdare into a busy industrial town.

The original settlement consisted of a cluster of dwellings on the banks of the Dare adjacent to the old parish church of St John the Baptist, about a quarter of a mile west of the confluence of that river and the Cynon. Certainly, by the end of the 18th century the houses were mainly aligned to the narrow road or rather track which ran through the valley. The village functioned as a centre providing the farms of the surrounding district with services such as the church, a cornmill, and probably other rural necessities such as an inn and a blacksmith.

By the beginning of the nineteenth century other discrete settlements were springing up around the ironworks at Hirwaun, Llwydcoed and Abernant, but the main development came with the growth of the coal industry from the middle of the century with the spread of housing down the valley following the sinking of new and deeper pits, and the expansion of the new colliery villages particularly in the Dare and Aman valleys towards the outward growth from the original core. The same period saw the development of the lower end of the Cynon Valley from Mountain Ash to Abercynon although the latter had already attained some importance as the terminus of the Aberdare canal.

The physical conditions and resources which made possible the industrial development of the Cynon Valley are to be found in its geology. In turn the latter can be appreciated fully only in the context of the geology of the South Wales Coalfield.

Essentially the coalfield is an elongated geological basin or syncline formed of Carboniferous rocks and extends some 90 miles from St. Brides Bay in the west to Pontypool in the east. The Carboniferous rocks consist of three main divisions, the oldest and lowest of the sequence being the Carboniferous Limestone Series followed by the Millstone Grit Series which are overlain by the Coal Measures. The Limestone and Millstone Grit rocks outcrop (that is, come to the surface) more or less continuously around the edge of the basin and therefore mark the limits of the coalfield.

The Coal Measures comprise the Upper, Middle and Lower Coal Measures. The Upper Measures contain a few workable coal seams particularly in the west but are largely composed of massive sandstones and grits. The Middle and Lower Coal Measures, consisting of mudstones, siltstones and a few subordinate sandstones include the thickest and most important coal seams in South Wales. Near the base is a fairly persistent sandstone, the Farewell Rock, so called because no workable coals were found below it

The coalfield is unique among the British coalfields in the wide variety of its coals, ranging from high quality anthracite through steam coal to friable highly volatile bituminous coal. The significance of these varieties as they affect the Cynon Valley will be dealt with later. Broadly speaking, anthracite occurs in the north-west and west, extending into Pembrokeshire; steam coal in the centre of the field particularly between the Neath and Taff rivers; and bituminous coal along its eastern and southern edges. This simple statement must be qualified because at any given locality the lower seams are more anthracitic, having a higher carbon content than those nearer the surface. Further, it should be stressed that nowhere is there a sharp division between the types; rather each grades imperceptibly into the other.

We will now look at that part of the coalfield lying east of the Neath Valley in more detail since further consideration of the whole is irrelevant to the development of the Cynon Valley. The broadly synclinal character of this section of the basin is modified by several features. In the first place it is asymmetrical in that the beds of the northern flank dip toward the centre at a shallow angle of between five and ten degrees, compared with dips on the southern limb of forty five degrees or more. The result is that in the former case the beds have a much wider outcrop. A second modification, albeit one which has little effect upon the Cynon Valley, is an upfold or anticline having an axis

Abergwawr Colliery aka Plough Pit or Powell's Pit. This was opened by Powell and Protheroe in 1849 and closed in 1875. It raised coal from the 2′9, 4′, 6′, 9′, No 2 yard, and 7′ seams.

trending approximately from Pontypridd to Maesteg. This has the effect of bringing nearer to the surface the productive seams of the Lower Coal Measures which, in places such as the Rhondda Valley in the centre of the basin, would otherwise lie at very great depths. In the Cynon Valley those seams reach their greatest depth at Abercynon. Thirdly is a series of normal, nearly vertical, faults running en echelon in a NNW-SSE direction. Those affecting the Cynon Valley will be dealt with in a little more detail later. Finally the Neath Valley follows the alignment of a major fault system—the Neath Disturbance. Although outside the Cynon Valley, related effects occur eastwards towards Rhigos and Hirwaun. The Neath Valley and Disturbance also mark the approximate boundary between true anthracite and the semi-anthracite and steam coals.

Topographically this part of the coalfield consists of a barren plateau formed of the tough Sandstones of the upper coal measures, scored by deeply incised river valleys having a dominant NNW – SSE direction. The plateau surface tilts southwards so that its summit level ranges between 600 and 450 metres (2000 – 1500 feet) in the north to about 240 metres (800 feet) on its southern edge.* Although the direction of the main rivers coincides with the alignment of the faults described above, there is no evidence of a causal connection except, of course, in the case of the Neath river. Neither does the direction of the rivers show any relationship to the nature of the underlying rocks. An explanation of the drainage pattern is outside the scope of the present study.

Let us now look at the Cynon Valley in detail. The most convenient way to define its extent is to regard it as being coterminous with the boundaries of the Cynon Valley Borough as it existed between 1974 and 1996, stretching from Rhigos to Abercynon, a distance of some 22 kms. (14 miles). With the exception of the north-western part around Rhigos and the anomaly at Ynysbwl where the Clydach drains directly into the Taff, the area so defined is drained by the Cynon and its tributaries. The Cynon of course is tributary to the Taff.

* All heights given in this chapter are above Ordnance datum (O D) i.e. the standard mean sea-level used by the Ordnance Survey.

It rises on the southern slopes of Cader Fawr about 5 kms. (3 miles) north of Penderyn and enters the coalfield just north of Hirwaun. From the latter place to Abercynon it has a relatively gentle average gradient of about 1/180, a factor which has facilitated the building of communications.

Although geology has not influenced the direction of the valley it has had a distinct bearing on the valley shape in cross profile. The northern part of the area from Rhigos to just north of Trecynon, lying in the Middle and Lower Coal Measures is open moorland lying between 180 and 220 metres (600 – 700 feet). It is bounded on the south by the Pennant Sandstone escarpment extending from Craig y Llyn 600 metres (1969 feet) OD to Mynydd Cefn y Gyngon. The northern limit is marked by a series of lower hills averaging 330 – 370 metres (1100 – 1200 feet) OD running from Moel Penderyn and Mynydd y Glog to the north western extremity of Mynydd Aberdâr.

From Trecynon south westwards to Mountain Ash the valley form becomes more apparent. On the south side the Pennant escarpment, maintaining its steep north-facing slopes, continues through Mynydd Bwllfa, Cefn Rhos Gwawr and Coedcae Aberaman. On the opposite side of the valley the capping of the Middle Coal Measures by Pennant Sandstones causes an increase in height southwards through Mynydd Aberdâr and Mynydd Merthyr. These Sandstones separated by subordinate mudstones form a series of well marked northward facing minor escarpments best seen in Twyn Gwersyllfa and Cefnpennar, reaching over 490 metres (1600 feet) OD in the latter. The summit profiles of these features is determined by the angle at which the strata dip towards the centre of the coalfield. The valley averages about 1.5 kms. (just under one mile) in width but the gentler slopes on the northern side give an impression of greater breadth. Here too the Cynon has formed a well-marked flood plain about 450 metres (¼ mile) wide in Aberdare but increasing to about 800

This is part of the Rhigos–Dunraven opencast site worked by Sir Lindsay Parkinson and Co. Disturbances of the strata can be clearly seen. The picture was taken in January 1965.

The late Glyn Davies

metres (½ mile) at Abercwmboi. Housing development on it is limited particularly in the south because its tendency to flooding is exacerbated by mining subsidence. On the southern side of the valley the Pennant escarpment is broken only by the two tributary valleys of the Dare and the Aman. The incision of these valleys into the Sandstone plateau has exposed the Middle Coal Measures and, in the case of the Aman, to some extent the Upper Measures and in both instances it has facilitated the exploitation of the valuable seams in the Lower Coal Measures. Of the three more important of the Cynon's left bank tributaries, Nantmelyn, Nant Hir and Nant y Wenallt, only the last has influenced colliery location.

At Mountain Ash the Cynon breaks into the Pennant Sandstone and from here to Abercynon its valley is much constricted. The valley floor, in places little more than 200 metres (200 yards) wide is flanked by steep slopes. Between Penrhiwceiber and Abercynon erosion of the Sandstones and intercalated Mudstones already mentioned has produced a terraced cross profile to the valley. At Mountain Ash and Ynysybwl erosion of the Upper Pennant Series has facilitated access to the underlying Middle and Lower Coal Measures.

Some modification of the topography was produced during the Quaternary Ice Age, notably in the last phase 25,000 to 15,000 years ago. This saw the southward movement of ice from the Brecknock Beacons coming up against the insuperable obstacle of the Pennant Sandstone escarpment. Part of the ice sheet, loaded with Old Red Sandstone debris, was diverted down the Cynon Valley practically filling it. Glacial erosion was not severe enough to produce a true U-shaped valley although some local oversteepening of the valley sides occurred. Locally generated ice also caused some modification of the Dare and Aman valleys as well as producing the Cwms of Llyn Fawr and Llyn Fach.

The main effect of glaciation here was depositional. The material deposited by ice is known as drift and consists of boulder clay, sands and gravels. Above Abercwmboi boulder clay predominates, blanketing the hillsides to heights of 300 metres (1,000 feet) and more. Between Abercwmboi and Abercynon particularly below 150 metres (500 feet OD) the clay is increasingly replaced down valley by sand and gravel. Below Mountain Ash the steeper valley sides are frequently drift-free. The thickness of these various deposits varies enormously from a metre or so to about 35 metres (120 feet). What information is available throughout the valley suggests an average thickness of 9-12 metres (30-40 feet). The effect is to smother the outcrop of the solid rock including coal seams and to increase the cost of deep mining. At Cwm Cynon colliery, for example, 87 feet of drift had to be penetrated before the underlying coal measures were reached.

The oversteepened valley sides have exacerbated the instability of the slopes and contributed to the occurrence of landslips notably along the Pennant escarpment and in the Dare and Aman valleys. The largest example however is found below Twyn Gwersyllfa on the eastern side of the valley.

More widespread are the heterogeneous deposits resulting from the downhill movement of soil, unconsolidated rock fragments, etc., chiefly under the influence of gravity, rainwash and freeze-thaw action These deposits collectively known as "Head" occur throughout the area except on the highest crags, covering much of the drift often to a depth of 2-3 metres (6-9 feet). Most appear to date from immediate post-glacial times although in some cases movement still occurs. As in the case of drift, landslips and head conceal the outcrops of the underlying strata.

It is of course the exploitation of its coal resources which is the raison d'être of the communities of the Cynon valley, but the topographical feature outlined have in large measure controlled the shape of their settlements. The broad valley and gentle southern slopes of Mynydd Aberdâr north of Mountain Ash have allowed urban development of a kind unusual in the coalfield, contrasting strongly with the linear development of terraced housing on the valley sides between Mountain Ash

This 1973 photo shows part of the Bryn Pica opencast site above Abernant, one of the more recent opencast sites. An American "Marion" excavator is making short work of loading coal into lorries.

The late Glyn Davies

and Abercynon on the slopes of the tributary valleys of the Pennar, Aman, and to some extent the Dare. In the latter case, in the constricted valley bottom, priority was given to collieries, their surface buildings and railway sidings.

The low southward dip of the strata has already been mentioned but even so this shallow gradient, between 1 in 11 and 1 in 6 is much steeper than the average gradient of the Cynon Valley floor—1 in 180. Thus coal seams that outcrop or occur at shallow depths in the upper part of the valley are found at ever increasing depths southwards. This can be illustrated with reference to the lowest workable seam in the area—the Gellideg:

Table 1

Colliery	Depth of Gellideg seam
Gadlys	133 metres (146 yds.)
Aberaman	217 metres (237 yds.)
Deep Duffryn	368 metres (403 yds.)
Abercynon	658 metres (720 yds.)

Hence towards Abercynon pits were necessarily deeper and larger.

It is obvious that any underground workings at right angles to the direction of dip, i.e. along the strike, will be horizontal. Thus, other factors being equal, the majority of permanent underground workings in the Cynon Valley ran approximately west to east. Similarly, where seams outcropped in the hillsides, they were worked where possible by levels running in the same direction.

We turn to the NNW-SSE trending fault systems. Broadly those affecting the Cynon Valley fall into two groups. The eastern group consist of the Twyn Disgwylfa fault and the Werfa system. The latter consists of the Werfa fault itself having a throw (vertical displacement) eastwards and two associated faults west of it which in the south throw westwards so creating a structural ridge – the Werfa Ridge. Northwards these minor faults are replaced by faults throwing in the opposite direction. In the southern part of the district the Werfa Fault is replaced by the Kilkenny Fault which again throws eastwards. The main faults of the western group are the Gadlys Fault, Bwllfa No 1 Fault and Bwllfa Nos 2 and 3 Faults. The last two continue into Hirwaun Nos 1 and 2 respectively. In the south are Cwmneol Fault, east and west Ynysybwl Faults and the Llanwonno Fault, all of which except the Cwmneol and Llanwonno faults throw westwards. The amount of vertical displacement varies from over 135 metres (450 feet) to less than 15 metres (50 feet). The range may vary considerably along the length of a single fault For example the displacement of the Gadlys fault at Aberdare is only a few feet whereas at Aberaman it is 115 yards.

Between the Werfa-Kilkenny faults in the north and the Gadlys and east Ynysybwl faults in the south the relative freedom of the Cynon Valley from major disturbances has facilitated deep mining. The topographical manifestations of faulting are few, being chiefly the occasional fissure and the odd small cliff feature. A notable exception is the scarp of the Craig yr Ysgol above Cwmdare, formed by Bwllfa No 2 fault.

The nature of the rocks influenced the character of the faults. In the resistant Pennant sandstones they usually appear as straightforward fractures but in the weaker mudstones and the associated coal seams of the Middle and Lower Coal Measures the fractures tend to split into a number of fault planes of different displacements and lengths, and different seams in the same area may be affected differently. Crushing of the coal is common in the vicinity of the fault planes. Further, these weak mudstones and siltstones of the Middle and Lower Measures contain a large number of structures such as minor folds and thrusts faults which are due to compressional forces. In the Cynon Valley the beds above the 9ft. seam are remarkable free of such structures and have been worked with no great difficulty. The nine feet seam itself, the most important in the valley and now largely worked out, is very badly affected in some places through disturbances and also by the presence of barren ground. North of the valley towards Rhigos the seams between the 2ft 9in. and the 9ft., i.e. practically all the productive seams of the Middle Measures are affected, possibly as a result of proximity to the Neath Disturbance.

During opencast operations near Moss Row, Abernant, this tram, still full of coal, was exposed in old workings and presented to the Dare Valley Country Park.

The late Glyn Davies

On a Wimpey site at Rhigos a 22RB excavator is tearing into a seam of coal. Opencast coal mining was introduced into this country in 1942 though it did not pass into the hands of the National Coal Board until 1952.

The late Glyn Davies

The cubical jointing characteristic of the bituminous seams in the east and south of the coalfield is poorly developed in the Lower and Middle Measures of the Cynon and adjacent valleys. It tends to be obscured by a series of joints known as "slips" usually ⅓ to ⅔ (1 – 2 feet) apart and forming an angle of about 50 degrees between the roof and the floor of a seam. Further in the Cynon Valley particularly, the strike of the slip is almost everywhere parallel to the main NNW-SSE faults described above. Working coalfaces were normally developed parallel to the strike and as far as manual extraction was concerned, in the direction opposite to the dip of the slips so that coal could be undercut. It has been argued that the relative ease with which the coal could be cut by hand was one of the factors which delayed the introduction of machine cutting into this part of the coalfield. The nature of the slips meant that the steam coal was produced in large irregular lumps, the size of which precluded the use of "Hopper bottom" wagons and necessitated the use of rectangular trucks with end doors.

The interbedding of the valuable steam coal seams of the Lower and Middle Measures of much of the coalfield, the Cynon valley included, with the relatively weak mudstones and siltstones, has created a major problem, that of "squeeze". When roadways were driven in these beds pressure caused the roof, floor and sides to close in. One result of this was that a very high proportion of the underground labour force was needed purely for maintenance, thus adding to the cost of extracting the coal.

Still other problems encountered in the exploitation of the coal seams derive from the conditions under which they and their associated beds were laid down; for example, breaks in continuity, seam partings and variations in the thickness and distances between seams.

The coal measures of South Wales were formed almost entirely of material derived from an adjacent land mass and deposited under deltaic conditions between about 315 million and about 305 million years ago. Deposition occurred in cyclic phases repeated many times. The coal seams were formed as masses of peat in great swamps which supported a dense tropical vegetation. Subsidence occurred and the decaying products of the forest cover were covered by a succession of deposits, muds at first then coarser material until sea level was again reached, providing the conditions for a new vegetation cover, the uppermost deposits providing the seat-earth for the new growth. The cycle then began again. The accumulation of sediments led to the compression of the underlying material, changing the mud and sand into mudstone and sandstone and the peaty material into coal. This ideal sequence known as a cyclotherm seldom occurred in practice; some phases were missed out, others duplicated. The thicknesses of the coal seams and their associated beds reflect differences in the amount of vegetal material, the rate and degree of subsidence and the type and amount of sediment brought in at any time.

Sometimes subsidences were small and localised and water was allowed into a limited area around which forest growth continues. More mud or silt would be deposited until the level reached again permitted the swamp forest to re-establish itself to form a continuous cover. Where growth was uninterrupted there would be a thick coal seam which, when followed into the area of subsidence would split into two, separated by a layer of rock. Such partings and split seams are common in the coalfield.

Further the coastal forests were traversed by numerous rivers and their distributaries, along the courses of which the growth of vegetation and subsequent formation of peat would be interrupted, resulting in large areas of barren ground in particular coal seams. Sometimes, particularly during flood periods streams would form new channels which would remove all or part of the already accumulated peat, replacing it with sand or mud. These "washouts" are fairly numerous and also affect the continuity of the coal seams.

There is strong evidence that minor earth movements occurred during Coal Measures times, precursors of the major activity at the end of the Carboniferous Period which resulted in the formation of the South Wales coal basin itself. The consequence was that some of the lower seams underwent folding and faulting before the deposition of the overlying beds which were therefore unaffected. Among the by-products resulting from the decay of the Coal Measures forests was the gas methane or firedamp (CH_4). Some was trapped under great pressure in the interstices of the coal itself and of those of the surrounding rocks particularly those immediately above the coal seam. Mining operations would disturb the strata and release the gas. Methane when present in air in the

Table 2

Classification and Sequence of Coal Seams and Ironstone Veins in the Cynon Valley

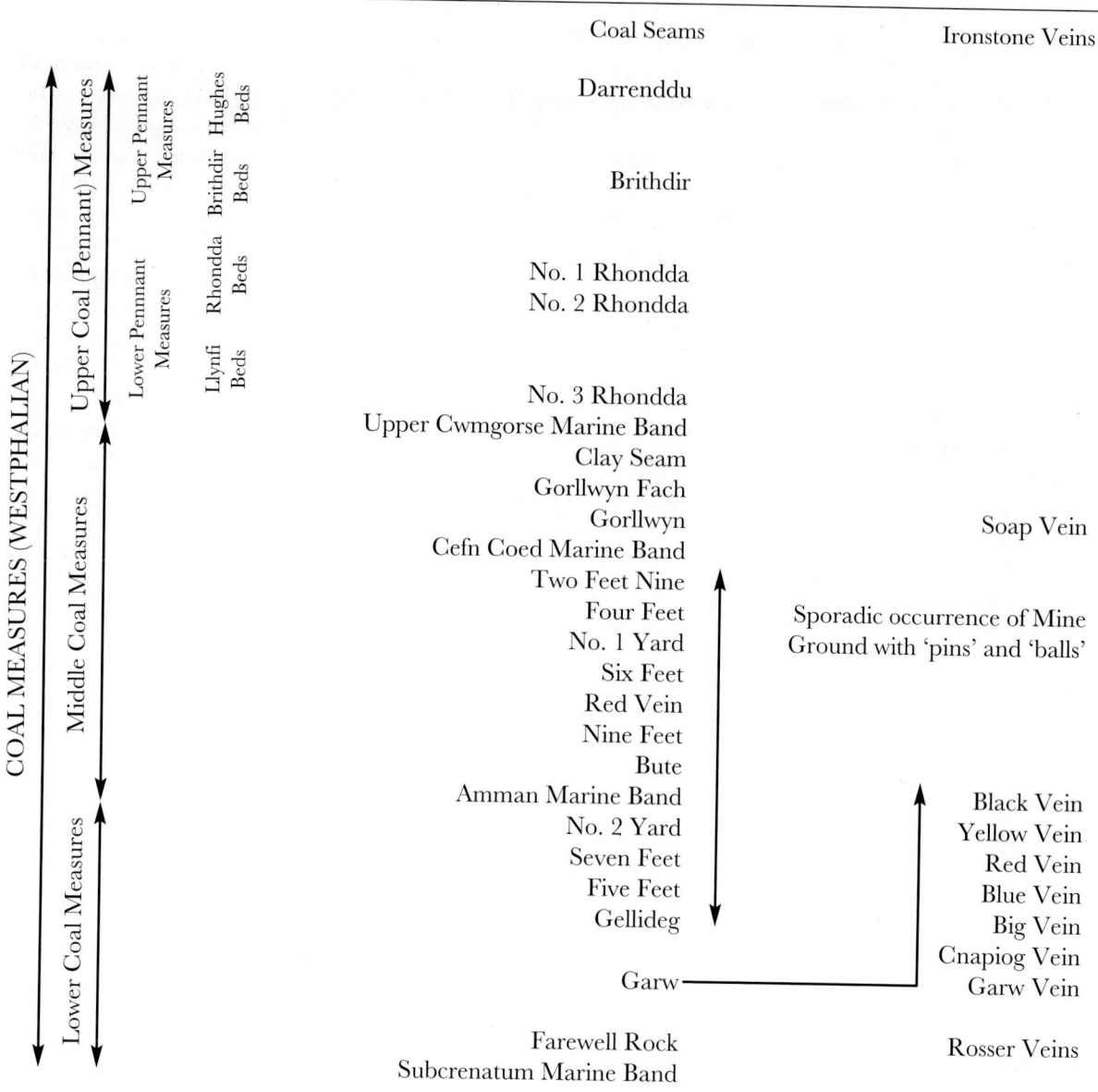

	Coal Seams	Ironstone Veins
	Darrenddu	
	Brithdir	
	No. 1 Rhondda	
	No. 2 Rhondda	
	No. 3 Rhondda	
	Upper Cwmgorse Marine Band	
	Clay Seam	
	Gorllwyn Fach	
	Gorllwyn	Soap Vein
	Cefn Coed Marine Band	
	Two Feet Nine	
	Four Feet	Sporadic occurrence of Mine Ground with 'pins' and 'balls'
	No. 1 Yard	
	Six Feet	
	Red Vein	
	Nine Feet	
	Bute	
	Amman Marine Band	Black Vein
	No. 2 Yard	Yellow Vein
	Seven Feet	Red Vein
	Five Feet	Blue Vein
	Gellideg	Big Vein
		Cnapiog Vein
	Garw	Garw Vein
	Farewell Rock	Rosser Veins
	Subcrenatum Marine Band	

COAL MEASURES (WESTPHALIAN)
Upper Coal (Pennant) Measures — Upper Pennant Measures — Hughes Beds, Brithdir Beds
Lower Pennant Measures — Rhondda Beds, Llynfi Beds
Middle Coal Measures
Lower Coal Measures

No attempt has been made to indicate the thickness of the seams, their distance apart or their character, i.e. whether they are simple, composite or split. The coals of the Upper Measures are of little significance and only the more important are shown. Massive Pennant sandstones occur in the Upper Measures from the Llynfi to the Hughes Beds, but in the main text, for the sake of simplicity, no distinction is made and the term Pennant Sandstone is used irrespective of the bed in which it occurs.

Again, in the text the older names, Coal Measures, Millstone Grit and Carboniferous Limestone are used in preference to the current designations, Westphalian, Namurian and Dinantian.

proportion of between 5% and 14% forms a highly inflammable mixture. The lower seams of the Middle Coal Measures in the Cynon Valley especially the famous 4ft. seam were particularly gaseous and methane was responsible for major explosions in the area during the latter half of the nineteenth century. (see also Chapter 7).

The foregoing summary of the major difficulties with which the winning of coal in the Cynon Valley had to contend is necessarily very generalised. Because of the great variations in the nature of the faults and in the seam characteristics a more detailed account is far beyond the scope and intention of the present work.

The wetlands in which the coal measures were formed were a freshwater or at least a brackish environment and extended from eastern North America to the Ukraine. However there were brief periods when subsidences were sufficiently great to permit a widespread incursion of the sea over the whole area of contemporaneous sedimentation in western Europe at least. These incursions resulted in thin deposits of marine sediments with characteristic assemblages of marine fossils. The widespread distribution of these so called "marine bands" makes them important marker beds for the modern classification of the coal measures and the correlation of its constituent seams.

Table 2 shows the sequence and names of the principal coal seams in the Cynon Valley. Originally the naming of the seams was done virtually on a free for all basis. They were named after their thickness or some other characteristic in localities where they were encountered or even after the locality itself. The variation in thickness and nature of the seams often within very short distances made correlation even in adjacent pits difficult, sometimes impossible. It was not until the mid 1950's that a satisfactory scheme was produced which was based on fossil assemblages in the associated strata, particularly the marine bands. The latter have enabled the British and European coalfields to be correlated with each other. In the Cynon and adjacent valleys the coal seams between the Garw and the 2ft. 9in. were equated with and named after the Aberdare sequence. Above the 2′ 9″ the less widely exploited coals have to some extent retained their local names outside the valley.

It is now necessary to deal with the coal types mentioned earlier. The classification into anthracite, steam and bituminous coals is based on rank i.e. the proportion of carbon present in the coal. This categorisation has been replaced by more scientific ones, but because it is more relevant historically, the older, cruder method is used here. The three main types are summarised in Table 3.

Table 3

	% carbon*	% volatile matter
Anthracite	93+	3-8
Steam Coal	91-93	8-22
Bituminous Coal	84-91	22-40

*Some carbon combined with hydrogen is present in the volatiles.

It should be noted that almost everywhere rank increases with the depth so that the upper seams contain more volatiles than the lower ones.

Anthracite, a hard, shiny, slow-burning coal used where a moderate supply of heat is required, was particularly suitable for baking, malting and central heating. It is not found as such in the Cynon Valley, but the lower seams between Hirwaun and Rhigos contain semi-anthracite having practically the same properties, and commercially no distinction is made, both types being marketed as anthracite. At the other end of the scale the more highly volatile varieties occur only in the upper seams above the 2ft. 9in., chiefly in the lower part of the valley. These were formerly used for domestic and coking purposes.

Most of the valley coals are steam coals, of which two sub-types may be distinguished—smokeless steam coal and dry steam coal. Both are virtually smokeless but the latter was particularly suitable for the manufacture of patent fuel since the lower volatile content balanced the addition of pitch which was used as a binding agent. In very broad terms dry steam coal was characteristic of the upper part of the Cynon Valley, while the smokeless variety was characteristic of the lower part. It was frequently used locally either singly or admixed as coking coal. The main use of both types however was steam-raising, particularly in naval and fast merchant ships. Their high calorific value, their resistance to weathering, their ability to stand rough treatment in transit and their high density resulting in less storage space per ton thus making them ideal for bunkering were the qualities which made them much sought after. They were the coals which were the basis of the fame and former prosperity of the Cynon Valley.

It should not be forgotten that the exploitation of the coal measures of this area were preceded by the extraction of another Coal Measure mineral, a low grade iron ore known as ironstone or mine. Originally the word miner meant a man who dug for mine. In the Cynon Valley as in the rest of the northern part of the South Wales coalfield, it was these ironstones which were the basis of the nineteenth century iron industry and at least until the mid-century they provided most of the iron ore used in the furnaces.

Chemically, ironstone is a carbonate of iron called siderite with an admixture of clay. The iron content is low averaging about 29%. It occurs in the form of bands or pins between 2.5 and 15cms thick (1 – 6in.), or as nodules between 1 and 30cms in diameter (0.5 – 12in.) embedded in shale. They occur sporadically throughout the Lower and Middle Coal Measures with a remarkable concentration between the Gellideg and Garw seams and immediately below the Garw (see Table 2). Near the top of the Middle Measures the Gorllwyn coal was associated with the Soap Vein, a "blackband" ironstone which contained so much finely disseminated carbonaceous matter that it could be roasted without any further additions of fuel.

One of the earliest methods of winning ironstone was by scouring. This consisted of damming a stream in a small valley where ironstone veins cropped out so as to cause the accumulation of a considerable head of water. The dam would then be breached and the violent outrush of water would erode the valley sides, carrying away the shale but leaving the heavier ironstone in the stream bed where it could be collected later. The process could be assisted by prior undercutting of the valley sides causing the mine ground to collapse. The best example locally lay just outside our area in Cwmgwrelych at Glyn-neath where the whole range of ironstones between the Gellideg and Garw coals was exposed. This was an important source of supply for the Abernant ironworks until the consequent silting up of the Neath canal and river Neath owing to scouring brought it to an end. There is some evidence that scouring was also used near Penywaun in Cwmnantyrhwch.

More important was "patching", a primitive kind of opencast working employed when the ironstone deposit lay at shallow depths beneath the surface strata which were removed and deposited in adjacent low, fan-shaped tips thereby often concealing further productive mine ground. Examples are Fothergills, Bryn Defaid and Bryngwyn patches.

Where ironstone outcropped on the hillsides levels would be driven in. This was commonly seen in the case of Hirwaun Common; Bute Level, Gorllwyn and Blackband Levels, Knobby Drift and Rosser Drift are examples. The Common was also a source of ironstone throughout the entire range from the Rosser to the Garw Veins. Where there were no convenient outcrops and the overburden was too thick, shafts were sunk; for example the Aberaman ironstone pit and the Dare pit at Gadlys. Occasionally pits and levels worked both ironstone and coal as at Treaman and Park Pit (Robertstown). Where ironstone alone was sought as in the veins below the Gellideg, the underground workings were on a very small scale as the low iron content did not warrant elaborate undertakings. Long after the demise of the local iron industry ironstone "Balls" (as the nodules were called) were collected in the normal course of working at some local collieries, notably Bwllfa and Werfa, for despatch to steel works where they could be used in the basic open hearth process.

Another product of the Coal Measures formerly of economic significance was fireclay. This was formed from the seat earths which supported the vegetation cover from which the coal seams were formed. Fireclay normally formed pale compacted clays underlying the majority of coal seams. They have a high silica content and are low in alkalis and soluble salts which have been extracted by the Coal Measure forest cover. These properties make them suitable for the manufacture of refractory products such as sanitary ware which, having a high glaze, had to be fired at high temperature. The fireclay mined at the Aberaman clay level provided the material for the manufacture of such ware at the Aberaman pipe works.

The firm of Douglas gained the contract to work the coal at the eastern end of the lower slopes of Cefn y Cynghor, that is, in the angle between Cwmdare Road and Hirwaun Road. In the right background can be seen the taller trees in Aberdare Park, and just left of centre is the house called "Four Winds" on Hirwaun Road.   The late Glyn Davies

At the Ffyndaf site at Rhigos a large nodule of ironstone protrudes from the face of the cut. Those deposits of ironstone and coal in this area which lay close to the surface formed the basis of ironmaking at Hirwaun from 1757.

John F. Mear

The more suitable of the vast quantities of shale and mudstone produced by mining were frequently used for brick manufacture at colliery brickworks such as Abernant River Level, Gadlys, Nantmelyn and Bwllfa.

Mention must also be made of the massive sandstones of the Upper Coal Measures. Above Cwmpennar the Pennant contained horizons of flaggy sandstones which were quarried for paving stone. Elsewhere the numerous quarries, mostly unnamed, scarring the hillsides from Cwmdare to Penrhiwceiber bear witness to the contribution they made to the valley's townscape up to the first war, elements of which are still visible in the older houses, chapels, churches, and other public buildings.

What did the early pioneers of coalmining know of the nature of the seams below the surface? The earliest references to coal working in the area are dealt with in chapter two, but some relevant observations may be made here. The terms of some of the leases mentioned, strongly suggest that the lessees and landlords had some knowledge of the disposition of the coal-bearing strata. The exploitation of the coal was, however, at first almost certainly to provide for limited local needs and was intermittent, unlike the development in the west where the coalfield reached the sea. The eastern part including the Cynon Valley remained unworked on any significant scale until the end of the eighteenth century with the establishment of the ironworks and the buildings of canals. Obviously much practical knowledge of the geology of the coal seams would have been obtained by development in the west.

The basin character of the coalfield was known by the end of the eighteenth century and was written about by Edward Martin who also described the occurrence of faults, pointing out that the occurrence of the latter was not always detrimental in that sometimes they served to bring coal seams nearer the surface. There was much information available but the extent to which it was known to, or acted on by, contemporary prospectors is doubtful. Coal had been worked on an increasing scale in the valley since the last decades of the eighteenth century mostly by driving into the outcrops. In 1815 Walter Davies wrote "The hill between Aberdare and Merthyr Tudful is perforated with levels". Interestingly, modern opencast working on Mynydd Aberdâr has uncovered old underground workings, but no trace of the primitive sinkings called bell pits has been found. Generally there was little need for them although reference to "sinking a mine" in some of the early leases suggest that some existed.

From the end of the 1830's the Geological Survey under Henry de la Beche was active in the coalfield and its results were increasingly used by the coalmasters. In the second half of the century some coalmasters themselves such as Thomas Joseph wrote learned treatises on aspects of coalfield geology.

In broad terms the story of mining in the area begins with levels driven into the hillsides in the north of the valley followed by small and relatively shallow pits and larger and more elaborate drift mines where conditions were favourable. Southwards, as the dip of the seams was greater than the fall of the valley floor, increasingly deeper and therefore larger pits were necessary and therefore the exploitation of the lower seams particularly in the lower part of the valley had to wait upon developments in the technology of winding, pumping, and ventilation.

The Navigation Colliery was opened by John Nixon in 1855 and closed in 1940. It had two shafts, one of which was divided into two by a timber brattice.

NMGW

Though sited at Llwydcoed, this was in fact the Aberdare Iron Company's works. The company bought the Abernant Iron Company's works in 1819, after which the two establishments were worked as one, the company using a section of Tappenden's tramroad for sending material from one works to the other. The Company also built a tramroad from Abernant to the head of the Aberdare Canal. When owned by the Fothergills the firm ran into difficulties and closed finally in 1875. When this photo was taken the site was occupied by the Tanybryn Brickworks, whose kilns are seen in the centre of the photo.

CHAPTER TWO

The creation of the iron industry and then the coal industry in the Cynon Valley were events which formed part of what has been called the industrial revolution, which in simple terms consisted of a tremendous increase, with the aid of steam power, in the scope and quantity of industrial activity, which turned Britain into the "Workshop of the World". The industrial revolution was a tremendously complicated phenomenon, which occurred in different ways in different places at different times, and it is not within the scope of this book to describe its origins and course except insofar as it affects the Cynon Valley. A few explanatory remarks are therefore apposite in order to put the development of the valley in its proper context with regard to the events in the rest of the country.

The industrial revolution is said to have begun in about 1740 when this application of steam power to industry began to make a fundamental and irreversible advance in industrial technical progress. The older steam engines developed by Savery and Newcomen were not rotative engines, i.e. they produced a to and fro motion only. Although this was suitable for the use for which these engines were developed, that is, pumping from mines, it was of no use in driving machinery which needed a rotary input, such as winding engines and the majority of ventilating fans. At first it was thought that the use of a simple crank would not serve to convert the reciprocating motion of the steam engines of the day to rotary motion, but it proved successful when tried, thereby enabling the engines of the day to drive machinery such as spinning mules, looms, lathes, colliery machinery such as winding engines, ventilators, pumps, etc., and this also paved the way for the invention of the steamship and the self-moving steam engine, i.e. the locomotive.

The first application of the "rotative" steam engine was to the cotton and woollen industries in the north of England, which were situated near sources of plentiful water so that water wheels could be used to power the mills. These were subject to disruption at times of drought and frost but the steam engines were of course less affected by these events. The introduction of steam to these industries had a great effect on the national economy, much greater than the later application of steam power to iron manufacture.

The presence of ironstone and coal in the vicinity of Aberdare has been dealt with in Chapter 1 and though the development of coal mining was the main reason for the expansion of the town and its environs, it should be remembered that Aberdare (but not Mountain Ash) was first an iron producing centre, in which the population increased over two and a half times between 1801 and 1831, the build-up period of iron manufacture in Aberdare. Nevertheless, the increase was not great in terms of numbers, and if rapid increase in population is regarded as an important indicator of the occurrence of the industrial revolution in a particular place, then in the Cynon Valley the industrial revolution cannot be said to have occurred in its proper sense until the later development of the coal industry. The older housing in Hirwaun, Trecynon, Llwydcoed, Gadlys and Abernant was built for workers who were mainly ironworkers, or who worked in the mines belonging to the ironworks. Had the later development of the steam coal industry not occurred, the building of settlements at Cwmdare and Cwmaman, the newer streets of Foundrytown, Aberaman, Abercwmboi and the development in the lower part of the valley would probably have never happened, and since the local iron industries had all virtually failed by 1875, the population would have moved on, hundreds of the original houses would have fallen into disuse, and Aberdare would have probably reverted to an insignificant village.

At this point we must mention the little we know about primitive coal mining in the area. In view of the tremendous amount of coal which lay underground in the Cynon Valley and its proximity to the surface in many places, it was inevitable that our long-distant ancestors became aware of its presence and of its value as a domestic fuel and for drying grain in the process of "malting", i.e. preparing it for brewing. No one knows who was the first to dig out coal, but it is known to have been used in Glamorgan during the bronze age 3000+ years ago. Coal was also worked on the outcrop by the Romans. By the 17th century landowners were aware that the coal lying under their lands was an asset

Abercwmboi Colliery was also known as Cap Coch Colliery. The original furnace ventilation was replaced by a 40′ Waddle fan in 1891. The pit was sunk by David Davis in 1851. It stopped raising coal in 1923 but the winder was kept in running order for many years after, as it was used as a pumping pit.   Brian Davies

valuable enough to warrant leasing out, and several references to these leases have survived from this early period. For example, in August 1578 Thomas Howell of Llantrisant leased part of a property known as Tir Llwyn Y Bedw from the Lord of the Manor. This property is thought to have been in the vicinity of Fedw Hir. Another adventurous son of Llantrisant, William Morgan, had a lease of the Earl of Pembroke (who owned a great deal of land in Glamorgan at that time) of the properties known as Bryn Pillog and Nant Melyn. This was in 1614 and they had to pay 5s 10d for the land and 5s for the right to mine the coal. It is not clear if this Nant Melyn is the one in Cwmdare, but a lease of 1631 is more particular, in that the Earl leased to Thomas Matthew several parcels of land including "Tir Wayne Wrgan" (Hirwaun Common) "with liberty to dig cole therein". In 1612 a small pit was opened at Rhigos.

Then in successive surveys of the possessions of the Manor of Miskin we find that in 1638 "Thomas Gruffydd houldeth the coale mynes in Aberdare . . . There are Coale Mynes on the Lord's Demesne Land called Gwayne-y-Person and Tire-y-Lloyne Bedw within the parish of Aberdare". In 1653 the right to all the coal in Aberdare was granted to John Thomas for 21 years, at a rent of 10s a year, and in 1678 the coal mines in Pym Pynt and Gwayne-y-Person were granted to William Owen for 5s a year for 5 years. The coal would have been sold in sacks, or bartered for lime from farmers in the limestone area of Penderyn. There was probably some "pirate" mining going on as well. The coal was mined by digging in the outcrop for as far as it was safe and afterwards repeating the process a few yards away. In parts of the Valley this practice was revived during the 1926 strike, the evidence for which is still visible today.

We find that in 1750 the presence of 4 small levels was noted:

1. Lefel Penrhiwllech. A level in the vicinity of the farmhouse of that name in Cwmdare is shown on the plan of the Dare and Aman branch of the Vale of Neath railway. It is doubtful whether coal could have been found at this altitude and the reference may be to some other part of the farm, which occupied the south flank of the upper Dare Valley down to the level of the river.

2. Lefel Bryn Gwyn (also known as Lefel y Bechgyn or Lefel Bryn Banerau Gwynion). Between Lluestai Llwydion (the old name for Nantmelin farm, Cwmdare) and Hirwaun.

3. Lefel y Garn. Not far from Ffwrness y Garn (alongside Nant y Derlwyn—to the east of Llwydcoed—where an unsuccessful and short-lived ironworks was built in 1773).

4. Lefel Penar on the mountainside above Cwmbach.

In 1793, according to "Gardd Aberdar", a man called Edward T Edward had a level "beside Tir-y-lluest". He made a channel to carry away the water and used it to bring out the coal in a specially constructed wooden boat. Reference is also made to a seam being worked "at the top end of Craig y Duffryn" and at Cwmpennar, but the coal did not prove suitable for malting. There was also a small coal works on the Ynyslwyd land and in other places.

In the face of this firm evidence of early coal mining it is surprising that there are two or three references to the fact that coal for domestic use was imported into the district. For example, Mr. Williams of Garth Hall, Llantrisant, told the famous geologist Sir Henry De La Beche that in about 1790 "the principal part of the coal used at Aberdare for household purposes was brought from Trebanog in Cwm Rhondda, a distance of 12-13 miles, on horseback over the mountains".

Very little written evidence about the practice of "Patching" (that is, the removal of coal or iron ore from near the surface) has survived. In September 1851 the CMG advertised an auction sale of the plant on a patch within 50 yards of the high road at the west end of Hirwaun Common. The plant amounted to: a 80 horse power steam engine with boiler and winding apparatus, 30 tons of bridge rails 26-29 lbs per yard, 20 iron wagons, 2,300 wooden sleepers 5 feet long, 4 tons of cast iron bars and plates, Blacksmiths tools, 350 yards of chain, 30 barrows, 100 yards of wheeling planks, lot of rollers on inclined plane.

Also farming stock at Beili Glas, the inn at Cwmhwnt, and 4 cottages.

From this description of the equipment of a patch perhaps a mining expert will be able to explain exactly how they went about it.

The Cardiff Times, 15th June 1935

Again, "An old mountaineer" writing in the Cardiff and Merthyr Guardian of 25th of June 1853 relates that about 100 years previously a miller at Cefnpennar was obliged to obtain coal for drying oats from Penwaun Gellideg near Merthyr, and the few inhabitants of Aberdare at that time were obliged some times to send for their coal to Darran Ddu in the parish of Llanwonno or, in the case of dwellers in the lower part of the valley, to Llanfabon.

The first important stimulus to local industry was the emergence of the local iron industry. There were ironworks in various parts of Glamorgan as early as the 16th century and the remains of one can still be seen at Cwmaman. They used charcoal made from locally grown timber for fuel, as it had been found that iron smelted with coal was spoilt by impurities such as sulphur in the coal. These ironworks were transitory with very low output and had virtually no effect on the industrial development of the then village of Aberdare. However, Abraham Darby at Coalbrookdale in Shropshire discovered in 1709 that coal could be used if it was first converted to coke. Nevertheless this method was not taken up at once, and the first coke-fired blast furnace in Wales, which was at Hirwaun, did not come into being until 1757, possibly on the site of a pre-existing charcoal fired furnace. The most bituminous coals made the largest and strongest coke and it was made by placing the coal in long shallow pits and igniting it. The coal was smothered by ash towards the end of the process. But it must be remembered that, like the ironstone, which lay adjacent to it in the ground, the coal required for use in the various ironworks was raised by the ironmasters on their own leaseholds. As Darby's discovery was gradually accepted by the ironmasters it resulted in other ironworks being opened not only in the Aberdare area, but in the whole of the northern edge of the South Wales coalfield, as the demand for iron rose to satisfy the needs of the industrial revolution and also to meet the demand for cannon arising from the Seven Years' War (1756-1763), a demand which was sustained by the later Napoleonic wars.

17

It is, perhaps, interesting to remember that to make one ton of iron as much charcoal as can be made from one third of an acre of growing timber was required, or as much coke as could be made from four and a half tons of coal.

In the Aberdare area, the works at Hirwaun was followed by others at Llwydcoed (1801), Abernant (1804), Gadlys (1827), and Aberaman (1845). None of these was large and not all of them were successful. The Gadlys works specialised at one time in the manufacture of armour plate for warships. The small scale of the enterprises in the Aberdare area was partly ascribed by the prominent mining engineer Thomas Joseph to the fact that many of the different kinds of coals in the valley did not make good coke. Indeed, he went so far as to state that for this reason, in the time before the steam coal was discovered, the most eminent and practical mining engineers of the district regarded the Aberdare coals as almost worthless. Sometimes the proprietors had to mix different kinds of local coal to make a usable blast furnace coke. For example, in about 1810, when Overton & Co. had the Hirwaun iron works they achieved this by mixing coke made from four different coals, namely the "dirty" vein mined at the Level Fawr near Penywaun, the upper four feet taken from patches near Bryngwyn, the Graig seam worked near Bwlch y Lladron and the old Gorllwyn level beyond the Hirwaun "great first downthrow west fault".

Generally speaking, although the rising population would have increased the demand for domestic coal, it is safe to say that the coal mines which were opened after the starting of the first coke-fired blast furnace in 1757 were mainly or wholly for the benefit of the iron works. Gardd Aberdare also states that there were about eight pits sunk between 1750 and 1836 for the same purpose. These would have been small, simple and shallow. But coal was required not only for making coke for use in the blast furnace but for use in processes relating to the further treatment of the iron at the works, namely in the puddling and balling furnaces, where it was used as coal not coke. Another major requirement was to fuel the blowing or blast engines which generated the powerful blast of air upwards through the furnace which was essential for raising its contents to the necessary temperature to melt the ore. When Neilson discovered in 1828 that pre-heating the blast improved the efficiency of

The lack of a canal from Aberdare to the seaboard brought into being the "Tappenden's Tramroad" referred to in a previous caption. This ran from the Abernant Ironworks through the Aberdare Ironworks and then crossed the River Cynon at Gelli Isaf by means of this bridge, built in 1834 on the site of an earlier structure dating from 1802. It was then joined by the Aberdare Canal Company's tramroad and afterwards ran through Hirwaun, over Cefn Rhigos and down the Penrhiw incline to the head of the Neath Canal at Glyn Neath.
The late Glyn Davies

The haphazard dumping of spoil suggests that this is an area which has been a patch, (probably the Bryngwyn Patches) where coal and ironstone were dug out from close to the surface many years ago. Now, in a time of industrial unrest (possibly in the 1911/1912 strike), miners are making an equally haphazard attack on the coal which is still there. Upper right a policeman is keeping an eye on things, or perhaps wishing he had brought a bag with him.

Doug Williams

the furnace, another requirement for coal arose. Finally, in those ironworks which processed their own pig iron instead of selling it on, there was a requirement for coal for the smaller steam engines which drove the rolls used to convert the finished wrought iron into bars and to drive other related machinery.

That portion of the Aberdare to Neath road between Penywaun and the west side of Hirwaun is overlooked to the south by the escarpment of Mynydd Cefn y Gyngon, the lower slopes of which have been subject to opencast mining which began in this district during the Second World War. This has obliterated most of the areas once known as the Bryngwyn Patches and Slade's Patch, where the gentle gradient of the seams enabled coal and ironstone to be worked during the heyday of the Hirwaun ironworks by the "patching" method described in Chapter 1. Above these slopes, the steeper gradient of the ground necessitated the use of levels for mining, and the escarpment has clearly visible signs of the inclines, tips, and the few traces of ruined buildings which were once so busy, but which are now all the more mute because so little is known about their method of working and the men (and women) who worked them. The upper slopes are also remarkable for the three "flues" lying against the mountainside like fallen chimneys. Nothing is known about these, but they presumably were associated with steam generation or possibly with the furnace ventilation of the workings but not with the dispersal of toxic fumes, which was the purpose of the similar structures used in the copper smelting industry of west Glamorgan.

19

These two engravings were made of the Middle Duffryn Colliery after the disaster in May 1852 which cost 65 lives. They are important because they they are the only detailed illustrations of a colliery of this period in the Cynon Valley. Note that, as often happened, the engraver was engraving things which he did not wholly understand. For example, in the upper engraving he has drawn one of the shafts of the winch in the foreground as a log of wood, and in the lower one the lifting bridge has been made too small to span the canal. Note also that he forgot to engrave the side of the boat in the right foreground.

ILN

21

The Aberdare Iron Works was situated at Llwydcoed on the farm known as Tir Ergid, and shallow pits and numerous levels for the extraction of coal and ironstone were made on the Tir Ergid property and on several other farms in the district. Near Shop Houses there were the Shop Little Pit and the Shop Level Pit, also known as the Tir Ergid Pit. Beyond Pentwyn Houses there was the Swamp Level, and the Patch Level is also recorded, as is the Dyllas New Drift. Near the latter was the Big Level, which opened in 1812, and this is specifically referred to as a source of coking coal from the nine-foot seam, though this seam, being a steam coal, would not normally be thought ideal for coking purposes.

The manuscript entitled "A Glimpse of the History of Llwydcoed" (original in Welsh) is the source for this information and it also mentions the River Level Pit and the Park Pit (that is, the one near Ysguborwen and not the one near Cwmdare), but this probably relates to the period after the amalgamation of the Aberdare and Abernant works.

The "Great Eastern" of 18,915 tons was the last and biggest of the three ships that Brunel built. She first put to sea in September 1859, but was not a commercial success until she was adapted as an intercontinental cable layer.

On the 11th of August 1869, a week before the "Great Eastern" started a return voyage from America it was stated in the Cardiff and Merthyr Guardian that an order had been placed with Rhys and Co. (Merthyr Dare Colliery) and Samuel Thomas (Ysguborwen Colliery) for 12,000 tons of coal.

The Gadlys iron works close to Aberdare town centre also obtained some of its coal and mine from Llwydcoed, from George Edmunds's Patch and Jenkin Richards's Patch on the upper part of the mountain, which are probably the sites visible there today. There was also a Dyllas level and drift in that vicinity and material from these sites were brought down the mountain by a tramroad, which terminated at "the yard at the bottom of Harriet St.". This was behind the houses which are opposite the Bridgend Inn. We are told that the trams were then transported "in Carriages" to the Gadlys works, probably along the Aberdare Canal Company's tramroad to the Robertstown Bridge and from there to the Gadlys works by means of the Gadlys Works tramroad. The works were also supplied with coal and mine from their nearby Gadlys and Dare pits.

The Abernant iron works was based on a lease of 99 years signed in 1801 by which the lessees, Jeremiah Homfray and

This photo is by the well-known local photographer J. Lendon Berry and shows a shaft being sunk at a local colliery. At the far side of the shaft can be seen the pump keeping the shaft clear of water.

James Birch, were entitled to extract mine and coal under several farms in the upper Abernant area. In 1819 the Abernant works was purchased by the Aberdare Iron Company following which the Llwydcoed and Abernant works were operated as one, the mine for both coming from patch working in the Llwydcoed area, and the coal from Abernant. In 1871 the company owned the following pits: Blaenant, Cwmbach, Forge, Mountain, Park and Tunnel. Abernant pit is shown as belonging to Richard Fothergill and Co. Richard Fothergill was then managing the Abernant works on behalf of his uncle, Rowland Fothergill.

In 1837 Crawshay Bailey, the successful ironmaster at the Nant-y-Glo works, purchased the Aberaman estate near Aberdare where he constructed three iron furnaces in 1845. As one of the proprietors of the Aberdare Railway, which opened from Abercynon to Aberdare in 1846, he caused the actual terminus of the line to be sited not at the principal station in Aberdare but near the bottom of Meirion Street, Trecynon, thus enabling limestone from Penderyn to be transhipped from the nearby tramroad to the railway, and hence to his works at Aberaman which connected to the Aberdare Railway by a spur made at Bailey's expense. The property also had supplies of very good coal, and in February 1849 a team led by the celebrated David Williams (Alaw Goch) found for him there the 9ft. seam of steam coal. Though the iron works had some years of prosperity Crawshay Bailey tried to sell it in the early 1860's. In 1864 the Aberaman Iron Works Limited was incorporated to buy the works. Its prospectus stated that the estate contained enough coal to produce 1,000 tons per day for 304 years. But this and other attempts did not succeed and the works came to an unchronicled end, as did all the iron works in the Aberdare area by 1875 with the exception of Hirwaun, which operated sporadically as a forge and foundry until the 1900's.

In taking the relationship of coal to iron as far as the end of the iron industry locally, we have run past the time of the important developments at Abernant-y-Groes in 1837 and it is to that we must now return after we have set the scene with a brief word about the general position of the south Wales coal industry in the first four decades of the nineteenth century. This Chapter has mentioned the mining of coal in the second half of the eighteenth century when its use was limited to malting, domestic use, and use in ironworks. The sending of local coal to other parts of the country was hindered by the remoteness of the north Glamorgan area, caused by the absence of good roads, thereby making difficult the first step in marketing—the transport to the coast for loading into coastal

This photo was taken in 1917 at Abercynon colliery. Presumably a Sumper is a man who excavates or maintains a sump, that is, that portion of a pit shaft which extends below the lowest stopping place of the cage.

Harry Rogers

23

shipping, which entailed the costly utilisation of packhorses. Other parts of South Wales did not have this difficulty. The southern border of the coalfield ran through Swansea Bay, Gower and the estuary of the Loughor and there was a detached section of it in Pembrokeshire. For ports such as Milford, Tenby, Saundersfoot, Llanelly, Burry port, Kidwelly, Swansea, Neath and Port Talbot the task of carrying coal to the ship was, therefore, relatively simple. Though much of the coal produced was used in the smelting of copper and in other metal manufacturing processes in the Swansea/Llanelly region, a coastwise export trade was built up, serving other ports on the Welsh coastline, Ireland and the West Country, from which there was fortunately a return load consisting of Cornish copper ore. The coal thus sold was bituminous coal and anthracite, but around 1824 coal proprietors such as R.J. Nevill from the Swansea/Llanelly area who already had outlets in the London area for their anthracite began to energetically develop a market there for their steam coals, and it was these entrepreneurs who must be mainly credited with the opening up of the sale coal trade in Welsh steam coal, and not Lucy Thomas of Waun Wyllt, Merthyr, the "trim little Welsh widow" whose primacy was asserted by Charles Wilkins, the Merthyr historian, the first but by no means the last to refer to her as the "pioneer or mother of the South Wales steam coal trade". Wilkins was wrong, for the consignment of Waun Wyllt coal which resulted in its superior qualities being noticed by the London coal sellers was sent in 1830, when George Insole was still directing his letters to Robert Thomas rather than to his "widow".

When the first canals with their associated tramroads were built around the end of the eighteenth century, Cardiff and Newport were able to ship coal at competitive rates, but it was mainly bituminous coal for domestic and foundry purposes. Following the foothold in the London market obtained by the Waun Wyllt coal, the consequent expansion of sales was very slow and confined mainly to the Waun Wyllt coal. However the quality of the coal, which was from the famous four-foot seam, was beyond doubt. The "Western Mail" wrote in 1874 "Merthyr is the birthplace of the celebrated, world-renowned, everywhere-praised four feet seam of smokeless steam coal", and

In this photo men are seen setting a "pair of timber" (roof support) in an underground roadway. Each "pair of arms" has been furnished with a horizontal "collar" and they are now engaged in "packing the roof" i.e. driving wedges between the collars and the roof.

Two colliers are here seen "holing" the coal seam in a way which, to the outsider, seems to be highly dangerous. The objective is to prepare the coal by undercutting in this way, so that the firing of a shot (a small amount of explosive) will bring down a greater amount of coal.

Another photo of a collier "holing out" the bottom of a seam. The coal has to be supported, but the two sprags set for that purpose will greatly hinder the collier if it becomes necessary for him to get out in a hurry.

Bryn Davies

25

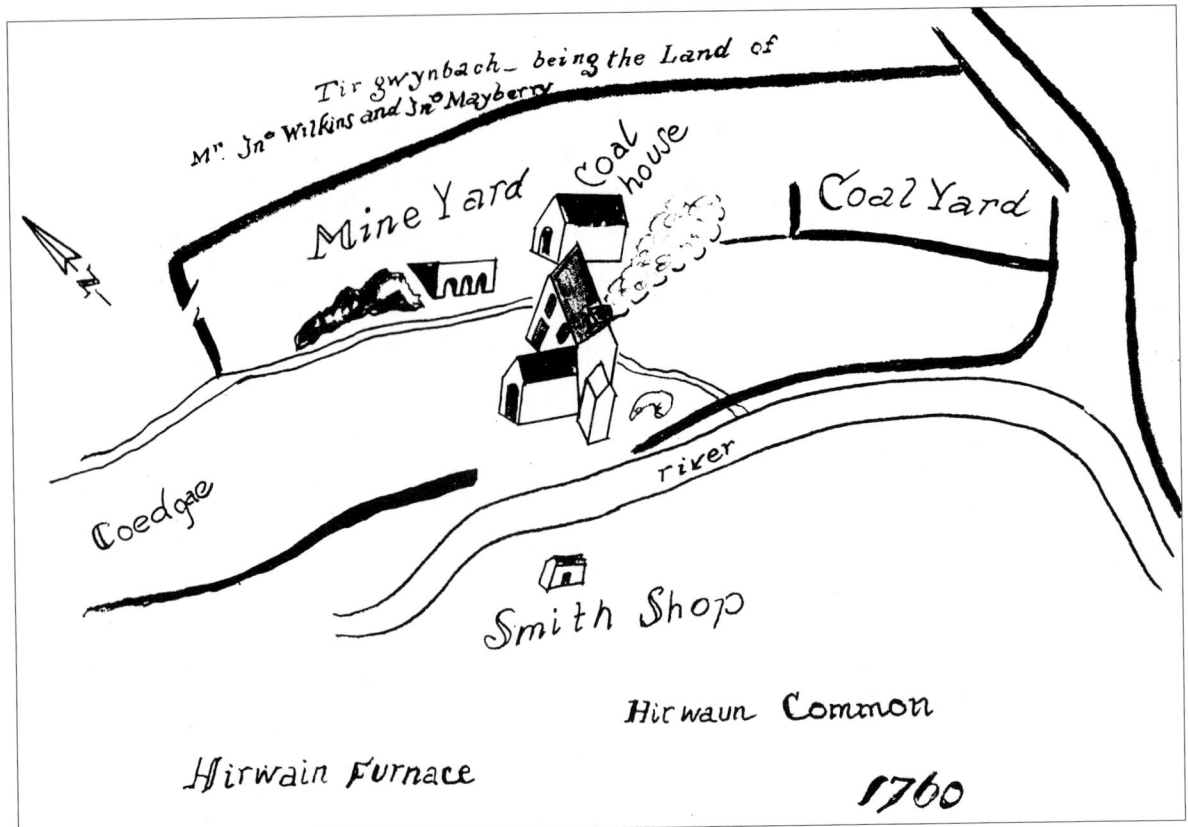

Tir gwynbach – being the Land of
Mr. Jno Wilkins and Jno Mayberry

Mine Yard Coal house Coal Yard

Coedgae

river

Smith Shop

Hirwaun Common

Hirwain Furnace

1760

Though this sketch, copied from a legal document, describes an ironworks (at Hirwaun) it is of some significance for the local history of coal mining because the references to "coal yard" and "coal house" and the date of 1760 support the claim that Hirwaun furnace was using coal to make coke for the blast furnaces soon after the date of the lease of 1757.   Doug Williams

Merthyr Dare colliery in Cwmdare was not the only one which, though far from Merthyr, hoped to boost its sales by including the word in its title. But when the great increase in the steam coal trade occurred the Merthyr ironmasters were more concerned to supply coal for their blast furnaces than for sale to others, and the initiative passed to the Cynon Valley.

Matthew Wayne (c.1780-1853) had been a furnace manager for Richard Crawshay at Cyfarthfa, and was well thought of. With the £800 which Crawshay left him in his will, Wayne went into partnership with Joseph Bailey at Nant-y-Glo ironworks. This turned out to be a success and enabled him to set up in 1827 as an ironmaster at Gadlys, Aberdare, in partnership with George Rowland Morgan and Edward Morgan Williams.

It is said that it was one of his sons, Thomas Wayne, who persuaded the father to look for the four-foot seam in the Aberdare area. Matthew agreed and a company was formed consisting of him, Thomas, his oldest son William Watkin Wayne, and the David family of Abernant-y-Groes, Cwmbach, upon whose land the pit was begun in June 1837. In early December of that year the famous seam was reached and the coal was exhibited in London on the 13th of that month. The modern Geological Survey map shows that at this pit the seam lies at a depth of sixty yards, not forty-nine yards as previously accepted. While this was going on the Waynes were still running the Gadlys ironworks and its associated collieries and mine grounds, despite which, they were referred to by a contemporary as "highly respectable parties but the *least enterprising* colliery proprietors in our district".

At first the development of the steam coal trade was slow. Steam locomotives were few in number and in any case they were fuelled by coke, which was not derived from steam coal, and it was not until 1856-1860 that a satisfactory method of using coal on locomotives was found. The coal was however ideal for marine boilers but steamships were also at that time not very numerous and not very big. Though there were in the U.K. an estimated 768 vessels in 1840, they represented a tonnage of only 87,539.

The Waun Wyllt coal had been placed on the London market in 1830, and now it was the turn of the Aberdare coal. In 1839 John Nixon, one of the mining engineers trained in the north of England, came to work in South Wales. In 1840 he came to an arrangement with Thomas Powell, who was sinking his first pit in the Aberdare valley, to introduce the steam coal to the French market on a commission basis. This he did, not without difficulty, but his reward, according to his biographer, was the witholding of the commision due to him from Powell.

As the 1840's approached there was an increasing demand for coal from naval and merchant steam vessels. There were of course steam coal collieries opening up in other parts of the coalfield, but the quantity of Aberdare coal was thought to be boundless while its quality and superiority over its Newcastle rivals was made clear by the results of official tests. Now the great expansion of coal mining in the Cynon Valley began. In addition to Abernant-y-Groes, by 1840 pits had been sunk at Blaengwawr, Blaenant-y-Groes, Cwmbach (No.9 Colliery), and Tirfounder. In 1843 the Lletty Shenkin, Middle Duffryn and Ynyscynon Collieries opened and these were followed by Upper Duffryn (1844), Aberaman and River Level Collieries (1845), Treaman and Werfa No.1. (1846), Cwmneol Colliery (1848), Abergwawr, Cwmaman, and Ysguborwen Collieries (1849), Deep Duffryn and Lower Duffryn (1850), Abercwmboi, Powell's Pit and Merthyr Dare in Cwmdare (1851), Bwllfa Dare Colliery (1857), Navigation Colliery (1855), and Nantmelyn in Cwmdare and Cwmbach New Pit, the Hirwaun and Aberdare Steam Coal Colliery and Park Pit near

The "Warrior" was the British Navy's first iron warship, which was built after a great deal of controversy. In October 1861 she made a trial of "Nixon's Aberdare Navigation Coal of the same quality as used in Her Majesty's Yacht Victoria and Albert." After making 14.354 Knots for six hours the trial was deemed successful and well reported on by her Master, Captain Denman. It was concluded that "Warrior" was the swiftest and steadiest of her Majesty's ships. She was refurbished some years ago and is berthed at Portsmouth.

The photo shows part of the slopes of Cefn y Gynghon where the profusion of iron ore and coal close to the surface encouraged the manufacture of iron at the nearby Hirwaun Ironworks. Apart from several tramroads and traces of buildings there are three or four structures lying on the mountainside which appear to be either flues serving as chimneys for steam-driven haulages, or chimneys for the furnace ventilation of the many levels on the slopes.

Doug Williams

The River Level Colliery was sited amid the ruins of the Abernant Ironworks. This drainage level runs from the colliery to the bank of the Cynon which at this place runs alongside but lower than the Aberdare Canal Company's tramroad. At some unknown time in the past it was thought necessary to support the roof of the level by means of a brick wall.   John F. Mear

Robertstown (1860), after which the opening of new collieries slowed down. Throughout the period referred to, many levels were opened in the district, some for the benefit of the iron works and others for house coal.

The steam coal colliery proprietors of the Cynon Valley found a rudimentary transport system awaiting them. This was the Aberdare canal and its feeder tramroads. The tramroads came first and were intended to supply the ironworks with their raw materials, namely ironstone, coal and limestone. In addition, one tramroad (Tappenden's tramroad) ran from Abernant ironworks to the head of the Neath canal at Glyn-neath. This took pig iron from that works and from the ironworks at Llwydcoed and Hirwaun to the Neath canal, the Aberdare canal not then being in existence. The Aberdare canal opened in 1812 with a tramroad from the canal head near Cwmbach to Tappenden's tramroad at Gelli Isaf bridge. Unfortunately, soon after, a severe depression occurred in the iron industry, which resulted in the bankruptcy of the Hirwaun proprietors and the Abernant proprietors in 1814 and the closure in about 1816 of the canal, which was almost entirely dependent on the ironworks. But in 1819 William Crawshay bought the derelict and vandalised Hirwaun works and renovated it. Having already gained control of the Glamorganshire canal he then took steps to acquire a controlling interest in the Aberdare canal, put it in good order, and by means of financial inducements he persuaded the Aberdare Iron Company to send all their iron down the Aberdare canal. There were other inducements. The Aberdare canal offered a shorter route to the sea and in addition the tramroad west of Hirwaun was in a very poor state, especially the great incline at Penrhiw, which had become disused by 1819. At about that time another tramroad was built from the Abernant works to the head of the Aberdare canal, and when the Gadlys iron works opened in about 1827 it was connected by a tramroad to the Aberdare Canal Company's tramroad at Robertstown bridge. Other short tramroads were built to collieries close to the canal.

From 1837 when the new pits mentioned above began to be dug down to the four-foot seam, it became clear that the canal would play a large part in taking coal down to the Glamorganshire canal at Abercynon and thence to Cardiff. In 1840 Crawshay persuaded the Aberdare Canal Company to purchase Tappenden's tramroad, ostensibly to "effect the necessary improvements to accommodate the increasing coal trade". The company's true motive may be deduced from the fact that when the sale was completed, that part of the tramroad between Hirwaun and Glyn-neath was allowed by its new owner to become virtually unusable, so that all traffic from the Aberdare area (including Hirwaun) had to use the Aberdare canal. Now the tramroad system assumed its final form. Iron from Hirwaun together with Penderyn limestone coming down the Hirwaun to Penderyn tramroad could be brought down over Hirwaun Common to join iron traffic from Llwydcoed, Gadlys and Abernant and coal from the pits in the vicinity of Aberdare as it made its way to the head of the canal. The owners of the canal saw a rosy future marked by increasing dividends, for not only was the coal trade expanding but the ironworks at Hirwaun, Abernant and Llwydcoed had resumed production some years previously and were working sporadically. But by 1841 Merthyr and Cardiff had been connected by the Taff Vale Railway, and in 1846 another railway joined Aberdare to the T.V.R. at Abercynon. Though the advent of the railway meant the eventual ruin of the canal, the increased demand for coal meant that there was at first enough business to keep canal and railway busy. This local boom was mirrored in many parts of the country as the railway network grew, and as steam-powered ships ploughed the shipping lanes of the world.

The great majority of houses demolished so far [in the district] were built before 1860. Five out of every six cleared were between 90 and 130 years old, with more than half concentrated in the 100-120 year age group. Typical examples include High St, Hirwaun; Cefn Place, Aberdare; Colliers Row, Aberdare; Timothy Row, Cwmbach; and Incline Row, Godreaman; These were all built between 1840 and 1860. In the light of this experience with demolition of houses in the post-war period, and bearing in mind the operative date of the byelaws, it is anticipated that virtually all the houses built before 1860 will have been demolished by the end of the century.

A forecast in the "Harmer Report" announced in June 1972. The report was rejected by Aberdare UDC by a majority of one.

This picture shows the Llewellyn family of Bwllfa, Cwmdare. Rees Llewellyn was the son of a farmer in Cwmparc, near Treorchy. He trained as a mining surveyor and afterwards became the manager of Bwllfa Colliery. On the right is Charles Edwards who married Rees's only daughter. Of his sons, David Richard (left) and William Morgan (centre, standing) became well known in Welsh mining circles.

The Rt Hon Henry Austin Bruce was, among other things, a shareholder in the Vale of Neath Railway and a critic of its engineer, I K Brunel. He became the member for Merthyr and afterwards for Renfrewshire. Later he became Secretary of State for the Home Department, and Lord President of the Council. He was raised to the peerage as Baron Aberdare of Duffryn in 1873 and was president of the committee whose report led to the Act which enabled the Welsh counties to establish intermediate schools. Aberdare was chosen for the site of one such school, which was recently demolished.

> *An inscribed stone on the inside wall of St John's Church records that David William Watkins "was buried perpendicularly" beneath the stone. It has long been thought that this means that he was buried standing up, but if the inscription is read to mean that he was buried "perpendicularly beneath" the stone, then the conventional method of interment can be inferred.*

CHAPTER THREE

At the time the four-foot seam of steam coal was discovered at Cwmbach in 1837 the land in the parish of Aberdare was owned by about 31 persons. Some of these persons led humble and inconspicuous existences on freeholds of only a few acres. Some of the bigger landlords, such as John Bruce Pryce of Duffryn and Crawshay Bailey of Aberaman also lived on their estates, but the biggest landlord of all, the second Marquess of Bute, was among the several "absentee landlords" of the South Wales uplands who lived in more congenial parts of the country. The second Marquess, John Crichton Stuart (1793-1848), had inherited from his father (Lord Mountstuart) great estates in South Wales and other places, which his grandfather (the first Marquess) had acquired by marriage to a descendant of the Earl of Pembroke, who had been given the property by Edward VI in 1547. When John Maybery took a lease of the minerals under Hirwaun Common with power to work them and to build a furnace for smelting the ironstone, the then lord of the manor was Lord Windsor. When he died his daughter Charlotte was the sole beneficiary under his will, and she therefore brought the Windsor estates with her when she married the first Marquess of Bute in 1766.

"With Britain claiming about four fifths of the world carrying trade, according to the statistical calculations of D. A. Thomas it could be said that South Wales products constituted about a third of the coal exports of the world."

Stated by Dr K. O. Morgan in his "Wales-Rebirth of a nation".

Though not now in use, the curling box, seen at the top of the picture, was a very useful part of a collier's equipment especially in low seams. It was placed on the ground in his stall and filled with coal by hand and then carried to the tram and tipped into it. In the curling box is the miner's shovel and pick (which he calls a mandrel). To the left of the shovel are his knee pads and helmet and to the right is his water-bottle or "jack" Below the mandrel is his grub box (also known as a snap box, bait box, or tommy box) and the "bar", which is passed through a hole drilled in the heavier tools and secured with a padlock. This prevents them being "borrowed " in the owner's absence. Also in the curling box (top right) is a methane detector which is not normally part of the miners' equipment.   Brian Davies

A close view of Nixon's headframe at Deep Duffryn. This colliery was the first in the Cynon Valley to be provided with pit-head baths.
The late Glyn Davies

The headframe of Deep Duffryn was noticeable from a distance owing to the curved lower stringers of the braces connecting each front leg of the frame to the corresponding rear leg.
Brian Davies

Deep Duffryn Colliery was sunk by David Williams in 1850 on the North-West side of Mountain Ash. Until 1869 it had water balance winding and a wooden headframe. After being taken over by John Nixon, it was supplied with a winding apparatus based on a ship's engine and a Nixon-designed ventilator. The Great Western Railway's line from Swansea to Pontypool Road (seen here) and the Aberdare canal (beyond the wall on right) ran past the colliery.

The late Glyn Davies

The second Marquess's freeholds in what was later termed the South Wales coalfield amounted to nearly 10,000 acres, the underlying minerals of which belonged to him. But in his capacity of lord of several manors in east and mid Glamorgan, he also owned the minerals beneath the commons in these manors, which amounted to some 26,000 acres more. From 1820, having become aware of the value of the coal and ironstone lying under his estate, he applied himself to its exploitation. Bute's preferred strategy was to grant leases for a term of years to entrepreneurs. An exception to this policy occurred in Rhigos, where he opened a colliery in about 1832 in order to provide employment for his tenants, who were said to be among the most poverty-stricken in Glamorgan. The venture met with many difficulties and in 1842 it was leased to David Davis, a shopkeeper of Hirwaun who, as "David Davis Blaengwawr", afterwards became a successful coal master. It does not appear that the Marquess ever attempted to make iron on his properties in the Cynon valley and John Maybery and his successors were the proprietors of the only ironworks built on the Bute estate in the Cynon valley.

Let us consider for a moment the extent to which the other landowners played a part in the opening up of the iron industry in the Cynon Valley. Samuel Glover, engineer, of Birmingham is known to us as having been appointed by the Court of Chancery as lessee of the Hirwaun ironworks during the minority of the owners, the two sons of Anthony Bacon, who had taken over the lease of the works in 1780. Glover also gave his name to a railroad built from Bryngwyn to the Hirwaun works. He acquired a number of adjacent properties at Llwydcoed, some of which were freehold. The first portion he bought was the Forest of Llwydcoed for which he paid £6,800 in 1787 to Samuel Hughes of Tregunter, Breconshire. After further purchases, on February 8th. 1800, he granted a lease of his properties for the purpose of building an iron works thereon to John Thompson of Quatt, Shropshire, John Hodgetts of Gothersley in the parish of Kinver, Staffordshire, and George and John Scale of Hansworth in the same county. The rent was £1,000 per annum, but no royalties were specified. Though the works were at Llwydcoed, they were known as the Aberdare Iron Company.

In the case of the Abernant ironworks, Jeremiah Homfray, "a great prospector in the South Wales mineral field", but originally of Worcestershire and his partner, James Birch of Aberdare, took a lease from Walter Wilkins of Maesllwch of farms in Abernant and in the Rhigos area. Wilkins came from a very old Norman family named "De Wintona" which settled in Glamorgan and Breconshire. After making a fortune in India he had returned to this country and settled at Maesllwch, becoming MP. for his county, Radnorshire. The lease granted Homfray and Birch power to dig out and use coal and ironstone and to build blast furnaces etc. upon the properties. Subsequently three members of the Tappenden family from Faversham in Kent became partners of Homfray and Birch, but in 1807 Homfray and Birch were bought out by the Tappendens, who themselves became bankrupt in 1814. Afterwards the works were taken over by the Aberdare Iron Company.

This is a close view of the Deep Duffryn headframe taken during the operation of fitting a new cage to the rope in about 1970. Safety helmets were not worn by surface workers at that time. It can be seen that the main legs of the frame, which was designed by John Nixon, are of a most unusual form, being made of flat-bottomed rails bolted at equal intervals to a number of iron hoops thereby making "tubes" albeit with large spaces between the rails. Two other headframes made in the same way were at Merthyr Vale Colliery.   Brian Davies

This view of Aberaman Colliery was taken in July 1962 at about the time of closure of the pit. This site was part of the Aberaman estate which was bought and developed by Crawshay Bailey who later built a private branch from the nearby Aberdare Railway to this colliery.

The late Glyn Davies

This is a slightly more distant and older view of Aberaman Colliery. The curved portion of the building on the left indicates that it was probably a fan-house. There were eventually a total of 5 shafts at Aberaman colliery which was opened in 1845 by Crawshay Bailey, who sold it in 1866 to the Powell Duffryn Company. It produced ironstone, coking coal and steam coal. By 1891 it had acquired a Waddle fan of 40 feet diameter and in 1909 it became the first Mines Rescue Station in South Wales. In the 1950s it became the headquarters of the NCB's No 4 area.

Gareth Thomas

Crawshay Bailey's interests in the Cynon Valley did not prevent him from retaining his interest in the Nant-y-Glo and Beaufort ironworks. By 1845 the sinking of the Aberaman pit was progressing and Bailey was the prime mover in creating the Aberdare Railway which ran to Aberdare from the Taff Vale Railway at Abercynon. This view shows the colliery with the stubby chimney of its ventilating furnace, but the presence of a small building at the foot of the chimney and a short tramroad leading to it with about six laden trams on it opens the possibility that here was a ventilation furnace at ground level rather than at Pit bottom.

Gareth Thomas

This photo of Aberaman Colliery contains a number of the company's wagons. The "PD" lettering on the wagons reminds us that when railways were becoming more widespread in the second half of the nineteenth century, private-owner wagons (That is, wagons owned by the user) were very numerous and were suspected of causing accidents owing to poor maintenance. The railways attempted to buy up these wagons but did not always succeed. But from the 1960's the railways tried to persuade manufacturers to revert to providing their own rolling stock, especially with regard to special purpose wagons. Gareth Thomas

This level at Ysguborwen was the first of Samuel Thomas and Thomas Joseph's projects in the Cynon Valley. It was rediscovered by History Society members in 1983 when this photo was taken of the keystone of the arch at the level entrance. It reads:

T(homas) & J(oseph)
S(gubor)wen
W
1850

Many alterations have since taken place, but it is believed to be still there.

John F. Mear

The Gadlys Colliery had several shafts sunk on its site some mining coal and one or two mining ironstone. They belonged to the Gadlys Iron Co whose blast furnaces were situated about ¼ of a mile away on the "Depot" site. This is a splendid view of the Colliery when it was in full swing. The pit in use was known as the Victoria Pit. Note to the left of centre the peculiar engine house for the winder, giving the impression that there was a vertical engine in there. The yard has an untidy scattering of pit-wood and at the bottom of the picture is a cutting through which runs the Dare River and, on a shelf, the Dare Valley branch of the former Taff Vale Railway which crosses over the river in the middle distance. Railway wagons bearing the colliery owners name (Lancaster Speir) can be seen (bottom left) and on the right a man can be seen standing on the plinth of the chimney stack.

We now come to the Gadlys ironworks. One Matthew Wayne, after working as a furnace manager at Cyfarthfa, became a partner in an ironworks in Nant-y-Glo. In 1820 he gave up his partnership and moved to Aberdare where, in association with two new partners, both local landowners, he built the Gadlys ironworks in 1827. The works (and afterwards coal mines) were built on land owned by one of the partners, George Rowland Morgan, and coal and iron ore were found underneath farms at Llwydcoed, some owned by Wayne and the rest by his other partner, Edward Morgan Williams. In about 1834 the Marquess of Bute granted the company a lease of ground on the lower slopes of the Graig at Aberdare where the Graig Colliery was afterwards built. Iron manufacture was discontinued in 1875 but the collieries remained in production.

A branch of the ancient family of Mathew had lived on their estate at Aberaman for some 200 years but the time came when the latest of the line, Edward Mathew, had no son to succeed him. Upon his death, therefore, his many properties were shared between his three daughters. The husband of one of the daughters, Hugh Lord, sold the Aberaman estate to Anthony Bacon 11, the son of the founder of the Cyfarthfa ironworks. After his death his executors sold the estate to the Yorkshireman, Crawshay Bailey, an extremely successful ironmaster of Nant-y-Glo. This was conveyed in 1837, though Bailey did not take up residence until 1844 after which he constructed three furnaces and sank pits. Aberaman was therefore the last of the Cynon Valley ironworks to be built. In 1864 the Aberaman Iron Company was formed to take over the ironworks but this did not succeed and in 1866 Bailey sold the Aberaman estate with its ironworks and (apparently under-developed) colliery to the Powell Duffryn Steam Coal Company, which turned its back on the manufacture of iron and concentrated on the mining of coal from the estate.

This brief summary of the role of the principal landowners in the development of the iron industry reveals that they all had different approaches, according to their personal circumstances and needs. At one end of the spectrum was the second Marquess of Bute who came into his inheritance in 1814, but due to eye trouble he was unable to follow his intention to take an active interest in the management of his estate until 1820. By that time most of the centres of iron manufacture on his estates had been set up.

The inside of the Gadlys winding engine house. Being driven by an electric motor the drum and its accessories were more compact than they were in the days of steam.

The late Glyn Davies

This is perhaps the best photograph of the Gadlys pit in its days of retirement. Although it closed in 1939 it was retained as pumping station until the 1960's and since the pumps were at the bottom of the pit and were attended day and night, this necessitated the retention of the winding engine. In this post-war view the colliery has been virtually cleared away though the Victoria pit is still in working order mainly in order to service the pumps at the bottom of the pit. Despite efforts made by the then Council, the National Museum of Wales and the Cynon Valley History Society (then in its infancy) it was not possible to save and preserve the electric winding engine or the headframe of the colliery, which was taken down in May 1972. The building on the left housed the winding engine.

Brian Davies

THE FOUR-GALLON CASK

A prominent feature and a common spectacle forty and fifty years ago on the roads leading from the town on Christmas Eve were men carrying small four-gallon casks, full of beer, upon their shoulders to their homes. These were bought in order to make merry over the holidays and to tide over the closing hours of Christmas Day. Many a comic episode occurred when some of these provident fellows could hardly carry themselves home leave alone the four gallon casks. Sometimes the casks were seen to be rolling down backwards over the Abernant road, Gadlys road, and Mill Street, while its owner would be struggling to his feet in an effort to re-capture the runaway cask. This custom also has disappeared, and the four gallon cask has gone out of use.

Although he was possessed of much less land than the Marquess of Bute, Walter Wilkins worked in a similar manner, granting leases for others to work, rather than working it himself. He apparently acquired lands in various districts and it was he who leased land at Abernant and other ironstone-bearing property near Pontwalby to Homfray and Birch, which became the basis of the Abernant ironworks. Samuel Glover, though acquainted with iron making, decided to lease the properties he had bought to others so that they could bear the cost and anxieties of industrial development.

At the other end of the spectrum, at Gadlys, Matthew Wayne with his partners George Rowland Morgan and Edward Morgan Williams set up ironworks and extracted ironstone from their own properties, and Crawshay Bailey did the same after purchasing the Aberaman estate, but not wholly successfully. These then were the only landlords to exploit their own resources of ironstone.

All the lessees of mineral property naturally had to pay for the privilege. Firstly, a rent had to be paid. It was a fixed annual sum irrespective of the amount of minerals raised, and was called a dead rent or certain rent. The effect of this was to guarantee the landlord some revenue even if the lessees did nothing with the land. It also stimulated a reluctant lessee to work the

Numerous levels flourished as part of the Abernant Iron Company and there was probably one called the River Level, a name which attached itself to this colliery which was afterwards set up in the 1870s in the midst of the derelict ironworks. There appears to be a standard gauge rope-hauled incline in the foreground behind which a heap of scrapped trams adds to the untidiness of the site.

minerals to get a return from the dead rent he had paid. When the mineral was found and brought to the surface the lessee had to pay a royalty of so much per ton, though this charge was not included in some of the early leases. Where minerals from an adjacent property had unavoidably to pass over (or under) the lessors land then a wayleave payment was also levied. These charges usually applied to whatever minerals were taken out of the ground such as clay, sand, stone and, next in importance to coal, iron ore, which was conveniently found in proximity to the coal, as explained in Chapter 1. In 1851-2 for example, the Aberdare Iron Company was one of the four large ironworks which were responsible for the bulk of the Marquess's mineral income, though the payments were mainly in respect of royalties on coal raised for conversion to coke for smelting.

It is likely that at about the beginning of the 19th century there were few persons in the Cynon valley wealthy enough to be able to invest in the local ironworks. This accounts for the number of Englishmen engaged in the development of local ironworks such as Jeremiah Homfray (Worcestershire), the Tappendens (Faversham), John Thompson (Shropshire), John Hodgetts (Kinver), and George and John Scale (Birmingham). Some of these had made money in trade and some had experience of iron making.

After the discovery of the famous four-foot seam in 1837 we have no

LEVEL AR-AVON ABERDARE.

Another view of River Level Colliery. The cages are wound by means of flat ropes which coil on themselves and thereby produce a "low gear" for starting from pit bottom which gradually increases during the wind. The opposite effect is produced on the descending cage. Unlike the other photo of this colliery, the headframe has a ladder to the top of the frame. Note the narrowness of the two external winding wheels which are provided with pairs of "horns" around their circumference to assist the proper coiling of the rope.

record of further pits opening in the next two years. No doubt this was a time when negotiations were taking place about the terms of leases. In preparing this book much effort has been expended on finding the dates of opening of the pits that are mentioned. The task is made more difficult by the fact that a source may not state whether a date of commencement signifies the date when the lease was signed, the date when sinking commenced, the date when the coal was reached, or the date when the first coal was sent to market. Another factor was that in some cases a lessee was allowed to take possession and start development before the lease was signed. For example, in the summer of 1853 Thomas Powell started to sink pits on land at Troedrhiwllech (Cwmdare) but afterwards refused to pay the second year's rent in respect of the property until he received the lease, after which he "proposed going on in good earnest".

One of the "new wave" of developers was David Davis, whom we have already mentioned, a successful grocer in Hirwaun who negotiated a lease and started sinking a pit to the steam coal at Blaengwawr in 1843. The first coal was sent out in 1845. The Aberdare Iron Company, which had

Blaengwawr colliery was opened in 1843 by David Davis. Eventually there were nine shafts there, four of which were airshafts. Like most of the early collieries in the valley, it had at first furnace ventilation and water balance winding. The surface buildings have now all disappeared.

The late Glyn Davies

Screens, Blaengwan Level, Aberdare. 217.

There were two Blaengwawr levels in Maesyffynon lane working (in 1903) the Graig and No 2 Rhondda seams. They produced house-coal (seen in the cart in the centre of the picture) and various sizes of coal for industrial use. The levels closed in 1935.

John F Mear

taken over the Abernant Iron Company in 1819, also opened a pit in the early 1840's at Blaenant, on the mountain above Abernant and another, the No. 9 colliery near Ynyscynon House. At about the same time the Gadlys Iron Company sank the Mountain Pit and drove various levels on their own property at Dyllas.

The man who ended by dominating the coal trade in the Cynon valley was the above-mentioned Thomas Powell who hailed from Monmouth and started business as a timber merchant at Newport. He sank a pit at Tirfounder and found the four-foot seam in 1842. He opened further collieries called Plough Pit (1849), Lower Duffryn (by 1850), and Middle Duffryn (1843). He also sank the pit called Troedrhiwllech or Cwmdare colliery, (afterwards known as Powell's Pit or Bwllfa No. 3) in Cwmdare, from which the first coal was sent out in August 1856. By the time of his death in 1863 he also owned the Upper Duffryn Colliery (1844) and other pits in south Wales amounting to nearly twenty in all. Powell did not concern himself with the making of iron at his works at Aberaman and most of his output was steam coal.

Chapter 2 ended with a brief mention of the Aberdare Railway, which connected with the Taff Vale Railway at Abercynon. Though nominally a separate concern the Aberdare Railway was leased to the T.V.R. when completed, and run by them until their amalgamation in 1902. The T.V.R., like most of the railways of the coalfield, were favoured by downhill running to the seaports and the return journey against the gradient was usually with trains consisting of empty wagons. This advantage did not apply to the rival railway, the Vale of Neath Railway, which was intended to run from Neath to Merthyr (using a tunnel through the Merthyr mountain) with a branch from Gelli Tarw junction to Aberdare. The plans for this line created a great deal of scorn when they were published, since it entailed a steep gradient to the summit at Hirwaun, at a place where Hirwaun Pond Halt (also known as Factory Halt) was built during the last war. Hirwaun Pond Halt was followed by a steep descent down to Aberdare which was of course a disadvantage for the VNR in that the gradient was against the loaded westbound trains.The branch opened in 1851, before Merthyr, and was extended, firstly to Canal Head and then down to Middle Duffryn. In this way it gained access to the several collieries in the lower Cwmbach area as well as those nearer Aberdare. Collieries in the Cwmdare and Cwmaman areas were reached by a branch of the V.N.R., the Dare and Aman branch, down which the first coal

The site of Treaman Colliery, now a football pitch. It was also called Nici-naci, Williams's Pit and Pwll Bara Menyn. It was sunk by David Williams Ynyscynon between 1846 and 1850 and closed in 1912. In the distance can be seen the roof of the Aberaman Hall.

Gareth Thomas

John Nixon was one of the northerners who created a niche for himself in the South Wales Coalfield. He sunk several collieries in the Cynon Valley and bought another (Deep Duffryn) from David Williams. He introduced engineering improvements in his pits and brought in long wall working and the double shift system. His main achievement was the introduction of Cynon Valley steam coal to the French market.

was sent in November 1854. Cwmaman was also served by a railway built by the Powell Duffryn Co. as an extension to an earlier line built by Crawshay Bailey as a spur from the Taff Vale Railway, which also had a short branch serving the collieries of the lower part of Cwmbach. The V.N.R's branch to Aberdare became its main line in later years when it was extended to Pontypool Road.

The two pits at Lletyshenkin were sunk in 1843 and 1850 by William Thomas. Also in 1843 Ynyscynon colliery was sunk by David Williams. Development then moved to the other side of the Cynon where Aberaman colliery was sunk in 1845 by Crawshay Bailey. By that year the River Level colliery had been brought into use at Abernant by the Aberdare Iron Company, and in 1846 David Williams inaugurated the Treaman Colliery and John Nixon the Werfa Colliery.

The Park Pit Cwmdare was opened by the Hirwaun Iron Company to produce coking coal and steam coal for the Hirwaun works. It is shown on the tithe map of 1847 but may have been open as early as 1830. If it was, it was the oldest deep mine in Cwmdare. In 1848 the Cwmneol colliery was opened by Carr and Morrison and in 1849 Shepherd and Evans opened Cwmaman colliery. In the same year Thomas and Joseph started the Ysguborwen colliery and Thomas Powell and Protheroe the Abergwawr colliery. At the half-way mark of the century the Aberdare Navigation Colliery and Bute Pit (Crawshay), Deep Duffryn (David Williams) and Lower Duffryn (Thomas Powell) were open, and in the following year they were joined by Abercwmboi (David Davis), Troedrhiwllech (Thomas Powell) and Merthyr Dare (David Williams) collieries. There now followed a period of consolidation of the existing collieries with only one pit more, (the Navigation at Mountain Ash—John Nixon) opening before 1857.

We return to yet another view of Aberaman Colliery showing a row of boilers on the right with the ventilation chimney behind. On the left Godreaman can be seen in the distance.
Harry Rogers

The steamer "Tafna" is seen loading coal for the Italian State railways at Cardiff Docks in about 1920. The name "Cwmaman" painted on the trucks shows the origin of the coal. Cynon Valley coal made Cardiff the largest coal exporting port in the world.

Doug Williams

Bwllfa coal awaiting shipment at Penarth Docks. The use of private owner wagons gave the coal companies plenty of scope for the free advertisement of their products.

Doug Williams

D. R. Llewellyn's patent fuel Works at the Gadlys Estate Aberdare.   Doug Williams

TBS Cwmpennar Pit was also known as Lower Duffryn, and was another of Thomas Powell's enterprises. It was open by 1850 and closed in 1927.
John F. Mear

The Tunnel Colliery was made by the Aberdare Iron Co and was open by 1865. It passed through a few ownerships and ceased to mine coal in 1904, serving thereafter as a ventilator for the Windsor level and Nixon's Werfa Collieries. No good photos of this colliery have come to light, which is a pity especially because of its proximity to the nearby Abernant Tunnel on the Merthyr branch of the former Vale of Neath Railway.

Doug Williams

It is not possible to say whether this pit at Bwllfa (Cwmdare) is the old pit or the nearby new pit. The picture is one of a set taken between 1867 and 1872 and the winding arrangements are of some technical interest.

Nantmelin Colliery Cwmdare. The headframe lacks sheaves and we may deduce that it is still under construction. The row of buildings in the foreground includes the smith's shop and on the left is the haulage engine house for the four ft drift which was completed in 1912, which is probably the date of the photo.
John F. Mear

This photo of Fforchaman Colliery in Cwmaman was taken in 1950. Also known as Brown's Pit it was opened following a lease dated 1856 and worked until 1965. Note the proximity of Glanaman road to the railway line and the dust nuisance likely to be caused thereby.
The late Glyn Davies

From the foregoing it will be seen that though the pioneers of the iron industry in the Aberdare area were almost all Englishmen with money to invest or experience in iron-making or other businesses, the coal industry was dominated by Welshmen, some of whom had already made money from iron manufacture or commerce. Some, like Thomas Powell, were Welshmen who came from outside the Cynon Valley. A few were English, some of whom were men of great ability, such as John Nixon from Tyneside and Crawshay Bailey from Wakefield.

Through the 1840's the development of the steam ships and steam locomotives, and the greater employment of steam engines for pumping in mines and as prime movers in mills and other factories in the U.K. as well as abroad, were responsible for the increased demand for coal. And it will be realised that the supply of suitable coal and the development of fixed and self-moving steam engines were factors which fed on each other, so to speak. The Cynon Valley played a large part in this expansion, for there was bituminous and steam coal in plenty, and at its western extremity, semi-anthracite coal as well. With regard to the use of coal in locomotives, it is not generally known that in their early days, locomotives were fired with coke made from bituminous coal because locomotives fired with coal could not comply with the legal requirement to consume their own smoke. Steam coal could do so, but it had a destructive effect on fire bars. However, modifications made to fireboxes became generally adopted in the 1850's (The T.V.R. in 1857), enabling locomotives to burn coal satisfactorily.

The area around Aberdare was responsible in the 40's and 50's for making Cardiff the leading port in the South Wales coal trade. The size of the undertakings varied greatly. The entrepreneur with only £100 or so to invest would drive a level into the crop of the seam, withdrawing and starting another when ventilation became a necessity and haulage costs became burdensome. To reach the steam coal

A pleasant picture of Powell's Pit, Cwmdare, taken before the removal of the metals of the former Dare and Aman branch (foreground) which took place by the 14th of July 1957. The colliery had closed in 1936 but some time later a new fan was installed in the flat-roofed brick building to the right of the base of the stack.   The late Glyn Davies

measures, which were deeper in the ground, shafts were a requirement and considerable expense was needed for haulage, ventilation, drainage, screens, sidings, rolling stock, and various surface buildings. These factors were behind the tendency towards larger and more expensive establishments funded by wealthier investors, but there still remained a number of smaller units such as the Bedwlwyn Colliery which operated from 1865 to 1901, in which period it was abandoned three times. A shorter-lived colliery was the Fforchneol Graig levels, which worked from 1921 to 1924 with a period of closure.

The Cynon Valley produced both iron and coal, but thanks to the influence of certain novelists and the film industry, when the popular mind thinks of iron, it thinks of Merthyr, and when it thinks of coal, it thinks of the Rhondda, Aberdare being generally ignored. In terms of production, there is some justification for this, for Merthyr at its peak in about 1845 was probably the greatest centre of iron making in the world. As regards the Rhondda, the earliest mining was confined to the bituminous coal in the lower Rhondda as it was deduced from the angle of dip of the seams in the Aberdare area that in the Rhondda the steam coal would be found at a depth which would make mining impracticable. However, this turned out to be untrue, and the steam coal was proved in the Rhondda Fawr in 1852. Thus began the rapid expansion of mining in the two Rhonddas, which overtook that of Aberdare by 1884 and expanded further, so that for the ensuing forty years it produced more steam coal than any other British district of the same area.

This is pit No 3 (mining housecoal) at Penrhiwceiber taken shortly before closure.
Brian Davies

Nevertheless, the pits of the Cynon Valley produced an enormous amount of coal over the years as can be seen in Appendix F. However, these figures should be treated with caution as inconsistencies sometimes occur, e.g. omitting to distinguish between small and large coal or between coal destined for ironmaking and that destined for export. Anomalies sometimes occured when coal was cut in one parish and brought to bank in an adjacent one.

Chapter 1 explained that the dip of the coal seams meant that the further one went down the valley the deeper the seams would be from the surface. For example, the Gellideg seam, which was found 146 yards below the surface at Aberdare was 170 yards below ground at Abercynon. Naturally this meant that the expense of mining increased as one moved further down the valley. This and the fact that there was no demand for coal for iron-making at Mountain Ash, probably accounted for the later development of mining in that area. The latter part of Chapter 2 has summarised the principal pits opened to 1860, after which the rate of new openings slowed down. At the lower end of the valley the Deep Duffryn (David Williams) and Lower Cwmpennar (Thomas Powell) pits were the first

This is the Bute washery under construction near Hirwaun Ponds alongside the coal sidings. There had previously been a brickworks on the site.   Doug Williams

of any significance in the lower part of the valley when they were commenced in 1850. The Lower and Upper Forest Levels were made in 1851 and 1857, and Nixon's Navigation Colliery was finished in 1855, after seven years' sinking. Nixon also bought Deep Duffryn from David Williams for £42,000. It was then producing 150 tons per day, but in two years, the installation of new winding engines and of Nixon's patent ventilator had helped to raise production to 1,000 tons per day. Developments were also occurring at Abercynon, where the Carne Park Levels were working by 1864, as were the Dyllas ironstone mine and patch. In this year the Meadow pit at Aberaman was sunk and the Tower Colliery No 1 drift was driven into the stretch of mountainside where the early workings for

---

Actual details of a water balance system for winding in use at Penclawdd in 1858.

TO COLLIERY PROPRIETORS AND OTHERS

TO BE SOLD BY PRIVATE CONTRACT the undermentioned articles belonging to a WATER BALANCE MACHINE for raising coal, viz
Framing complete for top of pit , cast iron shieves (sic) 5ft 7" dia with double breaks
Shaft for do. 7ft 9" long by 7?" square made of the best hammered iron.
Balance chain ¼" dia and 34 fathoms long.
Working chain ¼" dia 100 fathoms long
2 wrought iron cisterns to suit
160 fathoms of wrought iron guide rails about 8 tons

All the above have been in use at the Penclawdd Colliery near Swansea and are in good working order, but are not now in use in consequence of a winding engine being used instead.

Further particulars may be known on application to Mr. Dunkin at the colliery.

Dated Penclawdd, 28th September 1858

The Graig Pit was owned at first by the Gadlys Iron Co and was open from 1865 to 1916. The coal it raised was sent in standard gauge trucks down an incline which ran under the Dare branch of the GWR and over the Dare branch of the T V R terminating at the Gadlys Colliery. In the photo can be seen the wire rope connecting the trucks to the haulage engine in the open-fronted shed on the right.

It is believed that the women in the picture were probably employed on the screens at Llettyshenkin Colliery. The employment of women underground was made illegal in 1842.

coal and mine for the Hirwaun ironworks were made. In the following year Bedwlwyn and Graig Collieries were opened, as were the Pond Flash pits (Gadlys). The Tunnel Pit was open in the same year, though the date of commencement is not known. In 1866 the Upper Bryngwyn Levels were opened and the London and Merthyr Colliery, the Mountain Pit Abernant, and Pwllbach Pits were working.

In 1867 the Mountain drift and Pit were working and in the next year Fforchneol Colliery was opened. The Level Fach at Blaengwawr was working in 1869. At some time in the 70's the Level Francis Phillips opened in the Cwmbach tunnel area. The early 70's saw a flurry of activity In 1870 the Abergorki drift, the Blaenhirwaun drifts, the Tower Graig Colliery, and the Bute drifts were all working, and the Tan y Bryn level opened in this year or possibly earlier, and Brook level no 2 was in being in 1871, the year that Miskin Colliery opened. 1872 saw the opening of Penrhiwceiber colliery and the Forest level (Hirwaun) was known to be open in that year, as was the Prosper level. In 1874 the Coed Cae levels opened. The Gellideg and Gelli Isaf levels, the Llesty levels and T. Hopkins level were known to be open in the following year. The Gwrhyd Pit dates from some time after 1875.

> *On the 4th inst I was approached by Mr. William Jones (roundabout proprietor) who was desirous of passing his [traction] engine and vans under the incline bridge near Duffryn, Mountain Ash. The height to the underside of the bridge sheeting was insufficient and it was necessary to provide sufficient headroom that the roadway be excavated to a maximum depth of 2 feet and for a length of about 15 yards. I estimate the cost of same, including replacing the road at about £4 10s. The roadway is being restored today and I hold £5 in hand as deposit for the work from Mr. Jones.*
>
> **Report of the Mountain Ash surveyor July 1910**

By 1888 Nixon's ventilator (above) was installed at Deep Duffryn alongside the canal where it worked successfully for over thirty years. According to Nixon's biographer the ventilator was also installed at the Navigation Colliery and at the House of Commons. This assertion must be treated with caution as it is known that a Waddle fan did duty alongside the original shaft at Navigation.

Harry Rogers

Blaennant colliery belonged to the Aberdare Iron Company, having been built by them in the 1840's high on the mountain above the ironworks at Abernant. The building on the left (now removed) was made of poured concrete and housed the haulage engine for the incline which ran down to the ironworks. The incline running right to left behind the pond is the incline from the Mountain Colliery.

The late Glyn Davies

CHAPTER FOUR

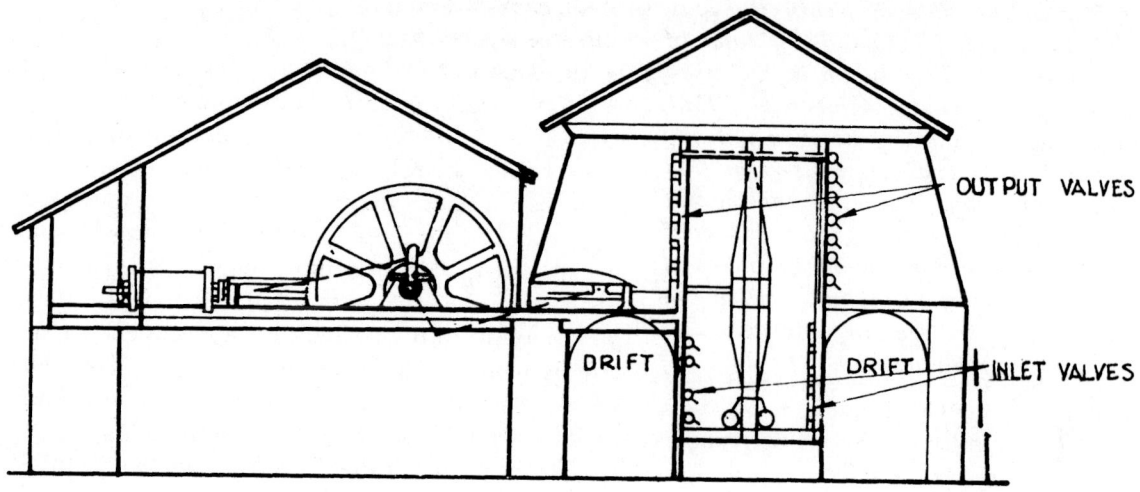

John Nixon's inventions have already been briefly referred to. This is a drawing of his well-known ventilator which consisted of two wooden rectangular chambers (one behind the other in this view) 30 feet wide and 21½ feet high. Each had a close-fitting rectangular piston fitted with rollers and running on rails within the "cylinder" The pistons were moved to and fro by an external steam engine. Each cylinder was furnished with simple "flap" valves, 168 acting as suction valves and connected to the fan drift and 196 acting as delivery valves open to the atmosphere, amounting to no less than 728 valves for the two cylinders.

Doug Williams

In this chapter we will look at the further development of mining in the valley, paying attention to methods of mining and the important subject of ventilation.

As explained in Chapter 1, the methods of coal and iron mining in South Wales, on the northern rim of the basin, would have been 'scouring', or 'patching', interspersed with a few shallow levels. There must have been a few shafts in being, reaching down to one or two of the topmost seams. But there was a sea-change in mining technology between 1850 to 1875 in South Wales and the Cynon Valley. One major turning point for Aberdare was the sinking of the "Abernant-y-Groes" shaft in 1837, with the famous 4ft seam of steam coal coming to light (described in Chapter 2). This triggered the necessity of deeper and yet deeper shafts on the valley floor and mountain slopes which, if successful, became the nuclei of villages such as Cwmdare, Cwmbach, Llywdcoed, Abernant and Cwmaman and eventually down to the South, where the Mountain Ash pits, followed by Penrhiwceiber colliery, and lastly, at the turn of the century, Abercynon Colliery, were opened. Other factors, chiefly the rise in demand also contributed to this "boom" in the steam coal industry locally, and in South Wales generally. Technical advancement was facilitated by the establishment of "The South Wales Institute of Engineers" in 1857. This created a forum for the discussion of the engineering aspects of mining with special regard to the improving of mining techniques. It seems that the engineers welcomed speakers who could inform them of different techniques practised in other parts of the country. An example of this was clearly evident when Mr. George Brown, a mining engineer from Northern England, spoke on "The Comparative Systems of Coal-Mining in the North of England and South Wales, with Regard to Accidents and Loss of Life". This lecture was presented in 1866 to a meeting in Swansea of the Institute, and was based on government inspectors' reports from both areas. It was apparent that Mr. Brown was correct in his argument, as his tables and lists proved. The methods of mining; the deployment of miners; the entire "shift system" was totally different from South Wales. The employment of extra officials and probably the theory and practice of "less pit room", was the final argument in ventilation standards. This phrase was expressing his views on the "long-wall" method of mining a seam, plus his recommendations for "double-shift" coal-getting from these long-wall coal-faces. By "Less pit room" Mr. Brown meant that if it was possible to concentrate the miners in one area of coal-face, and not scatter them, there would be less loss of life; ventilation would be simpler and thus more efficient; and there would be other associated benefits.

Mr. Brown should have come to Cwmbach about 20 years previously to form a view on the frequency of explosions in the collieries on the valley floor, especially those owned by Thomas Powell. The seams worked there had a poor safety record including much loss of life owing to the copious emissions of gas from the freshly opened seams. Improvements in systems and methods had to be introduced, often in the face of opposition from the coalmasters and in defiance of the requirements of the Inspector of Mines, one of four appointed by the Government in 1850. Access to this shared knowledge was vital for future changes, despite some protest from certain managers from the Cynon Valley. However, at Mountain Ash, John Nixon, a Newcastle man who was described as "a giant of that time", was, by the 1870's, very committed to improving the standards, efficiency and safety of his works. He was an engineer and businessman, who introduced improved ventilation methods into Deep Duffryn and Navigation collieries, and insisted upon "double-shift" coaling despite opposition from the colliers in his works.

In the 1870s mining methods and systems were settling into established routines, with conditions gradually improving below ground. Unfortunately, it was in 1875 that the iron industry collapsed in Cynon Valley, which resulted in a tragic closure of works together with their associated collieries. These events, however, directed the minds of the coalmasters towards the booming steam coal trade, and its newer methods of production in which the old system of working "pillar and stall" was being superseded by the long-wall method.

The pillar and stall method of working a new district involved driving two parallel roads through the coal to the boundary of the district. At intervals of about 20 yds, short roads would be driven at right angles. These were called stalls. At intervals of about 30 yds two stalls opposite each other would be extended to meet and these "cross cuts" could be further extended outwards. When as many stalls as were required were made, a plan of the new workings would appear as a grid of roads in which there would be included rectangular pillars of coal. When the coal had been worked in this way to the boundary it would be the turn of the pillars, which would be carefully extracted, working from the boundary back to where the operation began, having regard to the fact that the pillars were supporting the roof. This method is now known as "retreat working." In the Cynon Valley this final clearing of the pillars was called "working a Barry" and was frequently accompanied by a fall of the roof.

There were many different methods of long-wall working. With a well planned "longwall" advancing face method, even before the era of mechanised conveyor faces, as much as ten or twelve stalls would be driven at the same time into a seam, by two colliers and probably a boy, in each stall. As well as extracting the coal to the width of the stall, they would also hew and clear, beneath the roof and to each side, until the stalls would be linked up to each other, thus forming the coal-face. This is the longwall face. If the stalls are about 15 yards apart, which is about normal, there is now a face, for example, of six stalls, cutting coal from a combined face of 90 yards, plus "ribs" each end, giving an extra 10 yards of coal. This is now a face of 100 yards in length, with linked stalls. The stone "rippings" in each stall are shot-fired down, then packs of stone rubble support the side of each stall, as the face advances, as well as ensuring an airway for the entire face ventilation. This system was being worked by the 1890's in many of the valley's larger mines.

This photo shows Blaenant in its heyday. The colliery was served by a standard gauge incline connecting it to the Abernant works. Part of this incline can be seen in the bottom right hand corner and a standard gauge flat wagon is being lowered. This has an inclined floor so as to provide a horizontal surface upon which a number of loaded trams can be placed. The two stays running from the top of the headframe to the winder which resist the tendency for the winder to pull down the headframe are unusually long and are supported by vertical posts at midpoint. John F Mear

57

The Waddle fan was made in Llanelly and was popular in South Wales. This is the Waddle fan at the Navigation pit at Mountain Ash which was dismantled many years ago.
Brian Davies

A short distance from the original Navigation shaft a new pit was sunk in later years. This was known as the North Pit and this too was provided with a Waddle fan of 42ft diam. This is the fan (now dismantled) seen in the photo. The North Pit is in the foreground surmounted by a simple headframe.
Brian Davies

This is the engine of the steam-driven Waddle fan at the North Pit, Mountain Ash. Steam-powered Waddle fans could be supplied with one or two horizontal cylinders, but when two were provided the engine ran on one, the other cylinder being disconnected, as can be seen in this photo. The second cylinder would be re-connected and brought into use when the first cylinder needed maintenance or repair. The engine of this fan has survived but the rotor was too badly rusted to be saved.

Brian Davies

In the vicinity of the area shown in this photo, were the three Aberaman clay levels, part of the Aberaman colliery complex . Apart from mining coking coal they produced clay for the adjacent pipeworks seen in the above photo. They were one of the side industries of the Powell Duffryn combine. and stood alongside the Aberaman-Abercwmboi road. Part of the site is now occupied by the Kwiksave store.

The late Glyn Davies

The length of such a coal face would be pre-planned to include efficient means of transporting the coal produced in a shift, the number of horses required, etc. Management would also determine the amount of ventilation required for the face, and its share in the overall colliery ventilation system. A face such as described above was worked as a training face for new entrants in the "Libya" district of Tower No. 1 drift up until 1958, the one difference being the crude conveyors used in the face, as opposed to the use of horses previously.

Objections to working longwork methods were made by the colliers of the period, as they were losing the independence of "a stall to himself", wrote Mr. Bedlington, Colliery Agent, in 1870, who then made an astonishing statement, in retrospect. "Wherever it is possible", he said, "it would be better to drive the levels to the boundary, and then work back. Not always feasible, for want of capital or time". It has taken about 120 years for such coal faces to appear in the Cynon Valley, (and possibly South Wales). We refer to the 'retreat' method of cutting a coal face, now employed successfully, as explained above, by Tower colliery in the year 2000.

Longwall mining itself had changed immensely over many years, but by 1900, newer techniques from the northern coalfields were being tried in pits in the valley, one being the first electrical coal cutter in the valley introduced by D.R. Llewellyn, at the Windber Drifts in Cwmdare, in about 1905. It would probably have been used in a longwall face. (He had been studying American coal cutting methods prior to this turning point at a place called Windber near Paint Creek in Pennsylvania). This undercutting of a seam through a coal face enabled collieries to clear the face in less time, but the early coal cutters were unfortunately "cutting dry", that is, without the use of a spray of water to lay the dust. This increased air-borne dust quantities. By the 1930's, attempts at dust suppression were being improved, and by 1950 it was illegal to "dry cut" a face. (In coal mines the dustiness of the air varies between very wide limits, due to the differing operations in any one mine, and dust concentrations as high as 2000 milligrams per cubic 1.3yd. have been recorded during 'cutting dry'). This sort of figure would result in lung diseases, and could even cause a dust explosion.

Britain was at the peak of its power during the 1914-1918 war, when the Empire covered one third of the globe. The Navy and merchant fleets numbered thousands of ships powered by steam produced by the best steam coal. No better steam coal could be obtained than that of the Cynon and other valleys in South East Wales and the amounts produced and used were enormous. The Prime Ministers of Britain and Australia were Welsh-speaking North Walians. The contribution of Wales to the British cause and prosperity was very considerable.

Two stokers at Bwllfa Colliery with what appear to be extra-large shovels. Several of these boilers were used to meet the demand for steam for the winding engines, the fan and the haulages. NMGW

The Gloucester Wagon Works established a factory at Hirwaun in the angle between Broniestyn Tce and the railway line west of Hirwaun station. In the left middle ground can be seen a fan of sidings all occupied by wagons, while in the right foreground is the tramroad from Penderyn crossing the railway on its way to the ironworks (if still open) or to Hirwaun or Aberdare.

Ray Neale

Though this photo is about 94 years old it represents a vast improvement over the methods (if any) of affording first aid in the early days of mining. The wheeled stretcher was used for bringing a casualty out of the pit. The inscription on the ambulance reads: "David Thomas/Bwllfa & Merthyr Dare /No 1/Colliery ambulance." David Thomas was the miners' representative.

The lamproom at Bwllfa colliery where the miners' lamps were issued and returned, cleaned, mended, refilled and stored.

WIMM

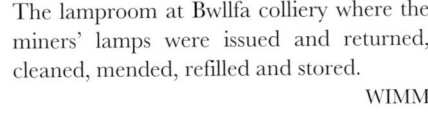

This picture of a more modern colliery lamproom shows the electric lamps that took over from oil.

Sir D. R. Llewellyn warns of "the burden of excessive coal (freight) rates upon the industry . . .

the individual self-propelled motor vehicle is so advantageous and so economical that the colliery owners, oppressed by the ridiculously excessive railway charges on coal are bound to adopt their use in increasing numbers".

The Cardiff Times 15th of June 1935.

"Conveyors and coal cutting machines were dispensing with the need for most of the skilled miners". This was stated by William Rhys Jones, under-manager at Cwmaman collieries, in his memoirs (written in 1945). It must also be stated that more modern methods were also making it easier for the miner to hew the stubborn seams. It was the same Mr. Jones who was present at the first installation of a compressed air coal cutter in the six foot seam at Aberaman, and was the first operator to cut a face in this manner, receiving personal congratulations from both maufacturer and higher management for cutting a one hundred yard face. (The cutter was produced by a firm called "Blackett & Co.") Later, at the same coal face, he would also be supervising the first installation in the valley of a face conveyor. It was an armoured chain type of conveyor, run by a small engine. This system of longwall mining was to remain, with certain improvements, until the advent of 'power loading'. The quicker methods of production also pointed towards the need for improved haulage systems below ground.

For details of cutting and conveying, see glossary—"Cycle (of coaling)".

Early levels (pre 1850), would probably be driven on the crop of a seam and quite simply worked by following the seam. Later, by the 1870s, a level would be likely to start slightly below the proposed entrance, where the required seam is evident on the crop. This lower gradient was to prevent water drainage from the loosened strata directly above the level mouth from entering the level proper.

Following this initial rising, when a stronger roof of the seam is evident, the drivage then follows the dip or rise of the seam to the boundary. As it progresses into the hill, various districts are developed and prepared for the highest output of coal possible. There were many levels in the Cynon Valley, and most of them would be small concerns, mining house coal from the topmost small seams, such as Werfa Graig (1910), Blaengwawr level and Mynach Du, (Ynysybwl 1891). The Clay level (1882), at Abercwmboi, was mining fireclay for the pipeworks in Aberaman, and also coal for coking purposes, and was part of the P.D.S.C.C. Ltd. works.

Llettyshenkin Colliery was opened by William Thomas of Waun Wyllt near Abercanaid in the Merthyr Valley, the coal from which initiated the sale of the four foot coal in London. The Llettyshenkin coal was sent down an incline to the lower Llettyshenkin pit near the valley floor into which ran a siding from the Cwmbach Branch of the Aberdare Railway. The Aberdare Canal also ran through the area.

John F. Mear

Levels did not need a massive investment, as a shaft would, for example, for a level owner would be selling coal almost immediately as his colliery developed, whereas a shaft might take some years to reach the required seams. (e.g. Deep Duffryn Colliery took five years.) The obvious development following the 'level' method was the 'drift'.

A drift is a tunnel or heading driven into a pre-planned coal seam through strata, at a fixed angle, which is mostly rock. It might pass through other coal seams, to reach the required seam. A drift will last longer, with fewer repairs and less maintenance. As most drifts incline downwards, a drift heading in the late nineteenth century would require almost constant pumping of water, and the angle of dip might be gradual to assist the haulage engine of the period. When the required coal seam was reached, then normal coal levels would be developed from the original drivage. A modern drift, such as the (new) Tower No. 3, driven in 1958, was completed far quicker than its predecessors, due to modern mechanical shovels, 50-plus shotfiring practice, and an extending heavy duty conveyor. But by the 1950s, in other coalfields, another complex mining system was introduced, the horizon mining method.

The nearest instance of this was in the Rhondda Fach when the Mardy Colliery connected beneath the Mardy mountain, with Bwllfa No. 1 colliery in Cwmdare in 1958. Prior to this method, when a 'link up' or development of an area of virgin coal was planned, a drivage heading would usually be driven to follow a coal seam.

In our area, there are invariably undulations occurring through faulting etc., and this results in transport systems which would vary in gradient as they followed the coal, which in turn would increase maintenance and running costs. Thus, with coal seams inclining in the general strata, it is feasible to consider horizon systems. Briefly, the method is, that the transport costs involved in following the undulations of a seam are obviated by the use of horizontal or near-horizontal roads beneath the coal which are driven without regard to the wandering of the seams. The coal-bearing seams are connected to the horizons by staple shafts containing a spiral chute which passes the coal down to the horizon, by means of which the coal is carried to the pit bottom or sent via a drift with belt conveyor to a surface washery.

Other advantages: (1) Efficient transport system with stone heading; (2) Repairs to roads driven in solid are minimal; (3) Highly inclining seams can be worked efficiently; (4) Ventilation is fairly constant.

A disadvantage was the very high initial cost of putting in such a major development.

Progress in improving the conditions of a mine and its workforce, was a slow process. By the turn of the nineteenth century, firms such as Powell Duffryn S.C.C. Ltd. had taken over most of the collieries in the Cynon Valley, (at one stage, only two mines remained outside their domain). The P.D. mines were improving slowly in mining practices, such as installation of face conveyors, coal cutters, etc. Then, in 1947, nationalisation occurred, which in the case of Cynon Valley collieries, was not that much of a leap forward, but an improvement, and a hope. When nationalisation occurred, there were twelve collieries working in the Cynon Valley, providing jobs for a large workforce. By 1990, only Tower Colliery remained.

Mechanisation, and an overhaul of all existing mining practices, was slowly grinding into gear, and by the late 1950s, the words "power loading" were being spoken. Self loading cutters were being mounted on longwall face armoured conveyors, which did not require colliers to fill coal directly from a coal face, except in the "gate" and "tail" stable area. Ploughs of German origin were being purchased, with rams pushing a face conveyor tight to the coal face. The plough travelled the face from end to end, ripping away the coal. There were new type tunnelling machines, tractor mounted, such as the "Duck-Bill Loader" (electrical), this was ideal for the mining of old pillars; also the "Dosco" arching cutter machine, used in tunnelling. These machines are being used today (2001) in Tower colliery, together with the 12 B.U. loader; the "Joy" loader filler, etc.,etc. All of these expensive machines were installed throughout most of the valley's pits. The technical advances were gradually improving the lot of a generation of miners.

By the 1980s, whatever the method of mining, longwall working, or pillar and stall, there was usually a machine to clear the product, and transport it to the surface for washing, sizing, and possibly blending, either on 4ft wide conveyor belts, (Tower Colliery), "double cage" winding, (Deep Duffryn Colliery), or in 12 ton skips, up a shaft (Abercynon Colliery). By the 1990s, Tower colliery was working a "Retreat power-loading longwall" face system.

This is a steam-driven fan at Bwllfa Colliery. It has two cylinders horizontally opposed of which only one at a time is in use, the nearest cylinder on this occasion. The connecting rod and the valve rods of the distant cylinder have been disconnected. The flywheel incorporates a rope drive to the fan off the picture to the left.   WIMM

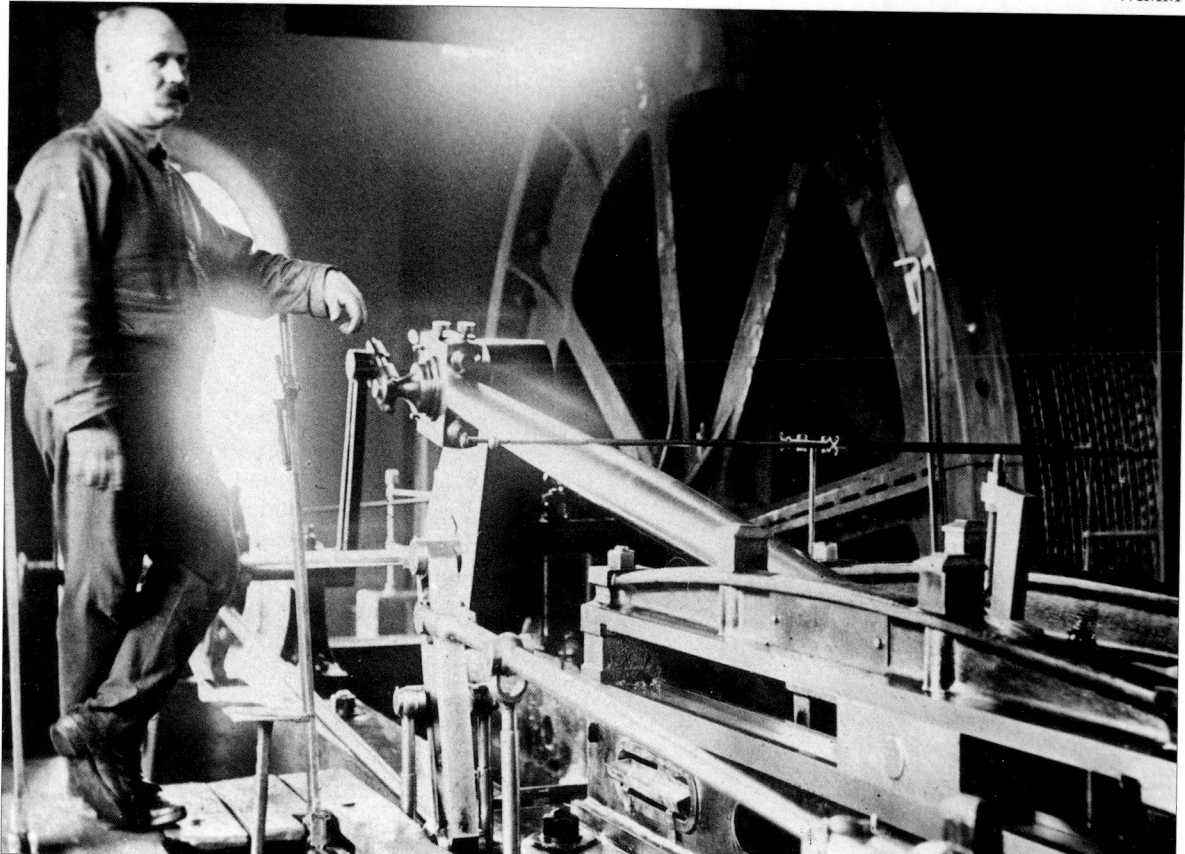

One of the winding engines at Bwllfa Colliery. The photo was probably taken by the then manager, H. H. Evans, who was a keen photographer, as was the engineman in the photo, Martin Palmer.   WIMM

Picking screens. The men are standing each side of a moving conveyor belt picking out and throwing aside pieces of shale, stone and other undesirable substances. Possibly taken at Llettyshenkin Colliery in the 1890's.　　　Bryn Davies

Ynyscynon Colliery, finally known as High Duffryn Colliery was the nearest to Aberdare of the several pits which had access to the Aberdare Canal in its progress down the valley. Originally the pit's name celebrated its first owner, David Williams, who sold it to the PD in 1866.　　　The late Glyn Davies

This is probably the last method of coal-getting to be worked at a pit in the Cynon Valley. Tower colliery has been using it for some seven years, and it has proved to be extremely successful to date. This method is the antithesis of any system that has gone before.

Quite simply, development headings are driven to the far boundary of the colliery. The coal face is then driven to connect the headings together, and then equipped with a complete "cover" of steel heavy duty chocks, from end to end. Each of these looks like a massive table which is hydraulically powered and can elevate to support the roof up to a height of eight feet. There are 201 of these chocks, which attach to the face conveyor, and they act not only as a total roof support but also as a means of pushing the face conveyor with rams tightly to the coal face, thus preparing the face for the next cut, (in a reverse direction). The chocks are also "self advancing" and the supports along the whole coal face (303 metres in length) are controlled by eight face workers. Two seams, the lower seven foot and the five foot, including a "dirt" band, are cut in one operation.

The entire coal face commences its cycle, cutting the coal "in retreat" towards outbye, from boundary towards the pit shaft. The face working at the time of writing, September 2000, is over three miles from the washery at the mouth of No. 3 drift.

The safety of the mine and of those who work in it depends upon adequate ventilation more than anything else. From the early days of mining levels, when there was nothing but natural ventilation, until the latest explosion in South Wales, miners have suffered death by suffocation, fires and explosions, large and small. Many of those incidents would certainly have been caused by poor ventilation. In 1803, an explosion occurred in a Rhigos level in which two were killed, and one was burned, one of which was a six year old girl. This was the first recorded incident of an explosion in the Cynon Valley, but certainly was not the last. The explosions of the 1840s to 1860s created an era of mine ventilation study, and many changes were taking place, especially in the legislation of this subject.

The main purpose of ventilation is to dilute the firedamp which seeps from the coal-bearing strata so as to render it less likely to explode and then to drive it out of the pit via the return road and upcast shaft. The other function of ventilation was to supply the miners for health reasons with a plentiful supply of fresh air. In the early days of mining the so-called natural method of ventilation was much used, probably because it cost little. If two shafts were sunk together to a fixed depth, and linked up horizontally at pit bottom by a heading, with the air in both shafts at the same pressure and temperature, a state of balance would exist owing to the weight of air being equal in both air columns. If one condition, of temperature or pressure, should change, the result would be a greater weight of air in one or other of

David Williams was better known in his lifetime by his bardic name, Alaw Goch. A successful coalmaster, he was also prominent on account of his literary and eisteddfod activities. Two settlements in the Rhondda, Williamstown and Trealaw, were named after him. He lived at Ynyscynon House.

Mr E. M. Hann was first connected with the Hetton Collieries in Durham and after gaining experience in various pits, he entered the service of the Powell Duffryn company in 1879, and was appointed manager of the New Tredegar and White Rose collieries. He eventually became General Manager of the whole of the PD collieries in which role he served for over 40 years.   John F. Mear

the shafts, causing an intake and return system of air to be commenced which could be enough to ventilate the mine, without the use of a fan or furnace to assist the air flow. This was used to some extent in South Wales, especially if the gas content of the coal was low.

In a survey conducted by Mr. Henry Davies M.E. (Mining lecturer and Geologist) in about 1891, he discovered that thirty three mines at least, were still using natural ventilation in South Wales. (N.B. This survey did not include every mine in South Wales.)

In certain weather conditions, in a hot summer for example, the direction of the air current could change, and the natural ventilation in a mine could be reversed. Depending upon the surface temperature and subject to its seasonal and daily variations, the strength of the natural air current can fluctuate, sometimes between night and day. At its best, natural ventilation produces only a small current, which may be controlled by changes in surface temperatures. To increase the current, one method sometimes used was the flowing of cold water into the intake. (Only used in a level with an adit below the workings.)

An obvious development of the "natural" system was to assist nature by lighting a fire at the bottom of the upcast shaft. It is well known that hot air rises, and the rising air served to draw in cool air through the downcast shaft. The drawback with this was that the air entering the furnace might have picked up firedamp on its journey through the workings, with predictable consequences. The risk of this was lessened by the introduction of the "dumb drift". The furnace was placed at a spot some yards away from pit bottom to which a supply of fresh air from the downcast shaft or from some other source could easily be brought for feeding the furnace. The hot air from the furnace rose up the dumb drift, which inclined towards the upcast shaft so as to join it about 30 yards above pit bottom. When in the shaft the rising column of hot air had an extractive effect on the foul air gathered at the bottom of the shaft.

Thomas Powell opened this pit in 1840 when it was called Tirfounder or Powell's Pit. It later became known as Old Duffryn Colliery. The site was one of many cleared after the Aberfan Disaster.

The late Glyn Davies

68

The Lady Windsor Colliery, Ynysybwl in 1914. The pit, initially known as Black Rock pit, was originally owned by Messrs Scott and Davies and afterwards by the Ocean Coal Co Ltd The sinking of this pit began in 1884, and the No 1 shaft was 2,047 feet deep. Eight seams were worked at this colliery throughout its life.

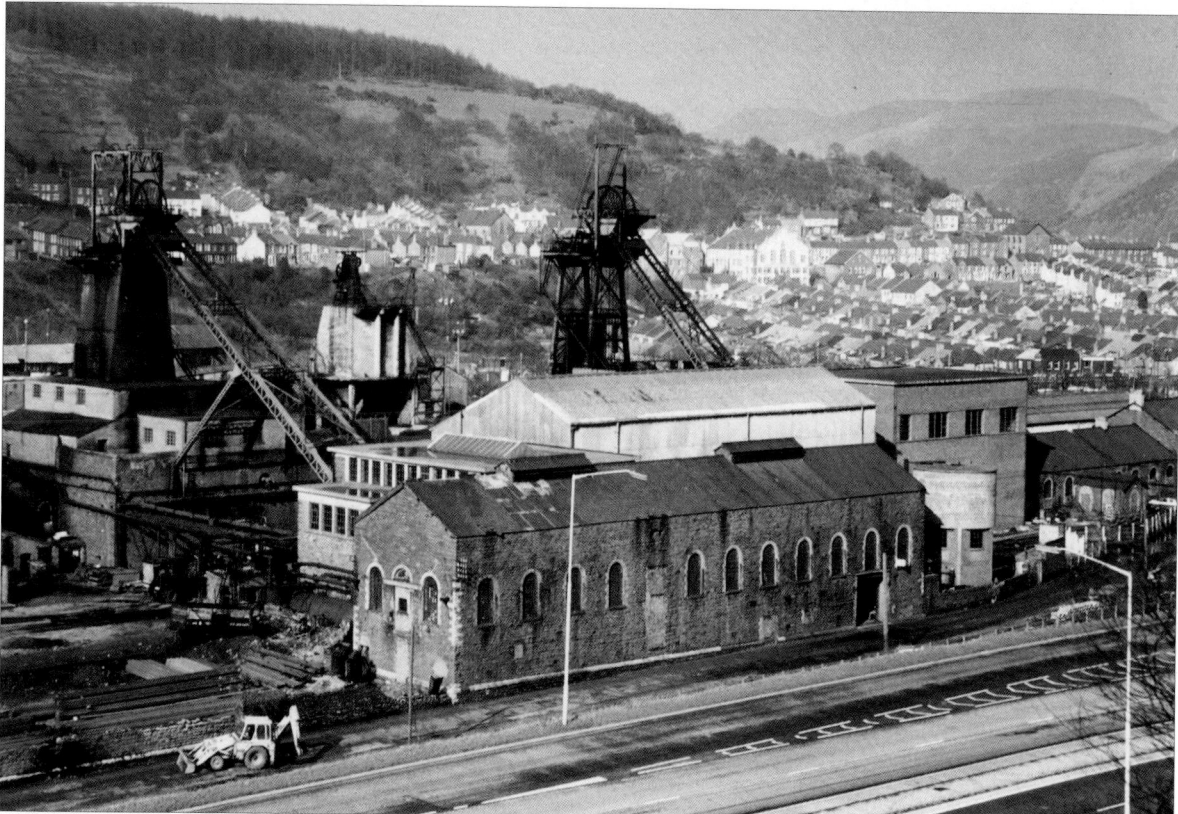

This photo of Abercynon Colliery was taken in 1975 when it had 13 years of life left. On the right above the houses can be seen the entrance to the Cynon Valley formerly called the Aberdare Valley. Following the disaster at Hartley Colliery in 1862 it was made obligatory for mines to have a second way out. At this colliery there were two shafts which were primarily for operational reasons, but also represented compliance with the law.

The late Glyn Davies

A way of using furnace ventilation "on the cheap" was used at "Middle Duffryn" colliery in Cwmbach, (and at many other places) prior to the disastrous explosions there. A shaft would be sunk to the required seam of coal and it was then divided vertically into two halves by a brick wall erected from pit bottom to over half way up the shaft. From this point, a brattice and wooden partition would be continued to the surface. One side of the dividing wall would be for the intake of air, and for winding purposes, while the other side would be used for pumping arrangements and the return foul air and gases (upcast). A ventilation furnace would be erected in the return airway near pit bottom, (in the case of the 'Middle Duffryn' example, it was just an iron basket of 18 inch diameter and hanging on a chain.) This furnace was supposed to ensure that the workings would remain ventilated. This was rather a dubious point in the Middle Duffryn example, as the first explosion here blew the dividing wall down. This was replaced later by a brattice and wood partition for the whole length of the shaft, which proved to be just as unsafe, and also proved fatal for the sixty five miners (including fifteen boys) not two years later.

The beneficial result of these disasters was that a law was passed stipulating that a deep mine must have at least two separate airways to the surface. This two way system was already being used in many pits in south Wales, but some of these concerns had neither fan nor furnace to stimulate the ventilation and were using "natural ventilation", (in some cases, up to 1891).

Steam-assisted ventilation was sometimes used in order to increase the speed of air ascending a shaft. This method was often used in the 1850's, up to the 1870's, and was sometimes used in conjunction with furnace ventilation. A series of steam pipes would be attached to the upper walls of the upcast shaft, steam jets pointing to the surface would be opened and the outburst of steam at pressure would assist in increasing the current of air through the workings. There were thirteen examples of steam ventilation in South Wales in 1891, with two examples in Cwmbach in the 1860's.

This is a view of Lady Windsor Colliery in 1974. In 1973 a £500,000 project had started to connect this colliery to Abercynon Colliery by means of two underground tunnels. A Horizon Mining scheme was introduced in the 1970's and this was very successful. All coal was raised at Lady Windsor.   The late Glyn Davies

70

To date, the most popular and effective way to ventilate a mine must be by the "fan". Quite simply, a fan ventilator is composed of a series of vanes set in a circular chamber with an inlet aperture to allow air into the system, and an outlet to expel the air at a higher pressure. Some fans are double inlet fans, and are smoother running. Sometimes the vanes can be curved to increase efficiency (wooden fans, 1920s on, would probably be curved). The motive power could be derived from slow speed engines, and driven by belts or rope, or direct from electric motors. An early example was the 'Guibal' fan, built of large diameter from 20 to 50 ft., and up to 12 ft. wide.

There are various fan types. Firstly the **'Waddle'** type. Probably because they were made in Llanelly, by the 1890s there were at least 62 of these installed in South Wales, as opposed to 20 'Guibal' fans.

Local Examples in 1891—**Guibal fan**: Used by Gorllwyn drift. (Bwllfa) 40ft. x 10ft. (This fan was also ventilating Bwllfa No 1 Colliery at one stage); **Schiele fan**: Used by Aberdare Merthyr (Steam Coal) Colliery; The **'Walker' fan** became popular later, and served the Midlands area well. Nantmelin colliery was still using a furnace in 1891.

As far as the Cynon Valley mines were concerned, the most well-known (but least used) form of ventilation was Nixon's ventilator, invented by John Nixon of Mountain Ash for Deep Duffryn Colliery. This was a displacement form of ventilator with enormous rectangular wooden cylinders. It worked well for the colliery for many years.

No 1 of the small fleet of locomotives which pushed and pulled wagons of coal to the main line sidings or to the Phurnacite plant, was passing carefully through the Navigation Colliery yard. Care was required because there was a right of way for pedestrians through the yard.

The late Glyn Davies

The required standard of ventilation is described as "An adequate amount of ventilation to dilute and render harmless all noxious and inflammable gases to such an extent that all roads and workings in a mine shall be kept in a fit state for working therein". This rule applies to all workings except abandoned workings which are normally sealed or fenced off. A district is not in a safe state if the air contains more than 1.25% of Carbon Dioxide or less than 19% of Oxygen, and the intake air is not free from inflammable gas. Ventilating methods have changed immensely since the days of an official who, upon suspecting a cavity in the roof of being full of firedamp, wrapped himself in a damp cloth then deliberately ignited the gas by means of a flame on a pole.

Ventilating science now has caught up with the computer age, an example being the intricate system now operating at Tower colliery. The current ventilation system in use there consists of a cluster of 12 fans of 100 hp each near the winder and another stand-by fan also on the surface. Underground there is a bank of 12 booster fans which are run constantly and auxillary ventilation. Gas emissions are subject to remote monitoring, and if the amount of methane in the return road of the current face exceeds a certain quantity a warning sounds in the control room on the surface and the power to the cutting machine at the face is cut off. In addition, a number of methane detectors have been installed and a methane drainage system is in place in all districts, the gas being pumped to the surface where it is used to generate electricity.

The engraver has captured the terrified look of this horse as he is lowered down a mineshaft in a harness. Though this is a depiction of a French colliery, horses in Britain sometimes went up and down the shaft by similar means when there was no alternative such as a drift.

Bryn Davies

Throughout the ages, horses have always been associated with the activities of man. Horses were carved into the culture of ancient nations in marble and stone. They played an important role in many wars, and in peace in practically every country in the world. The contribution of horses in the industrial world has been immense, and surely deserves a place in every book on mining, farming, transport, and many other walks of life.

The earliest known example of horses working below ground in the Cynon Valley would probably be in the "Lefel Fawr" drift on the Hirwaun common, where they worked at the 'powering', or turning of a whim, a machine for the pumping of water, in the nine foot seam. This was in the late eighteenth century. They were also used for winding.

Pit horses, in many areas, were called "pit ponies" whatever their size and stature. In the Cynon Valley generally, they were simply called "horses". The colliery horses working in South Wales were generally of the cart type, thick set and 14.2 to 15.2 hands. Ponies were used at pits with development work going on, and also where height of roadways had diminished. In 1938, there were approximately 7,400 horses employed below ground in South Wales and Monmouthshire. This represented 2,701,100 horse-shifts per annum, and

72

A view of the Phurnacite plant opposite Abercwmboi which was rarely seen not emitting smoke, steam or both. The growing demand for high quality patent fuel resulted in gradual expansion of the plant until the mid 1970s. However, in the mid eighties public opposition to the pollution created by the plant increased and this led to its closure in 1990 except for a small Ancit plant.

The late Glyn Davies

To occupy his time in retirement, Will Jones, former Master Haulier at Tower Colliery, bought this china horse and made a tram to fit it at the same scale. He then fashioned the horses "tack", the special harness which enabled the horse to pull a tram when used with the "shaft" (the U-shaped iron bar around the horse's hindquarters) and the "gun" (linking the shaft to the hitching plate of the tram).

John F. Mear

each horse got approximately eighty days of complete rest per annum. These horses consumed about 18,000 tons of corn, and 20,000 tons of hay, a total of 38,000 tons of feed per annum. They were fed, watered and groomed by 'ostlers', and inspected and supervised by 'farriers'. There were many horses that worked only forty five hours per week, and in most collieries all horses were limited to sixty hours per week. The master haulier was normally the person who decided on the overtime of a horse, and was the only man for such decisions. Senior to him would be the farrier, who was in control of all aspects of care relating to the men (hauliers) and horses in all of the stables in a mine.

The haulier was the man who "drove" a horse, that is, accompanied it throughout his working day, leading it as he walked at the horse's head. The shaft and gun, collar and assemblage of straps, etc., which made up the horse's "tack" was different from that found on horses used by farmers, tradesmen, etc.

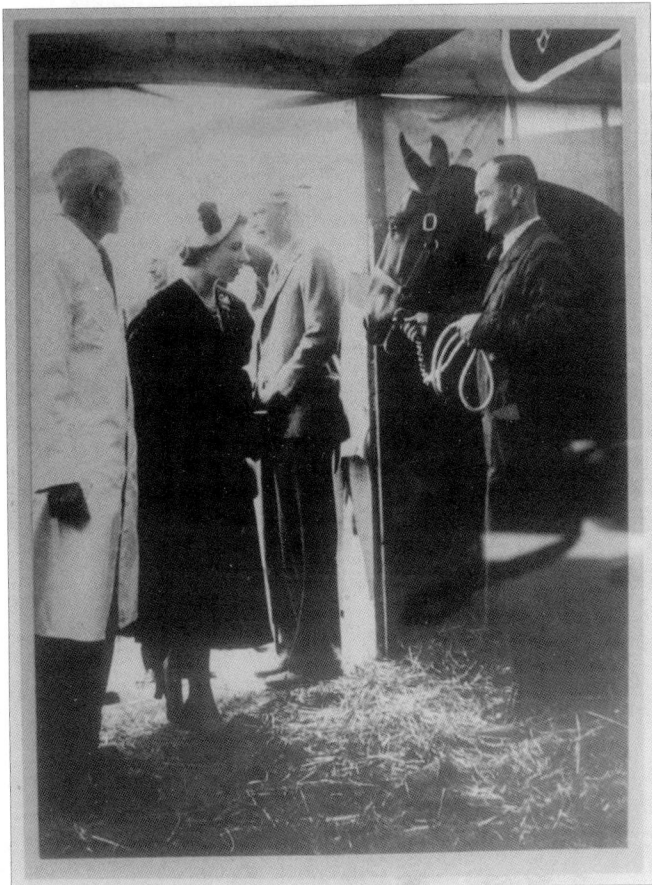

The farrier employed at the pit might be the buyer of horses for the company, as well as his other duties, and he would seek out the most suitable horse or pony at a sale or fair. In the Cynon Valley generally, due to the dipping seams and 'faulted' strata, his choice would probably have been for a strong stocky type of horse, that could hold against a full tram of coal when walking down a slope, and pull that same tram uphill around the next corner. The farrier would also assess a horse's temperament, check his age and fitness before the sale.

Mr. Peter Simpson was the farrier at Tower Colliery during the 1950's. There were five underground stables and one surface stable at Tower No. 1 drift. He was a strict official, who would normally attend one of the stables every day, but no-one knew which stable and which shift he would attend. Peter would always be waiting at the entrance of a stable at the end of a shift,

The Queen inspects the Tower Colliery Horse "Udal" at the Royal Agricultural Show at Newton Abbot, 11th of June 1952. On the right is Mr D. R. Williams, (Dai Pen Tip).

Two Tower Colliery horses exchange gossip when on their annual holiday. There are no longer any horses at Tower Colliery.

The late Glyn Davies

and he would thoroughly inspect every horse as it entered the stable, for evidence of injury or "roughing" against the lower roofs of the districts. Peter would also occasionally inspect a district in the workings, checking it out for possible hazards and bad conditions.

Mr. Howell Rowlands, of Aberdare, worked at the Tower collieries all his working life, starting as a young haulier, then as an ostler at different stables and finally as farrier of the mine, taking over from Peter Simpson. He talks of his farrier years as the most rewarding in terms of experiences, interest and fulfilment, despite being on call for twenty four hours. He recalls Inspectors' visits every three months, occasional outbursts of "greasy heels" among his charges and the sad times of having horses put down by a Mr. Boulton, a knacker-man of Merthyr. He remembers a haulier in the 1950's being dismissed for the cruel treatment of a horse; and he talks of the fine horse called "Hafod", who refused to take an empty tram into a heading. The haulier then sent for Howell the farrier who, after failing to move him on, sent for another horse, but before it arrived, the heading roof collapsed in front of them. The fall would have certainly have killed anyone in the vicinity. (Hafod was one of the last three horses to be sent from the colliery to retire to pasture at a "retirement home".) Hauliers generally accept the fact that horses underground gradually develop a "pit sense" as do most miners.

It was also the duty of a farrier to confer with a horse inspector and veterinary surgeon, if required. A farrier would also decide on the name of a recently purchased horse, and the local custom was to name it in relation to the month in which it arrived at the stable. If it arrived in January, its initial would be "A", in February "B" and so on. (Hafod above, would have arrived in August.) "A farrier must keep a book with a record of each horse, in a mine". (M.& Q., Part 2, p157, 1970). It appears that the raising of pit horses to the surface for holiday periods commenced in the Cynon Valley in 1952. The farrier would arrange this. Some horses would be raised in the pit cages, others would walk out via a drift, about six horses at a time. Mr. Howells recalls the "Holiday Fortnight" with nostalgia. He would always choose to put a quiet, steady horse first, to walk out via the drift. This was done so that other horses would walk behind it, and not bolt when smelling the open air, and seeing the daylight. It would be a busy two weeks following, attending to their needs on the surface.

An inspector of horses wrote in 1935 that there was not one case of cruelty to report. His report ended: "The Welsh miner is notoriously fond of dumb animals, and it is rare for him to fall from grace in this respect."

This picture of miners finishing their shift at Deep Duffryn was entitled "Into the light" by the photographer, the late Hans Hoyer.

We turn now to the preparation of coal for the market. Coal is mined to be sold, and to secure a good market, it must be properly sized, graded, cleaned by washing, and analysed. It may have to be blended with a different coal, depending on the customer's needs. The more the consumer realises the quality of the coal selected to suit his or her needs, the more will be the demand of the consumer. If a firm cannot maintain the standard of their coal then the customers will seek it elsewhere.

The colliery firms of South Wales, and especially in the Cynon Valley, have always enjoyed a reputation for mining good quality coal for the steam trade, for the shipping, railway companies etc. and particularly for the Admiralty. This stood them in good stead from about 1860 to the first World War, The Royal Navy especially so, as Cynon Valley steam coal was renowned for its smokeless quality, and for the rapidity with which it could raise steam when the navy needed speed, such as in times of war. It became the practice of the Admiralty to purchase Welsh steam coal, and following the "Navy Admiralty Test of Coal, 1876". (Blue Book), the Powell Duffryn Steam Coal Co. Ltd., was given the highest place, and they remained on the Admiralty's list until the Navy ceased burning coal. Much of this coal was mined from the Aberdare area and also from Nixon's Mountain Ash pits.

The highest quality coals were those which constituted the original Admiralty list, and the best of these were mined in the Aberdare and east Rhondda valleys. The composition of these coals is as follows:

1st. Admiralty Coal. (Steam)

Ash	3% to 5%
Volatile Matter	11% to 14%
Calories	8,000 to 8,400 K/Cal/Kg

The character of the coal in the whole of the South Wales coalfield can be approximately classified as: Steam coal – 48%; Bituminous coal – 30%; Anthracite – 22%.

The Admiralty-listed collieries in the Cynon Valley which produced such coals were: Aberdare/Merthyr (Steam Coal) C.C. Ltd.; British Rhondda, (Rhigos colliery); Bwllfa Colliery; Cwmaman Colliery; Duffryn Aberdare (Tower, etc.); Fforchwen (Cwmaman); Penrhiwceiber Colliery (described as clean, non smoking and economical).

The small dry coals were, by 1920, in great demand for patent fuel making, their low volatility being valuable in balancing the necessary addition of pitch as a binder. The local patent fuel industry took the lion's share of the British patent fuel export trade, 97% in fact in 1919.

An important aspect of coal preparation is the sampling of coal at the pit, and the best method of sampling coal at the face in the mine, was to cut a section from top to bottom in the seam, collecting the sample on a clean sack placed on the ground.

There are different sizes of coals needed for different markets, and this is achieved at the colliery screens. Even in the 1920s, the sorting, sizing, and washing of coal had advanced very rapidly, and great improvements had been made for the better handling of coal, and avoiding breakage, with the increasing value of the product. The principle of coal washing is based on the fact that the specific gravity of coal varies according to the type of coal and differs from the specific gravity of its associated impurities.

It will be remembered that in the early 1800s, mines such as 'Glover's' and 'Bryngwyn', were mining coal for coke production on Hirwaun common. The coke was used for the smelting of iron at the Hirwaun ironworks. There was also an attempt at working a coking coal level near Navigation colliery by the Nixon Navigation Colliery Co., in 1880, and lower down at Abercynon, the Carne Park level mined the Darren No. 3 seam coking coal, prior to 1874. Lady Windsor coal was also used for coke production.

Coke is made by coal being subjected to the influence of a high temperature and a limited supply of air so as to inhibit combustion. During this process of "destructive distillation" the volatile products (including coal gas) are given off and the remaining carbon coalesces and swells up to a larger bulk

---

Being the first writer to introduce the series of "Long Ago" I wish to comment [on the statement in an earlier issue of The Leader that John Nixon invented "Billy Fair play"]. It is true that Jeremiah Thomas (Jerry Billy) was the inventor of Billy Fair Play.* Jeremiah Thomas was not an Aberdarian as stated in the Leader. He hailed from the upper part of Pembrokeshire just on the border of Carmarthenshire. At the moment I cannot remember the name of the place. He and a brother or two were carpenters, and he selected the "hills", (as the saying goes) to work at his trade.He made a model of the "Billy" mechanism at the workshop to see if it would carry out the work for which it was intended ere it was put in operation at the screens. After some time he was promoted by D. Davis and Sons to mechanic supervising all the engineering department of the collieries . . .

It has been said in the columns of the Leader that Mr. John Nixon was the inventor of Billy Fair Play. That is not correct. Before ever Mr. Nixon came to South Wales the "Billy" was in operation at Blaengwawr, Gadlys, Aberaman, Ysguborwen and other collieries in the district. It was when Mr. D Williams (Alaw Goch) sold one of his pits at Cwmpennar that marked the advent of Mr. Nixon . . . a better master-owner than Alaw Goch never breathed.

* Nixon's biographer, J. E. Vincent, ascribed a number of inventions and innovations to Nixon not all of which can be verified. Billy Fair play was a device for weighing the amount of "small" coal in a tram. AL 25th Jan 1930.

than the original coal. There are a number of useful by-products arising from the process. The nature of the coke is dependent on the original composition of the coal that is being used, and also the seam and area of the coalfield whence it came. The No.3 Rhondda coal seam, (obtained from the upper Pennant Measures) was a first class 'dry' coking coal.

Although the Cynon Valley's collieries primarily produced steam coal, some also sold coking coal to various local firms, and exporting it for various by-products. The local main gas works at Aberaman, for example, was producing gas for public use from the coking of coal. (Some of which was mined at Aberaman colliery, and 'clay levels'). About 3,000 to 5,000 cubic feet of gas would be produced per ton of coal. This had a heating value of about 500 British Thermal Units per cubic foot, and was used for street lighting, gas engines, etc. in earlier times. The Powell Duffryn Steam Coal Co. Ltd., produced coke locally, with coal obtained from their collieries. Some local collieries that mined coking coal were Dyllas Drift; Gadlys (initially); Graig & Gorllwyn levels, Hirwaun; Carne Park; Abercynon; Mynachdu (Llanwonno) and 'Bwlch' (Hirwaun Common).

H. H. Evans was the epitome of the successful miner, progressing from pitboy to General Manager of the Cambrian Combine. Born at Trecynon, he moved to Maerdy to work in the pit there. He walked over the mountain to Aberdare for two winter seasons to attend the first mining night school. Eighteen years after working in a stall at Bwllfa Colliery, he became manager of the colliery. In 1910 he and two of his workmen (Gomer Jones, left, and W. R. Protheroe right) were awarded the King Edward medal for heroism after freeing a worker who had been buried under a fall at Bwllfa colliery. The three men are seen here outside Marlborough House after being decorated.   NMGW

This is almost certainly H. H. Evans at pit-bottom, Bwllfa No. 1 colliery when he was about to enter the cage. The long exposure used in his day has resulted in his moving lamp tracing its course on the negative.   NMGW

In 1902, a central washery was erected at the Middle Duffryn colliery, for the washing of small coal of the Powell Duffryn collieries in the Aberdare area. Completed by 1903, it became an instant success, as the washed product attracted a wider market, despite a higher price. This washery was the first erected in south Wales that was not used for the purpose of coke making. The P.D. company produced now, in addition to the by-products and coal itself, power in the form of electricity, gas and Benzole. The company's progress from 1900 to 1913 was "exceptional", and coal output for that period increased from 1,942,000 to 3,874,000 tons.

From these figures, it is obvious that the mining of and preparation for sale of coal was a successful activity for all the local coal companies until the 1920s, when more pits were closed in the Cynon Valley, due to the operation of market forces. However, by this time the role of Cardiff as the principal centre for the sale and shipment of the coal of the valleys leading thereto, had created a vast commercial centre around the docklands, and in the suburbs hundreds of Victorian villas were built for the affluent middle class which had been called into being by the business of buying and shipping coal. Then there were the thousands of terraced houses for the tradesmen and other workers. New docks were built to accommodate a cargo fleet with an eventual capacity of about two million tons.

In the 1923 edition of the South Wales Coal Annual there are listed no less than 78 firms of colliery proprietors and coal shippers, 31 firms of shipowners and brokers, and 13 firms of pitwood importers. Buyers would endeavour to gain contracts from the sellers on the most favourable rates i.e. low prices over long periods. Naturally, sellers wanted exactly the opposite. When a contract had been settled, "Tonnage" (i.e.transport) had to be arranged with chartering clerks. Then the trimmers had to be paid. Their job was to manually distribute the coal evenly in the holds so that the ship would adopt her correct attitude in the water. But by 1923 the coal industry of Great Britain had been in decline for ten years. The main cause of this was competition from foreign sources whose coal was not

George Elliot was another man from the north where he had become a pit Manager by the age of 24. He came to South Wales and was a member of the consortium which bought Thomas Powell's mining properties after his death, and formed them into the Powell Duffryn Steam Coal Co Ltd.

Crawshay Bailey was born in Yorkshire but left home at the age of 12 to assist his uncle, Richard Crawshay at Cyfarthfa. He became a successful ironmaster in his own right, and bought up many properties in South Wales for their mineral value (including Aberaman). In 1867 the Aberaman estate passed into the hands of the PD Co.

only cheaper but came from sources which were vast when compared with British reserves. Whereas the British coalfields amounted to 11,900 square miles, China had 4,000000 and America 280,000. And these were not the only competitors. In the period from 1913 to 1924 the output of coal in Spain had increased from 4,015,000 tons to 5,904,000 tons. Holland had increased output in the same period from 1,843,000 tons to 6,062,000 tons. And the competitiveness of the British coal industry had been blunted by unproductive mines and obsolete machinery-in other words, failure to modernise. However, competition also came from alternative sources of energy such as oil. By the mid-twenties coal had been overtaken and left behind by oil as the preferred medium for the propulsion of ships.

As a result collieries began to close down. Between 1922 and 1927 closures took place at Blaennant, Abercwmboi, Glyn Gwyn levels and Llettyshenkin. In an unwarranted moment of optimism Nixon's Navigation Colliery opened the Abergorki colliery in 1919, but the Nixon collieries all closed shortly after (though they were re-opened in 1929 by Llewellyn Nixon and Co).

In the case of Tower colliery, still mining coal successfully in 2001, the washing, sizing and blending still continues, but in a more sophisticated form. The end product is now classified as Anthracite, because the faces now mined are from the seams somewhere below Glyncorrwg, at the top of the Afan valley. The coal travels far before it reaches the washery and blending plant, to the west of Hirwaun. At the washery, a dense medium (magnetite), is added to the water, which deposits the waste material in the cyclonic movement wash. Froth flotation picks out small sizes, and the final products are large; small; beans and duff. Volatile blending is carried out for the end product destined for the Aberthaw power station.

We are glad that in all probability, gone are the days when two tired lines of labourers, too old for a coal face, would stand for a shift on a cold winter day alongside a 'picking belt', taking large and small stones from the coal hurtling past, and dropping them over the open side of the screen, into a truck below.

Taken at the Penarth Surveying School in 1921, the back row of this photo contains four local people. They are (l to r) Owen Jones Cwmdare, Sam Hopkins Hirwaun, Jack Griffiths Hirwaun, (and far right) Harry David Jenkins Cwmdare.

Doug Williams

This photo has faded badly since it was taken in 1903. All we know about it is that the men were "Werfa Colliery Workmen". The No. 1 pit opened in 1846 and the No. 2 pit in about 1879.

Bryn Davies

A view from Penrhiwllech of Bwllfa Colliery, Cwmdare, taken between 1910 and 1912. Note Bwllfa Row (also known as "Old Row") with its well-cultivated gardens and the paths from Bwllfa House (middle right, the residence of the Llewellyn family), one to the pit and another to the offices on the first floor of the building on the right.
Doug Williams

"*A collier ripping top stone down by the faint glimmer of a Clanny lamp, perceives near the point of his mandril the indistinct traces of a carboniferous fern. Although almost blinded by the dust he ceases work for the moment to more closely examine the fossil; the lamp is raised nearer the top, and a smile of amused gratification passes over his erstwhile set countenance. He leans on his mandril and smiles, for this was the fossil that his teacher had described to him, and fate had kept the fossil locked in that seam until this moment. The knowledge was now his.*" This was written by Mr. Henry Davies BSc., a lecturer on mining practice, and a geologist of note, as part of the introduction to his book on "The South Wales Coalfield, Geology and Mines". It was published in 1901, and doubtless became a great aid to mining students of the period, and for future historians also. Mr. Davies had not only presented a complete description of the geology of the coalfield, but had compiled detailed essays on many of the larger collieries, including mines of the Cynon Valley.

In 1905, Mr. W J Heppel, agent for Cwmaman collieries, arranged for Mr. Davies to give at Aberdare a series of sixteen lectures. Mr. Davies spoke on ventilation, safety, explosives, rescues etc. His talks were presented to the "Aberdare branch of colliery examiners" (officials of mines). (This title changed in 1934 to "National Association of Colliery Overmen, Deputies and Shotfirers"). During his lecture on ventilation, he stated that the Cwmaman Colliery officials had been complimented in a

Obviously taken at the same time as the previous photograph, this is Nantmelin Colliery. The drift plainly seen near the centre of the photo is "Bwllfa No. 4" Parts of old houses are seen here and there and this reminds us that people once lived near the pit top in this colliery. In the background the road to Bwllfa seems to have had a dressing of clean limestone, thereby making it very conspicuous.

Doug Williams

Government report, upon the excellence of their system. The lectures were published later in book form, for the education of miners and mining students generally. The meetings were surely exemplary specimens of quality education classes organised at the turn of the twentieth century. Not only were the officials attending the lectures impressed, but the hall was full for each talk.

The lectures were also presented in other valleys of South Wales, for this was the age for the education of miners, not just for the miners' sake, but for the coalmasters' need to obtain good colliery officials for the future. From such officials would also emerge the future management of collieries and works. By this time the industry had emerged from a "hole in the ground" concept, with many collieries changing to a modern approach. Practically every mining operation was being improved, below ground and especially so on the surface. Better surface planning, washing of coal etc., demanded qualified quality management.

An example of the success of such a mining student of this period was the life of Mr. H.H. Evans M.E., J.P. He was born at Windsor Street, Trecynon, Aberdare in 1865, and was educated at Ysgol y Comin School nearby. He started work as a collier boy in Bwllfa Colliery, Cwmdare, before his family

Thomas Powell owned pits in the Cynon Valley and others in the Rhymney Valley. In 1862, with 16 pits producing 700,000 tons of coal, he was probably the world's largest coal exporter. He is said to have refused to pay John Nixon the royalties due to him for having sold Powell's coal on the continent.

moved to Maerdy, Rhondda. He was the eldest of six children, was 20 years old, and still worked at Bwllfa Colliery, walking night and day to the family home in Maerdy. It was Christmas 1885 when his father died in the Maerdy explosion in which 81 miners were killed. Despite the burden of becoming suddenly the major bread winner of his family, he persevered with the mining classes at Aberdare, by walking over the mountain to the first mining night school in the area.

As a result of his dedication, he rose to be a manager at Bwllfa Collieries, and later became general manager of the Consolidated Cambrian Collieries. He was chairman of the Monmouthshire and South Wales Coalowners Association at the time of his death in 1935. He was once presented with the Edward Medal, (the "Miners Victoria Cross") for rescuing, with two other men, a collier trapped beneath a fall of 40 tons, at Bwllfa colliery. The other two men were W. R. Protheroe and Gomer Jones. (Mr. Evans presided at the fourth lecture by Henry Davies, on November 28th 1905, at Aberdare). Nothing was easy in those days of mining, but his motto was "He who suffers, conquers".

The local mine owners and colliery companies of the late nineteenth and early twentieth centuries initiated a more intense approach into mining education when, in 1913, they opened the "School of Mines" in Treforest, Pontypridd. Each company paid one penny per ton levy towards the upkeep and maintenance of it, at that time. There was another such school in Crumlin,

The Glyngwyn levels were in Miskin and were opened by the Nixon Navigation Coal Co in 1893. House coal was its main product and no less than 299 men were employed underground for this purpose in 1913. In 1925 it closed. The apparatus in the background was used for tipping the contents of trams into carts.

Harry Rogers

erected at about the same time. Later, as coal mining was diminishing in South Wales, the mining school at Treforest was renamed "Glamorgan Technical College" and in 1974 it became "Polytechnic of Wales", and is now the "University of Glamorgan".

The mining education system in South Wales has always been highly regarded, and it has produced many first class mining engineers, mining surveyors, mechanical and electrical engineers, etc. Some of these are still remembered locally. Two fine students arose to become N.C.B. South Wales area chairmen. Mr. Donald Davies M.E. BSc., a colliery manager 29 years old of Tower colliery in 1952, later to sit on the National Coal Board, and some years later, Mr. Phillip Weekes M.E. O.B.E., who was area director, and sat on the National Coal Board at the same time (1982).

Mr. Weekes worked his way upwards following his early years "on the coal", at a colliery in East Wales. Following his "retirement" he became chief adviser and chairman, and strong supporter of the buy-out of Tower colliery in 1994/5, and is still an able and strong supporter in 2001.

In 1950, the education of a boy trainee was a safe, systematic affair. Boys were recruited from school following a talk by a mining lecturer, or training officer from the local pit. A boy would be medically examined and passed fit. He would start work at a training centre, (the Cynon Valley centre was adjoining Aberaman colliery). He is then trained at specific work in a "pit", which is normally in a "gallery", a made up building that resembles an underground coal face, and he is supervised by a man trained in education with personal experience of pit work. The boys are taught about safety, mechanisation, first aid, and numerous colliery activities. Sporting activities sometimes took place.

Penrhiwceiber Colliery with its two headframes. The colliery was opened in 1872 by the Penrikyber (sic) Navigation Coal Co Ltd. Another shaft was sunk in 1912 and used for pumping. The colliery closed in 1985.

Brian Davies

When he qualified, which was highly likely, he chose a colliery to work in, and signed on. He was still a 'trainee', and even while working in a face, he was still under the wing of a training officer.

In every N.C.B. colliery, there was a training officer, with an office to deal with a trainee's problems. Later, there would be advanced training schemes, such as "staff training", mechanisation training courses, etc., and a boy could be well on the ladder to management. Miner's welfare scholarships, and even university scholarships were possible during the first twenty five years of Coal Board ownership.

In the nineteenth century the training of a boy would be a different experience entirely and would be almost certainly devoid of any methodical approach whatsoever. As a young lad aged about twelve, he would be taken to a stall below ground, given a "curling box" and a shovel, and he would labour in there by the faint light of a candle or two, until he would almost drop. Over the years stretching ahead he would be stronger in knowledge and body, and able to cope with dust, rats, water to his knees, and the occasional fatal accident in the district. He might change his job sometimes. About the age of fourteen, he might be driving a horse and tram of coal for a few more years, shouting at the "door boy" because he was not quick enough opening the ventilating door for his horse to pass, and being shouted at by the "gaffer" haulier as he was late returning to the "double parting". All of this was his education, and more to come, if he was lucky enough to survive and find work.

By 1850, the shipment of coal from South Wales to foreign lands had reached 3,351,000 tons. In 1900 it was no less than 58,405,000 tons.

There was a strong market for patent fuels in South Wales and the foreign export side was almost exclusively a South Wales industry. Of the 1,708,015 tons exported from Britain during 1919, no less than 1,649,193 tons were loaded from South Wales docks. Cynon Valley was well represented in this trade, firstly with Williams' patent fuel from Cwmbach in the 1860s and 1870s and later—after the Second World War by the Phurnacite Plant at Abercwmboi, which finally closed in 1990. A small 'Ancite' plant survived for a further eight years.

This is the Edward Medal awarded to Mr W. R. Protheroe who, together with Mr. H. H. Evans and Mr. Gomer Jones, were thus decorated by the King for saving the life of John Isaac, who in 1910 had been buried beneath a fall in Bwllfa Colliery.

The late Mrs. Rona Protheroe (Daughter in Law)

The nationalisation of the country's mines did not entail the prohibition of small licensed mines and there are several of these in that part of the coalfield west of Hirwaun. This was the scene at the Craig-y-Llyn Levels on the mountain at Rhigos in the summer of 1997. The workforce consisted of a manager, a fitter and 12 colliers assisted by three horses.

Bryn Davies

Nearly all of the coal raised at Tower colliery goes to Aberthaw Power station using a "Merry-go-round" train of hopper wagons which can discharge their contents without stopping. These wagons are being loaded with duff by a tractor shovel at the Tower Colliery railhead, which is now the terminus of the line. At this place the two tracks of the former Vale of Neath line have been left in place to enable the engine to "run round" its train.

John F. Mear

In this picture the train has arrived at Aberdare station where it is "waiting for the road" alongside one of the original platforms.

John F. Mear

There were at least two collieries known as "Park Pit" in the Cynon Valley and this is one of the shafts of Park Pit, Robertstown, which was closed in 1897 and filled in at a later date. The photo shows how the material used for filling up the shaft has subsided. Today there are strict rules governing the method and materials used in shaft-filling.   Doug Williams

This banner belonging to the Lady Windsor Lodge of the NUM dates from about 1970.
Brian Davies

The banner reads:

NATIONAL UNION OF MINEWORKERS.

LADY WINDSOR LODGE
YNYSYBWL

J. KIER HARDIE

"OUR DESTINY WILL BE DETERMINED, THROUGH THE IDIOLOGY OF SOCIALISM."

This incline was once the route of a tram-road carrying waste from Penrhiwceiber Colliery to the adjacent mountain. It was afterwards replaced by a conveyor which served the same purpose. After the closure of the colliery in about 1992 a conveyor was reinstated to bring the waste back down the mountain to be used as infill for the former site of the colliery.

Brian Davies

The northern boundary of the South Wales Coalfield runs north of Aberdare and because of the so-called saucer-like nature of the seams, some of them come to the surface in this vicinity. Since the coal and iron ore was so easy to mine, this area was subject to patching in the days of the iron industry, which is evidenced by the presence of spoil tips relating to that activity and the names of the patches e.g. Fothergill's Patch and Bryn Defaid Patch, on the old 25″ maps. This photo shows opencast mining taking place near the Dyllas a few years ago and the shallowness of the seam which the excavator is digging outt.

John F. Mear

Known as a "Free steering vehicle" (FSV) this device is used for the delivery of stores to the various worksites underground at Tower Colliery, which was the first colliery in the Cynon Valley to use such vehicles.

Malcolm Howells

The Cambrian Lamp Works now sited alongside the Aberdare Canal Company's tramroad and to the north east of the former High Level Station must now surely be the oldest business in the Cynon Valley. The original proprietors were E. Thomas and Williams Ltd. This illustration and the two that follow are from the firm's 1885 catalogue. The cover of the catalogue depicts (presumably) the patron Saint of miners, St Barbara, illuminating the workings by means of a Cambrian safety lamp or, according to an old miner with a twinkle in his eye, testing for gas.

Next to proper ventilation the use of safety lamps for illumination was probably the most important measure for the prevention of explosions. The first successful safety lamp was invented by Dr W. R. Clanny and the first mine in which it was used was the Herrington Mill Pit, the property of the Earl of Durham. Many types of safety lamp came into being, and when the British Government appointed a Royal Commission in 1884 to inquire into accidents in mines, they asked for specimens of existing lamps in use. Of the 250 or so sent to them and examined, four were found to be pre-eminent. Of these four, Evan Thomas's No. 7 lamp gave, upon the whole, the best results.

Doug Williams

LAMP No. 1 B.

Lamp No 1B. Although this lamp looks fairly ordinary at first glance, it has a number of refinements such as double gauze, electric ignition and magnetic lock.

Doug Williams

LAMP No. 1 A.B.

Lamp No 1 A B. This lamp was intended to meet the requirements of Managers and officials of mines, and was made of aluminium for lightness. Many years later in 1954 an explosion in Glyncorrwg Colliery in which 15 men suffered burns was found to have been initiated by a spark from an aluminium object. This resulted in the banning of aluminium products underground.

Doug Williams

Penrhiwceiber Colliery seen from the nearby hillside in the early 1980's not long before closure. The conveyor in the background was to transfer 'Ceiber coal to wagons standing in the siding whence the coal would be taken to the Phurnacite plant. When electrification of the colliery took place, a new winder was built (left background) and this neccessitated the turning of a headframe. The old steam winder is on right.

Brian Davies

In the centre of the photo is the headframe of the Tower colliery which started its life at the Bwllfa Colliery and was afterwards moved to Tower. The background is the vast chasm of the opencast workings adjacent to the colliery (now filled back).

Malcolm Howells

All is silent in the stables near pit-bottom and the farrier's cabin at the far end of the row is no longer used, for the last of the Tower's horses has been pensioned off.   Malcolm Howells

Nature is fighting back in this photo of Tower Colliery, where the steel girders composing the roof and wall supports are slowly bending under the increasing crush of the "roof". On the left is a pile of wooden "cogs" which will be used as supplementary support for the roof.

Malcolm Howells

Another site where steel supports have to be augmented by wooden cogs (right background) at Tower Colliery.

Malcolm Howells

This photo shows the cutting disk of a modern coal cutting machine at work. It is mounted on the face conveyor and at the rear of the machine is another disc which cuts the bottom coal, thereby cutting the whole seam.

Malcolm Howells

The interior of the Windber Level, Cwmdare. D. R. Llewellyn was the most successful of those entrepreneurs who opened levels to the thin upper seams cropping on the south slope of Mynydd Cefn y Gyngon. Not long after he qualified as an ME "DR" went to Canada and America to gain mining experience, and worked for the Berwind White Coal Co. at Windber near Johnstown, Pennsylvania. (note the transposition.) On his return he found that his father's firm had opened a level to the Gorllwyn seam and called it "Windber". On hearing that they were about to close the level as the coal was only 20″ thick, DR leased the seam from them and put in electric coal cutters. This was the start of his separate existence as a coalmaster.

Steve Grudgings

CHAPTER FIVE

"For many are called but few are chosen". This inscription in St. Elvan's Church is on a decorated window installed by Lord Merthyr in memory of the local captains of industry. It points to the highly competitive struggle which lay before those who aspired to wealth and renown through the development of the coal industry and reflects, perhaps, a feeling of satisfaction that the donor had no doubts that he was one of the few "chosen" for the highest position of eminence in this sphere.

The principal landlords and coalmasters were introduced in Chapter 3. Because of poor communications, steep gradients, poor soil, lack of neighbours of the same social standing and other factors, the larger landlords of the Glamorgan valleys such as (in this area) Bute, Kemeys Tynte, Gwynne Holford, etc. were "absentee landlords", living on their principal estates in more congenial places. Exceptions were Crawshay Bailey at Aberaman, John Bruce Pryce of Duffryn and Lord Aberdare's ancestors at Duffryn. As a result, the coalmasters rather than the landlords were the visible signs of authority in the valley, and if a family still held control of a colliery by the time of the second generation, as the Llewellyns did in Cwmdare, this led their families to adopt a kind of role-playing which owed more to the squire/labourer relationship than to the comparatively new employer/worker nexus. The degree of control exercised over the workforce was strengthened when a

During 1854 a house was being built at Aberdare for the Marquess of Bute's Mineral agent, W.S. Clark. On the 8th of December he slept in it for the first time and by the following March he was living in it. On the 16th of August 1858 he started building an estate office nearby. The house Clarke built (known as Mardy House, now demolished) he occupied until his death in 1864, whereupon the keys were handed to the brightest of his pupils, W.T. Lewis, who had been chosen as Clarke's successor. Lewis retired in 1913 and was succeeded by his nephew and pupil, R.T. Rees. This photo of Mardy House was taken in 1975 when it was the local tax office. Note the two boulders of coal flanking the door, a common practice at the residences of the South Wales coalmasters.

The late Glyn Davies

David Davis, Blaengwawr. His first attempt at mining was a level at Rhigos leased from the Marquess of Bute. Later, he turned his attention to Blaengwawr, Abercwmboi, and the Rhondda Fach.

1849. The terrible cholera epidemic of that year broke out here first of all in a house in Cobblers Row—a street of small houses opposite where the trap surgery (in Abernant Rd) now stands. Over 100 died in Aberdare.

1864. (Sept) A severe epidemic of scarlet fever raged through the town. Deaths from this fearsome malady are a daily occurrence.

1874. (Sept) A severe epidemic of scarlet fever broke out in Mountain Ash. It made great havoc among the young and took a heavy toll. Hardly a day passed without 3 or 4 funerals of children of tender age.

Mr. T. Thomas drew attention to the "obnoxious habit" of some inhabitants of throwing cockle shells into the street. It was decided that anyone found so doing should be summonsed.

From the minutes of a meeting of the Aberdare Board of Health in 1890.

---

coalmaster became a member of the Board of Health or was appointed to the Bench, and in an age when religious observance was increasing many workers thought it might be to their advantage to belong to the same chapel as their employer, thus submitting to yet another bond which could grant or withhold approval at will.

The image of a coalmaster in his large mansion overlooking and thereby dominating the houses of the workpeople is irresistible to the novelists who have portrayed the Welsh mining valleys, but the reality (in the Cynon Valley at least) is different. After taking a lease of one or more farms, the earliest coalmasters often lived "on the job" in one of the farmhouses at first. If the mine appeared to bode well, the farmhouse might be rebuilt on a larger scale, or a new dwelling built nearby, but in most cases the finished building was of a very modest nature, often with only about six bedrooms. Of the three largest, Abernant House (now the hospital) was a large house built on the site of an earlier one (Cynon farmhouse) by the proprietors of the Abernant ironworks. Aberaman House is a special case because it was a pre-existing gentry house belonging to the estate which Crawshay Bailey of Nant y Glo bought for the purpose of working the coal and iron ore beneath the estate. Duffryn house at Mountain Ash, once a modest farmhouse, is in the same category, and after being enlarged from time to time it was acquired with its demesne in 1747 by William Bruce, ancestor of Lord Aberdare.

The other "large" houses in the area were Plas Newydd at Llwydcoed (R.H. Rhys and the Waynes), Llwydcoed House (R.H. Rhys), Gadlys Uchaf (Bedlington and Roberts), Bwllfa (Rees Llewellyn and his sons), Glandare (Waynes and Rees), Ysguborwen (Samuel Thomas), Ynyscynon at Cwmbach (David Williams), Lletyshenkin, Cwmbach (R.T. & Daniel Rees), Brynawel in Foundrytown (William Thomas), Blaengwawr (David Davis sen), Maesyffynon (David Davies jun), Gadlys Isaf (G R Morgan), The Poplars Mountain Ash (John Nixon), Cefnpennar House (Rees Williams and Lord Aberdare's family), Mardy House Aberdare (William Southern Clark, Sir W.T. Lewis and R.T. Rees), Sunnybank (William Howells and Richard Williams), and Fairfield (Richard Lewis, Capt T.E. Malyon, D.R. Llewellyn, M.H. Llewellyn, and the National Council for Social services).

In an area where the industrial scene was dominated by two major industries, iron and coal, one would expect the social structure to be affected by the characteristics of those industries. One of the main characteristics of the coal industry was the separation of the sales and shipping functions which tended to be based at the ports, where they created a numerous and affluent middle class, but in the Aberdare area the middle class was very small in number compared with the vast number of miners and

Sited in a very pleasant environment, the Duffryn House (above) which has now disappeared was not the first to bear that name. There was a small farmhouse on the site in about 1400 which was enlarged and this passed into the hands of the Bruce family in 1750. The old house was replaced by this Gothic mansion in 1870 which became a County Grammar school in 1926. A new school having been built, the mansion was demolished in 1986.

Blaengwawr House taken in the 50's. It was built for David Davis, one of the successful shop owners who became a prosperous coalmaster, as did his son David Davis Jun, who lived near his father at Maesyffynon.   The late Glyn Davies

their families, and except for one or two cases the landed upper classes were absent, and represented only by their agents or trustees. In those parts of the coalfield where iron was made, at first most of the coal that was raised was used locally for making coke for the blast furnaces. Coal was also important for household use, malting, etc but most of it was sent away by rail to other parts of the country or to the nearest seaports for export. So although there were local ancillary industries such as Thomas and Williams's Cambrian Lamp Works and wagon making and repair, there were few "downstream" industries linked to the coal industry. The most significant were brickmaking and the manufacture of coal gas, but the produce of the former was usually confined to the colliery's own use and to the building of company houses.

The middle class in Aberdare therefore comprised the coalmasters and ironmasters, a small number from the secondary industries just mentioned, the richer townsmen and the professional people such as the doctor, the parson, the most eminent of the nonconformist ministers and the solicitor. Most of these had servants—among the coalmasters in 1851. Crawshay Bailey at Aberaman had five, in 1861 Samuel Thomas at Ysguborwen had six, Thomas Wayne at Glandare had five, Richard Fothergill at Abernant had eight, R.H. Rhys at Llwydcoed House had three and David Williams at Ynyscynon had four. The employment of servants enabled the inhabitants of these houses to live comfortable lives in pleasant surroundings which were not limited to the house. Duffryn House had a beautiful landscaped garden containing a rich variety of native and exotic trees, while the extensive grounds of Abernant House had deer, pheasants, large glass- houses and ornamental ponds.

It is time to look at the way of life of those who were *not* chosen. It is generally known that the growth firstly of the iron industry and later of the coal industry resulted in a great demand for labour

This is Ty Mawr situated on the north side of the Hirwaun Ironworks, built and occupied by the first proprietors of the works, the firm of Maybery and Wilkins, and occupied thereafter by their successors. When Francis Crawshay was put in charge of the Hirwaun works he declined to live in "The big house" and built a cottage for himself a little distance away which still exists. To show who lived there he had a large boulder of coal engraved with his initials and set up in the field in front of the house. When he retired he moved to Bradbourne Hall near Sevenoaks and, giving his eccentricity full rein, marched about his estate in nautical dress striking huge bells which he had in the grounds. This photo dates from 1950.

Doug Williams

With a few exceptions the first houses in Trecynon were built for the workmen of Ysguborwen Colliery. Of these, a few here and there were provided with only one bedroom upstairs as can be seen in this photo of Mill St. The reason for such an unsatisfactory arrangement is not clear. Of course, most of these houses have been modernised over the years and now provide much better facilities.

John F. Mear

which could not be satisfied by the existing workforce. The result was two waves of immigration, which caused young men to leave the agricultural district of mid Wales and west Wales, the West Country, Ireland and even more distant parts. During the second wave they arrived in various parts of the burgeoning coalfield and found work underground, as their predecessors had found work in the ironworks of the same area. There were also employment opportunities locally in the building and transport industries among others, as well as in the distributive trades, but some of the immigrant labour was required to take the places of those local men who had left agriculture for the higher wages of the pit. The resulting increase in population through the century was astonishing. The following figures for the population of the parish are taken from the ten-yearly census with percentage increase over the decade in brackets:

1801*	1486	
1811	2782	(87.2%)
1821	2062	(29.5% decrease)
1831	3961	(47.9%)
1841	3532	(10.8% decrease)
1851	14998	(32.6%)
1861	32299	(11.4%)
1871	37704	(16.7%)
1881	33804	(10.3% decrease)
1891	38431	(13.7%)
1901	43557	(13.3%)

* There are no reliable statistics prior to the first decennial census of 1801, but it is thought that the figure of 1,486 includes workers attracted to the new ironworks at Llwydcoed and Abernant.

> *The clerk to write to the Great Western Railway re non stoppage of last train from Neath at Llwydcoed Railway Station. The station serves upper part of Councils district where several tradesmen and thousands of inhabitants reside thus causing them either to alight at Hirwaun or Aberdare-a distance of between 2 and 3 miles.*
>
> **Aberdare UDC minutes 22 Jan 1897.**

The influx was bound to have had effects upon the Welsh language which were both positive and negative. Migration of Welsh-speakers from West Wales would increase the percentage of Welsh speakers. The arrival of non-Welsh speakers from Somerset or Ireland would decrease the percentage. But when immigrants came to work in ironworks or coal mines where the working language was Welsh then there was a tendency for them to pick up Welsh from their new workmates, probably interspersed with lurid Anglo-Saxon. And there was also the anglicising effect arising from the proximity of England. A recent analysis of Telephone Directory surnames representing over 63% of the Valleys' households reveals just over 50% of traditional Welsh surnames throughout the whole valley with roughly 54% being the fraction in the Aberdare area and 46% in the Mountain Ash area, the remainder being largely English with significant Irish and Italian minorities. Strife on the continent has led to the influx of Poles, Czechs and Hungarians among others. The resultant mix provided the Cynon Valley entry into the twenty-first century with a vibrant society of proud South Walians. Census figures always show spoken Welsh as more common in the Aberdare area than in Mountain Ash. Use of the Welsh language still continues in the valley. Much of the Welsh language spoken in Aberdare originally and later used throughout the collieries was based on the Gwentian dialect known in Welsh as "Gwenhwyseg". This was the Welsh spoken throughout South East Wales and Monmouthshire-probably derived from the language of the Silurians who originally inhabited the area. It is characterised by a mutation of the letter "a" so, for example, the Welsh word for fire (tân) becomes "tên". Many common words are modified; eistedd (to sit) becomes "ishda". The third person singular of the past tense ends with "ws". So "he walked" (cerddodd) becomes "cerddws". Welsh learning classes are popular and many activities are carried out using the Welsh language. The now established Welsh schools are an enlivening feature, and a locally produced newsletter "Clochdar", circulates monthly.

Now we must turn back the clock to mention the arrangements for local government which gradually evolved over hundreds of years. In the Middle Ages local government was in the hands of the Lord of the Manor and the shire i.e. County. As the manor declined in importance from the sixteenth century, the role of the parish, originally a seat of ecclesiastical government, expanded and became subject to administrative responsibilities which were discharged by a committee of ratepayers known as the Parish Vestry. This consisted of two churchwardens, four overseers and six other inhabitants of the parish. But in the nineteenth century the tendency was towards administration by means of "ad hoc" bodies, that is a separate body for each need. By 1880 the "ad hoc" bodies had proliferated and created a chaotic situation under which one could be liable for up to eighteen different rates. This chaos was remedied by the Municipal Corporations Act 1882 and the Local Government Act 1888 under which County Councils were formed and given administrative responsibilities. The Local Government Act 1894 created the Rural and Urban District Councils in place of the pre-existing Urban and Rural Sanitary Authorities and caused the demise of bodies such as the Parish Vestry and many of the ad hoc bodies. This two-tier (sometimes a three-tier) system remained in being until the creation of the unitary authorities under the Local Government (Wales) Act 1994.

Perhaps the most important of the obligations imposed by Parliament was the relief of the poor. Throughout most of Victoria's reign an oppressive and unpopular Act, the Poor Law Amendment Act of 1834, was enforced and caused great suffering. One of its main provisions was that able-bodied men and their families had to enter the workhouse to get indoor relief rather than stay at home and get outdoor relief. The workhouse was at Merthyr (afterwards St Tydfil's Hospital) and the Merthyr Tydfil Union (of parishes) was composed of nine parishes grouped into three districts the third of which consisted of the parishes of Penderyn, Aberdare, Rhigos and Llanwonno. The poor law was administered by an elected Board of twenty one Guardians assisted by relieving officers, doctors, a clerk and a treasurer.

This is Colliers Row, the first-built of four similar rows at Abernant (all now demolished) named Colliers' Row, Foremen's Row, Engineers' Row and Agents' Row. Colliers' Row was built in the 1850's and the other three in the 1860's.

The supervision of roads and bridges comes a very close second to poor relief. The parish was obliged to appoint a Surveyor of Highways, at first of their own choosing but after 1691 selected by the Justices of the Peace from the parish's short list. At the same time the number of days "statutory labour" per annum on the maintenance of the roads which every parishioner had to carry out was increased to six. This could be commuted by a cash payment. The Surveyor of Highways was usually unqualified and unskilled but men of higher quality came forward after 1835 when a new Highways Act permitted the levy of highway rates which, among other things, enabled the surveyor to be paid. The Act abolished Statutory Labour and permitted the creation of District Road Boards in those areas with a population of over 5,000. Local Road Boards could be established from 1848, but as late as January 1853 the local surgeon David Davis in giving evidence on the sanitary condition of Aberdare to the Government's inspector, Thomas Webster Rammell, stated "The roads are so bad that they are not fit for a horse to travel upon". In later years the Local Government Act 1888 transferred the entire responsibility for main roads to the newly-established County Councils.

The roads kept up by the Parish were generally those which communicated with other nearby towns or villages, e.g. the now disused road to Merthyr via Abernant. For the building of "long distance" roads such as the road from a place between Cilfynydd and Abercynon through Aberdare to meet the Abernant and Rhyd y Blew Turnpike at Hirwaun, the trustees secured statutory authority to

Glandare was another imposing coalmaster's house. It was built between 1846 and 1852 by which time its owner, Thomas Wayne, was in residence. He was the son of Matthew Wayne who established an ironworks at the Gadlys, Aberdare, in 1827 and in partnership with the David family, found the four foot seam at Abernant y Groes in 1837. Thomas died in 1867. By 1880 the house was inhabited by Daniel Rees, Civil Engineer. By 1920 Daniel Rees was dead and the house was occupied by his son, Robert Thomas Rees, Mineral Agent for the Marquess of Bute's Welsh estates and collieries.

In the mid-thirties the last of the family, Miss Annie Gertrude Rees, still lived at Glandare, but in the forties the house became a Bernardo's Home. Eventually the home became redundant and was knocked down, and the new St John Baptist (Church in Wales) secondary school took its place, being officially opened on the 4th of March 1976.

build and maintain them. They were called "Turnpike roads" and were financed by tolls taken at toll bars at intervals along the road. In 1830 there were four such toll bars or toll gates in the valley, situated at Hirwaun, Aberdare, beyond Mountain Ash, and Abercynon.

In narrower parts of the valley there were streets which ran directly up the valley sides giving access to the terraces which stood one above the other. Most of these streets were very steep, such as Pryce St., Mountain Ash which was examined in 1920 and found to be 1 in 4½. To pull a cart full of coal up this street required 5 horses.

A length of Parish road which remains today in as good a condition as it was when it was made in the mid 1850's can be seen to the east of the ruins of Penrhiwllech Farm on the mountainside overlooking Cwmdare. This was part of a road intended to be built from Cwmdare to the Rhondda but after passing Penrhiwllech it was apparently abandoned. The road had very little usage thereafter, with the result that it is still in remarkable condition.

The needs of public transport in the district were first met by the trains—the Aberdare railway to Cardiff in 1846 and the Vale of Neath railway to Neath and Swansea in 1851. These would have been supplemented by private horse-drawn vehicles and eventually by stage carriages subject to a degree of local authority control. In 1892 the Aberdare Board of Health licensed 48 omnibuses and 34 hackney carriages. According to William Bevan there were in Mountain Ash in 1896, 4 brakes, one wagonette and 12 cabs. The VNR had stations at Llwydcoed and Abernant on a branch which ran to Merthyr. When these lines were eventually taken over by the GWR the two stations in Aberdare were renamed Aberdare Low Level and Aberdare High Level, and their equivalents lower down the valley Mountain Ash Oxford St and Mountain Ash Cardiff Road.

In the nineteenth century if you lived in central Aberdare you lived in "The Village". If you lived across the river in the houses clustered around the lower part of Abernant road you lived in "The Trap", so called, says the legend, because there had been a pub in the vicinity, to which on pay day the passing ironworkers were irresistibly attracted. However, there is little or no evidence, documentary or other, for the existence of this Shangri-La.

Nearly everything in this photograph has disappeared. The main exception is Abernant road which ran in front of the houses in the background in which the Trap Road Cottage Hospital was set up in 1874 with 14 beds and 3 cots. Subsequently the Marquess of Bute made Abernant house available on moderate terms and it was opened as a replacement hospital for "the Trap" on the 17th of July 1917. The former hospital then became a doctors' surgery until it was demolished in the course of road improvements.

In 1913 the Aberdare Council-owned Electric Tramway system began operating with 36 vehicles, providing a service from the Cemetery gates at Trecynon to Aberaman. Branches from Trecynon to Cwmdare, Aberdare to Abernant, and Cwmaman to Abercwmboi were operated by trolley buses. Aberdare was the first undertaking in the country to start a service with both trams and trolley buses, and possibly the only undertaking to replace some trolley bus routes by trams. Mountain Ash did not have such a system but it had a service of buses operated by private companies which, in 1928, ran 28 buses an hour through the town, the speed limit having been revised from 12 to 20 mph. Aberdare Urban District Council finished its conversion to buses by 1935 and the trams and trolley buses faded from the scene. Bus services to places outside the council's area were operated by the Red and White and Western Welsh bus companies, both of which had depots in Aberdare. Interestingly, it appears that in Mountain Ash it was customary in 1923 for buses to pick up and drop anywhere on the route.

The Aberdare Canal, overwhelmed by competition from the railways and by subsidence caused by underground coal workings, finally closed in 1900. Afterwards the Aberdare and Mountain Ash councils each bought that portion of the canal which lay within its domain. The result was the building of the "new road" from Abercynon to Aberdare, the last part of which opened in 1933. In 1942 an increased demand for buses to carry workers to the ordnance factories was frustrated by a decrease in supply, the forces having priority in the supply of motor vehicles. As a result four red double-decker buses belonging to London Transport were lent to Aberdare Council and caused amazement as they ran through the streets of Aberdare.

Inevitably, Aberdare was affected by the "Beeching Axe" and the former TVR line closed to passengers on the 14th of March 1964 and the former Vale of Neath line did the same on the 15th of June 1964. Happily, the passenger service to Cardiff restarted on the 3rd of October 1988 and appears to flourish, as do the twice-daily trains of coal from the Tower Colliery.

Sir George Elliot and party outside Aberaman House. Before the industrial revolution the Aberaman estate had belonged for many years to the ancient Mathew family. Afterwards it had belonged to Anthony Bacon, Crawshay Bailey and others and had been much altered in the process. When this photo was taken Sir George Elliot was the occupier and he is seen here with members of his family and domestic staff.

What sort of houses did the immigrants referred to above find in the Aberdare area? We know that Aberdare existed as a village about 700 years ago but there is little surviving evidence of how people lived in those days. The "Bacon Drawings" of 1827/28 show scattered buildings in the village area, some roofed with thin stone tiles, and some with thatch. A painting in the National Museum of Wales made in 1812 reputed to be of "Elan Cottages, Aberdare" shows buildings with tiled roofs (see frontispiece). By 1841 the population was 6471, occupying 1171 houses. We may expect that most of these were built close to the Gadlys, Abernant, Hirwaun and Aberdare ironworks and the coal mines which served them. Hence Trecynon came into being as a result of the coal mines at Ysguborwen. But many of the Hirwaun workmen lived out of the parish, ie on the North side of the river. However, the greatest number of houses, 2750, was built between 1850 and 1859, the period in which the development of the coal industry was gaining speed and the larger ironworks were benefiting from the huge demand from abroad for rails. Some people think that the houses in the

area known as Greenfach which were demolished in the early 1960's to make way for the new library were the original properties on that site. In reality the original houses (possibly medieval) were demolished in the 1850's and replaced by Gadlys Row, Dare Place, Dare Street, Chapel Court, Green Street, and a confusing scatter of houses on both sides of the High Street. One also hears people praising the quality of the older houses, but the truth is that they were built very cheaply of undressed stone, with no "parpens" i.e. stones passing from one side of the wall to the other to bind the inner and outer skins together. As a result a common cause of failure in the old houses can be seen when the outer skin becomes bowed and subject to collapse. Often the mid nineteenth century houses have no foundations and have doors, for example, only half an inch thick. It was common however for the roof timbers such as the principal rafters to be made thicker than would be thought necessary today. However, a row of two or three cottages adjacent to Abernant house supported their roofs by means of cast iron trusses.

Rows of houses were put up by the ironmasters and coalmasters and later by other persons who had money to invest. Surprisingly, a number of cottages in Trecynon were built with only one bedroom. Most of the surviving cottages have been judiciously improved and are pleasant to live in. Often the new houses were occupied before the plaster was dry. Sometimes men took matters into their own hands, and Hirwaun Common became dotted with huts put up by squatters who used whatever material they could find. As early as 1788 the parishioners of Aberdare demolished the abodes of thirty-five of the squatters. This did not put an end to the practice and one of the first acts of the newly formed Board of Health in 1855 was to order the demolition of the huts on the Common. But matters appeared no better in 1867 when the Board of Health was informed that one David Price was living with four children in a one-roomed hut on Hirwaun Common thatched with brattice cloth. Nearby, William Tilley lived in a similar structure with his wife, three children and pig. However, matters improved gradually, and by the turn of the century there were over 6700 houses in the parish, most of which were built in compliance with a series of byelaws made by the local Board of Health from 1859 on, based on the Local Government Act 1858 and the Public Health Act of 1875. Broadly speaking then, the dwelling houses of the age of coal were better than those of the age of iron. But it would be a mistake to think that the sanitary reforms of the second half of the nineteenth century had done away with housing problems. The Aberdare Urban District Council decided in 1904 to conduct an investigation and appointed councillor Edmund Stonelake to do it. He reported: "Of the 396 houses visited the greater part was in very bad repair, and some in the last stages of dilapidation: windows and doors rotting away; water coming in through the roof; and in a large number of cases dampness in its most dangerous form viz, rising through the floor". In one instance he found that one WC divided into four stalls had to do service for the whole row of houses. In 1957, when a plan produced in that year by the then Glamorgan County Council involving drastic and far-reaching changes in the Aberdare district was made public, there was astonishment at the degree of public rejection which was evinced. The plan, which was supported by Aberdare Council, proposed the demolition of a very large number of houses and their replacement by new houses. The "South Wales Echo" of the 31st of January 1957 reported that "something like one third of the houses in Aberdare and the outlying districts would be demolished by 1971".

Dissent grew swiftly, and the bulk of the population, prominent citizens, the Chamber of Trade, and the local press were firmly opposed. It was felt that the plan was too drastic and wide-sweeping. For example, the Medical Officer of Health had classified 1218 houses as below standard.

A petition of 17,000 protests was gathered, weekly collections were made, Labour councillors were replaced by "Protectionists" in affected areas and feelings ran very high. A 400 yard-long cavalcade of 40 cars and 8 buses descended upon the Welsh Board of Health in Cathays Park, where "Cwm Rhondda" was sung outside and the petition was submitted. At a meeting with Henry Brooke, the Minister for Welsh Affairs, the Minister announced that a public inquiry into the Town Plan would be held. The inquiry started on the 27th of January 1959 and sat for 3 weeks and 2 days. On the 10th of October 1962 the Minister, Sir Keith Joseph, announced that the Plan would not proceed. It was afterwards learnt that the Ministers had been favourably affected by the way in which many of the houses had been repaired and modernised.

But this was not the last attempt to introduce widespread demolition to Aberdare. Drawn up by Dennis J Harmer and Associates, the "Harmer Plan" for the remodelling of the town and surrounding districts was made public at the beginning of June 1972. Immediately there was a public outcry at the proposal that 5,650 houses would be demolished under three ten-year programmes which would virtually wipe out all housing built before 1860, replacing them with 11,620 new houses built on 27 new sites. Eventually Councillors put the plan to the vote and it was turned down by one vote.

Towards the end of the nineteenth century building clubs had a revival in popularity and operated very successfully until the beginning of the first World War, many houses in the Aberdare area being built in this way. Having procured a suitable site, a number of persons would collectively borrow money to finance the building of a house for each of them. All members would pay subscriptions towards the clearance of the loan and incidental expenses. As each house was completed it would be allocated to one of the members by drawing lots. When all the houses had been completed and occupied and all debts paid the club would be wound up.

The wages earned in the coal mines were far greater than those of the agricultural areas of west Wales and elsewhere, with the result that the mining valleys of south east Wales became a veritable Klondyke. By the middle of the nineteenth century the population of the Aberdare district was over 1500 and Mountain Ash over 1000, with the numbers increasing rapidly. The insanitary condition of many of the towns in the industrial areas throughout the country led to epidemics, such as (in Aberdare) typhus in 1847, small pox in 1848, and cholera in 1848/49. Parliament reacted by passing the Public Health Act 1848, after which a vestry meeting at Aberdare decided to take the necessary steps to place itself under the provisions of the Act. First, the town had to be visited by an inspector from the Central Board of Health and a report made. This was done, the inspector being T W Rammell, whose reports on the towns of Merthyr and Cardiff contained, according to Dr John Davies, "some of the most unsavoury material ever to appear within the covers of an official publication". It was afterwards agreed that the 1848 Act should apply to Aberdare. Mountain Ash was in a different parish and its sanitary condition does not seem to have attracted the attention of the General Board of Health.

The Act enabled communities to elect a local Board of Health with the power to take steps to alleviate the environmental dangers which beset the worst-affected districts. In Aberdare the election for the twelve members of the first Board for the Cynon Valley was held on the 15th of September 1854, and those elected were; David Davies, Blaengwawr, (Coalmaster), Thomas Joseph, Mill St, (Coalmaster), Thomas Price, Rose Cottage, (Baptist Minister), John Jones, Aberdare (Druggist), Richard Fothergill, Abernant House, (Ironmaster), Rees Hopkin Rees, Llwydcoed, (Mineral agent), James Lewis Roberts, Aberdare, (Surgeon), Griffith Davies, Ynyslwyd, (Gentleman farmer), David Williams, Ynyscynon, (Coalmaster), Philip John, Aberdare, (Grocer), Thomas Wayne, Glandare, (Ironmaster), Crawshay Bailey, Aberdare, (Ironmaster).

Mountain Ash became a separate authority with its own Board of Health in 1867. At the first election Lord Aberdare became chairman of the Board. The other members were; Edward Thomas, Rees Williams, George Wilkins, David Coleman, John Griffiths, Howell Evans, The Rev David Jones, Thomas Jones, David Rees, David Clark, The Rev William Williams, Gwilym James, George Brown and David Morgans.

The single men who came into the district during the migration referred to above took lodgings and after settling in would send for friends and relatives to seek a share of the wealth of the coalfield. Inevitably there was a high degree of overcrowding, a practice which lasted into the twentieth century. But this was only one of the dangers inimical to the rising population. Not only was there no service of piped water to the hundreds of houses which were built before the byelaws came into being, but the water available from the springs and numerous wells was contaminated by death-dealing organisms. The main cause of this was the absence in working class dwellings of any means of sewage disposal other than throwing it into one of three culverts which ran from the town to the river, throwing it into the street, or putting it into ccsspits which were seldom emptied. The provision of a sewerage system

It is known locally that Cwmbach was the site of the first co-operative shop in Wales. Two workers at Lletty Shenkin Colliery, David Thomas and John Rees, became interested in the activities of the Rochdale pioneers in 1859, and together with ten or so others opened a co-operative shop on this site in Bridge Row in March 1860. In later years it was rebuilt in the form shown in the photo. When the time came for the building to be demolished the commemorative plaque seen on the wall was transferred to a nearby building.

115

and a supply of potable water were two of the eight recommendations made by T.W. Rammell following his inquiry in January 1853. However, it was not until September 1855 that the Board of Health did anything about it, and all they did was to dig three wells, one outside the Boot Hotel, another near the Welsh Harp Bridge over the Dare (near where Woolworths now is), another at the bottom of Gadlys Hill. It was not until January 1863 that the Board decided to appoint an "Officer for Health". In the following April there were still seventeen slaughter houses in the town, the filth etc., from which was taken to and dumped at one of three open spaces provided for the purpose. In September 1866 another piece of ground was taken for an "Ash Depot" (ie for sewage). This was where the Boys' Comprehensive School now stands

In 1857 the Board formed a Water Supply Committee but the committee's intentions (if indeed they had any) were forestalled by the formation of the Aberdare Waterworks Company in 1856. The company started work on a storage reservoir at Cwmdare the supply from which was turned on on the 12th of September 1859, but it was only available to the residents of Aberdare, Trecynon and Aberaman. In 1869 the Board took powers to purchase the water company and did so for the sum of £42,000. At that time the Chairman and at least two other members of the Board were directors of the water company.

The Board then took steps to extend the coverage of the undertaking to supply the whole parish and this was made possible by building two more reservoirs, each named after the stream upon which it stood, i.e. Nant-hir and Nant-moel. With increasing demand the supply was again found insufficient and in 1913 the Aberdare Urban District Council as the Water Authority agreed to purchase a minimum of 150,000 gallons a day from Merthyr Corporation.

However, dissension occurred in 1913 when the Corporation promoted a Bill for the setting up of the Taff Fechan Water Supply Board. Though the Bill was strenuously opposed by Aberdare Council, the Corporation won the day and the Taff Fechan Board was created with Aberdare UDC joining in 1921, followed by Mountain Ash. Other reorganisations have occurred over the years and today "Welsh Water" is owned by "Hyder" The situation in Mountain Ash was not initially as critical as Aberdare, but Lord Aberdare built the first small reservoir in 1862, followed by John Nixon with two more in 1868. It was not until 1886 that powers were granted in an Act of Parliament to make provision for both water and gas supply.

The Mountain Ash local board then took over with further reservoirs in 1892 and 1904 and the large Penderyn reservoir in 1920. The Mountain Ash population then stood at around 43,000 and Aberdare at 55,000.

Early in 1868 a fever epidemic raged in Cwmbach and it was not a surprize to one local observer at least:

"There is a row of houses called Duffryn Row numbering some twenty four houses running parallel with the canal. The row has only one privy to the lot, and it is in such a filthy state that it is impossible to get near it. A drain runs from under one of the houses to the canal and the effluvia is fearful . . . The filthy water in the canal is frequently stirred up by the boats navigating along . . . . Nothing could be a better fever producer".

Human nature being what it is, the provision of the public health facilities needed by well populated centres of industry in the nineteenth century lagged behind the demand, and ten years after the formation of the Board of Health the result in the Cynon Valley, as elsewhere, was recurrences of the epidemics of dreadful diseases such as typhoid and cholera arising from the pollution of drinking water by pathogens in faeces.

In 1865 the Inspector of Nuisances still had plenty to do, reporting to the Board that he had found the contents of a privy running through a pantry in Pleasant Row, of all places, and in the next year he had to call attention to the Bruce Arms at Aberdare where there was a well near a privy cesspool and an overflowing drain passing through the cellar. There were many such cases.

In the summer of 1866 it was feared that another outbreak of cholera was imminent and the Board of Health sprang to the fore, buying two whitewash brushes to lend to those who could not afford to buy one. (Whitewashing was believed to be an effective prophylactic measure). The first case was reported on the 10th of August.

In the intervening years the Board tried, in the absence of a

Quoits is a game of great antiquity, but the game was not taken seriously in Wales until 1896 when international matches with England were started. Soon teams sprang into being in many villages and towns in South Wales. This photograph is of Mr W Dice Davies who lived at Cwmdare for some years and worked at Bwllfa Colliery. "Dice" (as he was known) was Wales's most famous player, having been selected for Wales on 27 occasions and beaten only 7 times. He was champion of Wales 5 times and of South Wales 10 times.

proper sewerage system, to encourage the construction of properly constructed privies. The recommended method was to make a cesspit lined with masonry or brickwork of a finished size of four feet square and with a depth of not less than eight feet. This pit had to be surmounted by a brick or masonry hut four feet square and not less than seven feet high. A proper door and covering had to be provided.

In the year 1875 the Board at last turned their attention to the question of proper sewage disposal, a mere twenty two years after Rammell reported that the parish had no provision for drainage. Since Merthyr was facing the same problem the two Boards put their heads together and built a joint sewage farm at Abercynon. The construction of a main sewer in Aberdare began early in 1880, the Inspector of Nuisances reporting that 90 homes had been connected by October of that year and by August 1883 the number had risen to 3485 representing roughly 60% of houses in Aberdare and adjacent areas. The main sewer was later joined by a sewer from Hirwaun. With extensive subsequent house building, numerous extensions and enlargements to the original system have been made.

The disposal of domestic refuse has also been seen as a matter requiring careful management so as to avoid presenting a threat to health. But if there were no proper sewers until the last quarter of the nineteenth century we may be sure that the arrangements for the disposal of kitchen and other domestic waste were virtually non-existent, that is, they consisted of throwing it into ditches or on a midden, should such a luxury be present, or in default, into the middle of the road. Whichever course was adopted, the animal and vegetable content of the refuse became a resort for flies and vermin.

Because of the hilly nature of the valley, the railways of the Cynon Valley were not able to provide a passenger service for all parts of the district, and where such services were provided they were often on the fringe of the area concerned, as were Hirwaun and Trecynon stations on the Vale of Neath line. The advantages of street-based public transport, i.e. electric trams and afterwards motor buses, could not be denied and, together with the tremendous increase in the number of private cars, they presented formidable competition to the railways. This tramcar is standing at the western terminus of the system, at the entrance to Aberdare Old Cemetery.

When the local authorities began to collect domestic refuse, horse-drawn carts were employed to go from house to house collecting the rubbish and when full, taking the material to a distant tipping ground. The chief disadvantage of the horse and cart was its slowness on the journey to and from the tip. Its chief advantage was that usually the horse would learn the "round" and would stop where required, enabling the driver to assist in the filling. Despite this advantage, the carts began to be superseded by motor lorries in the 1930s. Until the second half of the twentieth century the refuse consisted mainly of the ashes from the previous day's coal fire on which any small items of cardboard or paper wrapping would have been burnt. In addition there would have been bottles and tin cans and any other rubbish such as broken china. As it would have made an obnoxious smell, animal or vegetable waste would not have been burned, but put straight into the waste bin, which would not have been one of the "wheelie bins" of today, but a bucket, demoted from indoor duties by the appearance of holes in its bottom. For a while after 1910 the refuse was burnt at the Council's "destructor" at Gadlys to raise steam for an electricity generating plant intended mainly to provide electricity for the district's trams. However the system was not very efficient and was discontinued.

Until now we have been considering public health and it is now time to say what we can about the day-to-day care provided by medical practitioners and others for the sick and injured. There is a record that in 1784 a doctor called Shon Rhys ap Ivan from Llwydcoed, together with the Reverend Thomas Morgans, Unitarian Minister of Blaengwrach, Glyn Neath, are said to have vaccinated 101 children against measles. In 1835 Parish notes tell us that in that year there were two surgeon doctors practising in Aberdare named Charles Forrest and Lewis Roberts. The population then was about 5,000.

The expansion of the iron and coal industries led to the appointment of "Company Doctors" such as the local practitioner, Dr Evan Jones, who was appointed Surgeon to the Aberdare Iron Works in

September 1864. He was well liked and had the reputation of being an expert surgeon. He held the position of High Constable for two years in succession and took an active interest in matters affecting the welfare of the town. In 1891 he was presented with a purse of gold containing £637 by the workmen of the district.

In the nineteenth century and the first half of the twentieth century hospitals were the resort mainly of surgical cases, and medical cases were treated at home. Fevers were treated in special isolation hospitals, one of which was built in Trecynon in 1877 and another at Mountain Ash in 1892. By means of a magistrate's order a fever case could be taken to hospital by force if necessary. Even in those days there were, sometimes, complaints in the press about the incompetence of doctors. One correspondent suggested that the miners should withhold their weekly contribution at the pits towards the salary of the Company Doctor and apply the money to the building of an infirmary at Aberdare, whereby they could have the privilege of choosing their own medical attendant instead of having to rely on the choice of the colliery proprietor. The Doctor Evan Jones referred to above was mainly responsible in 1874 for the establishment at Aberdare of the Trap Road Cottage Hospital which was supported by the Bute family. This had 14 beds and 3 cots.

In 1906 a number of like-minded friends met at the Cwmaman Institute for the purpose of organising an eisteddfod. A few months before the eisteddfod was to be held two or three serious accidents occurred at the local collieries, which highlighted the need for an institution where the victims of such accidents could be treated. As a result, the eisteddfod committee decided that the proceeds of the eisteddfod would form the basis of a fund devoted to the provision of a cottage hospital in the Cwmaman area. By 1910 when the fund amounted to about £600 and had obtained the support of the community, the committee was re-formed on a wider base with representation from the collieries and other bodies. It was found that over 90% of the workmen were in favour of the scheme but regrettably an industrial dispute caused the scheme to be laid aside for two years.

In January 1913 Mr. Hann of the Powell Duffryn Co stated that his company were prepared to erect and equip a cottage hospital behind Woodland Terrace Godreaman, and excavations were begun in June 1914. As a result of the Great War, materials became in short supply and the project had to be laid aside once more.

In the summer of 1915 it became known that the Marquess of Bute wished to close the cottage hospital at the Trap. However, he was prepared to let Abernant House on moderate terms. Furthermore, after discussions the Cwmaman and Aberaman Hospital Committee agreed to support the Abernant House General Hospital Scheme. The hospital was opened on the 19th of July 1917 with accomodation for 34 beds and 6 cots. On the 24th of January 1923 a temporary ward of 16 beds was opened because of pressure of demand.

On the 27th of September 1929 a fire destroyed the main building and two firemen lost their lives. The Hospital was rebuilt and enlarged to comprise 84 beds and was re-opened on the 25th of April 1933 by H R H the Duchess of York (The present Queen Mother).

In Mountain Ash a meeting held in "The Old Coffee Tavern" in 1895 agreed to take steps to obtain a hospital for the district. As a result, the "Cottage Hospital" which was paid for by Lady Aberdare was erected at Granville Terrace, Caegarw. Lady Aberdare also paid for a new wing in 1900 and for an operating theatre in 1908. A new larger hospital was opened in 1924, the original building being used as a maternity hospital, and later as a block of flats. The new hospital was financed by a Hospital fund supported by business and professional people and by the miners, who paid 6d per week. Further improvements and extensions were opened in 1937, and the running costs of the hospital were met by the proceeds of an annual eisteddfod

Many years ago it was the custom for parishioners to be buried inside the church. Then the churchyards of St John's, St Cynog's (Penderyn), St Gwynno's (Llanwonno), and St Mabon (Llanfabon) were made available for burials. The population rose rapidly and some of the chapels were permitted to inter within their grounds. The first public burial service in Aberdare to take place outside St John's churchyard took place in the Hen Dy Cwrdd in 1797.

The need for public cemeteries was exemplified by conditions in St John's churchyard where by 1861 it was impossible to dig a grave without exposing old coffins or remains. The number of interments (which included in 1849 no less than 100 due to Cholera alone) was such that it was closed in 1864 by Order-in-Council. Soon afterwards large cemeteries were laid out at Caegarw (Mountain Ash) and Hirwaun in 1866, Trecynon (Aberdare) in 1870 and others soon followed. Crematoriums opened at Pontypridd in 1924 and at Llwydcoed in 1970. It will not come as a surprise to discover that the first interment in Aberdare Cemetery was a miner, Morgan Jones, killed in a fall at Blaengwawr Colliery.

The two parishes of Aberdare and Llanwonno formed for administrative purposes the hundred of Miskin Higher. Crimes of a minor nature were dealt with locally in the courts of Petty Sessions, the ancestors of today's magistrates' courts. In the early nineteenth century courts were held in the Boot Hotel, Aberdare and occasionally in the Mountain Ash Inn. Law and order were maintained by Parish Constables of which there was at Aberdare one only in the early part of the nineteenth century. Law enforcement was put on a sounder footing in 1841 when the County Police was set up. Shortly afterwards there was built the first police station in the Cynon Valley at Windsor Street, Trecynon, and by 1851 there were 10 policemen based in the valley, but it was not until 1865 that a police station was built in Mountain Ash.

Until well into the twentieth century punishments could be very harsh, as in most other places;

1844. Two Aberdare youths, convicted of stealing apples from an orchard were sentenced to 14 days hard labour in the Cardiff House of Correction.

1855. Thomas Williams was convicted at Aberdare Police Court of stealing coal valued at 4d (less than 2p). and was sentenced to one month's hard labour.

1879. A £1 fine was imposed for the furious driving of a horse and cart down Abernant Hill at 10 mph.

Near Bethel chapel, Hirwaun, a Hirwaun undertaker, Rees Overton Jones, looks proudly at his new hearse.

The police also had a role to play in early fire-fighting measures. Before the formation of the brigades, there were hoses and ladders available and these were generally looked after by the police, who received an honorarium for their trouble. One such policeman was PC Morris of Cwmdare. When a fire started underground at Bwllfa colliery PC Morris was sent for and arrived with his hose. He then descended the pit with others to fight the fire.

The practicability of a system of fire fighting depends on the availability of a plentiful supply of water. During the 1890's hydrants began to appear and the local authorities set up fire brigades early in the new century. When the Aberdare brigade was asked to help to fight a fire in Mountain Ash's district the Aberdare brigade claimed and were paid a fee of £14/16/6d. for services rendered.

An indicator of the growth of the village of Aberdare into a town is the fact that in 1793 there were only two shops in Aberdare. The ironmasters soon opened truck shops (see chap. 7) and though these became illegal they seem to have been less unpopular in this area than in other places and they persisted until the mid nineteenth century.

> *Mr. Denton (Surgeon) begs to inform the public of Aberdare and its vicinity that he has opened a MEDICAL ESTABLISHMENT in Canon St, opposite the Temperance Hall, which he trusts will be of service to such as are suffering from a disease or accident; and hopes by attention and moderate charging to gain the confidence and continued patronage of such as may favour him. – 1858.*

The first Co-operative store in Wales was opened in Cwmbach in 1859 by a group of colliers, supplies being transported in by canal barge. The Co-operative movement afterwards made a huge impact in the area with Co-op shops opening throughout the valley, and the Society became a major provider and employer as the large population and initial prosperity ensured rapid commercial expansion. "Siop ni"(our shop) as it was known, featured prominently in valley life, the generous "divvi" (dividend) being a very popular and effective method of saving (The dividend could be as high as 17%). But now the Co-operative system has almost vanished from the valley.

Shops of all kinds formed the main streets of the settlements in the valley and the prosperity enabled the shops to be renovated to accord with the latest styles. The shops on the south and east sides of Victoria Square in Aberdare were built in front of the original properties, none of which now remain. One reputable chain of men's outfitters, namely Hodges, originated in Victoria Square and spread through Wales and the West Country. The large number of "front room" and "corner" shops are nearly all gone, as have the small bakeries and milk vendors. At one time these tiny shops provided a multitude of goods including colliers' chalk used by the miner for marking his number on the trams he filled and gunpowder for blasting underground.

To cope with the correspondence generated by the new commercial establishments and with the large population a main post office was opened at Aberdare at mid-century, and sub-offices were opened at Hirwaun, Trecynon, Aberaman, Cwmbach, Cwmaman, Abercwmboi and Mountain Ash. Mail for Mountain Ash was brought on foot from Aberdare. Business increased further with the introduction of the postcard and its accompanying half-penny stamp in 1870 and Cwmdare, Penderyn and Ystradfellte were added to the number of sub-offices. By 1897 28,000 letters a week were received by Aberdare GPO and 32,000 dispatched elsewhere, a far cry from the earliest days when letters were taken by a horseman from the primitive post office at the Black Lion to Merthyr, where they were collected by the Royal Mail Coach. In 1896 15,300 letters a week were delivered from Mountain Ash Post Office which was no longer "Near Aberdare". When telephones came to Aberdare in 1891, there were five subscribers only at first.

After the use of primitive candles and oil lamps (often evil smelling), the use of coal gas for illuminating dwelling houses and thoroughfares must have been a tremendous improvement. Indeed the historian of Mountain Ash, William Bevan, has recorded that when gas street lighting was first put in, people "were ready to believe that they lived in one of the chief cities of the Country". Although there had been a previous undertaking of which nothing is known, the first gas works of any significance in the upper part of the valley (The Aberdare Gas Company) originated at a meeting held on the 5th of September 1848, and a gasworks at Abergwawr was in use by the 24th of December following. Among the promoters were Crawshay Bailey and Thomas Wayne and only £1,500 of the

£2,000 capital was needed to set up the enterprise including the service pipes to the 150 (domestic) lights in use. In later years a gasworks was built at Hirwaun but this ceased to operate many years ago.

There were no gas lights in the streets of Aberdare at first except for four or five paid for by private individuals, but in 1856 a tender was accepted for the provision of 19 street gas lamps. Some people thought that street lighting was not a good thing because "the police might not be able to pounce on wary offenders". However, when the Gadlys Iron Works was in use the light from the furnaces was bright enough to facilitate the arrest of wrongdoers on more than one occasion. Some persons were wealthy enough to be independent of a public gas supply—when Abernant house was enlarged by the Fothergills in July 1861 a small private gas works was erected beside the tramroad on the west side of the property. The opening of gas works naturally meant a demand for suitable coal, mainly obtained from outside the valley.

As a result of the inadequacy and high cost of the gas supply, competitors stepped forward and despite the opposition of the Board of Health they formed the Aberdare and Aberaman Gas Company. They then obtained an Act of Parliament called the Aberdare and Aberaman Gas Act 1869, permitting them to set up a gas undertaking for Aberdare and Aberaman (the previous company was non-statutory). However, the Act did not empower the newly formed company to purchase compulsorily the undertaking of the Aberdare Gas Company, and had the effect of encouraging it to fight for its independence by improving its supply and reducing the price of gas. The Act, which applied to the area within the radius of 2½ miles from St Elvan's Church, emphasised that the supply was inadequate for the growing town.

The first gas works in the lower part of the valley was built by the Nixon Company in the Navigation Colliery yard. This provided light for the colliery, the streets of the district, dwelling houses, shops and places of worship. In 1887 the Local Board of Health took over the gas works and afterwards built a new works at Penrhiwceiber supplying gas to Mountain Ash, Abercynon, Ynysybwl and up to Abercwmboi.

Inevitably electricity finally supplanted gas for many purposes, though incandescent mantles became very efficient and remained in domestic use until the post-war period. Indeed, as the writing of this book began there was still one house in Cwmdare not connected to the electric mains, gas being used for all purposes. Mountain Ash Urban District Council began lighting its area in 1911, Ynysybwl being first, followed by Abercynon then Mountain Ash itself by 1922. Power was supplied by the South Wales Electrical Distribution Company. In the area of the Aberdare Urban District Council the situation was different, for in 1910 an electricity generating station was built at the old Gadlys iron works site, opening officially on 30th March 1911. During the first year 215 consumers and 142 street lamps were connected up, and by 1916 about two thirds of the district could draw upon electricity. However, all the Council's schools were still lit by gas and about 598 of the street lamps were still gas powered. Conversion of the supply from DC to AC occurred in 1935 and nationalisation of the industry in 1948. Nationalisation brought to an end the concession of virtually free electricity granted to chapels etc. by some of the colliery owners who generated their own electricity.

CHAPTER SIX

Until the mid eighteenth century only two places of Christian worship existed in the Cynon Valley. They were the parish churches of St. John in Aberdare and St. Gwynno at Llanwonno, curacies governed by the Vicar of Llantrisant and long established. Both churches are mentioned in relation to chancel repairs in church records of 1450. The Parish Church of St Cynog at Penderyn, of an antiquity comparable with that of Llanwonno, ministered to the needs of the northernmost extremities of the valley. Architectural evidence points to a date around 1200 for the foundation of St John's while several factors including the name of the early Saint Gwynno suggests an even earlier Celtic foundation for the church at Llanwonno. It has been estimated that the population around the year 1750 amounted to about a thousand, scattered through the valley, but concentrated mainly in the Aberdare area, and almost entirely monoglot Welsh speaking.

The Welsh translation of the Bible, authorised by the Anglican Church, had been available from the end of the sixteenth century but was little used throughout Wales for the following hundred years. However, increasing availability and proficiency in reading created a different situation in the eighteenth century. Some thirty or so of Griffith Jones's Circulating Schools (referred to below), invited by local clergy, had been active in the valley during the period 1736 – 1773; they taught bible reading and obviously made a significant contribution, and the results assisted in opening up the field of Christian worship.

John Wesley journeyed through Aberdare on the 6th April 1749, and preached at St. John's Church following a burial in the churchyard. He recorded "Few could understand so Henry Lloyd, when I had done, interpreted the substance of my sermon in Welsh". The protestant dissenters'

Chapter Six describes the dramatic events arising from "The Treachery of the Blue Books" in 1846-48. The two principal actors were the Vicar of Aberdare, John Griffith (right) and the Baptist minister of Calfaria, the remarkable Thomas Price (left).

movement had been growing and the first Nonconformist Chapel in the valley, Hen Dy Cwrdd, was established in 1751 at Trecynon by a group, previously worshipping at Cwm y Glo, across the mountain in the Merthyr area. Hen Dy Cwrdd became a Unitarian Chapel under the ministry of the the radical Thomas Evans (Thomas Glyn Cothi) who had suffered imprisonment for his radical political views. A splinter group formed the Welsh Independent (Congregational) chapel of Ebenezer nearby in 1811, but Hen Dy Cwrdd remained Unitarian. However, the building is now disused, though the cause is being maintained at Highland Place, Monk Street.

A Methodist chapel was established at the lower end of the valley at Ynysybwl in 1786, and was visited by John Wesley in that year, and around 1800 the Unitarians held meetings monthly in Mountain Ash at the house called Troedyrhiw. Meetings in houses, and later in the Farmers Arms in High Street, Aberdare followed the baptism of four adults in the river Cynon in 1791, and this resulted in the Welsh Baptist Chapel Carmel being built at Penpound (Monk Street) in 1811. Again, following meetings in the open air, houses and shops, the Methodists set up a chapel at Pentwyn Bach in Trecynon in 1806.

The population grew with the opening of the iron works and supporting ironstone and coal mines and so did Nonconformity with nine chapels in 1837 when the population reached eight thousand. The dissenters in Hirwaun initially worshipped together in houses, but in the early 1820's four chapels were established by the dissenting denominations, namely Nebo (Welsh Congregationalists), Soar (Welsh Methodist), Bethel (Welsh Calvinistic Methodist), and Ramoth (Baptist) causing the Anglicans

Bethel (Hirwaun) was built in 1823 and was the oldest of the nonconformist Chapels in Hirwaun and the largest in membership. It was rebuilt in 1838 and again in 1857. Prominent members of the Chapel were the Mathews of Ewenny and David Watkin Jones better known as Dafydd Morgannwg. But the backbone of the Chapel was the Bevan family. Ministers who gave sterling service were W. J. Williams 1866-1912, D. Teify Davies 1916-1943, followed by the bard Eurian Davies.

The Chapel was demolished to allow the building of the dwellings known as Bethel place and was rebuilt nearby, but the new building has since been demolished, and the congregation has joined an united Welsh Chapel in Nebo.   Doug Williams

The 1904 revival saw scenes of great religious fervour and worship which sometimes carried on until late at night. It is recorded that services were even held underground before the miners started work as in this depiction of such an event.

to say that Hirwaun was "Abandoned to the Dissenters". But the Anglican Church, despite having earlier sponsored the Welsh Bible and the circulating schools, was very slow to react to the population increase. The organisational and financial problems within the church resulted in an almost medieval situation. For example, there were no free seats in the parish church until 1850.

The Nonconformists, however, laboured manfully so that by the time of the population peak of nearly 100,000 in the first quarter of the twentieth century, the chapels in the valley amounted to no less than 140. Though the number of churches in the valley increased to 20 by the end of the century, the Nonconformists were forging ahead, not only in the centres of Aberdare and Mountain Ash, but in the outlying villages as well. The increasing success of Nonconformity meant that nearly every chapel had to be enlarged, the testimony of success being the plaque on the tympanum of the frontage proudly bearing the dates of the building and rebuilding. Activities such as "penny readings", "Band of Hope", Sunday School and even the temperance movement served pressing needs of the time, and in return the chapels, which were almost all Welsh speaking, unintentionally helped to perpetuate the Welsh language and culture. The chapels were in some cases supported by the native coalmasters, such as David Davies of Blaengwawr and his son of the same name, and one or two of them, such as Thomas Joseph, were actually engaged in their design and construction.

However, the situation of the established church improved greatly in the second half of the century thanks to such clergymen as John Griffith (later rector of Merthyr), the first Vicar of Aberdare. (The previous clergy had been curates). Other notable clergymen were Canon J.D. Jenkins, who achieved the unusual distinction of becoming President of the National Union of Railwaymen, and the Reverend C.A.H. Green, later Archbishop of Wales. They were all able men, Welsh speaking and

The driving force behind the 1904 revival in Wales was a former miner, Evan Roberts, who began to conduct informal services in Moriah Chapel in his birthplace, Loughor. But as the revival spread through Wales and the number of the converted increased, so did the doubts about Roberts' mental stability multiply, and in 1905, at the height of the revival, he withdrew to a friend's house in Leicester and remained in seclusion for the rest of his life.   John F. Mear

very active in church and civic affairs. A number of fine churches were established such as St. Elvan's. Despite funding problems this was built in 1851, sited on an eminence and dominating the Aberdare town centre with cathedral-like splendour. In 1858 the church was provided with a ring of bells. Some churches were founded wholly or partly by the landowners or coalmasters of the various districts and designed by prominent architects such as John Seddon, who designed St. Margaret's Church at Mountain Ash, which was paid for by John Bruce Pryce of Duffryn House. St. Fagan's Church was consecrated in 1854, and became a parish church in 1856, though the areas of Cwmdare and Llwydcoed were not included in the new parish and the two churches afterwards built in those places found themselves at first in the parish of Aberdare. They became part of the parish of St. Fagan in 1891. The Memorial Hall (Church club) built near the town centre and opened in 1895 in memory of Canon Bowen Jenkins (Vicar 1883-1893) provided a much-needed and well-used civic facility for many years until its demolition.

The neo-gothic style of the new churches contrasted with the austere functionalism of the chapels, which were often built of "rubble", i.e. un-dressed stone, covered with cement rendering incorporating a few elements of classical architecture, such as pilasters and mouldings. Chapels for English speaking congregations, being more recent in origin, tended to be more ornate even when small, such as Providence (Cong.) in Mountain Ash of distinguished appearance. More affluent chapels were able to afford a dressed stone frontage with sides and rear elevation of rubble.

There have been many long-serving and notable chapel ministers in the Cynon Valley. Dr. Thomas Price, the Baptist minister of Calfaria, Monk Street, was a remarkable man and a colourful character. He established eleven Baptist chapels, edited three Welsh newspapers, held classes on a range of subjects, ministered to over a thousand members and served on the Board of Health. Every month he led a hymn-singing band of worshippers through Aberdare town to carry out adult baptisms in the river Cynon at the end of Commercial Street. Those baptised wore long robes, the men black, the women white. He is also remembered for physically ejecting the minister of one of his daughter chapels who had become a Mormon. The chapel, Gwawr in Aberaman, then returned to the Baptist cause! He fiercely championed the local condemnation of the Report of the Education Commission of 1847 (Brad y Llyfrau Gleision), singling out for his strongest criticism the evidence given by the vicar, the Rev. John Griffith, on the state of morality and education in the parish (see below). Dr Price died in 1888 after a ministry of 42 years in the town.

The Reverend D. Silyn Evans served as congregational minister of Siloa Aberdare for 50 years (1880-1930). Far less flamboyant than Dr Price, he was another pillar of nonconformity, highly respected in the chapel and the town. The Reverend William Williams, minister of Rhos Baptist chapel, Oxford St, Mountain Ash from 1855 to 1891 was another revered figure, one of many such throughout the valley. The four main nonconformist denominations and the Unitarians have always been well represented in the valley with Congregationalists and Baptists the most numerous.

William Bevan lists 12 chapels, 5 Anglican places of worship and a Catholic church in Mountain Ash in 1896. Later the chapel total more than doubled. Abercynon, lower down the valley, did not develop until the late nineteenth century, the 1890's being the period of substantial chapel building. St David's (Anglican) church was built at the same time but the Roman Catholic Church was not built until 1925. English Baptist services were held in the colliery office at Penrhiwceiber until Bethesda chapel was built, and the English Congregationalists met in the railway station waiting room at Abercynon, and probably made good use of the Bible placed in every Taff Vale station waiting room.

There were notable religious revivals in Wales in 1859, 1879 and 1904. William Bevan tells us that a revival service in Bethania (Welsh Cong.) Mountain Ash in 1859 began at 10.30 am and lasted until 11 pm without a break. Unable to get in, some prayed outside and others sang. Scores of people returned to the faith reviving the tendency towards the enlargement of chapels. It is said that during one revival meeting a bemused individual, overcome with religious zeal, had to be restrained from re-entering Ebenezer chapel, Trecynon, with a ladder to "climb upwards"! In some instances, prayer meetings took place underground before work commenced. The 1879 revival was mainly Baptist and the 1904 revival was inspired by the almost mystical Evan Roberts. A Methodist from the Loughor area, Roberts with his supporting group of five young lady singers and evangelists began his first tour of the valleys at Mountain Ash and Ynysybwl. The fact remains, it seems, that many of the converts remained converted after these revivals. But it is also a fact that some persons were so much affected that they became mentally ill, and a small number took their own lives.

The chapel, born as elsewhere of spiritual and social needs, became for some time highly suspicious of the growing trade unions. Relationships between chapels and union members in some instances were quite hostile, resulting in complete alienation, and obviously it cast the chapels in an unfavourable light when such situations arose.

The Nonconformist cause had flourished also in the English-speaking population which increased rapidly in the late nineteenth century because of immigration, particularly from the nearer English counties. The astute Thomas Price opened the first English Baptist chapel in 1840 and there were

Abercynon Hall seen in 1994 against the trees which cover the mountainside. The camera is looking over the rows of houses on the lower slopes of the mountainside. The Hall has since been demolished.

upwards of 20 English nonconformist chapels by the turn of the century. The impressive Presbyterian church of St David was built near Aberdare town centre in 1879. The Christadelphians established a hall in 1897 and the Jewish community, which had grown with commercial expansion, held meetings in Dean St.

The rough and ready tumultuous "frontier town" district that was the Cynon Valley in the nineteenth century was fertile ground for the Salvation Army and much good was achieved by this respected body. There were three chapels (barracks), one in Woodland St, Mountain Ash, and two in Aberdare, one in High Street and one in Regent St, Aberaman. A remarkable Welsh-speaking Monmouthshire woman, Pamela Morgan, organised the cause in Aberdare. Mother Shepherd, as she was also known, had served in many areas and would, on occasions, lead processions and hold meetings dressed in Welsh costume. Crowds would be addressed from the steps and forecourts of public houses. She made her home in the Gadlys, Aberdare and later became a probation officer. All shops were closed on the day of her funeral on the 1st of March 1930, and the Glamorgan constabulary provided the bearers and escorted the hearse.

The "settling-in" of Roman Catholic immigrants was marked by the opening of the baptismal register for the area in 1854 and mass was celebrated by visiting priests in private rooms, usually in an inn such as the Bailey Arms (now Barclays Bank), Cross Keys in Green St, and finally the Cardiff Castle Inn (afterwards Victor Freed's music shop) now the B-wise store. St Joseph's church opened in Monk St in 1868, two years after the arrival of Father Dawson, the first resident priest in Aberdare. The Catholic school opened in 1878, as did churches in Hirwaun, Mountain Ash and Abercynon in 1878 and 1925. Father James O'Reilly served from 1882 to 1911 bringing about great improvements in the first three churches and a new school in 1911. He was well respected in the town and served for years on the Board of Guardians. A brand new school was opened off Monk St near the entrance to the country park at Easter 1998.

Survey figures for 1851 give religious attendance figures at 64% overall of the population. The figure now is far smaller and the situation much changed. The well organised Church in Wales and Roman Catholic Church are firmly established throughout the valley, and the English chapels by and large are similarly placed. The Pentecostal movement and Jehovah's Witnesses have an increased presence. The most obvious decline has taken place in the Welsh chapels. Until the 1930's in addition to its regular members, the chapels could rely on an appreciable attendance of casuals (ymwelwyr) but this has vanished. The decline in the Welsh language as the common everyday tongue of a large proportion of the valley people

The façade of Abercynon Workmen's Hall. Apart from the carved ball and pedestal ornaments on the edge of the gable this frontage is not heavily ornamented. This may be due to shortage of funds-note that the frontage is made of dressed stone which changes to brick at the corners. Perhaps the rendered side walls were made of rubble, as was often the case.

has meant a great decline in membership. Alan Vernon Jones has estimated that only 49 chapels are now in use out of a peak total of 145, 50 having been demolished, 15 closed and 31 otherwise used or converted. Membership throughout the valley is scattered and fragmented. It was the view of the late Reverend R.I. Parry, Minister of Siloa, a distinguished scholar, that too many chapels had been built, resulting later in many problems.

Utilisation of redundant chapel or church buildings has not always worked out satisfactorily but there are some pleasing results. Providence chapel in Mountain Ash has been mentioned previously. St David's Presbyterian church has been tastefully restored as office accommodation for social services and the flourishing senior citizens' centre on the site of the demolished Welsh church of St Mair presents a happy outcome.

The former immense predominance of nonconformity has certainly diminished in the valley, due largely to the reduced Welsh chapel presence, but the point must be made that when there was desperate need, particularly in the nineteenth century, they served the people magnificently. There can be no better summary than to quote

Penrhiwceiber Workmens Hall and Institute was opened in 1888 and is therefore one of the older generation of workmen's halls. Like many others it was altered to show films when they were introduced. The projection room was attached to the front elevation, ruining for ever the hall's chances of winning an architectural prize, but at least it is still there.

The late Glyn Davies

Canon E.T. Davies from "Religion in the Industrial Revolution in South Wales" (1966)—"The chapels made life bearable and meaningful to thousands of people both through their means of grace, and their character as social and cultural centres. The debt of the communities thrown up by the industrial revolution to the Welsh chapels is incalculable".

The promotion of religion has always been allied to the promotion of education, not least because a person who could read was enabled to have direct access to the scriptures. Another characteristic of the two subjects is the fact that the early days of both of them are difficult to research, firstly due to the paucity of sources and secondly due to the inaccuracy or incompleteness of such sources as do exist. The late Reverend R.I. Parry thought it probable that some instruction was given locally by travelling monks before the dissolution of the monasteries in 1535. It is also likely that Aberdare was included in one or more of several national and regional initiatives for the development of education in the seventeenth century, but there is no proof of this. At the end of the century the Society for the Propagation of Christian Knowledge was founded and this Society set up schools in Wales but the nearest reference to Aberdare was Llanwonno.

The work of the S.P.C.K. was carried on from 1740 by the "Circulating Schools" established by Gruffydd Jones and Madame Bevan. Teachers moved from parish to parish during winters holding classes in church porches or barns. The object was to teach the reading of the Bible and Church Catechism in Welsh. These are known to have been held in the Aberdare area from Ynysybwl to Ystradfellte.

Nixon's hall in the lower part of Mountain Ash is not there any longer having been destroyed by fire. This was one of the grandest halls and its round-headed windows gave it a chapel-like appearance. With decreasing financial support from a diminishing coal industry and a change in the public's needs, the maintenance of buildings such as this became more and more difficult.

The circulating schools eventually lost their financial backing and this resulted in a number of private venture schools being set up in the district, often by people who were themselves of little education. There were two works schools set up in Hirwaun in 1820. Called the Colliers' and Miners' School and Furnace or Fireman's School, they were among the earliest of their kind in Glamorgan. Supported by the Crawshays and run by the workers, they were funded by a stoppage of the workmen's pay of a halfpenny in the pound.

Before the intervention of Parliament in the provision of education for the young, two national agencies funded by voluntary contributions were active in the provision of education in the first half of the nineteenth century. Both of them had an effect in the parish of Aberdare. In 1811 certain members of the Church of England formed the "National Society for Promoting the Education of the Poor in the Principles of the Established Church". The reason for this action was the increasing success of the nonconformists in attracting more members to their causes, a success which resulted in a new chapel being completed in Wales every eight days. There were National Schools in Aberdare, Cwmbach, Aberaman and Trecynon. There were also a number of schools set up by certain collieries which were run under the National system. They were at Cefnpennar, Newtown, Miskin and other places.

A few years earlier in 1808 "The British and Foreign Schools Society" had been formed to provide non-sectarian education to all classes especially the poor. The schools it built became known as "British Schools". The first British School in the area, Park School (Ysgol y Comin), was opened on the 9th of October 1848. The second was opened in Hirwaun amidst difficulties caused by the lack of support from Francis Crawshay which had been originally promised. The school opened in July 1849 though the school room was not ready until June 1850. Subsequently British schools were set up in Llwydcoed, Cwmaman, Cwmdare, Abernant, Cwmbach,

John Davies (Pendar) listens to the reminiscences of his imaginary friend Dai (i.e. John Davies himself.)

I was thinking now of the first time I walked up to Hirwaun on a Xmas day. It was 62 years ago . . . Whispers had gone round that a big fight had been arranged to take place in a quiet spot somewhere near the Hirwaun/Penderyn tramway, on Xmas day, between Mike Ryan, Hirwaun, and Mocyn y Felin, Cwmaman. It was to be a first-class fight, and all the champions from Hirwaun down to the Mount were expected to attend. And indeed to goodness, they were there. Everything had to be done so secretly and quietly, because Old Thorney the bobby, who had not long been put in charge at Hirwaun, was so active and keen against prize fights, which were taking place so often in those days.

However, the pitch was arranged and the two champions began the fight, with a ring of about 50 on-lookers, mostly partizans, some shouting their bets. My uncle warned me when going towards the rendez-vous of the fight, to be prepared to run if the police came on the scene.

But lo and behold, when the fight began, there was PC Davies, Hirwaun, a very tidy bobby, so everyone said, standing by quietly, quite interested in the proceedings. Everyone thought then that there would be no interference on their part. But alas, when the fight was going along in fine style, the two men beginning to warm up to serious blows, who should burst into the ring quite suddenly and unexpectedly but Old Thorney and another policeman named Williams, shouting on all present to stand where they were, in order to have their names taken for aiding and abetting in the fight. Jaich Ariody, I wasn't going to stand there to give my name, so I ran away with a lot of other youngsters and some women. Of course the fight had to finish, and the names of the two men—Ryan and Mocyn—with some backers on each side, were taken by Thorney.

The next week at the police court held at the Lamb, Penderyn and at another court held about a fortnight later, the principals and some of the onlookers were bound over.

The poor bobby who looked on at the fight was fined 20s and costs and had an awful lecture by Mr. Maybery from the bench for having neglected his duty on the occasion of the fight, and standing as a passive spectator during the disgraceful proceedings. Old Mr. Thorney was raised to the clouds in congratulations from the bench for his good work in stopping the fight. AL 7/1/28.

Aberaman and Ynyslwyd. The dramatic and historic events which led to the building of the Park school cannot be omitted from this brief overview of the provision of elementary education in the valley.

In 1846 a Royal Commission issued a report on the state of education in the Principality of Wales especially into the means afforded to the labouring classes of acquiring a knowledge of the English language. The three chief Commissioners were clever young anglican lawyers with no knowledge of education, of Wales or of the working class. They were given clear instructions as to what they had to do which was to hear evidence from both dissenters and anglicans and to do so with courtesy, sympathy and impartiality. But the Commissioners failed to bring to their task the intellectual rigour which the work demanded. For example, they examined some 300 witnesses of which four in every five were anglicans.

The report showed that the state of education in Wales was dire. The premises were often unsuitable and the teachers were incompetent. In many parishes there were no schools at all. The non-conformists had to agree that there was much truth in what was said about the state of education in Wales. But the remarks about the immorality of the Welsh and of the women in particular were a different matter and a storm of indignation erupted over the Welsh countryside. The Commissioners were assailed in writing and speech and their report was referred to as "Brad y Llyfrau Gleision" (The Treachery of the Blue Books) and is so called to this day. The storm did not abate when it became known that some of the strongest criticism in the report had come from their Vicar, the Reverend John Griffith, and what was worse was the fact that his evidence was penned a few days, or at most two or three weeks after he first set foot in the parish. Furthermore, the vicar's only previous pastoral experience was as a curate in a village in Cheshire.

John Griffith deposed "Nothing can be lower, I would say more degrading than the character in which the women stand relative to the men . . . Promiscuous intercourse is most common—is thought of as nothing—and the women do not lose caste by it. Generally speaking there is very little sobriety. The men drink in beershops and are occasionally joined by the women. But on the whole the women drink at home. Nothing can be more improvident than the miners or colliers. Their religious feelings are peculiar to the Welsh. They are very excitable—have nothing like what is considered elsewhere a disciplined religious mind. They go to the meeting at six, come out at eight, and spend the remainder of the evening in the beershop. There is no religion whatever in my parish, at least, I have not yet found it."

The recriminations against the Commissioners were louder in Aberdare than anywhere else partly owing to the Vicar's folly in regarding himself qualified to contribute to the Commission. Then it was alleged that the Vicar, far from showing contrition, was continuing to vilify the morals of the Aberdarians by means of anonymous letters to the press.

The next scene took place at Siloa chapel in Aberdare where a public meeting was held on the 23rd of February 1848 with David Williams (Alaw Goch) in the chair. John Griffith declined an invitation to attend. The principal speaker was the Rev. Thomas Price, the redoubtable Baptist Minister of Calfaria, who moved a resolution which stated that the meeting felt surprise that the Vicar "being a stranger—having resided but a few days among us—should have deemed himself competent to furnish the information requested by the Commissioners; while at the same time it begs most distinctly to deny the whole of his statements . . . and this meeting further begs to express its decided disapprobation of his conduct". In this way began the somewhat turbulent career of the first Vicar of Aberdare. The non-conformists realised that they had to do something about the deplorable state of elementary education in Wales. The anglicans had to face the fact that the non-conformists had led the way in the provision of places of worship and Sunday Schools, and took action accordingly. But much harm had been done and for a while relations between anglicans and non-conformists were the worst ever. But the Vicar mellowed in time and when he left Aberdare in 1859 to become Rector of Merthyr he was regarded with respect by all sides.

The most enduring sequel in Aberdare to the Treachery of the Blue Books was the provision of extra school facilities in the shape of Park School (Ysgol y Comin). After the great meeting in Siloa in February 1848 the non-conformists of Aberdare elected a strong committee to proceed immediately with the construction of a British school under the chairmanship of David Williams. A quarter-acre site on the comin was obtained from the Marquess of Bute for £10 and the school and master's house were ready in about seven months! The formal opening took place on the 9th of October 1848 even though there were no pupils or teachers as yet. The school was to be wholly unsectarian and priority was to be given to the children of the poor (presumably what we would today call the working class), who had to pay 1d per week rising to 2d per week. Children from the middle classes paid 4d per week.

The appearance of the "British" and "National" agencies mentioned above did not result in the extinction of the private venture schools, which continued to flourish for years. But as a result of Forster's Act of 1870 which introduced free education throughout the land, a school board of nine members was set up in Aberdare, and another in Mountain Ash, which gradually gathered to themselves the British and National schools of their areas. The last British school to be handed over to the Aberdare Board was in Aberaman in October 1892. Though the 1870 Act called for free education, in reality charges were made, typically four pence per week, and in periods of unemployment parents were often

The Aberaman Public Hall and Institute dominated the shopping area of Aberaman. Like Nixon's Hall it had facilities for recreation as well as cultural and educational activities, and like Nixon's Hall it perished by fire.

unable to meet the fees, resulting in court action.

The momentum in the valley in elementary education was very soon to spread to a demand for secondary education. It is entirely fitting that the Intermediate Education Act for Wales was actually signed by Lord Aberdare in 1889 in his study in Duffryn House, a room which later became the headmaster's study, when the house became Mountain Ash Grammar School. This community can also be proud of the fact that two of the first fruits of that Act were the establishment in 1890 of a Higher Grade school in Clifton Street (transferring to Gadlys Central in 1907) and—more important —the establishment of Aberdare Intermediate School in 1896, and a new Girls' Intermediate School in Aberdare in 1913. Such was the enthusiasm for places, that overcrowding led to the opening of Mountain Ash Intermediate school in 1907. In retrospect, this mining valley can be proud of so many local people, educated in those early years, who have achieved distinction nationally.

Aberdare and Mountain Ash became Urban District Councils in 1894, Mountain Ash having absorbed Abercynon (formerly known as Aberdare Junction or Navigation) and Ynysybwl in 1880. Cefnpennar joined Mountain Ash in 1895. Subsequently the Councils's Education Committees took over the functions of the School Boards. Education eventually became a function of the Counties or County Boroughs, but became in recent years the responsibility of the new all-purpose authorities.

Much has been said about the desire of the miners for self-improvement through attendance at Mechanics' Institutes (which in Aberdare consisted apparently of a library and reading room) but the nineteenth century evidence for this hypothesis does not support this view. A reading room and library (inaugurated by the Rev John Griffith) was opened (probably in the long room of the Black Lion) in

1852. It subsequently moved twice, ending up in 1858 in the Temperance Hall (now the Palladium). At the annual meeting of the members of the Aberdare Mechanics' Institute in February 1855, the chairman, Mr. Rhys H. Rhys, remarked that as a Mechanics' Institute it was a perfect failure. "It was no use to mince the matter," he said, "the workmen did not avail themselves of it, it was nothing virtually but a Reading Room for the trade of the town." The report in the Cardiff and Merthyr Guardian went on to say; "This is the third time in the last seven years that a Mechanics' Institute has been given up at Aberdare. No institution started under better auspices than this. It lasted just two years as a Mechanics' Institute so-called and the subscribers have been obliged now to change its character . . . This is very sad, but so it is. Beer seems in greater demand than books." In June 1860 closure was being considered, owing to a decrease in subscriptions which had caused a debt of £28.

In October 1861, another report in the C.M.G. refers to the "floundering conditions" of the Aberdare Library though it does not say whether this was a renamed Mechanics' Institute or a different establishment. "The library and reading room are never heard of except when the exchequer is exhausted and assistance is required to keep the institution in existence. Some attribute this state of affairs to bad management and it is asserted that some individuals are continually pocketing the papers and periodicals, which is very disgraceful and ought to be put a stop to. 'The Times' invariably disappears before it has been in the room two hours and 'The Illustrated London News' and 'Punch' are sometimes never seen by some members. Efforts are now being made to better matters, and we hope something worthy of the stir will be accomplished for it is a sad consideration that this populous and wealthy town cannot support the only library of the kind ever established within its precincts."

From the C.M.G. of 22nd April 1865 we learn that the reading room was still in existence and called "The Aberdare Mechanics' Institute". The Committee of Management had called a General Meeting to decide whether it was advisable or not to keep the institution in existence any longer, as the annual receipts from subscriptions came to about £24 (and were collected with difficulty), while the expenditure was upwards of £40. It was stated that the honorary members (presumably the ironmasters and coalmasters) were reluctant to contribute to the institute when it was so little used. A proposal that the reading room be closed for a period to make the inhabitants feel the want of such an institution was not carried and the members voted instead to elect a fresh committee. This was done at a subsequent meeting.

In 1874 a proposal for an "Aberdare New Reading Room and Library" was made, with the most prominent local citizens (starting with Lord Aberdare) as Patrons or Trustees. A site in Canon St had been secured and £700 was promised towards the estimated cost of £5,000, but nothing came of the scheme. Then in 1887 the Marquess of Bute offered the plot of ground where the Constitutional Club now stands for a library together with a gift of £1000 towards the cost of books. This generous donation was turned down by the Board of Health.

Scattered local facilities began to be created by various Chapels and Churches and in 1900 the Aberdare UDC adopted the Public Libraries Act which enabled them for the first time to spend money on a library. In 1904 a public library opened in leased accomodation at the Memorial Hall and in 1917 it moved to the west end of Seymour St. From 1949 the library was at Siloa Hall until it moved into new accomodation in 1963.

William Bevan tells us that in 1896 there were three reading rooms in Mountain Ash maintained by the workmen of the area. Libraries were set up in the Workmen's Institutes and many years later these were taken over, expanded and maintained by the Council from 1964 with Mr. Harri Webb the poet as librarian. The central library at Mountain Ash, previously at Duffryn Rd, moved to new premises in Knight St in 1997. Cwmaman had a reading room as early as 1880 and was eventually provided with an institute with library, reading rooms, billiard room, games room, baths and other rooms.

The great hall in Darran road, Mountain Ash, was built in 1901 as a kind of market hall by a consortium of local businessmen. With an area of 21,000 square feet it was the biggest hall in Wales. But in its planned role it was not very successful and it was eventually used for eisteddfods, exhibitions, boxing and many other purposes including films.

From 1930 to 1947 it was used for the annual "Three Valleys Festival" (Merthyr, Cynon and Rhondda) . This was a festival of (mainly) song, inaugurated by Sir Walford Davies. Dr Malcolm Sargent was one of the principal conductors and one year he descended the Deep Duffryn Pit accompanied by an entourage of the the great and the good. They are (left to right): Mr. T. J. Thomas (Head Mechanic) Mr. T. Roderick (Manager) Mr. R. W. Burgess, Mrs. Burgess, Dr. Malcolm Sargent, Miss Margaret McLean, Mr. W. M. Llewellyn, Mr. W. A. Morgan, The Hon Mrs. J. H. Bruce, Mr. C. W. Dixon, Mrs. Dixon, Mr. W. O. Dyer, Mr. W. J. Bumford Griffiths, Mr. D. T. Evans.

135

A photo of Cwmdare taken near the Tonglwyd Fawr public house ("The "Ton") looking along Bwllfa road towards Bwllfa. This was probably taken before WW1 at a time when the streets belonged to the people and not to vehicles. When two people met in the middle of the road-well, it was just the place for a nice chat. The photo also shows that Cwmdare was not a typical mining village with the river, road and railway competing for the little space available on the valley floor, and the village itself was built well away from the pits thus permitting a more agreeable way of life.   Doug Williams

Obviously taken from Mountain Ash bridge, this photo shows the two running lines of the Aberdare railway on the left with a short branch to Deep Duffryn Colliery on the right. The houses on the left are the backs of some of the houses on the main road through the town.

Aberaman was provided with a similar facility. The well-known local historian the late Mr. W.W. Price was the secretary of the hall for 25 years. There were institutes at Cwmbach, Trecynon, and Abercwmboi and a miners' welfare hall at Cwmdare.

The facilities in the twentieth century were much better partly due to the advent of these Miners' Institutes. In addition to community activities, adult classes were provided by the Workers' Educational Association or by the extra-mural department of the University. The libraries in the institutes satisfied a hunger for knowledge (and for lighter entertainment) before public libraries in the valleys were established, some sooner than others. (Mountain Ash, for example, did not have a public library until 1965!) There are many examples of well-read politically literate working class men who became prominent leaders in the local community and beyond and who owe their post-school education to these libraries.

The fluctuating history of the Mechanics Institutes is more than counterbalanced by the reputation which the town of Aberdare enjoyed as a centre of religious and secular printing. A weekly paper in Welsh – "Y Gwron" (the Hero) ran from 1854 to 1860. The editor was the baptist minister Dr Thomas Price and the general approach was radical. "Y Gwladgarwr" (the patriot) ran from 1858 to 1882. The style was less intense, far more relaxed and the printing was better. "Y Gweithiwr" (the workman) appeared in 1859 but made no headway and was shortlived.

"The Cardiff and Merthyr Guardian" (CMG) was an English language weekly which appeared in 1833 and lasted until 1874. It is much thought of today as a valuable source of local history.

In 1862 the Aberdare Times appeared, guided by those who had run "Y Gwron". In 1898 it called the London Times "a miserable cockney print". It was incorporated in the "Aberdare Leader" in 1902. "Tarian y Gweithiwr" (the workman's shield) afterwards called "Y Darian", ran from 1875 to 1934. Championing the working class, it was very popular with a circulation of up to 15,000 copies a week, but began to lose impact after 1900. Policy changed after 1911 in "Y Darian", "A shield for the language, literature, purity and morals of our nation". Notoriety was achieved owing to a pacifist policy during the 1914-1918 war.

English was rapidly becoming the more common language in general with the turn of the century and, inevitably, the English press predominated. The "Aberdare Leader" began in 1902, took over "The Aberdare Times" before the end of the year, and established itself as the local paper. In 1911 it took over "The Aberdare and Mountain Ash Weekly Post" founded in 1906, and in 1934 it assimilated "Y Darian". Today called "The Cynon Valley Leader", it is very firmly established in the Valley. Over the years some twenty or so printers were in business in Aberdare. In addition to jobbing work such as pamphlets, programmes for concerts, etc, they produced a great number of periodicals and books relating to biography, poetry, local history, music and, of course, religion. Much of their output was in Welsh.

Working underground in the mines was both hard and dangerous and since man does not live by bread alone the miner tried to make the most of his leisure time away from the pit when he had bathed and fed. But not all miners felt at home in the company of books and the pursuit of knowledge. So it was that many or most miners took pleasure in out-door activities to entertain themselves in the short time available. Some of these activities were foot racing and whippet racing, prizefighting and cock fighting. The latter two activities became unlawful. Many miners enjoyed the more innocent activities of pigeon-fancying, walking and tending an allotment. As for the children, the streets were their playground and the games were handed down and sometimes modified to suit their needs.

But for the housewife, leisure periods were few and far between although we are told that in the middle of the 19th century they were inclined to visit the pubs-and there were many of them. 5 in 1793 and 49 of them as early as 1837 when the population was only 5,000. There were also many beerhouses, which were allowed to sell beer but not wines and spirits. It has been calculated that by 1872 at least 273 alehouses or beerhouses existed or had existed in the area from Hirwaun to Abercwmboi. In 1859 there were 12 pubs in Mountain Ash, including the oldest, the Mountain Ash Inn, built in 1809. The first working men's club opened in Aberdare in 1882 in the former Bruce Arms in Bute St (until recently the offlices of Marchant Harries and Co). We have all heard of the downside of pubs but the statistics above must surely indicate that the working men found good cheer in their "local" and entertainment too, for many pubs maintained a resident harpist to give a lead to the singing. This practice ceased when the magistrates forbade harpists to gain a living in this way. We are told that the method of showing appreciation of a song was to beat the table with the hand.

This is a photo of the Cwmneol Colliery in Cwmaman also known as the Lanky Pit and Morris's pit, after Carr and Morrison of the United Merthyr Coal Company Ltd. The pit opened in 1848 and closed in 1948.   GarethThomas

This pit was sited alongside Llwydcoed hill opposite the entrance to the former Creamery. Having been filled in, it was re-opened a few years ago, topped up, and re-capped. This pit has the oval shape (common in the early days) which was intended to provide space each side of the cage for the rods of the pumping engines of the Cornish type.   John F. Mear

The Dare Valley Branch of the former Taff Vale Railway branched off the main line at Dare Valley Junction Signal Box, about a quarter of a mile from the western end of the Taff Vale station in Aberdare. In this photo an engine has just left the main line and is propelling its rake of empty trucks up the branch. In the distance behind the locomotive can be seen the Council tram-shed. The shed was afterwards used by the buses which superseded the trams, but it was demolished in the early sixties and replaced by a new bus garage, which was itself knocked down a few years ago when the site was redeveloped.

D. K. Jones Collection

Photos of the Middle Duffryn Colliery are hard to come by, and this shot has a disappointing lack of detail. The pit was sunk close to the bank of the canal by Thomas Powell in 1843. It ceased raising coal in 1893 and became a pumping station until 1937 when it closed. A tramroad to a nearby tip was carried over the canal (on the left), the towpath, and the Neath-Pontypool line by means of the bridge in the distance. The canal closed to traffic in 1900.

John F. Mear

Many pubs included a "long room" on the first floor which was used by organisations such as benefit clubs. Many of the religious sects were formed at a time when going to pubs was not frowned upon, and some of them held their meetings and even eisteddfods in such long rooms until they had the means to build their own meeting house. Eventually, the rise of the Temperance Movement caused chapel-goers to turn their backs on the pubs.

For the mass of the population Cynon Valley was an outstanding example of the old adage that Wales is a musical nation. We have seen how chapels were closely linked with educational development, and therefore they were usually associated with the musical life of the Valley through eisteddfods and choral music. Eisteddfods, which had been somewhat aristocratic, became an outlet for the common man who aspired to better things. He could express himself not only in singing but also in literary competitions (like the quarry men of North Wales). More important socially was the enthusiasm of the working class masses as witnessed when four thousand paid to hear the oratorio "Samson" in the old Market hall whence Caradog's triumphant choir went to London and spread the fame of Aberdare's music and musicians.

While the tradition of eisteddfods in this valley goes back to 1820 with one held in the Swan Inn, later eisteddfods were held at the Mount Pleasant Inn in 1837, on Christmas day at the Market Place in 1870, at the Stag Inn, Trecynon (Y Carw Coch) and the one at Siloa in 1850 to raise funds for Ysgol y Comin. The first *National* Eisteddfod in 1861 was to be held on the "Comin Fach", that part of Hirwaun Common afterwards used by the Boys' County School (which is being demolished at the time of writing). This was to be an important event historically as it was the first organised under the new rules formulated at Llangollen in 1858, where the song which later became our national anthem was first heard. James James, who set to music words written by his father, Evan James, spent his last years in Aberdare and was buried in Aberdare Cemetery. The words were 'Mae hen wlad fy nhadau . . .' The large tent erected on Comin Bach was destroyed by a storm and the event took place at the Market Hall.

In 1885 the National Eisteddfod revisited Aberdare and the profits were to be donated to the three new University Colleges of Wales with which the working classes were closely associated. The Eisteddfod was held at Cae Smith on the Cwmbach road and was the first event of its kind to be lit by electricity. George Eliot MP the coal magnate was President and Matthew Arnold the poet, guest of honour. 11,000 attended and the chair was won by Watkyn Wyn with "Y gwir yn erbyn y byd" ["The truth against the world"] which subsequently became part of the rallying cry of the National Eisteddfod. The "National" was held again in Aberdare in 1956 and in Mountain Ash in 1905 and 1946, when the Queen was made a member of the Gorsedd of Bards.

There was strong prejudice for many years against many forms of entertainment among religious bodies. Thus the Methodists denounced the theatre as ungodly as recently as the last years of the twentieth century but other denominations took a more liberal attitude; with 200 pubs in the area in 1872, they saw a desperate need for alternatives but there was a shortage of public buildings. The Market House, called the assembly room, was the best, where good concerts were staged. The building of the Temperance Hall in 1858 was a very important event; it was called "a magnificent structure" and staged lectures, dramas, concerts, variety shows and public meetings. It also showed dioramas, which consisted of pictures painted on a wide canvas sheet which was rolled from one spool to another, with visual and sound effects, accompanied by a spoken commentary. In 1895 it became the "New Theatre and Hippodrome" and in 1918 it was renamed the "Palladium" and started showing films in addition to its usual fare.

In the second half of the nineteenth century there were five music halls quite near the centre of Aberdare. The street fair each year on the 16th of April was always popular, and so were the visiting circuses and menageries which would parade through the streets to advertise their arrival. Travelling fit-up theatres were eagerly awaited and a popular site for them was adjoining the Market using a solid stage and a canvas auditorium. From 1910 this place was the site of William Haggar's "Coliseum", a primitive cinema where he, a pioneer of film-making in Britain, showed the films he had made himself. In 1915 he opened a luxurious new cinema "The New Kosy Kinema" opposite his market yard pitch.

Cwmcynon Colliery was sunk on the bank of the Cynon. It had two shafts and was opened in 1889 by the Nixon Navigation Co Ltd. It closed in 1949.

The late Glyn Davies

Cwmaman Colliery was in fact a small cluster of collieries. Shepherd's pit (above) was the first, sunk in 1849 to the Gellideg seam. Then followed the Fforchwen and Trewen pits a little further up the valley. In 1921 work was proceeding on a new drift to the upper seams such as the Graig and the Gorllwyn. The collieries were acquired by the PD Co in 1935 and closed in that year.

John F. Mear

A mecca for entertainment in Mountain Ash was the Pavilion. Built in 1901 and having failed as a hotel, it was used for bioscope cinema, indoor fairs and skating, but though held to be the largest permanent structure in Wales, it did not come into its own until the 1930's with the Three Valleys Festival (Cynon, Merthyr and Rhondda), which became an annual event attracting a huge influx of people and choirs from far afield. It was associated with eminent musical figures such as Sir Walford Davies and Sir Malcolm Sargent. A Paul Robeson concert in 1938 demonstrated the strong links between the miners and the "aid for Spain" cause, many South Wales Miners having gone to fight in Spain for the socialist cause against Franco.

Fforchaman Colliery was a little lower down than Cwmaman. It dates from 1856 and was sunk by Brown and Protheroe, hence the alternative name "Brown's Pit".
Brian Davies

142

This postcard shows that the name "Brown's Pit" was commonly used for Fforchaman Colliery.

Gareth Thomas

Mention must be made of the strong amateur theatrical tradition in Aberdare. At one time many of the churches and chapels and some of the miners' institutes had their own amateur dramatic societies. The "Little Theatre" built in 1939 was an independent drama group which achieved national renown under the inspiring leadership of such stalwarts as the Reverend E.R. Dennis and Mr. Kalman Jones.

Holidays, as we know them today, were virtually unknown in the mining valleys in the nineteenth century except "Mabon's Day", a holiday on the first Monday of each month, won for the men by Mabon (William Abraham), the noted miners' leader. There was no holiday pay and the nearest thing to a holiday away for a miner and his family was day trips by rail, particularly to Barry or Porthcawl, organised by chapels, schools or collieries. In previous centuries various folk customs had been observed such as the feast of St John, the summer revels, and the Parish fairs which attracted travelling entertainers. These outdoor events and the vigorous street life of the town constituted the entertainment of the people before the advent of music halls and other facilities for communal enjoyment which have been described above. The zenith of street life was probably in the 1926 strike, when there were concerts, jazz bands with gazookas, character bands, carnivals, sport days and the like.

Competitive sport is an important feature of life in an industrialised society; indeed for many, the most important aspect of their leisure time. Cycling running and boxing were important in the Cynon Valley in the late nineteenth century, and gambling was associated with them. The one most particularly associated with the Cynon Valley then was cycling, professional and semi-professional (in the Cardiff area the analogy was baseball). In the 1890's cycling with pneumatic tyres suddenly became much cheaper. "The Swan" and "Lamb and flag" in Aberaman helped produce a group of professional world champions, notably Tom and Arthur Linton and Jimmy Michael who broke world records in America.

Professional and semi-professional runners competed in "Powderhall sprints". Boxing developed from the earliest days—with bare fist fights on hillsides fought to a finish—to organised controlled contests producing several champions such as Boyo Rees and not a little gambling. There developed, for two reasons, a particular affinity between boxing and the mining valleys: it is a very hard and

143

dangerous sport and the working conditions in the mines and ironworks were equally hard and dangerous: and secondly professional boxing was for many the only source of additional income especially in periods of high unemployment and so there grew the legend of the hungry fighters of the deprived valleys of South Wales. Boxing booths were set up in fields, notably the Poplar fields in Mountain ash and a professional team would invite challengers from the public attending.

These fights could be literally called "blood and sawdust" affairs; indeed one notorious manager in Mountain Ash would refuse to pay out to the challenger because there was too much blood! The pavilion became a Mecca for boxing in South Wales, drawing up to 15,000 spectators, and put Mountain Ash on the map. Boyo Rees from Abercwmboi became a famous local hero. Many champions including Tommy Farr had their early experiences at Mountain Ash Pavilion. Wrestling in the Market Hall enjoyed a temporary boom around 1912.

Cynon Valley has interesting and contrasting histories of the two football codes. The world often associates rugby with the South Wales valleys and Mountain Ash, formed in 1875 and sponsored by the Hon W Bruce, has a claim to be the oldest rugby club in the country; "The Old Firm", so-called, it is believed, from the hawker outside the original ground shouting "Come and buy from the old firm".

There was never any shortage of powerfully-built miners for the pack but in 1895 the formation of the Northern Rugby Union drained playing resources with the trail North. The lure of the professional game was a reflection of the modest financial means of the working class amateur players. The club has had a chequered history sporting very successful teams including internationals and suffering several financial crises particularly during miners' strikes. After several temporary grounds it moved to "The Rec" and more recently to the Duffryn ground. Aberdare, in sharp contrast, can claim to be a birthplace of soccer in South Wales in 1893 when rugby was already the Welsh national sport. It began in Aberdare park, then the Ynys Meadow where the first attendance was 10, admision was 3d and ladies went free! By the end of the century it was established and won cups and leagues, defeating Sheffield United, the English cup winners. Thanks to the efforts of the Llewellyn family, coalmasters, they were reformed in 1921, entered the football league and enjoyed, with the help of some imported players, a brief period of success and large gates plus "the best supporters' club in the world", only to fold in 1927.

Since the Powderhall Sprints in the latter years of the nineteenth century, there was little athletics activity until the famous Nos Galan races were started in 1958. These New Year's Eve races in Mountain Ash were to commemorate the legendary runner Griffith Morgan, a shepherd of Llanwonno, better known as Guto Nyth Frân whose phenomenal running made him a hero and who dropped dead in 1737 after accepting and winning a challenge. His grave is in Llanwonno churchyard. These races have been a huge success thanks to the enthusiasm of their founder, Mr. Bernard Baldwin. They included a run from Llanwonno to Mountain Ash bridge by a mystery runner with an Olympic style torch, a a four mile race around the streets and a 100 yards sprint. Like boxing in the earlier years, this Nos Galan event put Mountain Ash and Cynon Valley on the sporting map.

Cricket had its beginnings further back than other major sports though it was first played without proper pitches. The Aberdare cricket club was formed in 1861 and played its first match against Mountain Ash. In 1862 Trecynon Cricket Club was formed. The game was then played at Abercynon Park in the 1890's and at Robertstown and in Aberaman under the auspices of the Powell Duffryn Company. Also in the nineties Aberdare Hockey Club was the premium club in that sport in South Wales.

As for more genteel and gentle sports, we must mention golf, tennis and bowls of which the first two were associated more with the middle classes. Aberdare Valley Golf Club was founded in 1907 and opened in 1908 on a farm owned by Lord Aberdare and expanded from 9 to 18 holes. In 1923 there was a split leading to the formation of the Aberdare Golf Club, and the original club became known as Mountain Ash Golf Club. Abercynon Golf club was also formed in 1921. Tennis had an earlier history for the Aberdare Tennis club began in the 1890's and the Mountain Ash club was formed later in the same period. These were two of the oldest tennis clubs in the whole of South Wales.

Since the early years of the twentieth century bowls may be said to have superseded tennis as a popular working class summer sport in this valley. As with other sports the miners' welfare clubs were

A group of colliers taking a meal break in the Dyllas Level. As will seen from the "peg and ball" oil lamps this was a "naked light" mine. The photo dates from the early twentieth century.

Idris Edwards

"The Independent Order of Rechabites" was one of a number of benefit societies which arose in the nineteenth century. It was one of a few such societies which partly based itself upon the Freemasons. Its principal tenet was abstention from all intoxicating liquor. The photo is of the Grand Lodge Reception Committee at Aberdare in 1914.   Doug Williams

important in fostering games and as an example the first rough bowling green was created in 1912 leading to the formation of the Aberaman Welfare club in 1913 followed by that of Aberdare Park and Town. In 1926 a valley league was formed to include Abercynon, Aberaman, Aberdare, Mountain Ash Hospital and Nixons and the sport has continued to prosper with the recent development of indoor bowls culminating in the opening of a prestigious new arena in Mountain Ash.

An interesting minor sport of great antiquity was "Quoits"which involved throwing a heavy cast-iron ring at a mark. Known as "the miner's game" quoits enjoyed a boom in 1896 when international matches with England were started. In the twenties and thirties Newtown was a noted centre for quoits. The game has waxed and waned several times since then and nearly all of the quoits grounds have disappeared. The ruins of a clubhouse and pitch at Bwllfa Dare still exist. This was built at the cost of the Llewellyn family of Bwllfa House. Wales's most famous player at quoits was a local man, W Dice Davies (known as "Dice"). He lived in Cwmdare for some years and worked at Bwllfa Colliery. He was selected for Wales on 27 occasions and beaten only 7 times. He was champion of Wales five times and of South Wales ten times.

The most popular indoor recreation in the institutes was billiards and snooker, followed in later years by table tennis. Three of the best known institutes were Cwmaman, Aberaman and Trecynon.

In the last two Chapters we have seen how, in the course of the nineteenth century and beyond, the rapidly growing mining population of Cynon Valley evolved into a bustling thriving community, which acquired by slow degrees those necessities, institutions and amenities for a fuller, healthier and more caring society. Life was still hard for the vast majority but by the end of the century it was less harsh, more civilised and aspiring to better things-men did not live by bread alone. It is time now to look in some detail at the working conditions, in this most dangerous occupation, the mining of coal.

CHAPTER SEVEN

To say that the job of the miner is unpleasant and dangerous is a statement against which few would seek to argue, except perhaps to say that it is not as bad as it was in years gone by. The dangers affecting the miner at his workplace deep in the earth included the emission of gases from the coal, leading to explosions or suffocation, explosions of coal dust, inundation, accidental fires, injuries caused by machinery and haulage, the inhalation of dust and falls of roof. Although explosions in iron ore mines were rare they were not unknown. For example, an explosion which seriously burnt nine persons took place in such a mine known as David Williams's mine at Cwmwenallt on the 31st of May 1841, and another, which killed 11 persons, at the Black Vein ironstone pit in June 1848. There have been similar accidents in other places.

When we recollect that the coal and oil which are found underground in various parts of the world are products of decayed vegetable matter it comes as no surprise that the the gas known as firedamp is of similar origin. For all practical purposes firedamp can be regarded as being methane. It issues from the coal and other strata in the form of a slight but continuous emission and continues to do so even when the coal has been brought to bank. Indeed, several explosions of fire-damp have occurred after the coal has been sent to the docks and put on board ship, such as the "Neptune" which blew up at her berth in Cardiff Docks in 1848, killing the chief mate and seriously injuring the captain. This fate was also suffered by the brigantine "Gertrude" at Cardiff in 1850. Both ships were loaded with Powell's coal. A Russian Barque full of coal also blew up in Cardiff docks at the end of October 1856 despite the fixing of warning notices.

Sometimes the pressure of gas would be so high as to burst out from the strata, when it would be termed a "blower". Blowers containing well over a million cubic feet of gas have been known. When some workmen employed by the Gadlys Iron and Coal Company were sinking a shaft about half a mile from Aberdare, a powerful blower was encountered. This was piped to the surface and ignited

The Lower Duffryn Rescue Team, No. 1 Squad. Left to right, standing: S. Eley, T Harding, C. Fluke. Sitting: H. J. Morris (superintendent and instructor), W. H. James, Richard Griffiths (Captain), A. Moore (Manager).

after which it burned with a flame 9 to 10 feet high. In the pit, however slowly or quickly the gas was emitted, it would tend to mix with the air in the vicinity. Such a mixture, if consisting of between 5 and 14% of methane is explosive, highly so when the proportion is around 9.5%. The steam coal region, in which the Cynon Valley is situated, and the four foot seam in particular, were notorious for the amount of firedamp given off, and the frequency and severity of the explosions which occurred as a result. It should be added that in several cases the use of naked lights was a contributory factor in causing explosions.

However, once such explosions began to be studied it became apparent that certain aspects of the explosions could not be explained by the known facts, and by 1912 it was accepted that coal dust in suspension in air not only worsened the effects of a firedamp explosion but was itself an explosive agent when subjected to a naked flame. "Blackdamp", also known as "stythe" or "chokedamp" was a mixture of carbon dioxide and nitrogen. After an explosion "Afterdamp" was often found. This was a mixture of gases but mainly carbon dioxide and carbon monoxide. The former was poisonous inasmuch as it would not support life and the latter was not only poisonous but explosive when mixed with air in a certain proportion.

The ventilation of the Upper Duffryn Colliery was the subject of comment after the explosion of the 2nd of August 1845 when 29 persons were killed, of which 4 were under 18 years old. The verdict of the jury was that the ventilation was inadequate to ensure the safety of the men employed. The mine was owned by Thomas Powell.

The deadly effects of an explosion were also apparent in the Lletyshenkin explosion of Friday, the 17th of August 1849 when the 53 dead were either burnt or asphyxiated by the afterdamp. The dead included 14 boys under 16 years of age, of which one was 10 and another 8. It seems that in this pit also, the ventilation was insufficient and the use of naked lights had triggered off an explosion of the firedamp, but the verdict of the coroner's jury recommended that a separate ventilation system be used to take away the gas emitted in old workings. Owner: Mrs. Rees and others.

This is the Cwmaman rescue team. They are wearing breathing apparatus and appear to be carrying out an exercise in a concrete-lined culvert.

Mrs Colin Davies

The Middle Duffryn Colliery was the scene, on the 12th of December 1850, of an explosion which took the lives of 9 workmen. The pit was owned, according to the Cardiff and Merthyr Guardian, by "one of the most extensive, public spirited, and humane colliery proprietors in this or the adjoining counties Thomas Powell, Esq, of The Gaer". The Coroner, George Overton, is also praised by the editor of the CMG for conducting the inquest "with the most rigid impartiality" with the assistance of the Government Inspector of Mines, Herbert Mackworth, "a gentleman of great scientific attainments".

The same colliery was the scene of the Cynon Valley's worst mining disaster, when an explosion killed 65 men and boys on the 10th of May 1852. On this occasion the CMG stated that the explosion "tends to show the hopelessness of ensuring the non-recurrence of similar accidents, for it is affirmed that measures had been taken, in the ventilation of the works, to make the air courses, and the condition of the workmen as perfect as human ingenuity and skill could render them". Mr. Mackworth's report on the explosion mentioned the "gassy" nature of the seam being worked which had resulted, since the year 1845, in four very serious explosions which had taken 159 lives. After the December 1850 explosion the then inspector, Mr. Blackwell, had condemned the use of naked lights and the brattice (a vertical partition in a shaft enabling it to be used simultaneously for two purposes, e.g. downcast and upcast airways). However, the brattice had been retained, as had the ventilation furnace and the use of candles, and the pumping shaft was shut off by a door from the ventilation. Mr. Mackworth concluded, "I am compelled emphatically to condemn the entire neglect of the safeguards insisted on at the former inquest. The loss of 159 lives in the Aberdare Valley by explosions, all of them arising from the peculiarly dangerous state of the firedamp in the four feet seam and the overlying strata, demands the entire exclusion

The presence of four policemen at Bwllfa new Pit can only mean one thing—a strike. One workman and an office worker appear to be intent on keeping one or more of the boilers going, probably during the 1911 strike.
John F. Mear

of naked lights and the ordinary furnace and the adoption of strictly-enforced rules and a larger ventilation". So much for the "perfection" of the ventilation mentioned by the obsequious "Guardian".

So far little had been said about the culpability of the owner, Thomas Powell, even in the forthright report of Mackworth. There is a hint in the exchanges between Overton and the foreman of the jury that Overton was inviting the jury to criticise Powell. The inquest was held on only three of the dead, Thomas Pritchard, Owen Evans and John Richards. The jury's verdict on Thomas Pritchard was "accidental death" with an expression of regret that the 1850 recommendations had not been complied with.

The coroner asked if the jury thought it necessary to make any allusion to the mode in which they came to their death.

Mr. John Lewis, grocer (foreman): "We have no opinion or recommendation to give in the matter further, being of opinion that all the deaths were occasioned by the same cause-the explosion-which occasioned the bursting or breaking open of the stoppings, thereby preventing the action of the fresh air, and consequently the death of the parties".

The Coroner: "Would you like to consider that matter, or to make any special verdict?"

Mr. John Lewis: (after speaking to his fellow jurors) "No, we do not think it necessary to give any further opinion or recommendation".

The Coroner: "If you would wish to consider it, perhaps you can do it. Perhaps you'll take a few minutes to consider it"?

Mr. John Lewis: No, we have considered it. From the evidence we had we are of opinion that the bursting of the stoppings prevented the action of the fresh air and caused the after-damp to be so fatally effective".

The Coroner: (after speaking to Mr. Mackworth) "Would you like to consider it? Perhaps you would like to make a special verdict."

Mr. John Lewis : "No, we would not".

Another juror: "It was purely an accident".

Mr. John Lewis: "Yes, I have said that more than once. We have considered that in considering the whole case".

The Coroner: (after another short consultation with Mr. Mackworth) "Do you wish to attach anything to your verdict in the case of John Owen"?

Mr. John Lewis: "No, Sir"

The Coroner: "Very well, if you do not wish to attach anything to it there is an end of the case".

Despite the sycophantic remarks of the Editor of the CMG Powell was probably a most unpleasant and ruthless man who had a lot to be ashamed of in the conduct of his mines and in his business relationships. At one time he refused to pay John Nixon the commission he was owed for selling Powell's coal in France. When Nixon began to speak of legal proceedings Powell said "Now, Mr. Nixon, I was never afraid of the law. I had a lawsuit with Lord Bute and I beat him, and I will beat you too. To hear you talk about agreements! I have never in my life made an agreement that I could not get out of, and all that are against me I get out of".

But Powell was not the only proprietor with a callous disregard of the welfare of his workers. On the 26th of May 1855 Mackworth wrote to "Mrs. Rees and others, Proprietors and Trustees of the Lletty Shenkin Colliery, Cwmbach". The letter began; "I hereby give you notice that I am not satisfied that since the last five explosions of firedamp which have occurred in this colliery, the necessary precautions for safety have been or are being carried out". The letter went on to repeat criticisms of the ventilation arrangements, the use of naked lights, the danger to life caused by props which had not been set by experienced colliers and many other matters.

An unusual view of the wooden headframe of Bwllfa New Pit taken from the front of the winding engine house, with some light maintenance going on.

John F. Mear

However, Thomas Powell seemed determined to do as he wished in his own collieries. The result—further explosions, this time in the Lower Duffryn Colliery. 12 men were killed and 12 injured on the 6th of November 1860. In the same pit 2 were killed and 1 injured on the 1st of December in the same year. Although the first accident was caused by a man opening his lamp, insufficient ventilation was implicated in both accidents. Powell died in 1863 and in 1864 The Powell Duffryn Steam Coal Co was formed to purchase Powell's mines from his estate. Had Powell lived until 1906 he might have turned over a new leaf upon hearing of the Courrierres explosion in that year which, having a death-roll of 1100, was the greatest disaster in the annals of mining. The next most serious explosion was the Senghenydd disaster in 1913 (439 dead).

The disasters which have been mentioned above took place in situations which entailed the use of

150

child labour, one of the most disgraceful aspects of Victorian Britain. The following quotations are from the journal of the Rev William Roberts, South Wales agent for the British and Foreign Schools Society. He visits Hirwaun:

14th. Feb. 1855
The state of education in this place is in a deplorable state; there are some sort of two schools in connection with the works. The teachers are shamefully deficient as to their morals and competency, one of them being in the habit of swearing and cursing the children in the school, and the other drunk half the time.

Earlier, on 22nd May 1828, an appeal was made to the National Society for a school in Aberdare, "For there are 300 boys and 400 girls between 7 and 13 years requiring cheap and gratuitous education." Parents would be expected to pay 2d. or 3d. a week.

Such was the sad situation for children in the Cynon Valley in the first half of the 19th century, and earlier. Even if there was a school to attend, it would probably be attended but rarely. With mouths to feed within the family, the child of six or seven years, and sometimes younger, would be carried into a level before dawn, and return home 12 hours later. For that shift he or she would sit, cold, weary and lonely near an air door, possibly with a candle, and wait for the passing of a horse and tram with a haulier, who would expect the door to be opened for them. Another child would be working with the father, filling a tram with coal or ironstone, and always susceptible to injury from the coalface. The father would claim an extra tram for the child, which might make his wage sufficient for next week's food and rent bills.

This situation was not rare, it was essential for the children of most families to work hard and long in order to boost wages. Women would also be recruited for mining work, for that was also expected of them, despite injury or worse. A twenty one year old surface worker at the Gadlys Graig colliery, a Miss Anne Butler, was killed on the colliery incline on 9th November 1866, while trying to stop a runaway coal journey of full trams. Mr. John Dixon, schoolmaster at Hirwaun in 1842, when Hirwaun ironworks school was in being, stated that shopkeepers' children would have greater advantages and continue longer at school, and he regretted that the girls are taken so young to work, especially into mines. He also commented on their "very coarse behaviour, and swearing is common".

In order to compile a document on "Children's Employment" in "Reports from Commissioners, 3rd February 1842, Robert Hugh Franks Esq. travelled Glamorgan and Pembroke to enquire into the condition and employment of children and young persons engaged

In the Aberaman Williams' pit, 1862, [at 11 years of age] I was miraculously rescued when it was flooded by billions of tons of water that broke in from the abandoned mine Abernantygroes, if I remember the name. As I was in the innermost part of the pit, my way of escape, they thought, was cut off. But the brave William Roberts carried me on his back half a mile with the water almost to his chin, and I weeping and saying "Cha i byth eto weld mam a nhad" ("I shall never again see my mother and father"). And the hero replied "Cei, cei, mae'r dŵr yn mynd i lawr" (Yes yes, you shall, the water is going down"). If I should visit dear old Wales again I would diligently seek for his grave in the Aberdare Public Cemetery— the Westminster Abbey of Wales. I would also find out the grave of William Williams, Dumfries Street, who perhaps at still greater risk rescued me from the Blaengwawr explosion—to die later that evening, as they thought, because I was so horribly burnt that the rescuing party could not identify me, and I semi-conscious and voice very husky and throaty because of the poisonous afterdamp in my body. I could only whisper that my name was John Thomas. But there were several John Thomases among the boys. The cautious foreman of the rescuing party asked "Have you a brother working in this mine, or on the top of it?" "Yes, Griff" I replied. "Griff y Gôf you mean? "Yes." "Why, the boy is Johnny Kitty!" they concluded. To distinguish me from other John Thomases they called me after my mother's name, Catherine".

The Rev. J. A. Thomas of Chamberlain, South Dakota. In A.L. 26 Jan 1924.

[Griff y Gôf was Mr. Griffith Thomas, Cwmdare, then a blacksmith and afterwards chief mechanic at the Bwllfa collieries.]

in mines and manufactures. At the top of the table that he later published is the following reference to the Plymouth Colliery in Merthyr parish. "It was a large colliery for those days, with a total of 675 workers employed, (and was owned by Messrs. Hills.) Of those, there were 90 boys aged under thirteen years; and 25 females," each working at least six days a week.

The following are taken from various such documents and reports:

1) David Thomas: "I am a trammer, and I have been working here for four months; I am seven; I work the same time as James Davies but I work harder and I earn twelve and a half pence a week: I have not been hurted yet; I cannot read and I don't attend chapel."

2) Evan James: (16 years). "I have been employed 7 years; I have not been seriously injured; I never could read; has 3 sisters and 1 brother in work; none can read; Jesus Christ is the son of God."

3) Mary Jacobs: (14 years). Trammer; Works with sister; Works in part of the mine, pushing trams for three years; We work 12 or 14 hours sometimes.

4) William Firth: Aged 6 years: "I hurry with my sister and they pay me sometimes: I don't like to be in the pit; It tires me; I was crying to go out this morning."

5) Morgan Davies: Age 9 years; Worked for 2 years; Earns 8 shillings a week (40p.); Occasionally been hurt; but never laid off work more than a week; No schooling; Is now learning A.B.C.

The Coronation Drift was opened by D. R. Llewellyn in 1912. On Monday the 16th of June 1913 these four men were involved in a catastrophic fall of roof at the drift. We know their names but we do not know which is which. John Evans and W. J. Llewellyn were both killed and Waldo Evans seriously injured. The fourth man, Jack Rosser was unscathed.

Doug Williams

There are far too many such stories in this vein to relate them all. It is to be hoped that all these children mentioned survived such hopeless times.

Some nine years on in 1853, the Vicar of Aberdare, Mr. John Griffith, had given notice of a motion to the Merthyr Board of Guardians, regarding the problem of orphan paupers. He explained his motion, stating that "There was an abundance of employment for all ages and sexes, yet these pauper children were not employed." He added that "Coal mining was one species of employment from which they were entirely excluded, and I recommend underground employment."

He added that if there was no close family to assist them at work, then they could be apprenticed "at ten years of age, to some steady, well known man." The man could have remuneration for expenses, by taking his apprentices wages. Of the orphans, he stated: "That they are the seed-bed of nearly all the crime in the parish."

The motion was seconded by Mr. David Davies, Blaengwawr (one wonders why). The motion was passed eventually, with the term "orphan" to include all children without a father. "Legitimate" and "illegitimate" being classified apart.

When approaching Bwllfa Dare from Cwmdare there is a wooded area on the right with tramroad inclines and spoil tips. This is the area known as "The Windber" to Cwmdarians. There have been over the years over 20 levels in this area working the thin seams found in the upper part of the Middle Coal Measures. The above photo shows the surface features of Windber Colliery. It had a building over the mouth of the drift (just above the centre of the photo) in which there was the haulage engine. The trams of coal ran under the road to screens on the site of Nantmelyn Colliery which were served by a siding from the Dare Valley branch of the T V R.

John F. Mear

153

In March 1870 Richard Fothergill III arranged for two working colliers, Mr. Thomas Thomas, Cwmdare, and Mr. Lewis Morgan, Rhondda, to go to London to take part in the committee proceedings of the Regulation of Mines Bill. However, the Bill was postponed and the miners took part instead in a discussion on the Bill at the residence of Lord Elcho.

Eleven years later, (1864), Mr. David Davis' employees, door boys all, of Abercwmboi colliery had withdrawn their labour upon the refusal of Mr. Davis to increase their wages. This action moved the owner into requesting the colliers to perform the boys work themselves, and thus acquiring the boys wages on top of their own. The men refused on safety grounds, and Abercwmboi colliery remained idle for nine weeks. On the 16th July 1864 a compromise was achieved and the door boys returned to work. Prior to the strike the boys were receiving seven shillings per week (35p.), as opposed to eight shillings (40p.) in other collieries. The boys achieved the average wage of the district, which was 7 shillings 8½ pence.

Mr. Franks, commissioner, writes of the work performed by children, and describes a typical door boy as "cold, wet and not half-fed, the poor child, deprived of air and light, passes his silent day." Yet another job for boys and girls would be 'carting'. They wear a leather girdle around the waist, attached to a chain between their legs, which is attached to a coal filled drag cart. The child then drags the cart on all fours in a low seam, to a terminus for trams to be filled, and hauled to pit bottom by horses.

Another method of transporting coal in a seam that is inclining at about 40 degrees, would be the windlass, operated by women and boys. "This work is so severe, that their shift is but 10 to 12 hours duration."

Mr. Franks mentioned at this point that the Welsh windlass was an improvement on the "odious system adopted in Scotland in similar veins". Mr. P. Kirkhouse, overman of the Crawshay works, including Hirwaun, quotes "400 children all working underground, of these, 50 may be females".

Far too many children did not survive the working conditions, or accidents at work; instances were commonplace, as the lists below signify:

Fatality figures of children listed below represent boys and not girls.
Some of Cynon Valley details: (from 1851 to 1861)

Werfa colliery chain disaster:	Total of 11 killed including 3 boys (aged 11, 12 and 16).
Middle Duffryn explosion:	Total of 65 killed – 15 boys (1 boy aged 10; 5 boys aged 11; 4 boys aged 12; 1 boy aged13; 2 boys aged 14; 2 boys aged 16).
Lower Duffryn explosion:	Total of 19 killed including 7 boys (2 boys aged 10; 1 boy aged 12; 1 aged 14; 3 aged 14).
Blaengwawr colliery explosion:	Total of 13 killed including 4 boys (10; 13; 14 and 15 years).

Apart from the boys killed in such disasters, another 33 single fatalities of boys also occurred from 1851 to 1861 in the Cynon Valley, taking the total to 62.

N.B. There may be many more, as the records scrutinised were not completed in some instances. The figures do not include any seriously injured or burnt children, as these were not included in any list of the period. Newspaper cuttings from the past show occasionally details of a child's death in a colliery, but seldom the burnt or injured child.

Below are listed sad examples of newspaper cuttings:

April 6th 1861: William Davies, aged 9 years, was returning home from work in the Lower Duffryn colliery. Tired, he stumbled and fell under the trams of the incline, mutilating his legs. The unfortunate boy failed to survive amputation.

Oct. 18th 1864: Werfa colliery. A boy of 12 named Charles Protheroe, whilst working in the stables near pit bottom, fell into the shaft sump and drowned. A month later, it was revealed that the boy was 11 years old, and should not have been employed underground, as it had been illegal since 1862. A government inspector charged the agent of the pit, a Mr. John Williams, with unlawfully employing the boy. Convicted, he was fined 5 shillings and costs.

Dec 2nd 1865: Powell's pit, Cwmdare. Henry Andrews, aged 8 years, fell asleep in a coal truck in the early morning, whilst at work on the surface. "Tipping" of small coal resumed and killed the boy. An overman was reprimanded for employing such a child.

One must also wonder as to the financial straits of the boy's family for permitting such a tragedy. The list goes on and on, which is beyond the understanding of new generations, who could never contemplate a child of 5 years suffering such cruel labour. Parents were probably desperate to gain a few extra shillings and the mineowners were ready to turn a blind eye to it.

It took until the 1840's for the Government to appoint commissioners to investigate child labour, and it took until 1862 for legislation to be considered on the subject of legal age limits.

In 1864 there were 438 doorboys working in the mines of the Cynon Valley. It is interesting to note the employment of doorboys in collieries came to an end in 1897. Following a dispute between "Nixon Navigation Collieries' Company", and the hauliers of these pits, the Cambrian Miners' Association interceded and persuaded Mr. H Gray (agent) to concede that all hauliers be paid sixpence a day, for the opening of all doors underground when required. (Prior to this, only the dayshift hauliers were paid this duty.) It was also agreed to discontinue the job of doorboys.

N.B. Mr. Carlton Smith, giving an account of a visit to the mining districts in 1833, said "children are sent down the mines with bread and cheese. Sometimes they could not eat due to dust and bad air, and the heat would melt their candles. They were frequently beaten by men for whom they worked."

As for more recent times, it was on July 1st 1957, that an order (Employment of Young Persons order) was made providing that no male person who has not attained the age of sixteen shall be employed below ground in a mine of any class, etc." (M & Q Act 1957).

A photo taken underground at Windber Colliery, Cwmdare in 1938, where a coal cutter is at work in a seam which is 18″ high. Windber is said to be the first place in the South Wales Coalfield to introduce electric coal cutters. They were introduced by D. R. Llewellyn in October 1905 and they marked the beginning of his independent business career.

Collieries, West	A family, consisting of parents and two children. Husband earning £1.5s.pw.			
		Expenditure per week		
		£.	s.	d.
Glamorganshire	16 lbs of flour	0	3	0
and Carmarthenshire	1 lb of butter	0	0	11
	1 lb of cheese	0	0	9
	Animal food	0	2	3
Report by	2 ozs. of tea, at 4½d	0	0	9
R.W. Jones Esq.	2 ozs of coffee, at ½d	0	0	3
	1¼ lb of sugar at 8d	0	0	10
Appendix	Soap & sundry articles	0	1	9
	Drapery, averaging	0	4	0
	House-rent &c.	0	2	6
	Expenses, clubs, ale,&c.	0	1	9
		£0	18	9

The shafts by which men, coal and materials were taken up or down the pit, as the case may be have always been places of high risk In September 1851 a "bucket" used at Wyrfa (or Werfa) Colliery for taking men up and down the pit broke up and 14 men were killed. Owner: Mr. John Nixon and others. At Cwmneol pit in Cwmaman on the 29th of November 1855 a cage containing eight men was being wound up the shaft. For some reason it failed to stop at the surface and, turning upside down as it went over the sheaves, flung the men down the shaft to their deaths. A similar but less grievous accident occurred at Pwll Als (Park Pit) in Cwmdare in January 1868. The engineman allowed the engine "to take one stroke too many", which caused a fatal accident. He had been on duty for two days. There have been numerous cases of men falling from the cage or being struck by a falling object but overwinding accidents were virtually eliminated by safefy devices which included the automatic detachment of the winding rope if necessary combined with means to hold the cage securely while the men got out. It seems doubtful that such measures were in place at Bwllfa No 3 in 1910 for twice in three months the cage became detached from the rope and fell down the pit.

Another threat to the miners' lives is the flooding of the mine. It is unusual for there to be no seepage of water into an underground workplace.When this is noticed it can, if necessary, be kept under control by being pumped out of the pit. However, great danger is present when breaking into old workings either by accident or design, for there may be the accumulation of many years of water drainage there. The most famous instance in the coalfield of this type of accident happened at Tynewydd colliery in the Rhondda Fawr on Wednesday the 11th of April 1877, when four men and a boy were rescued after ten days imprisonment by water in a rising heading. In the Cynon Valley a flood in the River Level Colliery took the lives of 6 men in 1896 after which the pit was closed for several years.

Accidental fires underground may be a result of explosions or of faulty machinery or electrical equipment. Obviously the need to keep the ventilation operating in order to remove smoke and to induce fresh air for breathing conflicts with the need to keep airflow to a minimum so as not to feed the fire.

Much of the activity at the coalface is done in confined places and in proximity to machinery with moving parts. In addition, the use of trams to bring coal out of the pit has necessitated underground railways with "journeys" of trams hauled by steel wire rope. It is not surprising that the history of mining is littered with accidents, slight and severe, involving machinery, and trams seem to be involved in the majority of cases. The terrifying effect of a breaking wire rope when under tension could be followed by the running away of a journey of loaded trams which might, on a lucky day, stay on the rails and come to a halt. Otherwise the derailment of the trams would often result in a man being crushed against the wall of the workings. Many accidents were caused by the practice of men riding on the trams and falling off, which often had fatal results.

The ground in which the coal seams lie is sedimentary, which means that it was deposited in layers of various thicknesses. Apart from coal, these deposits consisted of clay, mudstone, siltstone, ironstone, and various kinds of rock. The various layers (or strata) were laid down horizontally but were in many cases distorted by subsequent massive movements of the earth's crust, as Chapter 1 has explained. Consequently, when the working away of a seam of coal or any other material takes place beneath a stratum of rock which has broken up due to the deformation mentioned above, then it is liable to collapse if its support is taken away. Then there occurs a "fall" of roof, with men trapped underneath if they could not get quickly out of the way. Miners were often able to detect warning noises emitted by an unsafe roof—these were termed "picking" or "pouncing".

The remoteness of the scene of mining accidents and the lapse of time which is thereby incurred made it essential (and required by law) for first aid facilities to be provided at stations underground and at the surface. In addition, suitable stretchers must also be made available at the first aid stations. On the surface a first aid room had to be provided.

The explosion of firedamp underground usually resulted in workmen with blast injuries and severe burns, as well as men who were trapped by a fall of ground caused by the explosion, or by spontaneous falls. In the former case the rescue of those men was extremely dangerous owing to the presence of the poisonous afterdamp. Over the years many different kinds of breathing apparatus were developed for the use of the rescue team or teams maintained by each colliery, as well as devices for the revival of apparently suffocated persons. When an accident occurs which appears to need highly trained rescue workers the Dinas rescue station takes charge from the start and their team is always the first to approach the incident area. The mine's own rescue team(s) will give support as required.

People who have to do with dangerous substances or machinery often acquire a very nonchalant attitude to them, sometimes with disastrous results. In the mid nineteenth century and well into the twentieth it was not unusual for miners to have to provide their own gunpowder which they purchased from a local shop. Complaints were sometimes made that men went to bed drunk and lit their pipes when there was a barrel of gunpowder under the bed. In one case, the barrel was thought to have been put near the fire to dry. The resulting explosion took off the roof of the house and left the man seriously injured. In another local case dating from 1850 a woman threw into the fire a small ball of gun-cotton which she had found in a box. She and her mother were killed.

We do not any longer see so many old miners (and some not so old) visibly suffering from the effects of Pneumoconiosis caused by prolonged inhalation of the very smallest particles of stone dust and coal dust which can be liberated by the mining of coal and many other minerals. The disease with its frequent coughing and shortage of breath has caused many thousands of premature deaths in the coalfield, often accompanied by bitter wrangling about compensation. Miners were also subject to the

---

Ground disturbance caused by mining (known as subsidence) has created problems over many years. It occurs when the "roof" above a worked-out seam collapses into the old workings. Sometimes the collapse is of such a nature as to extend as far as the surface and to affect buildings, roads, gas and water pipes, etc, though at the surface the sinking of the ground was often only a few inches. Nevertheless, it was not a rare sight to see a building so badly affected as to need the support of buttresses or even to require demolition. The following are from reports made by the Surveyor of Mountain Ash Urban District Council:

May 25th, 1923. During the last week there have been signs of a general movement near the Town Hall. The kerbstones have been crushed in 3 or 4 places and in 6 places the paving stones on the footpath have been squeezed up and out of place.

Oct 17th 1938. Subsidence in the Mountain Ash area is still causing a large number of leakages in the water and gas mains and your staff are continually searching for and repairing leakages.

In March 1996. Penrhiwceiber Junior school, built in the 1880's was demolished due to the cumulative effect of subsidence.

eye disease, Nystagmus, usually caused by inadequate lighting. Other afflictions include beat knee and beat elbow, and synovitis of wrist, and contact with rat's urine can lead to Weil's disease. In recent years miners with a long experience of using power tools underground have been found to have "Vibration White Finger". An old enemy of the miner was Dermatitis, a skin disease caused by exposure to certain liquids and types of dust.

In the mining industry as in many others, it has been the case that improvements in the measures for the protection of the miners have met with opposition from the mine-owners, and in many cases it was found necessary to enforce compliance with good practice by means of an Act of Parliament. The first Mines Act in this country was passed in 1800 and was entitled "An Act for the Security of Collieries and Mines" Another Act of 1843 excluded from underground work all women and girls as well as boys under 10 years old.

An explosion at Haswell Colliery in the North of England, where all precautions had been neglected resulted in the death of 95 men and boys in 1844. After much delay the Mines Regulation Act of 1850 was passed and this was followed by a second Act in 1855 but neither Act was effective. It was not until after the tragedy at Hartley Colliery in Northumberland in 1862 that it was made compulsory to to have a second outlet to a mine.

Further Acts were afterwards passed, so that today, when the coal industry is but a shadow of its former self, mining activity is bound by Acts of Parliament and Regulations, etc made thereunder which affect every aspect of underground working from accidents to ventilation, and including dust in mines, explosives, electricity, first aid and rescue, firedamp drainage, lighting, locomotives, mining qualifications, plans, safety-lamps, shafts, smoking, and tipping operations.

In Bwllfa Colliery yard competitors for a timbering contest practise their skills in putting up timbers.

NMGW

158

At the Bwllfa Colliery Offices a workman turns away from the pay-office window and begins to count his money to check whether he has had his due. The office was on the site of Bwllfa Dare Colliery and remained in use for some years after the colliery stopped coaling in November 1938.

NMGW

From opposite ends of the valley:

THE VISIONARY "BLIND RHYS"
Rhys Hopkin Rhys (1819-1899), a native of Llwydcoed.
Blinded by an explosion during an experiment at the Dowlais works in 1847; A towering figure in early local government and later instrumental in providing early reservoirs, the sewerage scheme, Aberdare cemetery and the magnificent Aberdare Park opened in July 1869.

THE BOXER "DAI" DOWER
(1934-), a native of Abercynon.
British, European and Empire Fly-weight champion in 1955. World Championship title fight in 1957 but unsuccessful. Renowned for his great skill as a boxer and his always pleasant, modest demeanour.

This pit, the De Winton pit, was also known as Park Little Pit and Pwll Spite. It lasted only from 1899 to 1903. This photo is believed to show the sinking of the No. 2 pit. Its wooden headframe had provision for one cage only. Its underground workings in the Bute seam were connected to the workings of the Number Nine Pit in Cwmbach. James Lewis leased it at first from the Marquess of Bute, to whom it afterwards reverted. In 1915 the PDSCC Ltd took over the lease, but they did not work the pit.   Doug Williams

160

CHAPTER EIGHT

The practice of grouping together for mutual comfort and security is known in the animal world and has been paralleled in human activity. There can be little doubt that this instinct underlies such harmless activities as quite young children forming "gangs" in the playground as well as groups of adults forming together whether for innocent activity or for more nefarious purposes. We might expect, therefore, that workmen's unions had existed for many years before the Industrial Revolution in the form of local trade associations, but the coming of that Revolution certainly caused skilled craftsmen to combine to protect their interests. Unfortunately, these early efforts coincided with the French Revolution (1789) causing the ruling classes to view the efforts of the workmen to form unions as dangerous and revolutionary. Consequently, the Combination Acts of 1799 and 1800 (complementing the 'Conspiracy Laws' of 1795-6) were passed, making it illegal for workmen to form unions to press for more money, or for fewer and shorter working hours. Slowness in the growth of trade union organisations in the early years of the nineteenth century, can be accounted for in the main by this anti-trade union legislation passed by the Government.

This hostility towards trade unions by Government and employers resulted in many workers turning to Friendly Societies to unify and enforce their interests. Many examples of local sporadic action took place in Glamorgan in these early years, but nothing that could be called 'continuous association' is to be found until about 1831.

The Combination Acts proved to be unsuccessful—loopholes were found in the laws whereby the unions claimed they were Friendly Societies, which had been legalised by Lord Rose's Act of 1793.

In 1824, a Parliamentary Select Committee Report recommended the repeal of the Combination Acts. The Report was accepted and the Acts repealed, thus legalising combinations of workmen. This helped to prepare the ground for the first trade union organisations in the 1830s.

In 1820-21, the iron industry had seen labour conflict in Aberdare and it is possible to see trade unionism emerging from these events. Although by 1824 trade unions were legal, they were not tolerated by the employers who had the necessary powers to control the workers who, unfortunately, did not possess the organisation or understanding to stand their ground in a dispute. Nevertheless, there is no doubt that the workers were involved in disputes with their employers but these initial actions were carried out surreptitiously. Local tradition has claimed that the Red Flag— that became the standard of the trade union movement—was first raised on Hirwaun Common in 1831, when a white flag was dipped in sheep's blood before a march on Merthyr.

Despite the coal industry being labour intensive with the sinking of new pits in the area, there does not appear to have been any organised union activity in Aberdare before 1831. On the other hand, the coal-masters quickly appreciated the need for presenting a united front in dealings with the men, particularly when faced with the informal industrial action that doubtless occurred. However, the coal-masters, whilst recognising the problem of organised labour, did not establish a united organisation to deal with the coal industry until 1856, when the Aberdare Steam Coal Proprietors' Association was formed. Trade union activity did not at this time take root among the miners of Wales in general, and Aberdare in particular, simply because of the lack of trade union tradition and expertise, together with the lack of co-operation between the pits and the various coal-fields. Being unskilled work in the early days, new labour was easily recruited from the many immigrants flooding into the area seeking work. In addition, the large flow of men seeking work was deterring the advance of unionism, as known trade unionists could be sacked and easily replaced from this constant supply of alternative labour. Nevertheless, some informal collective worker activity occurred in the 1840s with some strikes and disputes breaking out in the Aberdare Valley, as the workers fought to maintain their wage levels. Some evidence indicates industrial militancy continued into the 1840s and 1850s and the development of the steam coal trade, particularly in Aberdare, saw a greater degree of unionism being organised by these new colliers as compared to those employed by the ironworks. In addition, links

This is Samuel Thomas of Ysguborwen who was originally a Merthyr shopkeeper. With his brother-in law, Thomas Joseph, he took up mining in the Cynon Valley. He lived at Ysguborwen house.

Sir W. T. Lewis, later Lord Merthyr, was firstly mineral agent of the Marquess of Bute before acquiring interests of his own in the Rhondda and Rhymney valleys. He was the founder of the South Wales and Monmouthshire Coalowners' Association. His residence was Mardy House, Aberdare (now demolished).

were now forged between the sale-coal colliers of Glamorgan and Monmouthshire.

The conditions existing in the mining industry were always likely to lead to disputes over wages and conditions, this never more apparent than when new mines or seams were being opened. While the main clashes between masters and employees were over wages rates, it should not be forgotten that from time to time other matters strained industrial relations. One classic example was the belief by the masters of the connection between the colliers and Chartist activities. Once established this concept was difficult to eradicate. Any combination of workmen was viewed with deep suspicion by the owners and this was aggravated by the continued Chartist activity in the area until about 1844, when trade improved.

Very closely linked to the disputes over wages and conditions was the dissatisfaction with the Truck system of payment. Owing to the relatively isolated geographical locations of many of the new communities, it was necessary for the employers to provide provisions as well as houses for their workers. Thus began the company shop, or Truck shop, which together with the 'long pay' system, by which workers were paid monthly or even longer, was to be the cause of bitter disputes. Under the Truck system, workers were not paid cash, but with goods from the employers' shop, or coupons only redeemable in the same shop, thus lowering the value of workers' wages. This system was beneficial to the employer because, if he wished, he could overcharge his workers, take advantage of 'economies of scale' and buy cheaper, and it gave him a hold over the employee who could not leave his work while owing money to the company. Used initially during the iron-making years, by the time the steam coal industry was established the shops were a well-known feature of the Cynon Valley. Truck shops were opened in Aberdare from between 1803 and 1881. The first was set up at Hirwaun in October 1803 by Edward Overton, and others were opened at Llwydcoed for the Aberdare Ironworks, by the Scales Brothers; at Dover House, Gadlys for the Gadlys Iron-works by the Waynes; at the Trap, Abernant Road for the Abernant Ironworks by Richard Fothergill; at Cardiff Road, Aberaman (opposite the present day Blaengwawr Public House) by Davis of the Blaengwawr collieries; and at Aberaman (near the site of the Old Band Institute) by Crawshay Bailey.

The Trellwyn Methodists have built a church,
The front looks like an abbey,
But thinking they can fool the Lord,
They've built the back part shabby.

From "The Sand in the Glass" with acknowledgements to the author, Michael Llewellyn, and to John Murray (publishers) Ltd.

Although declared illegal by the Truck Act of 1831, the system remained in existence for many years after this Act and was, in fact, adopted by some coal masters as the industry expanded. However, opposition to this system resulted in the formation of the Aberdare Anti-Truck Society supported by workers, traders, shopkeepers and the local Nonconformists. Under the provisions of the Truck Act court action was taken against Richard Fothergill in 1851.The case was proved and Fothergill was fined £5.00 with costs. The extraordinary sequel to this event was a well-attended demonstration held on Hirwaun Common to protest *against* the finding. Despite the conviction Fothergill's Truck shop survived but all was not lost. The workers established their own shop—'the workers' shop'—to compete with the company shop and this eventually led to the setting up of the first Co-operative Society Stores in Wales at Cwmbach in 1859. Fothergill's Shop continued trading, surviving a brief protest by Abernant workers in 1861 until it finally closed in 1868.

However, the suspicious and antagonistic atmosphere, fanned by the possibilities of industrial conflict, was not improved by the tactics employed by either side in disputes. In almost all strikes, the coalmasters' standard reaction was to employ outside labour in an attempt to weaken the men's position. The men's reaction frequently led to violence and it was reported in May 1843 that coal levels at Llwydcoed, owned by the Gadlys Iron Co, were raided, mining equipment destroyed and candles and powder scattered far and wide.

These "raiders" were the 'Scotch Cattle'. This was the name given to an illegal, secret society, formed by bands of workers from the valleys of North Glamorgan and Monmouthshire, who attacked owners and workmen against whom they had grievances. They were active from 1820 to about 1840, but recent research has suggested they were still active in 1860 in Aberdare.

Their activities included the holding of open-air meetings at night accompanied by horns, drums and gunfire; sending warning notes to blacklegs and informers; organizing attacks on owners' properties; and midnight visits to the homes of fellow workers they wished to intimidate. The society adopted a red bull's head as its symbol and the leader's identity was never revealed, but was known as 'Tarw Scotch' (Scotch Bull). Various suggestions regarding the name of this illegal society have been made, such as the practice of using cattle skins as a disguise, or because they 'scotched' those who accepted lower wages, or simply because they were black-faced with a ferocious appearance. This dispute of May 1843 lasted for four months before collapsing owing to the miners having no outside help. This effectively killed off any hope of establishing a trade union movement in the area for many years.

Another favourite tactic used by the coalmasters was the discharge note—a certificate given to each worker who satisfactorily completed his contract at one colliery—that had to be produced before he was employed at a different colliery. While this was a legitimate procedure, it was frequently used in an oppressive manner as a device to victimise colliers and to break strikes. These events left feelings of bitterness lingering long after the disputes that caused them had been settled, and the presence of the immigrant workers remaining in the area became a constant reminder of the opposing interests of the colliery owner and his workmen.

Census returns show Aberdare's population grew from 3,961 in 1831 to 37,704 in 1871, an increase of approximately 900%. In particular, the Aberdare parish in the 1850s, when the population increased from 14,999 in 1851 to 32,299 in 1861, has been described by Dr John Davies as "the most dynamic place in Wales". This increase was due to the inflow of migrants seeking work in the new coal-mines, with by far the largest number of immigrants during this period being agricultural labourers from West Wales. Although not bringing any tradition of organised labour, they had already learnt the advantages of concerted action in the building of their Noncomformist Chapels in the strongholds of Welsh dissent in such areas as Pembrokeshire, Cardiganshire and Carmarthenshire.

These workmen quickly adapted to the needs of their new surroundings in the building of many chapels for their way of worship and in the setting up of many Friendly Societies. More importantly, they began to take an interest in the formation of labour unions for industrial negotiations with their employers.

That this action was necessary is evident by the number of strikes that took place in the Aberdare Valley over the employers' actions in reducing wages. Between 1849 and 1852, Aberdare suffered the effects of a depression in the coal trade accompanied by a series of strikes and disputes over the reduction in wages. Following a strike in 1848, the men were compelled to accept the employers' terms, but the tension and unrest arising from the acceptance of these terms lasted almost two years finally resulting in the 1850 strike.

One of the earliest examples of co-operation between Glamorgan and Monmouthshire colliers took place in early 1843, when a strike at Tredegar spread to Aberdare, where workers in sale-coal pits came out in sympathy. The strike however was short-lived and the men returned to work with a wage reduction of 2d. per ton of coal produced. One reason for this failure was the fact that each colliery operated individually in negotiations with the owners, there being no central labour organisation available, simply a federation of individual collieries. The total inadequacy of individual action was clearly demonstrated in 1845 when 150 colliers employed at Powell's Pit, Cwmbach, went on strike for an advance in wages. This strike resulted in several of the leaders being successfully prosecuted by Thomas Powell for leaving their workplace without notice.

By 1847, there is evidence of localised unions when a four-month strike in Aberdare and in new pits in the lower Rhondda was organised. In 1849, a union was organised by Aberdare colliers to resist the

Under powers granted to them by the Powell Duffryn Act 1872, the PD company had built direct lines from the entrance to the valley of the Aman to both the Taff Vale Railway and the Great Western Railway. As a logical extension of their activities, the PD Co built in 1902 a washery and in 1904 a power station both of which could be served by the new lines referred to, and also by the TVR and GWR. In this photo the washery is on the left and the power station is in the right background. In the nineteen twenties the power station used to sell bulk electricity to the District Council.

The late Glyn Davies

The numerous amalgamations which resulted in the PD becoming the largest exporter of coal in the world also resulted in such things as centralised workshops and other economies of scale. This enabled them to repair their own locomotives and other items of machinery with tools such as this massive centre-lathe, and wheel lathes capable of handling locomotive wheel sets.

John F. Mear

discharge and/or hire of workmen without their joint consent. In January 1850, colliers at Gadlys Pit stopped work in an effort to gain an advance in wages—the owners replied with proposals for a wages reduction. Soon most of the colliers in Aberdare were out on strike and Thomas Powell responded by importing 150 colliers from Gloucestershire. Matters did not improve and one demonstration at Hirwaun Common drew a crowd of about 7,000 people and this so worried the police that soldiers were called in to assist in the event of trouble. Fortunately, the meeting passed without trouble breaking out. As the strike went on, it was inevitable that some men returned to work but when these 'blacklegs' were intimidated by strikers, some prosecution followed. Recent research by D. Gareth Evans has suggested that it is entirely possible that the 'Scotch Cattle' were involved in this strike in 1850, though their usual area of activity was in Monmouthshire.

In 1860 at Level yr Afon, Abernant, a strike occurred in protest at a wages reduction that highlighted the violence always likely to accompany such action. After failing to heed warnings not to work by three separate union members on three separate occasions, a known blackleg was killed by a bomb thrown into his house. One other known 'blackleg' was allegedly excommunicated from Siloa Chapel, Aberdare for his actions—despite the general opposition to unionism by the Nonconformists. As far as can be ascertained, this strike was the last time mention was made of the 'Scotch Cattle' in the Cynon Valley.

The large number of strikes in the mining industry during the 1850s in Wales in general and Aberdare in particular, provides a clear indication that some degree of 'organised' worker activity was in the process of establishing itself. Attempts to establish a colliers' union were made but these were quickly stamped out by the coal-masters. Under the stimulus of the 1850 strike, Aberdare colliers came together to form the 'Glamorgan Union Of Colliers', which was to have branches at every colliery where at least forty colliers were employed, with a subscription of 4p. per month. But these efforts were only responses to times of crisis and simply ephemeral, as indeed were the efforts of the English unions to set up more durable organisations in South Wales.

Apart from the power of the coal-masters, strong trade union activity was slow to develop due to several factors including the following: the geographical layout of the area, with its many long, deep

165

and narrow valleys made inter-communication very difficult; the varied quality and different types of coal, each with its own conditions, customs and labour; and the influence of the ironworks on the coal industry posed its own particular problems. Another important factor holding back the formation of trade unions, was the determined opposition of the Nonconformist clergy. These religious leaders held that unions were anti-religious, and, such being the power of the Chapels, this opposition was considered a serious threat by prospective trade unionists. In addition, the leaders of the Nonconformist denominations were strongly against any form of working class combinations, considering the oaths taken by union members to be blasphemous.

Clearly, these conditions were not conducive to the establishment of strong trade unions. Not even the movement into the coal-field of large numbers of immigrants with some organisational experience —but no history of trade union activity—did anything to strengthen the situation.

However, a disastrous strike in Aberdare took place in 1857 when the employers announced a reduction of 15% in wages. The strike lasted seven weeks, with troops again called to maintain order, but the miners were forced back by privation and had to accept the original terms plus a further reduction of 5% to compensate the owners for losses incurred by the strike. By this time, the coal-masters, realising the men were becoming more aware of the need for joint action to gain their objectives, set up their own trade organisation. In 1856, the Aberdare Steam Coal Proprietors' Association was active, with wage rates its main concern, but with each colliery owner free to negotiate his own terms, the Association was not very successful. Therefore, the 1860s saw a re-alignment of both owners and workers in preparation for the anticipated troubles that lay ahead.

On 14th March 1864, at a meeting at the Windsor Hotel, Cardiff the coal-masters set up their own formal association. The steam-coal proprietors resolved to form the Aberdare Steam Collieries Association with the object 'the care of all matters connected with the Steam Coal of the district' and 'the protection and benefit of the trade generally'. Several factors made the Association a formidable organisation with its various rights and obligations clearly set out and, with its membership confined to the Aberdare Valley, the Association was compact. Furthermore, it included several of the more influential firms in the industry and its members were working the most famous of Welsh steam coals. By 1870, it was strengthened by the inclusion of other areas to form the South Wales Steam Collieries Association. There is little doubt this Association was formed as a direct consequence of the more active interest the men were taking in trade union activities plus the increased demands that had been made upon the coal-masters in 1863 and 1864.

The development of the Rhondda Valleys coal-field during the 1850s and 1860s ensured work was plentiful, although there were brief spells of over-production and unemployment. Consequently, this time was comparatively free from industrial strife, with wages being fairly high. It is important to note that up to 1871 not one strike of importance was caused by a demand for increased wages-strikes were invariably called in attempts to prevent the reduction of wages.

It is considered that trade unionism virtually disappeared until the late 1880s, as the lower paid workers transferred their efforts into other related movements such as Chartism, Co-operative Shops and Short-time committees. However, during the same period, trade unionism made some advances among the skilled workers but these did not benefit the very large number of unskilled workers. However, any attempt at organised trade unions for the unskilled was effectively prevented by the double objections of both skilled men and the coalmasters. Nevertheless in July 1871, some evidence of local trade union activity can be detected in the Cynon Valley, when miners organised a concerted attack against the migration of Staffordshire men to work in the pits at a time of a local dispute. Although only a local dispute, it indicated there was the belief that collective action by the workmen was necessary to maintain or improve their conditions.

As early as 1869, several local unions had been set up and the Amalgamated Association of Miners (A.A.M.) formed in Lancashire, spread to the Aberdare Valley. This action coincided with a recession in the coal trade and, adding to this situation, a new militancy was appearing amongst the miners in the early 1870s.

On 1st June 1871, after a wage demand had been refused, the men, encouraged by the President of the A.A.M., went on a strike which lasted for twelve-weeks that was seen as a test of strength between the union and the employers. In the Cynon Valley, all the following pits were on strike: Bwllfa;

Nantmelyn; Gadlys; Abergwawr, Blaengwawr; Cwmneol; Fforchaman; Aberaman; Abernant; Werfa; High Duffryn; Old Duffryn; Llettyshenkin; Middle Duffryn; Abercwmboi; Lower Duffryn and Navigation. This strike was finally resolved when the men settled for no reduction in wages and a small increase with further advances to be negotiated later. This was the first time that the Miners' representative, at that time Thomas Halliday, had been allowed to give evidence to the arbitrators—the coal-masters had finally recognised the union organisation.

The union further benefited from this success, as in Aberdare alone, in 1871 membership increased from 310 in February to over 6000 in June, and in the boom years of 1872-73, the union was able to consolidate its position. By 1873, the union membership in South Wales was probably at least 30,000 but this success was short-lived. A temporary recession in late 1872, resulted in the employers calling for a reduction in wages causing a strike on 1st January 1873. The A.A.M., now at the height of its powers assisted the men by payment of strike money, at 10 shillings per week. This strike, involving all South Wales pits, was the greatest that had occurred to this time and was fought with great bitterness. Lasting until May, the miners finally accepted defeat returning to work with lower wages and the acceptance of the Sliding Scale—a device whereby wages were determined by coal prices. Resulting from the payment of strike pay, the A.A.M. became bankrupt and was dissolved.

The first Sliding Scale agreement was reached on 11th December 1875 with wages adjusted every six months and this responsibility was placed in the hands of a Joint Committee of five owners and five miners representatives. For the first eighteen years, its president was William T. Lewis, an autocratic leader and strong opponent of all forms of collective bargaining and its vice-president was William Abraham, better known as Mabon.

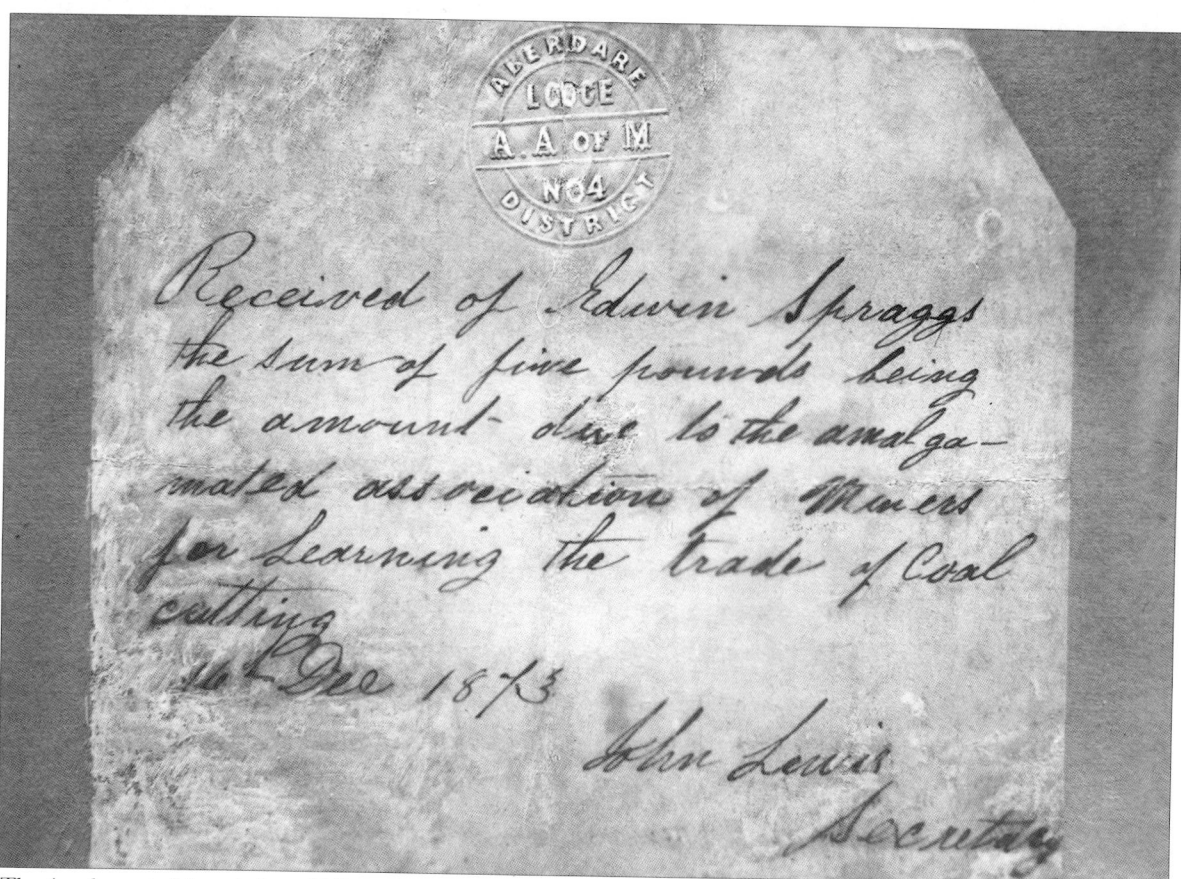

The Amalgamated Association of Miners had a branch in the Aberdare district and attracted a lot of support after winning disputes in 1871 and 1873. This receipt shows that in the latter year one Edwin Spraggs paid the Association £5 "for learning the trade of coal-cutting". Did the association really conduct classes in coal-cutting? If so, did the beginners learn this trade at the coal face, and if so, who was the benevolent coalmaster who allowed trainees to have the run of his property? Or was it a device by which the union got more money from new members? But 1874 saw the beginning of a decline in Trade Union support, and after 1875 the AAM gradually faded away.

John F. Mear

William T. Lewis was born in Merthyr in 1837. After completing his education, he obtained work in the office of W.S. Clark, Chief Mineral Engineer to the Marquess of Bute eventually becoming his chief assistant. When Clark died in 1864, Lewis succeeded him, moving into the official residence at Mardy House, Aberdare (now demolished with The Beeches Nursing Home erected on the site) plus a salary of £1000 per annum. He developed a large practice as a Mining Engineer and in 1867 became a colliery proprietor in his own right, with interests in Pontypridd and Rhondda. In 1872, Lewis was instrumental in the formation of the South Wales and Monmouthshire Coalowners Association, whereby all the interests of the coal and steel makers were combined, in direct response to the miltancy of the workers and the growth of trade unionism. After taking a leading role in the 1873 strike and lock-out, he is alleged to have formulated, with others, the Sliding Scale, that allowed miners' wages to be determined by the selling price of coal. In 1855, he was knighted and eleven years later he was given a baronetcy for his service to the community. In 1911, he was created Baron with the title Baron Merthyr of Senghenydd. He died in 1914.

William Abraham was born in Cwm Afon, near Llanfabon in 1842. The son of a working miner, he began work in the mine as a door-boy at the age of ten. From 1872, he was the Miners' Agent for the Loughor District of the Amalgamated Association of Miners until the collapse of the union in 1875. He was the natural choice to lead the miners following the collapse of the union and he filled the position with great success. He was a remarkable leader, a consummate operator and a thorough Welshman in the approved style, a Liberal and Nonconformist. He was to be known by a Bardic name, Mabon, which remained with him until he died. During tough negotiations with W.T. Lewis, the head of the newly formed Coal-owners Association, he hammered out the agreement setting up the famous Sliding Scale. Between 1875 and 1902, he was Chairman of the Miners' side of the Sliding Scale Committee and this, together with the monthly one-day holiday he gained for the miners, was to be his memorial. In 1885, Mabon became the first Welsh working class MP in the Rhondda. Mabon was an advocate of co-operation between owner and labour, avoiding strikes wherever possible and using arbitration to settle disputes. Politically, he was associated with the radical wing of the Liberal party, a Home-Ruler and friend of Gladstone and Lloyd George. In 1909 he was forced to join the Labour party by the miners but he did not appreciably change his political opinions. He resigned his seat in 1920 and died two years later.

The Sliding Scale had met with opposition from the start, owing to the price of coal falling during the first four years of its operation. This caused anger amongst the miners with agitation mounting for a minimum wage, independent of prices, and an eight hour day. The younger miners, led by William Brace bitterly attacked Mabon and the owners. Attempts were made to rebuild a union based upon what remained of the A.A.M., and by 1880, there were a number of small district unions in the coalfield, the strongest being the Cambrian Miners' Association led by William Abraham.

By the late 1880s, large-scale industrialisation was deepening the rift between employer and employees; class feeling was emerging and each class sought to improve its own status. Political consciousness was awakening in Wales as was the realisation that opportunities were beginning to open up for the working class. Although it would take another twenty years before the Trade Unions formed their own political party, the seeds were firmly sown.

By 1893, those who opposed the Sliding Scale had an organisation around which they could gather—this was the Miners' Federation of Great Britain founded in Newport in 1889. Spurred on by the size of the rapidly growing coal companies, the miners realised the need for a united front. Following a long lock-out, from September 1897 to the end of March 1898, when the miners were again defeated, the chief lesson learned was the need for a more centralised union. Consequently, on 11th October 1898, the South Wales Miners' Federation (later to become known as the 'Fed') was formed, receiving immediate approval with 104,000 joining by the end of 1899. Its first President was William Abraham.

The demise of the iron industry had provided the opportunity for the coal industry. The financial power of companies who had seemed destined to die with the iron industry, was renewed by a transfer of their efforts into the coal industry.

Those far-sighted men had seen their wealth increase with the new South Wales Steam Coal—a term that within a short time was to set standards of coal value throughout the world.

Without doubt, the Aberdare Valley was in the forefront of this new development as the following production figures indicate.

1844	71,031 tons.
1856	1,173,459 tons.
1870	2,342,792 tons.

At its zenith in 1913 the South Wales coal industry had increased production levels to almost 57,000,000 tons which was one fifth of the total British coal output. Furthermore, 70% of this output was exported, a much larger proportion than that of any other coal-field, and the industry directly employed about one third of the Welsh labour force. These figures indicate how deeply Wales had become dependent upon the coal industry that included the mining, sale and transportation of the product.

During the First World War, the coal industry played a vital part in the war effort with coal needed for industry and fuelling the warships but this did not prevent the South Wales coal-field from becoming involved in industrial conflict. Much unrest was brought about by the belief that the miners were being exploited by the coal-owners, leading to a strike in July 1915. The Powell Duffryn and other companies, who were charging up to 50% more for coal since the outbreak of the war, paid very high dividends to their shareholders, but refused the miners a pay rise to compensate for the increasing costs of living. Government intervention declared striking unlawful but this was a serious mistake. The miners were infuriated but, in reality, the law was completely unenforceable—how could a workforce of over 200,000 be punished? The South Wales miners went on strike from 15th to 21st July 1915 and the fact that only the South Wales coal-field was involved in the conflict, can be regarded as proof of their militant attitude and of the unique importance of Welsh coal. Further unrest occurred in January 1916 over the Conscription law, and in April 1916 over the issue of the 'closed shop' with the huge profits of the mining companies remaining a constant source of bitterness. Finally, in the face of this conflict, the government responded in November 1916 by taking control of the South Wales coal industry, a policy that was extended to all British coal-fields in February 1917.

Other serious problems caused by the war would not be manifest for some years. The demand for coal production was huge, yet colliery development was ignored and plant and equipment difficult to obtain. The more accessible, richer seams were worked out, many pits were exhausted in the rush to keep supplies flowing and there was little incentive to modernise. Consequently, by the end of the war the coal-field was crying out for investment that would enable the more difficult seams to be worked. If the coal-field was to survive, a great deal of money was needed to modernise the old mines with further investment necessary to open new ones.

It is appropriate to mention those Valley men, many of whom left the pits to serve their country during the First World War. Within the first week of the War, recruitment centres were set up in Aberdare and Mountain Ash and there were no shortages of volunteers to fight, with most recruits destined for all branches of the Army. Most of the volunteers went into the 'local' regiment and served with one of the battalions of the Welsh Regiment, with the South Wales Borderers and the Royal Welsh Fusiliers also having their share of local men. To date, it has not been determined how many men left the mines to serve their country but in all probability, it was a large percentage. Interestingly, at the end of the War when the Army was demobilised, many local men were among the first to return home having been given priority demobilisation in order to return to work in the mines.

On 8th March 1923 a crowd estimated at about 14,000 witnessed Sir D. R. Llewellyn reveal the grey granite of the cenotaph in Victoria Square, Aberdare, erected to honour the memory of the men of the Aberdare district who fell in the Great War. Similar scenes occurred at other times throughout the Cynon Valley. Well over 1,000 men had died. Sadly, many other names were to be added to the names of the fallen in the valley, as elsewhere, in 1945.

CHAPTER NINE

The First World War marked a turning point in the fortunes of the South Wales coal industry; particularly was it so in the case of the steam coal producing district, which of course included the Cynon Valley. However for reasons mentioned below, the disastrous consequences were not immediately apparent.

By 1914 Welsh steam coal had established itself as the premier fuel for the world's navies, including the German fleets, and it was increasingly used by merchant shipping, especially the faster vessels. After the outbreak of war there was an insatiable demand from the Royal Navy and from allied fleets, and every effort was made to increase production in spite of a diminished workforce. In the initial enthusiasm to enlist in 1914 and early 1915 thousands of miners had flocked to the colours and many continued to do so in later years despite the fact that coal mining was a reserved occupation. Details are not available for the Cynon Valley, but the following figures for the Glamorgan coalfield show the decrease in manpower during the war years.

Table 1

Year	No. of Miners.	Output ('000 tons)
1913	156,675	38,033
1914	156,938	35,847
1915	134,004	33,110
1916	141,310	34,151
1917	144,531	32,133
1918	144,189	30,865

Although some miners were released, those that remained were the young and able-bodied, so that the mining workforce had a measure of imbalance tilted towards those who were too old or too young for service. To meet the demand for coal, the easiest, thickest and most accessible seams were exploited without regard for future development, and maintenance work was kept to a minimum.

The result was that by the end of 1918 the mines were in a very dilapidated condition. The demand for coal continued mainly in order to make good the loss of production from the damaged coalfields of North East France and Belgium. In December 100,000 miners nationwide received an accelerated demobilisation and the Cynon valley received its quota. The following figures show the jump in employment in the Glamorgan coalfield.

Table 2

Year	No. of Miners	Output ('000 tons)
1919	169,837	31,058
1920	179,983	30,252

1920 recorded the highest ever figure for miners employed in Glamorgan, exceeding the 1913 total. Yet largely because of the deterioration in the condition of the mines, output per man/shift had fallen and output was below that of 1913.

Over the years a considerable degree of horizontal integration had taken place in the South Wales coalfield and this was particularly the case in the Cynon Valley. By 1919 ownership of the valley's collieries was virtually in the hands of the Powell Duffryn Steam Coal Company, and the Llewellyn family. The former's collieries consisted of Aberaman, Cwmneol, Fforchaman, Llettyshenkin, Lower Duffryn, Blaennant and River Level. Some of the smaller collieries acquired by Powell Duffryn since 1864 were closed, having originally been bought for their leases. Their mineral takings were now worked from adjacent pits and in some cases they were used for drainage and ventilation.

When its coal mines were nationalised the PD Co retained a number of related businesses in the fields of engineering, coal processing and distribution and shipping. It was not until May 1996 that the company made the final break with coal mining by disposing of the last of its solid fuel interests to concentrate on its shipping and engineering activities.

D. R. Llewellyn (later Sir David), the eldest of the Llewellyn brothers was more indirect in his approach to appropriation. By the 1920's his clutch of directorships was Byzantine in its complexity. He was chairman of the following companies in the Cynon Valley alone; Bwllfa and Merthyr Dare Steam Collieries Ltd (Bwllfa Nos.1–4) and the Cwmaman Coal Company Ltd. (Cwmaman and Fforchwen), D. R. Llewellyn Ltd. (Windber, Dyllas and Llwynhelig), Duffryn Aberdare Colliery Co. Ltd. The last named was formed in 1919 specifically for the purpose of acquiring from the Bute estate Tower Colliery and 4,000 acres of mineral-bearing ground extending from Aberdare to Glynneath, in face of fierce competition from the Powell Duffryn Company. He now controlled about one seventh of South Wales coal production.

Most of the collieries in the lower part of the valley belonged to the Nixon Navigation Co. They were Abergorki, Cwm Cynon, Deep Duffryn and Navigation. In 1929 these were absorbed in a merger brokered by W. M. Llewellyn, D.R's younger brother, to form a new company, the Llewellyn Nixon Collieries Co. Ltd. There remained Abercynon owned by G.K.N., and Lady Windsor in Ynysybwl, belonging to the Ocean Coal Company. In 1930 the Llewellyns merged all their mining interests to form Welsh Associated Collieries and in the following year this new company acquired Abercynon as well. In 1935 Powell Duffryn and W.A.C. merged to form Powell Duffryn Associated

This photo is of a new drift being made by the Cwmaman Coal Company in 1918 to reach the upper seams such as the Graig and Gorllwyn. One wing wall is completed and masons are working on the other. Other modernisation included the replacement of horses by haulages driven by compressed air.

Doug Williams

172

Collieries Company Ltd. Three Cynon Valley collieries remained outside the domain of the colossus and continued to do so until nationalisation. Lady Windsor Colliery (Ocean Coal Company), Rhigos Colliery (British Rhondda Colliery Company), and a small independent colliery—Werfa Dare, owned by the Williams Brothers.

To return to 1919. The period immediately following the war was one of continued prosperity. Because of the demand from Western Europe, particularly as has been indicated, from France and Belgium, the price of coal reached an unprecedented height. The South Wales miners were determined to consolidate the gains they had made during the war and early in 1919 through the South Wales Miners' Federation, they demanded reduced hours, increased wages and the nationalisation of the industry, which was still under government control. The government was prepared to concede only one third of the wage demands and the miners voted by an overwhelming majority to strike. The Prime Minister, Lloyd George, bought time by promising an immediate Royal Commission to consider the miners case. The latter agreed provided that half the commission's members should be nominated by them.

The commission under Judge Sankey reported on wages and hours in March, recommending an increase of 2/- per shift and a reduction of hours from eight to seven. The proposals were accepted by both sides, the strike was averted and the commission returned to work to consider nationalisation. Although the chairman and half the members favoured nationalisation, the government considered the large minority against it was a sufficient reason for them to reject the recommendation. However all members agreed on the desirability of nationalising the coal itself since amongst other things the employers objected to the payment of minimum or dead rents which the royalty clauses involved.

The industry continued buoyant through 1920 but concern about inflation and the huge profits the employers were making resulted in another strike in October 1920 which was settled in November by the offer of another 2/- per shift.

This is the Bute pit on Hirwaun Common, where a boiler explosion took place on the 19th of January 1883. A stoker, Morgan Powell, was standing in front of the backplate of the boiler when it exploded and he received mortal injuries. Three men standing nearby were also hurt. The wooden headframe, the engine house, various out-houses and part of a stack were blown down. The colliers underground took another way out of the pit and were unharmed.   Doug Williams

This brief period of post war prosperity was a false dawn. The collieries of France and Belgium had now recovered, and further their damaged machinery had been replaced by modern, more efficient equipment including mechanical coal cutters and conveyors. Poland too had become a serious competitor in the European market and Germany was paying its war reparations in coal. The United States had captured much of the South American market and European countries were no longer prepared to pay high prices for Welsh steam coal. The price of the latter f.o.b.* at Cardiff at the beginning of December was £26 per ton. Within a few weeks this had halved.

By early 1921 Cynon Valley collieries were working part-time. In some cases—Tower and Bwllfa Nos. 2 and 3—notices of closure were given and a levy was raised among the workmen at Bwllfa Dare and Windber, which were still working, to help their colleagues at the former pits. Then came a further blow. The government announced that it would relinquish control of the mines on 31st of March and they would be returned to the owners. The latter immediately reneged on the November 1920 agreement, arguing that the reduced price of coal made it impossible to pay the wages conceded by the government. The new terms which cut wages by up to a half, were rejected by the miners and a lockout followed at the beginning of April.

It was generally admitted even by the coal owners that wages were too low but they were adamant they could not afford more. D. R. Llewellyn stated that dividends would be suspended until conditions improved. He also gave permission for his Hirwaun workmen to pick coal from nearby colliery spoil tips.

Meetings were held throughout the coalfield declaring full support for the miners from the railwaymen and dockers. The government declared a state of emergency . The latter withdrew and the miners carried on alone for 3 months until they too were forced to capitulate at the end of June at greatly reduced wages.

The following year the great demand for training and education in the mining industry along with a hope for the return of more prosperous conditions, led to the opening of a mining engineering laboratory attached to the Boys' Intermediate School, (later the Boys' Grammar School—now demolished). In 1923-24 there was a slight improvement and production and exports increased as a result of the French occupation of the Ruhr and a coal strike in the United States. From the end of 1924 it was downhill all the way.

Two events should be mentioned. In 1921 there had been built near Skewen, at a place to be known as Llandarcy, Britain's first major oil refinery, ironically the producer of the fuel that was to replace completely steam coal. Secondly in 1925 the government announced a return to the Gold Standard thereby increasing the value of the pound and causing overseas customers to pay more for British goods, including coal.

Throughout 1925 into 1926 relations between the coal owners and the workforce became even more strained. The former argued that the only way to make Welsh coal competitive in the world market was for the miners to work longer and accept lower wages. The miners replied that their wages were already at subsistence level and they were not prepared to work more than 7 hours a shift in the hazardous conditions underground. Their answer was increased investment to improve working conditions and for the introduction of more machinery. With regard to the latter, in spite of the introduction of an electrical coal-cutter in the Windber colliery early in the century the degree of coal face mechanisation in the Cynon Valley, as indeed throughout the entire steam coal district, was very small. In no small measure this was due to geological conditions. There had however been a considerable increase in the use of conveyor belts.

In 1925 the government averted a strike by giving further subsidies and by offering another Royal Commission. Nearly all local collieries were working part-time. Then in 1926 the coal owners delivered an ultimatum, demanding swingeing and immediate wage cuts. The S.W.M.F. backed by

* "Free on board", i.e. delivered to the ship free of charge.

the Miner's Federation of Great Britain, rejected the demands completely, adhering to the slogan coined by A.J. Cook, the president of the M.F.G.B., "Not a minute on the day, not a penny off the pay". On the 30th April the miners were locked out by the employers. Immediately the T.U.C. called a general strike of all its affiliated unions. On 4th May the entire country came to a standstill.

In Aberdare and Mountain Ash as in other towns there were central strike committees which virtually took over the local administration, organising supplies for essential services and authorising necessary transport movements.

Then on the 12th May the T.U.C. capitulated. Nationwide the miners stood alone until late in November, with the onset of winter, they too were forced to yield, returning to work and accepting the employers' conditions of a reduction in pay and an 8 hour day.

The summer of 1926 was one of severe deprivation for miners and their families. Meetings were held regularly at the Miners' Institutes at Abercynon, Penrhiwceiber,* Mountain Ash, Aberaman, Trecynon, and the Palladium, Aberdare, (which had inherited some of the functions of the old Temperance Hall), and increasingly in the amphitheatre of the Plough Tip in Aberaman. These meetings, addressed by miners' leaders and Labour M.P.s were forums in which ways and means of continuing the struggle were discussed. The men were not entitled to relief from public funds, the allowance for their families was meagre, the assistance provided by the cash strapped Board of Guardians was barely at subsistence level. The miners themselves were dependent upon small, irregular cash payments from the S.W.M.F. Free school dinners were provided for children and provision was made for shoe repairs. Besides scavenging spoil tips, outcrops were worked for coal. The alignment of small depressions seen today east of the Treherbert road near the Tower colliery dates from this period. The resources of small shopkeepers had been strained in 1921, but the support, though similarly limited, of the local Cooperative Societies was invaluable. Communal kitchens were set up but those needed money to maintain them. An outcome which in some ways was perhaps one of the most significant features of 1926 was the way in which the community, thrown on its own resources, organised a vast number of activities which served the triple function of giving people something to do, provided entertainment, and helped to raise funds to run the kitchens. These activities included carnivals, concerts, swimming galas, sports, cricket and football matches, and of course jazz bands. "Zulus" , "Toreadors", and "Pirates" equipped with gazookas were part of the daily scene in Aberdare and Mountain Ash. 1926 was the high noon of community spirit and solidarity in the valley.

* In his book on Cynon Valley place-names, Mr. Deric John points out that over the years there have been many mis-spellings of the word "Penrhiwceibr" of which the NCB's "Penrikyber" is the worst.

THE NONCONFORMIST CAUSES

In general the traditional ritual of the established church is much simplified or absent, clerical dress is less formal or not used. Greater emphasis is laid on the preaching of a sermon.

METHODISTS (METHODISTIAID)
Established by John Wesley, and most akin to the Anglican Church. Central organisation arranges the circulation of ministers.

BAPTISTS (BEDYDDWYR)
Baptism is reserved for adults and regarded as personal acceptance of the sacrament.

UNITARIANS (UNDODWYR)
As the name implies, they believe that God is not a trinity but one person.

CONGREGATIONALISTS or INDEPENDENTS (ANNIBYNWYR)
Individual congregations manage their own affairs with church government (The Congregational Union) exercising moral authority.

PRESBYTERIANS (PRESBYTERIAID)
Formerly known as CALVINISTIC METHODISTS (METHODISTIAID CALFINIAID)
Congregations are governed by elders of equal rank. In England and where, in Wales, English is the medium of worship, the Presbyterians and Congregationalists have combined to form the United Reform Church.

The spirit and experience of the period have been memorably recorded by Edwin Greening and several of the above details have been drawn from his account.

The South Wales Miners Industrial Union (backed by the employers) was insignificant in the Cynon Valley, and blacklegs were relatively few. The hatred they incurred was out of all proportion to their numbers and the stigma attached to them persisted even through their families for decades.

The "Aberdare Leader" for 28th April 1928 gave a list of local collieries which had closed since 1926.*

Table 3

Colliery	Owner	No. of men affected
Blaengwawr	Aberdare Graig Coal Co. Ltd.	100
Bwllfa No. 3	Bwllfa and Merthyr Dare Steam Coal Co. Ltd	703
Fforchwen	Cwmaman Coal Co.	720
Tower	Duffryn Coal Co.	456
No. 2 Drift	do.	56
No. 3 Drift	do.	72
Dyllas	D. R. Llewellyn & Sons	165
Aberaman	Powell Duffryn Steam Coal Co.	1172
Navigation	Nixon Navigation Co.	2011
Clay Level	Powell Duffryn Steam Coal Co.	15
Lower Duffryn	do.	816
Blaennant	do.	437

The irregularity of the coal seams produced some curious results. Before the advent of piped water many houses had wells, many of which were in the cellar. It was not unknown for methane to seep from the wall of the well and cause an explosion if exposed to a naked light. At one time in the Cwm the gas bubbled up through the bed of the River Dare and could be ignited and used for cooking by picnicers. In both these cases the seam from which the gas came must have been near the surface, as was the seam in Aberaman (said to have been the four-foot) which was visible in the cellar of the Victoria Inn, which was at No. 440 Cardiff Road. The Victoria Inn closed in 1916.

Aberdare UDC minutes 25th June 1897

Some remained permanently closed either because of the exhaustion of their reserves or because those reserves could be easily worked from adjacent collieries. These were Blaengwawr, Dyllas, Clay Level and Blaennant. The remainder, along with Bwllfa No. 1, the Bwllfa No. 2 complex, Cwmaman, Windber, Llwynhelig, Tirherbert, Cwmneol, Fforchaman, River Level, Werfa Dare, and in the lower part of the valley, Deep Duffryn, Abergorki, Cwmcynon, Abercynon and Lady Windsor were to continue part time working for a decade. The Cwmaman complex (Cwmaman, Fforchwen and Trewen) closed in 1935 and Llwynhelig and River Level in 1939.

Until 1914 South Wales had produced 20% of Britain's coal and had accounted for 60% of her coal exports. The steam coal industry particularly was geared to supply the needs of shipping and the export market. The steam coal valleys had no alternative industrial base to fall back on. Several of the Cynon Valley collieries were on the Admiralty First List—Cwmaman, Fforchwen, Trewen, Cwmcynon, Deep Duffryn, Navigation, Penrhiwceiber, Aberaman, Cwmneol, Fforchaman, Lower Duffryn, Blaennant, and River Level. By the 1930's the Royal Navy had almost completely gone over to oil and the Merchant Navy was following suit. And this applied too, to the ships of other nations.

Between 1927 and 1937 the number of men employed in the valley's collieries fell by half, from just under 20,000 to 10,000. One third of this number travelled up to ten miles from their home to their place of work.

For many the only alternative was to move out of the area completely. The maximum population for the valley as recorded

*Taken from a statement by the Secretary of State for Mines, in answer to Parliamentary Question No. 108.

by census returns was 98,292 in 1921. This gain over previous years was due to inward migration and natural increase, i.e. the excess of live births over deaths. In fact the inward movement continued for two or three years after 1921. From 1927 onwards the situation was dramatically changed, the movement of people was reversed.

Table 4

	Popn. 1921.	Popn. 1931.	% Intercensal Decrease	% Natural Increase	% Decrease due to Migration
Aberdare	55,007	48,746	11.4	5	16.4
Mountain Ash	43,287	38,386	11.3	9.9	21.1

It will be seen from the above figures that the true loss due to migration was offset by natural increase.

In 1928 the Industrial Transference Scheme was established. Working through Employment Exchanges it was intended to facilitate the movement of unemployed men from areas such as South Wales to parts of the country where they could train for new employment. Single men under thirty-five years old were given preference. In March of that year two young miners from Aberdare left for Syston near Leicester to train as moulders. They were the first from South Wales to move under the arrangement. In spite of financial assistance provided, the scheme was not a success, and throughout the next decade, far more left independently than under the scheme.

In 1934 the eastern part of the coal-field was designated a Special Area whereby new industries were to be encouraged to set up in the area. In 1936 an industrial survey of South Wales was published which underlined the limited effect of the Special Area legislation. The following table taken from it shows the extent of continued migration during the early '30's.

Table 5

Loss due to migration 1931–35

	April 1931–June 1933	June 1933–June 1935
Aberdare	870 (1.78%)	1650 (3.39%)
Mountain Ash	813 (2.12%)	1700 (4.43%)

In four years over 5,000 people had moved away from the valley. Their main destinations were those parts of England where light industries, particularly the motor car industry, were expanding—Oxford, Dagenham, Coventry and Slough with its new trading estate. Other destinations included the anthracite coal field, southwest England, the south coast and even the United States and Canada. For those who remained the worsening situation is revealed by the following figures.

Table 6

Number of coal miners unemployed in Cynon Valley

1931	1932	1933	1934	1935
5,058	6,303	7,633	7,878	7,682
27.0%	34.8%	42.5%	43.8%	44.6%

The 1930's were the years of the hated means test and hunger marches. Free milk and free school meals were provided for the children of the unemployed. The Miners' Institutes from Trecynon down the valley to Abercynon were centres of social functions. They provided facilities for recreation such as billiards and films as well as excellent libraries and reading rooms. It was a period of political awareness. The Left Book Club flourished in Aberdare and later several valley miners left to join the International Brigade in Spain.

The collieries worked sporadically, often on a day to day basis. Notices of available work were flashed on cinema screens, or notably in Aberdare were displayed outside W. Cable's newsagents shop at the lower end of Canon Street, opposite to the entrance to Whitcombe Street. The site is now occupied by the Halifax Building Society office. The Coal Act of 1938, which nationalised coal royalties, had no effect upon local employment.

The establishment of the Treforest Trading Estate in 1936 drew a trickle of people from the valley at first, but it was to prove an important source of employment in later years. The following year Aberdare Cables was set up in Trecynon, the first light industry unrelated to coal mining to come to Aberdare. Again at first it provided only a small measure of relief but eventually it became a major employer. In the same year the Powell Duffryn Company installed the Phurnacite patent fuel plant in Abercwmboi using a process designed by the French Disticoke Company to utilise the fine sizes of the dry steam coal produced by local collieries. It did not become operational until 1942 but it was to have a considerable impact in later years.

In 1936 the Settlement was opened in Aberdare. It was made possible by the gift of Fairfield House by M. H. Llewellyn, the youngest brother of D.R. and by grants from the National Council of Social Service in Wales. The prototype was Toynbee Hall in London's East End and the idea was for a group of people to settle in a depressed area and to study and make provision for the needs of the community. It was linked with a number of social service centres throughout the valley. The activities provided were numerous, ranging from cultural pursuits including literature, French, Welsh, politics and current affairs to practical classes in carpentry, shoe repairing, quilting and dressmaking. Particular emphasis was given to Keep Fit classes.

These are the Tower drifts No.1 (left) and No. 2 on the mountainside above Hirwaun in the 1950's. The five similar trams are of a type known in the Tower colliery as "Bombies"and they were popular because if "raced" they could hold about 1½ tons of coal. The tram without sides was known as a "Sulky". With the aid of four steel posts put into sockets on the frame, timber, pipes etc could be carried. The No. 1 drift dating from 1864 worked the 6ft seam and the No. 2 drift (1894) the 9ft.

The late Glyn Davies

A "raced" tram. It was an acquired skill to load a tram so as to hold the maximum amount of coal combined with the minimum amount of loss during its journey to the surface. When a collier had filled his tram he would chalk his number on it. The white chalk patches were caused by successive colliers attempting without the help of water to erase the number of the last user before putting his own number on it. Note the sprag in one of the wheels which prevents the tram from running away.

NMGW

Rearmament in the later 1930's had at first little impact upon the Cynon Valley. After 1939 the situation changed. Again there was a great demand for coal for wartime industries, but again there was a movement out of the coal industry of young miners, employed and unemployed predictably at first into the armed forces and then into other industries which appeared in the valley such as the shell factory at Robertstown and the Royal Ordnance Factory at Hirwaun.

With the collapse of France in 1940 the export trade ceased abruptly but there was an increasing demand for coal for the armament industries. In 1942 the mines were once more placed under government control, operating through the Ministry of Fuel and Power.

These factors led to a shortage of labour which persisted in spite of a scheme to recall former miners from other industries and from the forces. Men under 25 registering for National Service were given an option of serving underground. Few volunteered and eventually in November 1942 the War Cabinet agreed to compulsory recruitment. The plan was the brainchild of the Minister of Labour,

Ernest Bevin, who decreed that one in ten of men between the age of 18 and 25 available for call-up should be chosen by ballot for pit work. Cynon Valley received its share of "Bevin Boys" who received preliminary training consisting of a 4 week course at Oakdale Colliery in Monmouthshire. On completion of the course, the conscripts were posted to mining areas and those who were lucky enough to be posted to a colliery near their homes would live at home, others in lodgings, but locally the majority were accommodated in hostels in Hirwaun and Mountain Ash. The scheme caused much controversy because of the adverse reaction between recruits and established miners. Boys from a mining background were easily assimilated, others less so. However without them the labour force would have been disastrously low.

The shortage of labour meant that the miners were in a strong position, and they made the most of their bargaining power. The most serious dispute which involved all the Cynon Valley collieries was over the Porter Award in March 1944. This amongst other things tried to minimise the differential between the wages of skilled and unskilled workers. It was settled by giving a substantial increase in the minimum wage.

The last year of the war saw the formation of the National Union of Mineworkers, the old South Wales Miners' Federation now becoming the South Wales District of the larger union. The spring of 1945 also saw the publication of the Reid Report. The Reid Commission had been set up by the wartime National Government to report on the condition of the mining industry. Its conclusion will be one of the matters mentioned in Chapter ten.

CHAPTER TEN

The fall of France in June 1940 had taken away over 70% of Britain's overseas coal market. This naturally lead to the closure of pits and this in turn lead to men leaving the industry and taking up other employment or service in the forces. By 1942 this was one of the factors which had brought about an acute shortage of coal, and in that year opencast coal mining was introduced into this country by the Mines Department of the Board of Trade. The National Coal Board became responsible for opencast mining in 1952, forming an Opencast Executive for that purpose. The Executive had four regions and the South-Wales coalfield was included in the South Western region of the executive.

The earliest opencast sites were opened under the emergency provisions of the Defence of the Realm Act 1939 and one such was Ffyndaf on the north western edge of Hirwaun Common. The removal of the exploitable coal from the six foot and nine foot seams and the restoration of the site had been completed by 1953. In the early days the depth of the excavation was limited by the size of excavating plant available, and steam-driven plant was still in use. This meant that at Ffyndaf the maximum depth of the excavation was about 25 yards, whereas the more recent Ffyndaf B site was excavated to a depth of over 100 yards. Later, further sites were opened under the same powers on the lower slopes of Mynydd Cefn y Gyngon on the land between Cwmdare and Tower No 1 Colliery. These sites yielded 1,059,020 tons of dry steam coal over the next decade though much coal was "lost" due to previous deep mine workings. Were it to be anounced today that a similar site was to be coaled, there would be a call before work started on the site for the rescue excavation of the old tramroads, levels and other remains of the age of iron.

At the beginning of the 70's further sites were opened to the west of the sites mentioned in the previous paragraph, firstly at Rhigos. In 1980 Ffyndaf was revisited and fresh coaling began, which came to within 200 yards or so of the famous Tower No 4 Colliery. The Ffyndaf B site produced 1.7m tons of coal which was sold as high quality anthracite. The next site to be exploited was the Ffyndaf Additional, after which restoration was commenced.

The sites so far mentioned are all on Hirwaun Common, broadly speaking. There remain areas of coal under the common which are of interest but they are partly under ground occupied by the Tower No 3 drift and the overland conveyor, so no action on this front is likely until the end of deep mining in this vicinity.

The sites on the north side of Aberdare include the conspicuous Bryn Pica site. The first opencast working in this area was the Tir Ergyd site from 1961 to 1963. and this was followed by the so-called Bryn Pica site of 30 acres which was worked from 1963 to circa 1983. By this time the NCB were applying for planning permission to extend the site, thereby creating 200 jobs and producing 1.2 million tons of valuable coal. There were protests at this development and a public enquiry was opened in April 1974. On the 19th of December 1974 the Secretary of State for energy, Eric Varley, announced his approval of the scheme, subject to a small number of changes to the boundary of the original plan. Now the site has been restored. There have been several other small opencast sites such as Croesdy and Dyllas.

Let us go back to the end of the second World War when, to everyone's surprise, a parliamentary election resulted in a landslide victory for the Labour Party. The ensuing Labour Government then moved to refashion the Welsh economy by providing a wide base for industry and making it more competitive, while doing away with the depression and great unemployment which had bedevilled the pre-war economy. The Labour Party had been committed to nationalisation since 1918, and upon taking office it proceeded to nationalise the major industries including the nation's coal mines, which passed into public ownership on the 1st of January 1947. The coal industry was not the only industry to suffer from the effects of failure to modernise its infrastructure and methods. However it is the coal industry alone which we are dealing with and it is to that industry's difficulties that we direct our attention.

It is in the nature of coal mining that the first coal to be extracted from a new pit, being nearest to the shaft, is the cheapest to bring to bank. When the nearest coal has been all extracted, that coal which lies at a distance can only be brought out with the expenditure of more money on haulage, ventilation, roof supports and (sometimes) pumping. Hence older pits tend to be uneconomic and this was one of the reasons why coal output fell throughout the war while costs rose. In fact, a "Times" leader stated in 1944 that the cost of home-produced coal was the most alarming of the factors affecting the future of the basic British industries. Other factors were the persistence of bad feeling between management and men in the industry, and the loss of most overseas customers because of the war.

The coalmasters had introduced amalgamations in the 1930s to attract the benefits of scale, resulting in the closure of a number of uneconomic pits. In 1945 the Reid Report "recommended that the viable existing pits should be reconstructed and pits with low productivity closed. In their place new pits would be sunk which would be closed when they in turn became uneconomical to work. At

Taken in about 1976, this shows two underground haulage inclines at Deep Duffryn Colliery, Mountain Ash.

NMGW Dept of Industry

This photo of Nant-y- Fedw Level in 1967 shows how nineteenth century techniques remained the best choice for private mines until well into the twentieth century. In the background can be seen Mr. Harry Rogers of Abercynon, who worked at Nant y Fedw at that time. Mr. Rogers' interest in the history of mining has led to him being regarded as an authority on the mining history of the Cynon valley, as the compilers of this book have found to their advantage.   Harry Rogers

the same time Harold Wilson , in his book "New Deal for Coal", called for a massive investment programme of from £150m to £300m as part of a national plan which would incorporate some of Reid's proposals and full national ownership of the mines. Predictably, the latter suggestion formed the basis of the Coal Nationalisation Act of 1946.

At nationalisation the 958 largest surviving pits in the country were taken over by the state leaving some 400 small pits to shift for themselves as private pits under licence. The Cynon Valley pits which became part of the National Coal Board's estate were Aberaman, Abercynon, Abergorki, Bwllfa, Nantmelin, Cwmcynon, Cwmneol, Deep Duffryn, Fforchaman, Penrhiwceiber, Rhigos, Tirherbert, Tower and Werfa Dare.

The future prospects under nationalisation were governed by the fact that, as Harold Wilson pointed out, the coal industry was facing the post-war period with higher wages, costs doubled, and with productivity more than 10% below the pre-war figure. Optimistically, the Reid Committee called on miners and their leaders to join with mining engineers "in an entirely new spirit of co-operation for a united effort to raise the productivity of the industry to the highest level". But industrial relations in the period preceding nationalisation gave no grounds for expecting that this appeal has any chance of success. The first plan for coal, drawn up in 1950, called for 240m tons a year, made possible by an investment of £520m. This did not produce the required result, and in the best year, 1955-56, when 228m tons were brought out, 17m tons of coal had to be imported. But by then the NCB was facing competition, at first from Middle East oil. This, of course, led to a decrease in demand and the inevitable gradual closure of pits which were only marginally effective. In this way 264 of the NCB's mines were closed between 1957 and 1963. By 1970 the number of active pits had dropped to less than 300, and in the Cynon Valley only Abercynon, Bwllfa, Deep Duffryn, Penrhiwceiber, and Tower were still open. In those pits which had a good prognosis the long-awaited introduction of mechanisation underground took place, leading to a loss of jobs at the coalface. Those of the remaining pits which could not improve their productivity were gradually closed. So it was that, for differing reasons, the number employed in the mines went down. In a bid to cut costs in a dwindling industry, in March 1967 a massive national reorganisation of the NCB's mines took place. The South Western Division, which comprised the six areas of the South Wales Coalfield (of which Aberdare was number four), was abolished and replaced by two new-style areas, East Wales and West Wales. Aberdare found itself in the West area with its headquarters at Tondu.

An NCB statement about the changes said that many of the collieries in South Wales were "poised for increasingly effective operation . . . In terms of output per man/shift (OMS) the figure has gone up from 21 cwt to 27 cwt over the last six years. The efficiency of colliery operations in South Wales has never before reached that level." Hindsight tells us that this was an unfortunate time to make such an optimistic statement, for from 1969 coal would never again contribute more to the nation's primary fuel intake than all other sources put together. It was stated above that Middle East oil had begun to compete with coal in 1957. Now, in the late sixties, natural gas from the North Sea began to challenge the supremacy of coal. In 1971 coal had to take second place to oil and in 1974 its share had dropped to one third. In the Cynon Valley Abergorki Colliery closed in 1968 as did two levels at Tower Colliery in the following year.

The requirement of Aberthaw Power station is for "duff", that is coal of a particle size of no more than ³⁄₈". To make redundant the level crossing on the Hirwaun-Neath road and to otherwise speed up the movement of coal to the washery and sidings near the Pontypool–Neath line, and dispensing with the use of locomotive and wagons, this overland conveyor was built by Aberdare Engineering in 1963. This took the washed duff direct to the railhead on the former Pontypool–Neath line which had been left in place as far as Hirwaun Pond so that the railhead could be served. Subsequently, washing etc took place at the colliery and the duff was sent by the conveyor to a covered loading bay alongside the railway, where about 36 hoppers continue to be loaded by tractor-shovel twice a day (see colour section).   The late Glyn Davies

At first the shedding of jobs did not lead to great hardship, because there were plenty of jobs available outside the industry and also because redundant miners were willing to take work in other collieries or indeed other areas. But when the figures for 1967 saw the number of redundancies (12,900) rise to over six times the highest previous annual figure the NCB realised that it could no longer find jobs for all those men who wished to stay in the industry. Not for the first time in the history of industrial relations in the coalfield, activists pitched their tents at the door of the official leadership and accused them of being ineffective.

The militants wanted industrial action "to secure a change in fuel policy" to exact better conditions and rewards, and protection from the worst effects of redundancy. This revival of direct action was fuelled by a strike in South Wales arising from the lack of progress towards an improvement in surface workers' hours. The strike spread and soon there were 130,000 miners defying their leaders. The strike lasted 14 days or so and proved to the miners that they were powerful enough to ignore their own leaders if they thought it necessary.

Another confrontation was sparked off by the next annual pay

In the sixties, this dramatic and costly accident happened near the Tower Colliery. An engine was bringing down some loaded wagons from Tirherbert Colliery when the wagons took charge and demolished the screens, which then fell upon the engine and some of the wagons. In this picture the conveyor, which has partly torn free from the screens, has been given temporary support by a "cog" of sleepers.   Doug Williams

claim. In 1971, at a time when the Heath government was committed to an incomes policy which sought to impose an 8% ceiling on on all pay awards, the miners presented a claim for 17% for face workers, 47% elsewhere underground, and 44% for surface workers. This constituted a gap between the negotiators which could not be bridged. A poll of the miners delivered a vote in favour of strike action and notice was given that a national strike would take place on the 9th of January 1972. This was the first major strike since nationalisation.

After 7 weeks the miners were granted more than ⅔ of their pay claim. But by that time 12 major generating stations were closed down, 1.4m workers were idle and a total shut-down of the economy was less than 14 days away. This humiliating defeat for the government was brought about by the deployment of "flying pickets" and a well-organised stranglehold of the nation's power supplies. Though he was until then hardly known outside Barnsley, his part in organising the blockade brought Arthur Scargill to national attention and gained for him a meteoric rise through the NUM hierarchy. Later in 1972 he won the post of Compensation Agent for the Yorkshire NUM and soon after a place on the union's national executive. In 1973 he won the succession to the Yorkshire presidency. In 1981 the national presidency was his. Following the NUM's 1973 annual conference a pay claim which was resisted led to an overtime ban which duly led to another national strike in February 1974. The prime minister, Edward Heath went to the country asking the rhetorical question "Who governs Britain"? He was defeated and the ensuing Labour Government settled with the miners on extremely favourable terms.

One of the capital schemes in the plan for coal was the Mardy Colliery project announced in February 1949 by the South Western Divisional Coal Board. It proposed to develop an area which had lain fallow since the German occupation of France in 1940 had badly affected the coal export trade from south Wales, resulting in the closure of the Mardy pits.

The district, which was scheduled for development at a cost of £4m, contained the only reserves of coal remaining in the upper Rhondda Fach district. It was proposed to reopen the Mardy pits and connect them by underground roadways to Bwllfa No 1 colliery in the upper part of the Dare Valley. Both the Mardy and Bwllfa pits would be rebuilt, and the former would be the outlet for coal and spoil, as well as the means of access for most of the workmen. Bwllfa would be used for ventilation and for access for the miners living in the Aberdare area. On the completion of the project Bwllfa No 2 and Ferndale pits would close and the workmen transferred to the new project. Full output was expected to be reached by the mid fifties when 2,800 miners would be producing 4,000 tons a day. The district was said to contain reserves of 100m tons of coal which would be worked from up to 12 seams. Construction of the project took place in 1951-52 but it seems that the Mardy scheme did not become as successful as had been hoped and the result was that the Mardy complex was connected eventually with the "Tower" workings, nor was there much of an improvement when the Fernhill workings in the Rhondda fach became part of the overall scheme.in about 1969. The reason for the disappointing outcome was unfavourable geological conditions.

On the 12th of April 1962 there occurred the worst accident ever to have taken place in the long history of the Tower Colliery. At 10.30 a.m. an explosion ripped through the panel G district from the N2 Development heading in the 9 foot seam. The force of the blast and flame ripped down roof supports in the vicinity of the explosion, but there was no fall of roof. Nine Tower men died that day,

It was in the sixties that there occurred the worst accident ever experienced at Tower Colliery. On the 12th of April 1962 an explosion took place at 10.30 am which claimed nine lives. This was not the worst colliery accident to affect the western end of the district, for an explosion at Rhigos Colliery on the 10th of July 1941 took the lives of sixteen men. This photo shows the interment of some of the victims of the April explosion at Bryn y Gaer Cemetery (off the road from Hirwaun to Penderyn).

Doug Williams

This was the scene at Bwllfa on the completion of the link-up with Mardy colliery. The New Pit winder (left) has been allowed to remain but the Old Pit winder (left, off picture) has been demolished. Nearly everything else on the site had been erased. A concrete headframe has been made over the shaft of the new pit and the building nearest the camera contains the compressor and miscellaneous equipment such as the methane monitoring apparatus. The further end of the building contains the winding engine and fan.

The late Glyn Davies

and eleven others were injured, some badly. The reasons for the explosion were, firstly, a ventilation fan had to be switched off in order to extend a power cable further into the heading. This was normal practice for that time. (The fan that was stopped was on the same power feed as the remainder of the mining machinery).

The new cable was found to be twisted and damaged near one end and power had arced across the cores when the current was once more switched on (Apparently it had been dragged to the heading by a horse). The build-up of fire-damp in the heading was obviously reaching "explosibility" percentage (9.5%) in the general body of the still air when power was resumed and the cable blew. With every explosion that occurs, something is learned. From this explosion a new regulation came into being which ensured that electrical power to a fan switch must be entirely independent and not be in the same field system for machinery, etc.

Among the hazards of mining mentioned in Chapter 7 is flooding of the mine. In about 1974 an inrush of water from opencast workings adjacent to Tower No 4 occurred. The water ran into old workings near Tower No 4 Pit Shaft. This exacerbated the pumping problems at Tower, causing problems which remain to this day.

Another inundation of the nine foot seam took place in June 1982 from old workings of the Rhigos colliery which were beside and above the Northern part of the lease area. The water entered the N.17 gate road and resulted in the loss to Tower of future nine foot seam reserves. Fortunately, neither of these incidents caused death or injury.

The ground formerly occupied by the Middle Duffryn Power Station was afterwards taken over by the Phurnacite plant and this coal blender was built on the site.
The late Glyn Davies

This is the image which most people keep in their minds when the Phurnacite Plant is mentioned.
The late Glyn Davies

Further developments included the underground linking up of Abercynon and Lady Windsor collieries and this photo shows the scene when the break-through was made.

NMGW

With accelerating pit closures the scene in this photo became more common. A glance at the uprights of the headframe shows that we are watching the filling-in of the Deep Duffryn shaft,

- The late Glyn Davies

189

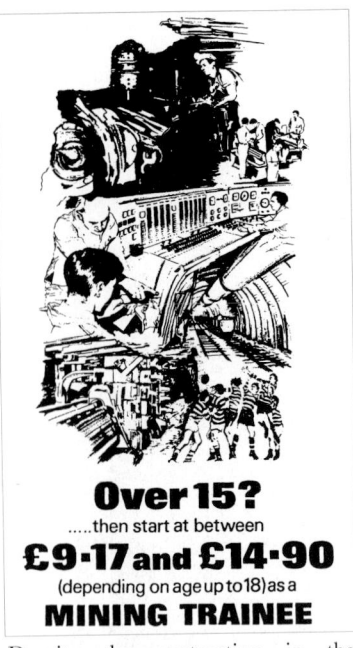

Over 15?
.....then start at between
£9·17 and £14·90
(depending on age up to 18) as a
MINING TRAINEE

Despite the contraction in the industry, the NCB were still trying to attract youths into mining as this 1971 advertisement shows.　　Bryn Davies

The two potent symbols of the traditional method of coal mining are the steel headframes over the pit and the massive spoil heaps consisting of the mudstone and siltstone which has to be worked away before the miner can get at his coal. In 1964 the Civic Trust published the findings arising from a study which it had made of derelict lands in this country. Among other things it stated that the presence of industrial dereliction engendered a "derelict land mentality . . . which bred a brutish insensibility, bordering on positive antagonism, to the life and loveliness of the natural landscape it has supplanted. It debases as well as disgraces our civilisation". In 1968 a Welsh Office report stated that in South Wales there were about 17,000 acres of derelict industrial land situated at more than 1,300 separate sites, and that, pro rata, less reclamation had been done in Wales than in England. In that year derelict land in the Aberdare urban district amounted to some 850 acres at 22 sites, of which the largest was the Bwllfa Dare complex of tips comprising, with its adjacent land, 284 acres.

Following discussions with the County Council, various Government departments, the Coal Board and other bodies the Cynon Valley Borough Council pioneered a scheme to turn the floor of a large part of the Dare Valley into a Country Park. Reclamation work started in May 1971 and the park was opened on the 5th of December 1973.

The park was: 1. The first to be recommended for approval by the Countryside commission; 2. The first to be established by a District council; and 3. The first to be created largely on reclaimed derelict land.

With ever greater standards of health and safety being imposed, many of the pit shafts which had been filled in years before were revisited, topped up where necessary, and new capping provided. Very often they were then surmounted by a concrete marker.
　　　　　　　　　　　　　　　　　　　　　　　　　　　　　John F. Mear

190

An example of the correct method of scraping out the coal dust from a bore-hole using a metal scraper. This clears the hole of fine coal dust which could otherwise be liable to burn or even explode during shot-firing. In the background can be seen part of the rammer with which the shotfirer will insert the explosive and detonator and then "stem" the hole with an inert material.

Harry Rogers

191

In November 1974 the enormous tip created by the Abercwmboi Colliery was gradually being levelled out, bringing to view the Phurnacite plant behind it. The colliery closed in 1923.   The late Glyn Davies

Following the implementation of the Beeching Report the passenger service between Pontypool and Neath was terminated on the 15th of June 1964. With indecent haste the work to single the High Level line (above) began the very next morning together with the severance of the track at Cressely Crossing, Mountain Ash. However the link at Aberdare between the High and Low level lines remained in place and so the trains of coal from Tower Colliery and from the Robertstown opencast loading plant, and limestone trains from the Penderyn Quarries were able to cross to the Low level line at Aberdare which remained in working order, though the passenger service had ceased in the previous March.   The late Glyn Davies

Furthermore, the very substantial improvement to the area's environment was recognised by a Prince of Wales award in 1972. Since its opening the park has been improved by the construction of an interpretation centre, administrative offices and catering and residential facilities.

The Aman Valley was also an example of heavy industrial dereliction and the intention here was to rejuvenate the area and use it for house-building. So far the Upper Cwmneol and Bedwlwyn tips have been removed and the former Fforchaman Colliery site and associated waste tips have been cleared and levelled. Coal recovery operations at the Cwmaman, Blaenaman Fawr and Fforchwen tips have expedited the clearance and land-shaping of those sites.

The course of industrial relations between the Coalmasters and their successor, the National Coal Board and the National Union of Mineworkers has always been a stormy one and space will not allow a blow-by-blow account of the confrontations in the turbulent 1970's and 1980's. We will therefore confine our remarks to the local effects of the 1984 strike and its consequences.

In March 1984 there began the strike in the nation's coal industry which was probably the most costly in British industrial history. One estimate of the cost came to £3.25 billion and this did not include the estimated loss to each miner of £9000 and the loss arising from the 38 working faces out of a total of 490 which did not reopen. The leader of the NUM, Arthur Scargill, called on all members of the union to withhold their labour. In the resulting pit-head ballots only ten of the twenty-eight mines in South Wales voted to comply with the request. Nevertheless the strike went ahead. Many weary and impoverished months later the men marched back to their mine, defeated but not dismayed. But in the eighteen months since the strike ended twelve of the pits of the South Wales coalfield had closed including Mardy, and, as Dr John Davies has remarked, at the end of the 1980's there were more Welshmen working in banks than in pits. The strike was stated above to have been the most expensive in British industrial history. Certainly it was one of the most important if only because the number of pit closures which occurred after the strike caused a decrease in the number employed in the mines which permanently/diminished the the status and power of the union.

Moving now to more recent times and to two Tower pitmen who are riding on the roof of the moving cage as they inspect the sides of the pit. Peter May and Keith Garland are connected by a light chain to the massive "Bridle Chains" which secure the cage to the pit-rope.

Malcolm Howells

Many readers will be surprised by the spacious nature of the main roads underground and the standard of illumination in the Tower Colliery. This is No 4 conveyor belt looking inbye.

A picture that needs no caption!

The late Glyn Davies

In 1992 the last round of pit closures began and by April 1994 Tower was conspicuous for being the last deep mine in South Wales and, though allegedly profitable, the necessary steps were being taken to close it down.

A public campaign began for the purpose of reversing the decision to close the pit, which succeeded in its purpose. However, British Coal hung on to their intention and the pit finally closed on the 23rd of April 1994.

The actions which then followed to prepare and put into being a workers' buy-out caught the attention and, indeed, the approval of people of all political persuasions up and down the country. Apart from valuable support from the Local Authority and the Wales Co-operative Centre, enormous public backing was received from all those who had benefited from Tower's solidarity in the past. But most significantly, £2 million was raised by the 239 miners who had pledged £8,000 each from their redundancy payments. On the 23rd of December 1994 ownership of the colliery passed into the hands of Goitre Tower Anthracite Ltd. On the 2nd of January 1995 the Tower miners marched back to their pit and took possession of it.

The mine is owned by the above-mentioned company the shares of which are owned by the company's employees equally. There are no other shareholders. The workforce are all highly trained and experienced in their duties, and most of them are doing the jobs they were doing previously under British Coal. The present working coalface is 600 metres below ground and 3 miles from pit bottom and from this the colliery produces 500,000 tons of Anthracite a year, 75% of which is sold to Aberthaw Power Station. Two new faces are in preparation for mining reserves when the need arises. 290 persons are directly employed and a further 85 are employed by contractors underground and on the surface.

The surface buildings and spoil heaps associated with Tower No 3 (the New Drift) are on the lower slopes of Twyn Canwyllyr, which overlooks a large tract of Hirwaun Common, where the coal and ironstone for the Hirwaun ironworks was mined from the middle of the eighteenth century. We hope that for many many years it will be possible for the local history experts of the day to say to visitors "This is the site of the earliest of the systematic coal workings of the Cynon Valley and as you see, coal is still being mined there today."

A final contribution from the Rev John Griffith, who sent the following letter to "The Times" castigating them for an article they had printed which had referred to the mineworkers as "pine-eating and champagne-drinking brutes":

"I have lived among them for nearly 50 years and I know what their earnings are on average as well as that of any master that employed men. I know that earnings of some of them have been great. But, then, have they not earned them? Were they not fully entitled to their earnings? Do they not risk life and limb for them? Do they not descend into the earth every day of their lives leaving wife and children behind, and no man can say whether they shall ever again see them? Have we not seen men killed by the scores and even hundreds at one swoop? Do not the annual returns of her Majesty's Inspectors of Mines show that men are so killed every day of the year, of whom the public know nothing? When a great explosion happens, and scores and hundreds are hurled into eternity at once, all England hears and shakes and pities. But the number killed annually as individuals nobody hears of, nobody cares for, nobody pities. And yet this number so killed, one by one, far exceeds the number killed wholesale. But these leave behind widows and orphans like the rest. Now sir, I ask when a trade is attended with so much risk as this, ought the men who labour in it to be well paid, especially when those who profit by their labour accumulate fortunes that are almost fabulous, except to those who have ears to hear and eyes to see, what is passing around them? It does, therefore, make my blood boil to hear men spoken of as "Pine-eating and Champagne-drinking brutes" when I know the facts are quite the other way, to take the average all round. Of course, I admit that they earn much in good times ; that they spend good what they ought not to spend, in rioting and drunkenness; and let me ask you sir, who has told them of this more pointedly than I have, as Vicar of Aberdare in the past and Rector of Merthyr in the present?

195

A mystery picture! This picture post card was presumably sold in the Aberdare area and is entitled "Tower Colliery, Hirwain". Many persons learned in local history have scratched their heads over this picture, the problem being that it is not the Tower Colliery! It appears to show a new headframe and winder under construction on a site previously used for a purpose which cannot be deduced from the ruins on the left. In addition there are short rows of houses in the background and these do not fit in with the landscape near the Tower. The History Society would like to know which pit this was.

REMINISCENCES

The sound, in streets near collieries, of the tramping feet of colliers coming off shift at mid-day or at night. Each man with a block of wood under his arm. (Free coal and firewood were part of the wages).

The unremitting toil of the collier's wife, blackleading fire-grates, shining brasses, the wash-tub (twbin golchi), scrubbing boards, hand operated mangles (sometimes) smoothing irons, heated in sequence before a coal fire, mounds of ironing, the bath tub ready before the kitchen fire or in the scullery, in preparation hopefully, for the returning uninjured collier.

Loads of coal deposited in the streets outside houses or in back lanes, the coal carried into the coal shed (coal cwtch) and neatly stored.

Huge public funerals, hundreds of men in mourning, often with bowler hats, walking behind a horse-drawn hearse. Magnificent hymn singing at the graveside, no hymn sheets, the words well known.

A proliferation of allotment gardens. Quite large plots, well kept, giving self-sufficiency in potatoes and other vegetables. Horse manure readily available and cheap.

Buses, usually double deckers, carrying miners to outlying collieries The Aberdare Council Transport Dept provided a service to Aberpergwm and Empire Collieries (Cwmgwrach) for over 31 years. At one time there were enough workmen to fill six double deckers and one saloon bus, but numbers decreased and the Council service ceased in 1959.

Early morning hooters, sounding from pit-heads, the first at 5a.m., rousing colliers for the morning shift.

Widespread unemployment in the 1920's and 1930's with much hardship.

Appendix A

Table of Mines
(The Davies/Godsall list)

Preliminary Notes

1. In the Davies/Godsall list which follows, over 300 mines in the Cynon Valley—large and small, successful and abortive, are recorded in alphabetical order, and numbered for easy reference. The list therefore acts as an index of the many mines which used to exist in the Valley, and accordingly the mines themselves are not included in the general index at the end of the book.

2. Where more than one name is found in the first column (column A), this indicates that there were more than one pit or colliery under the same ownership in that locality. However, names in square brackets are alternative names for the preceding headword, e.g. [Nici-Naci] for Treaman. Where it can be ascertained, the National Grid Reference of each site is given in column B.

3. Abbreviations used in the table are:

NCB	=	National Coal Board
CC	=	Coal Company
SCC	=	Steam Coal Company
PD	=	Powell Duffryn
WAC	=	Welsh Associated Collieries
PDACC	=	Powell Duffryn Associated Collieries
PDSCC	=	Powell Duffryn Steam Coal Company

4. The letter W against a date in one of the date columns D (opening date) or F (closing date) means that although the date of opening or closing (as the case may be) is not known, the colliery was known to be working at some time during the year in the column. The hash sign (#) followed by a number directs the reader to the note bearing that number in Appendix B.

5. The shaft details column shows firstly the number of shafts and/or levels, and then information about the type of ventilation and winding arrangements. The depth and function of shafts are noted.

6. Proprietors are shown in chronological order, with information about disputed ownership, lease reversions and temporary closures.

7. The "seams" column (column H) shows the seams worked. Where these are denominated by the thickness of the seam, they are shown in imperial measurements as, for instance, 4′ (four foot seam), or 2′9″ (two foot nine seam).

8. The general information column (column I) lists the colliery's products and notes explosions and other disasters with information about numbers of deaths and injuries. Any other significant facts are also noted.

9. Finally, the compilers of this book apologise for certain minor errors which have crept into the Table of Mines when the book was almost ready for the printer and when the cost of rectifying the mistakes was punitive. The entry relating to the trial level at Ynysybwl should have been placed at the end of the list and not at the beginning. Furthermore some slight puzzlement may have been caused by the omission of the number 43 in the list and of the letter 'E' in the heading. As no loss of information has been caused by the errors, it has been decided to let the errors stand.

	A	B	C	D	E	F	G	H	I
	Colliery Name	Location	Shaft Details	Date Opened		Date Closed	Proprietor	Seams	General Information
1	A Trial Level. (Ynysybwl)	Above & behind 'Crawshay Street', Ynysybwl.		By 1893. #121.				Darren Ddu, also called 'Cefn Glas'	The seam worked ended at the Llanwonno fault. Section of seam in Ynysybwl area as follows; Top coal (inc. shale) - 4" Middle coal - 22" 'Holing' shale - 6 to 8" Bottom coal - 8"
2									
3	Abercwmboi Clay Levels.	Abercwmboi (near Graig Street). SO 022001.	3 Levels, air pit 117'. 2 Levels opened by 1891. Furnace ventilation, at this time.	1882 W #19 (Vol. 1)		1940's #20	PDSCC Ltd. #21 (p.29) From 1935, PDACC. #1 (29.06.1935)	2'9" & fireclay.	Products: 1. coking coal, 2. manufacturing (clay for pipeworks). 19/11/1903 - 3 men killed by roof fall. Levels were closed and reopened 3 times. 73 men employed in 1914. Clay Levels were part of Aberaman Colliery complex.
4	Aberaman Colliery & Blackband Pit.	Aberaman. SO 016004. SO 015002.	Total 5 shafts. 710' to Lower 4' seam. Blackband Iron vein 255'. Furnace ventilation initially, and water-balance winding. Main downcast shaft was oval in section (16'x10'). By 1891, Waddle fan (40' diameter). Upcast shaft 10' diameter.	1845 #7 (p.67)		1962 #24 (p.510)	Crawshay Bailey. #25 (p.131) From 1866. PDSCC Ltd. #21 (p.7) From 1935, PDACC Ltd. #27 From 1947, NCB. #26	4', 6', 9', Bute, Yard, 7 & Gellideg seams.	Products : ironstone, coking coal, and steam coal. Blackband shafts opened in 1840 by David Williams. 06/1848, 11 killed in Blackband Pit explosion 14/03/1858, 2 killed. 25/06/1872, 1 killed (16 years old). Total killed in explosions 1848-1881, 18 men and 1 boy. 1900, linked below ground to 6 other Powell Duffryn Collieries. 1905, first mechanical conveyor in South Wales. First Mines Rescue Station in South Wales (1909). 1949, NCB Training Centre, No.4 Area. No.4 Area HQ by 1950's. 1,215 men employed in 1918. In 1955, output was 143,873 tons.

	A	B	C	D	F	G	H	I
5	Abercwmboi Colliery. [Cap Coch Colliery].	Abercwmboi. ST 030096.	2 shafts, 1027 to Gellideg seam. Furnace ventilation in 1869. Waddle fan in 1891 (40' diameter).	1851 #28	1923 #19 (Vol. 1)	David Davis #28 (D.D.). 1866, David Davis & Sons. #29 (p.23). From 1881, PDSCC Ltd. #21 (p.7).	No.2 Rhondda, 29", 4', 6', 9', Yard, 7. Graig seam worked in 1914.	Products : steam coal and house-coal later. Explosions - 24/12/1866 - 3 killed. 15/10/1870 - 5 killed. In 1864, 9-week strike of Doorboys. Coal later worked from Aberaman Colliery. Pumping Pit until 1970. Produced 90,410 tons in 1869.
6	Abercynon Colliery. [Dowlais New Pit]. [Dowlais-Cardiff Colliery].	Abercynon ST 082946.	2 shafts North Pit 2220' to 9' seam, South Pit 2259'. Shafts 20' diameter, ventilated by Schiele fan (21' diameter). Water problems during sinking, completed by1906. Speed of cage-wind 50' per second.	1889 #30 (p.96).	1988 #31 (p.5).	Dowlais Iron Steel & CC. #31 (p.5). From 1903, GKN. #31 (p.5). From 1931, WAC. #31 (p.5). From 1935, PDACC Ltd. #31 (p.5). From 1947, NCB. #32.	Upper 4', 6', 5', 9', Bute seam.	Product: steam coal. Total of 18 men killed during shafts sinking; of these, 7 men killed in shaft fall in 1893. Haulage accident on 05/05/1906, 5 men killed. Linked below ground to Lady Windsor Colliery, Ynysybwl in 1973. 'Skip Winding' introduced in 1971 (10 ton Lift). In 1914, 200 horses working, 2,561 men employed. In 1984, 500 men employed. Output in 1913 was nearly 500,000 tons.
7	Aberdare Graig Colliery.							See Blaengwawr Level. Title also used for Graig Colliery.
8	Aberdare Level. [Horseway Level].	Gadlys, adjacent to Robertstown Bridge. SN 000032.	Level in 6' seam. Airshaft in Aberdare Park.	1868 W #33		Hirwaun Iron Company. #34. Later, probably, PDSCC Ltd. #35	6' seam.	Product unknown, probably steam coal. Connected to Park Pit in 6' seam. Later, a horseway and watercourse.
9	Aberdare Navigation Colliery. [Rhydywaun Colliery].	Hirwaun Common. SN 972044, SN 975049.	1 Drift and upcast shaft 120', and Rhydywaun Level 1861 W.	1850 W #19	1892 #36 (p.17)	In 1850 Rhydywaun Coal Company #36 (p.17). From 1875 Rhydywaun Brick & Coal Company Ltd. #37 From 1878, Bute Estates. #36	Yard, 7, Gellideg.	Steam coal and fireclay. Outputs: in 1864, 630 tons. In 1869, 4,098 tons. Furnace ventilated, with naked lights in use in 1891.
10	Aberdare-Merthyr (Steam Coal) Colliery, Hirwaun.							See- Hirwaun-Aberdare Colliery.

	A	B	C	D	F	G	H	I
11	Abergorchi Drift. (Abernant).	Abernant (West of Blaennant Colliery) SO 021046.	Level with upcast shaft 63' deep. Furnace ventilation in 1891. (5,220 cu.ft./min)	1870 W #38	By 1921.	From 1870 Aberdare Iron Company. #3 (08/04/1915). From 1875 Aberdare & Plymouth CC. #3 (08/04/1915). From 1882, James Lewis. (Aberdare Works and Colliery Co.) #118. From 1911 PDSCC Ltd. (not worked). #3 (08/04/1915).	Abergorchi seam (Graig seam).	Product : house-coal. The 1903 output was 20,526 tons. Naked flame lamps were in use in 1891. The drift closed for some time in 1905. 'Stall' system of mining was worked in the drift.
12	Abergorki Colliery. [Gorllwyn Pit].	Mountain Ash ST 053987.	1 shaft 621' in depth. Connected to upcast shaft by 1956 (Upper Forest Level).	1919 #26	1968 #24 (p.510)	In 1919, Nixon Navigation CC Ltd. #1 (29/01/1929). From 1929, Llewellyn Nixon Ltd. #1 (11/05/1929). By 1936, PDACC. #1 (01/02/1930). From 1947, NCB. #26.	Gorllwyn. (washed peas, nuts & small).	Product : steam coal and house-coal. 389 employed in 1954. B.R. Edwards was Manager in 1928. 1954 output - 98,154 tons.
13	Abergwawr Colliery. [Plough Pit]. [Powell's Pit].	Aberaman. SO 014014.	5 shafts, 528' to 7' seam. Furnace ventilation and water-balance winding initially.	1849 #4 (09/06/1849).	1875 #29 (p.22)	1849, Tom Powell & Protheroe. #40 (No.52). From 1864, PDSCC Ltd. #40 From 1865 to 1870, ownership in dispute (Law suit). From 1870, Powell Bros. #40. From 1873, PDSCC. #40.	29', 4', 6', 9', No.2 Yard, 7.	Product: steam coal. In 1872, boy of 12 killed by a roof fall, on his first day at work. North Shaft later became upcast for Aberaman Colliery. In 1869 a surface boiler explosion killed 4 men.
14	Abernant Clay Level.	Abernant area.	Level, furnace ventilated, producing 2,000 cu.ft./min.	1891 W #30 (Item 69)		In 1891, James Lewis (Aberdare and Works Colliery Co.). #30 (Item 69).	29' & fireclay.	Product: steam coal & fireclay. Naked flame lighting in 1891. It is possible that this level is 'Patch Level', by another name.
15	Abernant Colliery.							See- No. 9 Colliery.
16	Abernant y Groes Colliery. [Cwmbach No.1]. [Cwmbach Colliery].	Cwmbach SO 024019.	3 shafts and 1 horseway drift. Furnace ventilation and water-balance winding. Pit bottom in 9' seam at 489'.	1837 #7 (p.67)	1896 #22	In 1837, T. & M. Wayne & Co. (Aberdare Coal Company). #15 (Map). By 1863, Messrs. T. Powell & Son. #2 18/04/1863. By 1869, PDSCC Ltd. #21 (p.10). By 1895, James Lewis. #2 (22/06/1895).	4', 29', 6', 9', Bute, Yard, 7.	Product: steam coal. First deep pit sunk in Cynon Valley for the sale of coal. Colliery abandoned in 1896. Coal reserves then worked from Llettysiencyn Colliery. Abernant y Groes Colliery triggered the Steam Coal Era in South Wales, and shipped coal to London in 1838. 10 fatalities in 6 separate explosions from 1852 to 1881, including a boy of 11 years in 1855. Produced 94,691 tons in 1869.

	A	B	C	D	F	G	H	I
17	Abernant y Groes Level. [Coronation Level].	Cwmbach SO 028019.	Level.	1952 #41	1955 #41	D. Leonard & Co. #42 (09/06/1952).	Graig.	Product: house-coal. Licensed Private Mine. This level struck old workings with wooden rails, and a wooden tram being found.
18	Bedwlwyn Colliery. [Gwdi-Hw Level].	Cwmaman ST 008988.	2 levels and airshafts. Furnace ventilation.	1865 #43 (p.10)	1901 #22 (Vol IV)	From 1865, James Kenway & Sons, #44, later Bedwlwyn Coal Co. #43 (p.11). From 1892, Cwmaman Coal Co. Ltd. #43 (p.11).	No. 2 Rhondda.	Product: house-coal and coking coal. Colliery abandoned 3 times:- 03/06/1865, 19/01/1892, and 30/03/1901. J. Kenway also worked a local quarry and coke works. Produced 10,203 tons in 1869.
19	Bevan's Level.							See- Bryngwyn Levels.
20	Bevan's Pit.							See- Fforchneol Colliery.
21	Black Grove Level.	Ynysybwl (Clydach Valley).	A level with a downcast airshaft (16' Dia.) 99ft. in depth, producing 3,900 c.f.m.	W. 1888. #61	Abandoned 1894. #61		Darren Ddu seam. In (This seam crops in the local cemetery.)	Product: Housecoal, coking coal, & manufacturing. 1888 A Mr.Rhys Roderick was the manager, with 21 men underground.
22	Blaengwawr Colliery.	Blaengwawr SO 006020.	Total of 9 shafts (including 4 airshafts). Furnace ventilation and water-balance winding initially. Pit bottom in 7 seam at 483'.	1843 #28 (D.D.)	1926 W #8	David Davis 1843-1866 #28 (D.D.). David Davis & Sons, 1866-1885 #28 (D.D.). Closed from 1885 to 1914 #26. From 1914, PDSCC Ltd. (Production by 1917). #39.	4, 6, 9, Bute, 7 and Gellideg.	Product : steam coal. The colliery was used as a 'Satellite' pit for Aberaman Colliery and Gadlys Pit later. Explosion on 06/03/1861, 13 killed; naked flame lamps were in use at this time. 4 other explosions from 1845 to 1866 - total deaths 5. A boy, 10 years old, was killed by a roof fall in 1864. Produced 56,157 tons in 1869. A Mr. Morgan Jones, collier, was killed at the pit in Oct. 1860. His was the first burial in the cemetery at Aberdare.

	A	B	C	D	F	G	H	I
23	Blaengwawr Levels.	Blaengwawr (Maesyffynon Lane) SO 005019, SO 002019.	2 Levels.	1903 W #1 (15/08/1903)	1935 #10 (p.105)	In 1903, owned by Aberdare Graig CC Ltd. #46 (1911). From 1916, D.R. Llewellyn & Sons. In 1930, WAC Ltd. #1 (01/12/1930). 1935, PDACC Ltd., who closed it. #10 (p.105).	Graig and No.2 Rhondda.	13 men were employed in 1911. Explosions:-31/12/1914, 1 man killed; 19/01/1925, 3 men killed and 3 men burned (naked flame lamps in use at the time). Produced house-coal, washed small coal, nuts & beans (industrial use).
24	Blaenhirwaun Drifts.	Hirwaun SN 935050.	Two Levels.	1870 W #36 (Map 9)	1913 #36 (p.21)	Initially, M. of Bute, (Duffryn Aberdare Coal Co.) #36 (p.21). D.R.Llewellyn & Sons acquired the mine in 1913 and closed it. #36 (p.21).	Gorllwyn and Graig.	Workings connected to Tower Colliery (No.1 Drift). Produced house-coal and steam coal.
25	Blaennant Colliery. [Old Balance Pit].	Abernant SO 021045.	2 shafts. 722' to Gellideg Seam. Furnace ventilation and water-balance winding initially.	1840s #17 (p.54).	1927 #1 (06/08/1927)	Aberdare Iron Company (Bankrupt in 1875) #25 (p.130). From 1875, Aberdare and Plymouth Co. #3 (08/04/1915). From 1882, James Lewis. (Aberdare Works and Colliery Co.) #3 (08/04/1915). From 1899, Bute Estates #3 (08/04/1915). From 1915, PDSCC Ltd. #1 (06/08/1927).	Graig, 29", No.1 Yard, 4', 6', 7, 9', Bute, 9', Gellideg.	Product: steam coal. Manpower in 1911 was 511; in 1915, 200 men. Outputs :- 1906 - 90,712 tons. 1924 - 65,669 tons. From 1870 to 1896, there were 3 explosions with a total of 3 miners killed.
26	Blaennant-y-Groes Pit.							See- Cwmbach New Pit.
27	Blaennant-y-Groes level							See- Lefel Francis Phillips
28	Brickyard Level (part of the Bwllfa complex).	Cwmdare (Near Reservoir). Within Nantmelin Take.	Level.	1888 #47(p.65)	1928 W #46 (1928).	From 1888, Bwllfa & Merthyr Dare SC Co. Ltd. #47 (p.72). Lineage of ownership as in Bwllfa No.1 Colliery up to 1928. #47 (p.72).	Gorllwyn (abandoned Sept. 1914). An unknown seam was worked from 1914 to 1918.	Product: steam coal. 72 men employed in 1912. The Manager at this time was Edward Pugh.
29	Brithdir Level.							See- St. Gwynno Level.
30	British Rhondda Colliery.							See- Rhigos Colliery.
31	Brogden's Graig Colliery.							See- Hirwaun Common Colliery
32	Brook Level (No. 1) [OldAbernant. Level].	[Old]Abernant. SO 018030.	2 Levels.		1882 #38	Aberdare Iron Company (Bankrupt in 1875). #3 (08/04/1914). From 1875, Aberdare and Plymouth Co #3 (08/04/1914). From 1882, James Lewis. (Aberdare Works & Collieries Co. Ltd.) #3 (08/04/1914).	4', 6, 9'. These seams were abandoned in 1870.	Product: steam coal. The colliery was linked below ground and used as a horseway to Blaennant Colliery. (Probably No.2 Brook Level.)

	A	B	C	D	F	G	H	I
33	Brown's Pit.							See- Fforchaman Colliery.
34	Bryn Defaid Collieries. [Bryn David], [Bryn Level].	Llwydcoed. SO 002059, plus other locations in the same area.	Levels, airshafts and 'patches'.	1738 W #48 [4(612)1]	1870 W #2 (07/06/1870)	In 1738, unknown. In 1770, George Bowser (Ironmaster) #49 (Vol 1 - p.257). By 1870, Aberdare Iron Company. #2 (07/05/1870).		Ironstone and coal were worked by W. Bowser in 1770. Coal at that time would be used for coke production for the smelting of iron. First recorded fatal accident (known) in a Cynon Valley mine; a Daniel Simon was killed by a roof fall in 1738.
35	Bryngwyn Colliery (Old).	Hirwaun Common. SN 976045.	1 shaft & 1 level 60' to 4' seam. Furnace ventilation.	1775 W. #50 (p.13)	1861 #36 (Map 8.).	Accredited to Hirwaun Ironworks Co., with subsequent owners. #50 (p.13).	(Iron) Knobby, Blue & Rosser veins. (Coal) Graig, 4', Gorllwyn.	Produced ironstone and coking coal, and steam coal later.
36	Bryngwyn Levels (Upper). [London & Merthyr Colliery], [Cefn Merthyr Colliery], [Forest Level].	280 yards to north-west of Lower Drift.	New level into 2'9" seam in 1866.	1866 #2 (20/05/1866)	1883 #2 (12/04/1883)	See Bryngwyn Lower Level. (From 1866).	See Bryngwyn Lower Level.	See- Bryngwyn Lower Level. Mr. H. Kirkhouse was agent for Bryngwyn (then called London & Merthyr Colliery) in 1870.
37	Bryngwyn Levels (Lower). [Kirkhouse Drift], [Bevan's], [Rosser Drift].	Hirwaun Common. SN 973042, near Ty-Rhos.	2 drifts initially, with an upcast shaft. (60' to 4' seam). Furnace ventilation.	1840's W #36 (Map 6)	1883 #2 (12/04/1883) (advert. for the sale of the colliery)	F. Crawshay (lease holder before 1860). #2. From 1860, Kirkhouse Bros. #37 (1860). From 1865, Herbert Kirkhouse only. #37 (1865). In 1866, London & Merthyr CC Ltd. #2 (20/05/1866). In 1870, Cefn Merthyr Collieries (Lockett & Judkins). #47 (p.75). In 1872, Bryngwyn Coal Co. (Bwllfa CC Ltd.). #47 p.75. (J. Howakon, Prop.). Reputed also at one stage, D. Bevan (pre-1868).	2'9", Gorllwyn, Upper 4', No.2 Gorllwyn and ironstone veins. Also 4', 6', 9', 7 and No.1 Rhondda.	Product: initially coking coal; steam and house-coal were produced later. A new method of loading coal directly into railway trucks at the new level's mouth was operating in 1866. In 1883 the colliery was advertised for sale. (NB - a J. Howakon, proprietor, was involved 1872 - 73). Explosion in Oct.1863, 3 injured. Inrush of water in March 1870, 200 men were employed at this time.
38	Bryn-y-Gwyddel Levels.	Llwydcoed. SO 006068, near the top of the Dyllas Hill.	2 Levels.	1950 W #18 (No.51)	1965 #41	Bryn-y-Gwyddel Coal Co. (J. & D. Davies). #18.	9' seam.	Licensed Private Mine.

	A	B	C	D	F	G	H	I
39	Bush Level	Near Mtn./Ash, to the south of Graig Cottage. (Upper Miskin)	Level		3/4/1917 #122	Local public house landlord. (Bush Inn.)	No.2 Rhondda seam section 1ft.2ins., with fireclay bottom.	The level was driven into a water adit, and was closed in a short time.
40	Bute Drifts. [Hirwaun Drifts], [Oliver's New Drift].	Hirwaun Common, South of Tirherbert Road. SN 938054.	2 drifts, connected at one stage to Tower Old Drifts in the 9' seam.	1870 W #36 (Map 9)	1930's #51	In 1870, Duffryn Aberdare CC (Bute) #36 (p.16). From 1919, D.R. Llewellyn & L. Guret (Cambrian Coal Combine) #51 (p.221). From 1930, WAC Ltd. #36 (p.23).	6', 9'.	Product: steam coal. The drifts were flooded by an inrush of water in 1930's, presumably from Blaenhirwaun drifts. Became pumping station for Tower Colliery washery until 1983. Finally sealed in 1986. Output in 1903 - 10,022 tons.
41	Bute Level.	Llwydcoed. SO 001057.	Level.	1897 W #53				
42	Bute Pit, [Bute Merthyr, [Abergorki Level], [Gutter Level].	Hirwaun Common. SN 954046.	1 shaft (downcast, 552'). Furnace ventilation and water-balance winding initially. Later, an upcast shaft on hillside to west of Tower No.1. A drainage level also connected to Bute Pit (Gutter Level).	Pre-1850 #36 (Map 8).	1906 #54	In 1850, Hirwaun Ironworks Co. (Crawshay). From 1864 to 1871, Hirwaun Coal & Iron Co. Ltd. (T.C. Hynde). From 1872 to 1882, Aberdare - Rhondda SCC Ltd. #37. Up to 1906, reverted to and worked by Bute Estates (Duffryn Aberdare CC.) #3 (06/08/1919).	4', 7', Abergorki, 9', 6', Upper Yard, Upper 4'. Connected later to Tower Colliery upcast shaft. Iron veins: Black, Rosser, Knobby and Llyfrau up to 1850.	Products: iron ore and coking coal. Later, steam coal. 5 explosions from 1854 to 1882 with 5 deaths. A surface boiler explosion on 27/01/1883 killed one man. In April 1872, a boy of 8 was killed underground on his 3rd day at work. An Overman was fined £10. NB. The Company and works were acquired by Aberdare - Rhondda SCC Ltd. for £50,000 in 1872. The furnace ventilating the pit was at the mouth of 'Pant Level'.
44	Buxton's Level.	Cwmdare. (Windber) SN 970032	Level.	1906 #10 (P.104).		D.R.llewellyn & R. Buxton (Agent and partner). #47 (P.65)		Part of the Windber complex.
45	Bwlch Colliery.	Hirwaun Common. SN 966040.	2 levels.	1900 #46 (1901)	1920's W #56 (p.35)	Humphries & Griffiths. #1 (p.4) 04/12/1909. By 1909, D.R. Llewellyn & R. Buxton. (Formed Bwlch Colliery Company Ltd.). #1 (p.4) 04/12/1909.	No.2 Rhondda.	Products: semi-bituminous house-coal, also washed small coals (steam). The Colliery employed 95 men in 1911, the Manager being Mr. D.L. Jones.

	A	B	C	D	F	G	H	I
46	Bwllfa Dare Colliery & Gorllwyn Drift. (Bwllfa No.1 Colliery) (Bwllfa No.1 Colliery)	Cwmdare SN 971024. The drift was 20 yards West of No.1 shaft.	2 shafts, later a level. Old Pit depth 600'. Sinking commenced 1853. Water-balance winding and furnace ventilation initially. New pit, depth 450', sunk in 1867, ventilated by a Guibal fan. New shaft diameter was 14½' x 10'. The drift was working by 1891, and was later used as an upcast for Bwllfa Dare Colliery. A second drift was driven in 1924.	1853 #47 (p.73)	1938. Finally, 1989 #47 (p.73) The drift closed in 1938	Sam Thomas & Joseph. #47 (p.72). From 1856, S. Thomas & Lewis. From 1857, Ebenezer Lewis. From 1862, Lewis, Lockett, & Marychurch. In 1864, Bwllfa Coll. Co. Ltd. From 1873, J. Brogden & Sons. From 1876: Bwllfa & Merthyr Dare C. Co. Ltd. In 1886, in the hands of trustees. From 1890, Brogden & Budgett. Also in 1890, Bwllfa & Merthyr Dare Steam Colls. Ltd. In 1891, Bwllfa & Merthyr Dare Steam Colls. (1891) Ltd. From 1928, Bwllfa & Cwmaman CC Ltd. From 1930, WAC Ltd. From 1935, PDSCC Ltd. From 1942, PDACC Ltd. In 1947, NCB.#47 (p.72), 1953 to 1989.	Graig, Gorllwyn, 2'9", 4', 6', 9', Bute, New Seam, (Brass vein) Yard, 7' and fireclay. The section of the Gorllwyn seam in the drift was 2' 8".	Product:- mainly dry steam coal (large nuts, peas and duff). Production ceased in 1938. Pit later used for ventilation, transport of men and materials, pumping, etc. until closure. Following nationalisation (1947) Bwllfa No.1. was refurbished, and in 1958 became linked underground with Mardy Colliery. Coal was then raised at Mardy. Disasters:- 3 killed 1878 (naked flame lamps). 5 killed by smoke from shaft fire on 27/12/1867. 5 other miners killed in 5 different explosions 1859-1876. Produced 108,823 tons in 1869. Output by 1921 was 1000 tons per day. Manpower was 1,133 in 1913. Mr. G. Kirkhouse was Manager in 1869, and a Mr. W. Wilmer Manager in 1875. The drift was connected below ground to all the Bwllfa collieries, and indirectly to Gadlys and River Level collieries.
47	Bwllfa No.2 Colliery.							See:- Nantmelin Colliery
48	Bwllfa No.3 Colliery.							See:- Powell's Pit. (3)
49	Bwllfa No.4 Drift.							See:- Nantmelin Drift.
50	Capcoch Colliery.							See:- Abercwmboi Colliery.
51	Carne Park Colliery. [Parc Newydd Colliery].	Abercynon ST 077995 Adjacent to, and to the west of the Taff Vale Railway.	Levels. Plan shows 2 levels, 1 airshaft (45'). 4 abandoned levels nearby. Flue ventilation initially, with naked flame lighting.	1864 W #60 (1864)	Mid 1960s. #41	In 1864, proprietors unknown. In 1873, a Mr. McCullough. #60 (1863). In March 1874, up for sale. #2 (07/03/1874). By 1910, Carne Park Colliery Co. Ltd. #1 (05/08/1911). In 1911, bankrupt, taken over by Receivers. #1 (05/08/1911). By 1914, Carne Park Colliery Co. Ltd. (R.N. Huxtable). #46 (1914). In 1919, Richardson Bros. #61. Later, Jones & Co. Ltd. #61. By 1957, D. Leonard & Partners. #41.	Darren No.2 - 2'6" section of coal.	Product : up to 1874, coking coal for ironworks. Later, house-coal and manufacturing. Level was 90 yards south-west of St. Donat's church, and was capable of producing 40 tons of coal per day in 1874. The colliery was leased from Dr. Nicholl Carne, who was the landowner. The colliery was not nationalised in 1947

	A	B	C	D	F	G	H	I
52	Cast House Level.	Abernant. SO 010634, near River Level Colliery. Shown on Abandoned Mines Plan, NCB, 1970. (Ab. Lib.).	Level in 6' seam, plus an airshaft.	Pre-1830 #26		Abernant Iron Co. in 1870. It is not known whether it survived the collapse of the company in 1875.	6' seam. #38.	Product: by 1870, steam coal. The upcast airshaft, sunk to the 6' seam, was surmounted by a 30' stack.
53	Cefn Cwsg Drift.							See- Lower Duffryn Colliery.
54	Cefn Merthyr Colliery.							See- Bryngwyn Levels.
55	Cefn Pennar Pit.							See- George Pit.
56	Cigarette Pits 1 & 2.	Abernant, SO 016036, near the 'Rhos Wenallt' public house.	2 shafts, one on each side of the old Merthyr road. 60' in depth.	1880s W #62	1900 #8 (p.97)	James Lewis. #8 (pp.96/97). (Aberdare Works & Colliery Co.) By 1900, Bute Estate. #8 (p.97).		The colliery used naked flame lamps, and smoking was allowed, hence the name. Possibly part of the Gwrhyd Colliery complex.
57	Cnapiog Drift.							See- Knobby Drift.
58	Coed Cae Levels.	Abernant. SO 014039.	Levels.	1874 #2 (08/08/1874)			4' seam.	Explosion on 01/08/1874, Fireman and 3 colliers burned. Naked flame lamps in use.
59	Coed-y-Gam Drift.					Probably Abernant Iron Co.		See - Dyllas Collieries.
60	Coronation Drifts.	Hirwaun Common. SN 945043, sited above old Tower Colliery, Old No.1 & 2 Drifts (350 yards).	2 drifts linked below ground to Tower Graig Colliery, which later became the ventilation return drift. One drift marked on plan as 'Gorllwyn Drift'. (Possibly the old Gorllwyn drift)	By 1912 #36 (p.19)	1939 #36 (p.27)	1912, D.R. Llewellyn & Co. Ltd. #29 (p.84). In 1920, D.R. Llewellyn & Sons Ltd. #3 (29/10/1919). From 1930, WAC Ltd. #66. From 1935, PDAssCC Ltd. #66.	Gorllwyn and Graig.	Product: house-coal and manufacturing. In 1932, produced washed peas, beans and small. No.1 drift, from 1958 to the present time (1998) provides piped water to Tower Colliery faces for dust suppression etc. Naked flame lighting in the 1920s. The drifts were excessively wet with 15 pumps in constant use.
61	Coronation Level.							See- Abernant-y-Groes Level
62	Craig-y-Duffryn Levels. [Duffryn House Levels].	Duffryn Estate, Cwmbach, 250 yards above the canal.	A series of small levels 250 into the crop of theseam.	1794 #67 (p.105)	1836 #67 (p.105)	J. Bruce Pryce (father of the first Lord Aberdare). # 4 (25-6-1853).	The seam was between 15" and 22" thick.	Coal for the roasting of oats in 'Duffryn Mill' and the heating of Duffryn House.

	A	B	C	D	F	G	H	I
63	Crichton Drifts.	Cwmbach, 250 yards NE of No.9 Colliery.	2 levels plus an airshaft. (One level was of a previous mine)	1913 #68	1916 #22	Bute Estates. #3 (08/04/1916). From 1915, PDSCC Ltd. #3 (08/04/1916).	No.1 Yard and 4'.	Product: house-coal. Crichton was linked in No.1 Yard seam to Tunnel Colliery workings and also to Werfa Colliery workings. Tunnel Colliery upcast shaft was used for return ventilation. Naked flame lamps used in 1914.
64	Crimea Level.	Cwmbach, est. 100 yards west of Crichton Drift. SO 016026, drift heading North-West.	Level plus an airshaft.	1885 W #69	1885 W #69	Aberdare & Plymouth Co. #3 (08/04/1915). From 1882, James Lewis. (Aberdare Works & Colliery Co.) #3 (08/04/1915).	2'9" and 4'. The 4' cropped just above the level.	Product: steam coal. Linked underground to Windsor Level, Patch Level and No.8 Level in the 2'9" seam.
65	Croesdy Level.	Llwydcoed. SO 001043, near Ysguborwen Colliery, and Croesdy Farm	Level and airshaft (5' dia.). Also 'patch' worked here. Furnace ventilation.	1880 W #70		Due to its proximity, was probably part of the Ysguborwen Colliery complex at one stage.	Seams and veins unknown.	Product: probably ironstone. Earlier, from patches. Layout of levels evident on map (Geo. Survey, England and Wales, 2nd edition, 1901).
66	Cwm Level.	Abernant. SO 015058	1 Level, & an upcast air-shaft. (28' to yard seam, &43' to 6' seam.)	1871.W. #2 (22-4-1871)	1888. #118.	1. Aberdare Iron Co. #3 (8-3-1915). 2. Aberdare Works & Colliery Co. (By 1885) (J.Lewis) #118.	Yard seam, plus a drivage into the 6' seam. The 4' seam AB.1870's.	Product: Steam coal. The seams were dipping to south at 2" / yard.
67	Cwm Level. [Dare Fechan Level].	Gadlys, near Cwm Farm. SN 996024.	Level.		1910 #22	Dare Fechan Coal Co.	Gorllwyn.	Product: house-coal. Sited alongside old tram road of Gadlys Graig Colliery.
68	Cwm Nant-yr-Hwch.	Hirwaun Common, just south-east of Penywaun.	Level or Patch.	1663 #49 (p.257)		Mynyffee and Martin. #49 (p.257).		Product: ironstone for smelting at 'Cae Luce' furnace, Llwydcoed.

#	A	B	C	D	F	G	H	I
69	Cwmaman Colliery, (includes:- Fforchwen Pit, Trewen Pit and Llewellyn Drift). [Shepherd's Pit] Being the original Shaft.	Cwmaman. SS 997995.	Shepherd's Pit 1131' to Gellideg seam, furnace ventilation and water-balance winding initially. Fforchwen sunk later (from 1873 to 1899). Trewern Pit sunk by 1912 (main ventilation shaft for colliery). Llewellyn Drift (No.4) driven in 1918.	1849 #4 (30.11.1849)	1935 #43 (P8)	T. Shepherd & Evans (later owned by H.J. Evans only). #4.(30.11.1849) In 1873, Cwmaman Coal Co. #43. (P7). From 1918, D.R. Llewellyn. #3 (16/01/1918). In 1928, Bwllfa & Cwmaman C.Co. Ltd. #71 (08/05/1928). In 1934, WAC Ltd. #1 (01/07/1930). In 1935, PDAssCC Ltd #1 (29/06/1935).	2'9", 4', 6', Red Vein, 9', Bute, Yard, 7' and Gellideg, Graig and Gorllwyn worked from the drift.	Product: dry steam coal and house-coal from the drift. Explosions:- In 1865, 1 killed. In 1911, 2 killed. In 1932, the colliery's total manpower was 1,870 men & boys. In 1869, produced 74,411 tons. At one time, it had supplied coal for much of the London Underground Railway system, its coal recognised as being of the finest quality.
70	Cwmbach Colliery							See- Abernant-y-Groes Colliery.
71	Cwmbach Little Pit.							See- Pwll Bach Colliery.
72	Cwmbach New Pit. [Pwll Blaennant-y-Groes], [Cwmbach No.2], and Flue Pit.	Cwmbach 'Tunnel' area, 350 yards south of Tunnel Colliery. SO 027021.	3 shafts. Main intake shaft, pit bottom in 7' seam at 498'. Two upcast flue-shafts with furnace ventilation initially.	1860 #26 (sec. 5)	1897#22	In the early 1860s owned by Aberdare Coal Co. (Wayne) #26 (sec.5). By 1870, Messrs. Lewis (James Lewis). #2 (25/06/1870). Aberdare Works & Collieries Co. Ltd. By 1899, it was acquired by PDSCC Ltd, who abandoned it and worked the 'take' from Llettysiencyn Colliery #35.	2'9", 4', 6', 9', Yard, 7' and Bute.	Product: steam coal. The colliery was exporting coal to Cuba in 1866. Naked flame lamps used in 1880, causing explosion with resultant 1 death. Flue pit sunk in 1865 to the east area of the pit to open up reserves of virgin Yard seam. 740 tons of coal produced in 1872.
73	Cwmbach No.1.							See- Abernant-y-Groes Colliery.
74	Cwmcynon Colliery (Nos.1 & 2).	Penrhiwceiber ST 059979.	2 shafts. Main shaft (intake) sunk to 1,523' in the 7' seam.	1889 #2 Sinking Commenced, (06/04/1889)	1949 #24 (App.V)	Nixon Navigation Co. Ltd. #2 (06/04/1899). From 1929, Llewellyn-Nixon Collieries Co. Ltd. (W.M. Llewellyn). #1 (11/05/1929). From 1930, WAC Ltd. #1 (12/01/1929). From 1935, PDACC Ltd. #1 (29/06/1935). In 1947, NCB.	2'9", 4', Yard, 6', 9', No.3 Rhondda, 7', Gellideg. Abergorki seam abandoned in 1901.	Product: steam coal. Manpower in 1911 was 1,392. Below ground link-up with Navigation, Deep Duffryn and Upper Forest Level, the latter used as upcast return level at one stage. The Manager was Mr. Arthur Jenkins from 1915 to 1928.
75	Cwmdare Colliery							See- Powell's Pit (No.3).
76	Cwmdare Colliery.							See- Bwllfa Dare Colliery.

	A	B	C	D	F	G	H	I
77	Cwmdu Uchaf Levels. [Cwmdu Level].	Robertstown, east side of the River Cynon, 180 yards to the west of Park Pit, near Robertstown.	Levels.	1888 W #2 (07/04/1888)	1906 W #1 (22/09/1906)	Unknown. Prior to 1888. In 1888, PDSCC Ltd. #2 (07/04/1888).		Product: unknown. The output for the year 1905/6 was 7,559 tons of large coal, and 3,791 tons of small coal.
78	Cwmneol Colliery. [Morris's Pit], [Lanky Pit].	Cwmaman. ST 007998.	Two shafts: South (No.1) Pit was sunk to the 7' seam in 1848, the 'Lanky' Pit (upcast) in 1850, also sunk to the 7' seam at 1,078'. Water-balance winding up to 1855 and furnace ventilation initially.	1848 #72 (p.38)	1948 #24 (App.4)	Carr & Morrison (United Merthyr C.Co. Ltd.). #72 From 1865, Aman-Aberdare Coal Co. Ltd. #2 (13/05/1865). From 1868, PDSCC Ltd. #72. NCB in 1947, and closed in the following year.#26.	2'9", 4', 6', Red Vein, 9' Bute, 7' and 5'.	Product: steam coal (in 1859 it was sold as 'Carr's Merthyr Coal', and was exported from Cardiff Docks). 350 tons daily were produced at this time. There was a winding disaster on 28/01/1855 when 8 men died in the shaft. Cwmneol was stopped in 1893 and reopened in 1898, working the lower seams. The name 'Morris's' was derived from Martin Morrison, an initial proprietor. The 'Lanky' Pit was so called as its winding system was designed for small 'Lancashire' trams. 56,368 tons produced in 1863.
79	Cwmpennar Pit.							
80	D. Rees Jenkin's Level.	Cwmdare. SN 972034.	Level. #47(p.65).					See- Lower Duffryn. Gorllwyn seam worked.
81	D. Roberts' Level.	Hirwaun Common. 160yds. to the west of Level Fawr.	One level evident on Hirwaun Common plan. #120	Pre-1847. #120.				
82	Daniels' Level.	Above Troedyrhiw Trwyn Farm. SO 0166-9147 (Ynysybwl)				Mr Iago Daniels. #61	Darren Ddu seam. (Known as Darren No.2. in Cynon Valley.)	Products: Housecoal & Coking coal.
83	Dare Fechan Level.							See- Cwm Level.
84	Dare Inn Level.	Cwmdare. SN 981029.	Level.	1920 W #73	1931 W #73	Bwllfa & Merthyr Dare Steam Coal Co. (1891) Ltd. #73.	Driven into the 9' seam.	Its main use later was as a drainage adit for Bwllfa No.4 level in the 9' seam workings.

	A	B	C	D	F	G	H	I
85	Darren Ddu Level.	Near Ynysybwl. SO 0650-9280.	A level & an airshaft, (6' Dia.x 240' deep) furnace ventilated, providing 5,000 c.f.m.	W.1850 #61.	W.1931 #61	David & John Thomas (from Ynysddu). #61. In 1931, owned by "Darren Ddu Colliery Co." #46	Darren Ddu seam.	Products: House coal & steam coal in 1931.Working method, longwall face with naked lighting in 19th. century. Manager in 1875 was Zebediar Beecham, and John Coles in 1891. Ten men employed in 1931.
86	David Williams' Level. [Cwm Wenallt Level].	Abernant, exact location unknown, described as "Near the Balance Pit" (Blaenant Pit?)	Level.	1841 W #5 (29/05/1841)		David Williams. #5. (29.05.1841)	Iron ore vein, adjacent to coal seam.	An ironstone mine. On May 23rd, 1841, an explosion occurred, seriously burning 9 miners, 2 of whom were boys. Several of these were not expected to live. Naked lighting in use at the time. Product: Steam Coal and ironstone.
87	Ddu Allt Level.	Near Ynysybwl		W.1922 #61				
88	De Winton Colliery. [Park Little], [Pwll Spite].	Abernant, below and to the west of Aberdare Hospital gates. SO 005029.	Two shafts. Wooden headgear on main shaft. 225' to Yard seam. The upcast pit was the South shaft.	By 1899 #2 (07/10/1899)	1903 #1 (07/03/1903)	1899, James Lewis. #1 (07/03/1903). (Aberdare Works & Colliery Co.) Reverted to M. of Bute later. In 1915, acquired by PDSCC Ltd., who did not work it. #35.(J.Lewis dead by 1901, worked by executors until closure).	4', 6', 9', Bute and Yard No.3. Bute and 9' abandoned in 1901. (9' plan shows pillar & stall system, Bute seam shows longwall method).	105 employed in 1900; women were employed on the surface. The manager was Mr. Paul Williams M.E. A working plan shows a connecting heading in the Bute seam into No.9 colliery, Cwmbach. The 'take' of DeWinton lease was small, so an area was sub-leased in the Bute seam from the Wayne's Merthyr Colliery.(Gadlys). (Beneath 'Maes-Y-Dre'), Aberdare.

	A	B	C	D	F	G	H	I
89	Deep Duffryn Colliery.	Mountain Ash. ST 045994.	Two shafts:- Shaft 1 - 16' dia by 1891, 1,167 to 7' seam. Water-balance winding initially with wooden headgear until 1869. Shaft 2 - 8'6" dia (upcast) furnace ventilation up to 1869. Nixon's Patent Ventilator used by 1888. No.1 shaft was deepened in 1924, and again in 1953 to the Gellideg seam.	1850 #13 (pp.36-39)	1979 #12	David Williams (Ynyscynon). #3 (12/04/1913). In 1856, John Nixon. #3 (12/04/1913). By 1870, Nixon, Taylor & Cory Co. Ltd. #2 (16/04/1864) (Nixon - Navigation Co. Ltd.) In 1929, Llewellyn Nixon Coal Co. Ltd. #1 (11/05/1929). From 1930, WAC Ltd. #1 (01/02/1930). In 1935, PDACC Ltd. #1 (29/06/1935). NCB in 1947.	2'9", 4', 6', 9', 7', 5' and Gellideg.	Product: steam coal. David Williams sold the pit to John Nixon in 1855 for £42,000. Nixon later was famous in South Wales for his inventions such as the 'Billy Fair-Play, a fair method of weighing coal, and long-wall and double shift methods of coal extraction from the coalface. Manpower and production peaked in 1913 with 1,515 men working. The WAC company opened the pithead baths in 1933, the first in the Cynon Valley. Production in 1867 was 129,663 tons. A boy of 10 was killed in 1871, and a boy of 12 killed in 1880. On final closure, 390 men were transferred to other local pits.
90	Dowdswell Level.	Near Ynysybwl.		W.1900			Darren Ddu seam.	
91	Dowlais New Pit							See- Abercynon Colliery.
92	Dowlais-Cardiff Colliery.							See- Abercynon Colliery.
93	Drain Level & Pit.							See- Ysguborwen Colliery.
94	Drift Rees Llewellyn.							See- Tirherbert Colliery.
95	Duffryn House Levels							See- Craig-y-Duffryn Levels.
96	Duffryn-Dare Colliery [Ping-Pong].	Cwmdare. SN 985027.	Level and airshaft.	1901 #47 (p.61)	1910 W #25 (p.138)	In 1898, Waynes Merthyr Co. Ltd. #25. (P.138.) By 1902, Llwydcoed Collieries Ltd. (Lancaster). #25.	2'9".	Product: steam coal. In 1910, 93 employed including women on the surface. Mr. T. Ashworth was Manager in 1910.

213

	A	B	C	D	F	G	H	I
97	Dyllas Collieries, including:- Old Drift, Mountain Balance Pit, [Coed-y-Gam Drift.]	Llwydcoed, SO 006058, SO 003059.	Numerous drifts, levels and airshafts driven to the Gellideg coal seam and ironstone initially. Furnace ventilation. Water-balance winding method in Mountain Pit.	1840s #1 (20/05/1924)	Coed-y-Gam Drift W.1920's	Up to 1865, Gadlys Iron Co. (Waynes). #2 (25/02/1865). In 1877, Waynes Merthyr Co. Ltd. #2 (02/06/1879). In 1898, Dyllas Colliery acquired by Lancaster Steam Coal Co. Ltd. 47#(P.61) In 1914, acquired by D.R. Llewellyn & Sons. #8 (Vol II, p.100).	4', 6', 9', 5', No.2 Brass, plus various ironstone veins (ironstone also worked on 'patches' system).	Product: ironstone and steam coal later. Dyllas used naked flame lamps until at least 1913. This resulted in 5 minor explosions, causing 5 deaths and 3 burned between April 1893 and December 1913. A serious inrush of water occurred in September 1912 in the 5' seam; no lives were lost. 252 men employed in 1911.
98	Dyllas Drift and Waun Fawr Level. [Llwydcoed Colliery].	Llwydcoed, SO 005054.	Level and airshaft. Upcast shaft 48' in depth.	1902 W #9 (p.2)	1929.W #1. (5.01.1929)	Llwydcoed Collieries Co. Ltd. initially. #9 (p.2). In 1906, owned by W.P.Powell & Co. #3 (15/03/1913). By 1914, D.R. Llewellyn & Sons. #29 (p.84). In 1935, PDSCC Ltd. #26. (Not known if worked by P.D.Co.)	6', 9', No.2 Brass, 4', 5' and Bute seam in 1915.	Product: steam coal, also coking coal. 170 men employed in 1928. The Manager was Henry Jones. Mr. R. Buxton was the Company Agent during the '20s. Output in 1903 was 49,067 tons. Due to the slump, 'half-time' was worked from 1921 to 1928. 300 men employed in 1912.
99	Dyllas Drift Ironstone Mine & Patch.	Llwydcoed.	Drift, probably with an airshaft.	1864 W #2 (02/02/1864)		Waynes Merthyr Co. Ltd. #2. (25.02.1865)	Iron veins unknown.	A young woman called Mary Rees was killed by a fall in February 1864, whilst working in a 'mine' patch.
100	Dyllas Level.	Llwydcoed.	Level.	1955 W #19 (P.603)	By 1960	Dyllas Drift Co. Ltd.		Licensed Private Mine.
101	East Drift.							See- Hirwaun-Aberdare Colliery (Aberdare / Merthyr SCC. Ltd.)
102	Evan Bryant Mine.	Hirwaun Common, SO 959049, near Knobby Drift.	Level.	1849 W #36 (Map 8)		E. Bryant. #36 (p.285).	Cnapiog vein.	Product: ironstone.

	A	B	C	D	F	G	H	I
103	Fforchaman Colliery. [Brown's Pit].	Cwmaman. SS 999995	Three shafts (Two upcast). No.1 Shaft - 14' dia x 680' deep. No.2 Shaft deepened to lower measures in 1906. 915' to below Gellideg seam.	1856 (lease) #10 (p.18)	1965 #24 (App.5)	Brown & Protheroe (& Co.), 1856 to 1864. #72 (p.89). From 1864, United Merthyr Colliery Co. Ltd. #72 (p.90). From 1868, PDSCC Ltd. #21 (p.19). From 1935, PDACC Ltd. #1 (29/06/1935). From 1947, NCB.	29", 4', Yard, 6', 9', Bute, 7', 5' and Gellideg.	Product: quality steam coal - quoted in 1859 as 'Never saw coals of such good quality' (Lab. tests in London). Explosion on 18/12/1869, 3 killed. Safety lamps were the only lamps used at Fforchaman at the time. In 1957, 767 men were employed and annual output was 175,000 tons. 'Brown's Pit' was so called after James Brown of Monmouth, one of the first proprietors. Output in 1863 totalled 60,430 tons. An 8 year old boy was discovered working in the pit in 1866. His mother had lied about his age. Mr. Trevor Ryder was manager in 1956.
104	Fforchneol Colliery. [Bevan's Pit].	Cwmaman, near 'The Globe' Inn. SO 008002.	Two shafts 240' to Graig seam. By 1881, the shaft had been shortened to 105', probably due to water problems.	1868 #44 (P.8)	1893 #44 (p.9)	Bevan Bros. from 1868 to 1871. #44. Rees Bevan and Family, 1871 to 1879. #2 (30/04/1892). From 1879, the Fforchneol Colliery Co. Ltd. (owned by W. Thomas, Brynawel), for £500. #44. (P.9) The same year, it was sold to a Mr. Render of Manchester for £1,500. #72 (p.126). A Mr.F.B. Millar was reported as owner, in 1881. (Ab. Times cutting).	Graig seam & Fireclay	Product: steam coal and fireclay. The pit was sunk between the Gadlys and Cwmneol faults. The first owner, D. Bevan, was killed in a shaft accident in 1871. Fforchneol did not work on most winter months due to very wet conditions. A brickworks was erected and working by 1886 using fireclay from the colliery. Produced 5,313 tons of coal in 1876/1877. The Manager at this time was a Mr. Snape.
105	Fforchneol Graig.	Cwmaman. Located on land adjoining Fforchneol farm, near the 'Globe Hotel'	Levels.	1921 #1 (24/10/1921)	1924 #22	Fforchneol Graig Coal Co. Ltd #1 (24/10/1921). By 1924, Godreaman Graig Coal Co. Ltd. (owner William Thomas of Gorseinon). #1 (24/10/1921). The first owner, & Managing Director of the company was a Mr. A.O. Hughes, of 'Glenbrook' Aberaman.	Graig seam worked.	In February 1924, 1 killed and 2 injured in a roof fall near mouth of the level. There was no-one in charge of the mine at this time, and help for the trapped miners were rescuers fom Cwmneol Colliery. The level was closed from 1922 to 1923. Candles were in use for lighting. 7 men employed on a 'day-to-day' basis.
106	Fforchwen Pit.							See- Cwmaman Colliery.

	A	B	C	D	F	G	H	I
107	Forest Level	Hirwaun Common. SN 955042.	Level.	1872 W #22		London & Merthyr Colliery Co. Ltd. #22.	Seam un-named	Product: steam coal. Forest Level was part of the Bryngwyn Levels complex.
108	Forest Levels: 1. Lower. [Newtown Level], [Wretched Level].	Mountain Ash (Newtown) ST 057986.	Level.	1851 #13 (p.37)	1891 #13 (p.39)	(Lower) Jenkin Williams. #13 (p.37). From 1853, William Simons of Merthyr. #13 (p.37). Later acquired by Aberdare Iron Co. (Fothergill). #13 (p.37). From about 1870, Nixon Navigation C. Co. Ltd. #13 (p.37).	No.3 Rhondda; section of seam was 2'2".	Product: mainly house-coal. 2 miners were badly burned in an explosives accident in 1888. Forest Levels were listed in 1876 as 'Fforest Tredegar'. The combined Forest Levels output in 1887 was 58,086 tons.
109	Forest Levels: 2. Upper. [Mercy Level].	Mountain Ash. SO 053991.	Level.	1857 #13 (p.37)	1876 (p.37) #13	(Upper) William Simons of Merthyr. #13 (p.37). Aberdare Iron Co. (Fothergill) later. #13 (p.37). From about 1870, Nixon Navigation Co. Ltd. #13 (p.37).	Seams, etc, as in Lower Forest.	The Upper Forest Level was connected to Cwmcynon Colliery later, as upcast. Catalogue of Abandoned Mines Plans also refer to this link-up.
110	Forest Slope, including Black Band Level.	Hirwaun Common, near Bryngwyn.	Level.	Pre-1850 #65		Unknown (possibly worked by Hirwaun Ironworks, who were producing iron by this time, and their railway was nearby).	Black Band Ironstone & Gorllwn Seam	Product : the Black Band vein of ironstone for smelting, and the Gorllwyn coal seam for coking coal initially. An early map shows the mine marked on the crop of the Gorllwyn seam.
111	Forge Pit, including No.3 Level, [Pond Level].	Abernant. SO 012030. The colliery was adjacent to the forges of the Abernant Ironworks.	Three shafts including an upcast airshaft, and one level (No.3). Furnace ventilation initially, and water-balance winding. Main shaft: 207 to 9' seam, dia. 16' x 11'. Upcast (No.2): 10' dia.. 231' to 9' seam. No.3 level worked the 4' seam, and was also used as a horseway for Forge Pits. The shafts were re-capped in 1997	1851 W #2 (17/10/1863)	1910 #22	Aberdare Iron Co. (formed 1823), bankrupt in 1875. #35. From 1875, The Aberdare & Plymouth Works. #3 (08/04/1915). From 1882, Mr. James Lewis. (Aberdare Works & Colliery Co.) #3 (08/04/1915). In 1899, the lease reverted to Bute Estates. #3 (08/04/1915). From 1915, PDSCC Ltd., who never reopened the colliery. #35	Red Vein (described as 'Dirty Vein'), 9, 6, Bute, Gellideg and 7.	Product: steam coal. Explosions:- 22/06/1860, 1 killed, 21/09/1863, 1 killed, 14 injured & 4 horses killed. Naked flame lamps in use at the time. Main pumping shaft for River Level Pit from 1882. A schoolboy, Gordon Bennet of Seymour Street was killed by falling down the shaft in May 1919. The Pond Level was working in 1875

	A	B	C	D	F	G	H	I
112	Fosters New Level. [Park Level].	Hirwaun Common. 132yds. S/West of mouth of Level Fawr.	One level evident on Hirwaun Common plan. #120.		Closed by 1840's.	A Mr. Foster. #120.		A small concern, possibly part of Level Fawr complex.
113	Four Feet Drift							See- Tower Colliery, No.1 Drift.
114	Four Feet Drift							See- Nantmelin Drift.
115	Furnace Level.	Abernant.						See- River Level Colliery.
116	Gadlys Colliery, Old Pit and New Pit, [Victoria Pit]. (By 1844). Plus 1 Airshaft. (Also linked later to 'Pond Flash' Airshafts.	Gadlys. SN 998026.	Three shafts plus a horseway drift to the 4' seam. Old Pit: 430' to 5' seam. Furnace ventilation initially, and water-balance winding. New Pit: (Downcast) 436' to 7 seam. Shaft dia. 17 x 12'. (Upcast) 195' deep, shaft dia. 10'. Waddle fan, in 1891 (40' Diameter, 63,960 C.F.M.	1820 W #23 (pp.127/128)	1939 #6 (27/02/1939)	In 1820, Mathew Wayne (Wayne & Co.). #23 (pp.127/128). In 1863, known as Gadlys Iron Co. #16 (item 14). In 1877, Wayne's Merthyr Steam Coal Co. #2 (02/06/1877). From 1892, acquired by Lancaster & Spiers Co. #1 (22/03/1924). Later, PDSCC Ltd. #6 (27/02/1939).	Graig, Upper Yard, 29", 4', Yard, 6', 9', Bute, 7', 5' and Gellideg.	Mineral leases totalled 350 acres. Product: coking coal initially, steam coal and fireclay later. Explosions:- total of 21 killed from 1850 to 1897. Of those:- 24/4/1848 - 5 killed. 04/10/1871 - 4 killed, 6 burned. 24/10/1872 - 4 killed. Ventilation shaft for River Level Colliery, Abernant later, and coal reserves worked from that colliery under PDSCC Ltd. In 1891, was working longwall system. Naked flame lamps in the new pit.
117	Gadlys Dare Mine Pit. [Pwll Mwyn].	Gadlys, situated near western end of Maelgwyn Terrace. Gadlys.	One shaft.	1861 W #2 (18/09/1861)	1901 #35	In 1861, Gadlys Iron Co. #2 (18/09/1861). During 1880s, Wayne's Merthyr Coal Co. #35. PDSCC later. #35.	Ironstone - Rosser Vein plus others. Coal - Lower Yard and 5'.	Product: initially, ironstone and coking coal (in 1863). Probably steam coal later. Gadlys Dare Mine was part of the Gadlys complex, and linked underground. Explosions:- 25/07/1863 - 1 killed. 06/11/1865 - 1 killed. 23/02/1872 - 1 killed. 22/10/1875 - 9 Sinkers burned in shaft explosion. Linked up underground to Pond Flash Pits later. Shaft re-capped in 1997.
118	Gadlys Graig.							See Graig Colliery (Aberdare).

	A	B	C	D	F	G	H	I
119	Gelli Isaf Levels.	Trecynon, 300 yards south of Gelli Isaf Farm. SN 991041	3 Levels & an air shaft.	1901 # 112.	1909 #39 (item 6)	In 1903, Mr. T. Morgan. #1 (Parish Returns, 07/03/1903).	Gellideg, worked from crop.	Product: steam coal, with 4,293 tons produced in 1906. Abandonment plans show the seam worked to boundary.
120	Gellydeg Level.	Llwydcoed. SO 042017.	Level.	1875 W #2 (11/12/1875)		Gellydeg Colliery Co. Ltd. Share offer 11/12/1875. #2 (11/12/1875).	Gellideg seam worked.	
121	George Pit. [Cefn Pennar Colliery].	Cefn Pennar. SO 042017.	No.1 Shaft :- (downcast), oval in section, 16 x 5'6" dia., 1,215' deep. No.2 Shaft :- (upcast), 16 x 8' dia., 1,458' to 7 seam. Ventilated by Guibal fan 40' in diameter.	1881 #29 (p.23) (Coal raised in 1885)	1905 #1 (22/09/1906)	PDSCC Ltd. #29 (p.23).	29", 4', 9' and 7'.	Product: steam coal. The colliery worked 'double-shift' and 'longwall face' methods of mining operations, with safety lamps. Workforce in 1891 was 341 below ground, 61 on the surface. It was unremunerative and was closed in 1905, the seams being worked by Lower Duffryn Colliery. The Pit was named after Sir George Elliott. In 1903, 7,717 tons were produced. The manager for much of its life was Mr.G.M. Green
122	Glandare Mine Pit.							See- Pond Flash Pits.
123	Glover's Levels, Old and New.	Hirwaun Common.	Levels.	1813 W #77 (p.5, 1813)		Hirwaun Ironworks Co. #77 (p.5, 1813).	9'.	Product: coking coal, for Hirwaun Ironworks.
124	Glyngwyn Levels.	Miskin, Mountain Ash. ST 049986.	Two levels plus an airshaft 51' in depth, (5' X 5' Dia.) Furnace ventilated, (12' X 9') Producing 8,370 C.F.M.	1893 #13 (p.44)	1925 #78 (p.13)	Nixon Navigation Coal Co. Ltd. #13 (p.44). In 1929, the colliery was acquired by Llewellyn-Nixon CC Ltd., who never worked it. #1 (09/02/1929).	No.3 Rhondda, abandoned about 1915. Rider seam abandoned in 1925.	Product: house-coal. In 1913, 299 men were employed below ground. No disaster occurred in Glyngwyn despite the use of naked flame lamps. Mr. Tagg. Williams was Manager in 1915, using longwall face system.
125	Godre Hirwaun Colliery.							See- Park Pit, Cwmdare.
126	Gorlwyn and Black Band Levels.	Hirwaun Common, near Long-Range Level. SN 973040.	Two levels.	1840s W #65		Possibly owned by Hirwaun Iron Co., who were directly involved in obtaining of ironstone and the product for their ironworks.	Black Band vein of ironstone and Gorllwyn coal seam.	Product: ironstone and coking coal.

	A	B	C	D	F	G	H	I
127	Gorllwyn Colliery. [Gothlyn Level], [John Bird Levels], [Old Gorllwyn].	Hirwaun Common. SN 948054. (Near Bute Pit).	Two drifts and an airshaft. One level driven through Hirwaun No.1 fault into the 9' seam.	1813 W #77 (p.5)	1871 W #37	Pre-1813, Bowser, Overton & Co. #77. From 1818, Hirwaun Ironworks Co. (Crawshay). #23 (p.17). 1861 to 1863, J.Bird & Co. (bankrupt). #37. In 1864, Williams & Co. #37. By 1865, Williams & Rhys. #37. From 1866 to 1871, Powell & Rhys. #37.	Gorllwyn, Graig, 9' and 4'.	Product: initially, coking coal for the ironworks. In 1861, house-coal. Sample annual tonnages :- In 1863, 18,000 tons. In 1870, 8,250 tons.
128	Gorllwyn Drift, (Cwmdare)							See- Bwllfa Dare Colliery.
129	Gorllwyn Level.	Hirwaun Common. SN 933044.	Level.	1912 W #79		D.R. Llewellyn (Aberdare Graig Coal Co.). #36 (p.19).	Gorllwyn and Graig.	Product : house-coal. This level was used as a companion drift for Coronation Drift, evident on a Rescue (Mines) plan, 1938. May have originally been a level of the earlier Gorllwyn Colliery.
130	Gothlyn Level.							See- Gorllwyn Colliery, Hirwaun.
131	Gotre Machine Drifts, Lower and Upper.	Hirwaun Common. SO 948054. near Bute Pit.	Two drifts and an airshaft. One level driven through Hirwaun No.1 fault into the 9' seam.	1825 W #80 (p.142)	1866 W #2 (17/02/1866)	In 1820, Hirwaun Ironworks Co. #23 (pp. 127/128). In 1859, closed with ironworks. #23 (pp. 127/128). In 1865, owned by Hirwaun Coal & Iron Co. (T.C. Hinde). #2 (04/02/1871). Bankrupt in 1871. #2 (04/02/1871).	2'9" and Upper 4' ; 5' later.	Product : coking coal initially. The Crawshay Company drove the colliery from the horizon of the 5' and Gellideg seams.
132	Graig Colliery. [Gadlys Graig], [Aberdare Graig], [Pwll-y-Graig].	Aberdare (in Ty Fry area). SN 995021.	Two shafts . No.1 shaft :- 744' to 5' seam, dia. 17' x 12'. No.2 shaft (upcast) :- 528' to 9' seam, dia 9' x 9'. Furnace ventilation initially, flue pit for Level Fach 20' deep x 20' area.	1855. #17 (No.59)	By 1916 #22	In 1861, Gadlys Iron Co. #2 (11/01/1868). By 1877, Wayne's Merthyr C. Co. Ltd. #2 (02/06/1877). By 1892, Lancaster & Spiers C. Co. Ltd. #1 (22/03/1924). Later, PDSCC Ltd., who never worked the colliery. #9 (p.2).	2'9", 4', 6', 9', 7', 5' and Gellideg. Graig seam crops at pit top and was worked by the level.	Product:steam coal; Level Fach - house-coal. Explosions :- 07/08/1869 - 4 badly burned. 27/02/1892 - 1 killed and 11 burned in shaft explosion (Candles in use). 7,500 tons produced in 1905/1906. Working method in 1891, Longwall and Pillar & Stall. A young girl, Ann Butler, was killed on surface work in 1866.
133	Graig Level (Aberaman).	Exact location unknown.	Level.	1878 W #19 (p.40)	1895 W #2 (26/01/1895)	PDSCC Ltd. #2 (10/04/1866).	Graig.	A serious shotfiring accident occurred in January 1895.

	A	B	C	D	F	G	H	I
134	Graig Level.	Cwmdare, near Lluestau-Llwydion Colliery.	Coal level.	1888 W #47 (p.65)		Abott & King. #47 (p.65).	Graig.	Product : house-coal. The level shown on the working plan of the Windber Dare level.
135	Graig Levels	Near Ty-Fry, 220yds. to west of Graig Cottage. On the Graig seam crop. (Part of the Graig Coll. complex.) (Above).	Two Levels. (Old & New).	Est. 1860's. #114.	10/9/1898. #114.	Wayne's Merthyr Co. Ltd. (Worked on lease from the Earl of Windsor.)	Graig Seam. A total section of 5' 1" was worked, of this, 2'2" was coal; & 1' 8" was fireclay.	Products: Probably house coal & fireclay. The colliery was abandoned due to unprofitability. Method of working was 'Long work stall.'
136	Graig Levels.	Hirwaun Common. SO 901046.	Two levels.	1801 #23 (p.18)	1876 W #37 (p.45)	Hirwaun Ironworks Co. (W. Crawshay) prior to 1859. #2 (21/12/1861). From 1861, acquired by John Bird, together with Gorllwyn Colliery. #2 (21/12/1861). Bird bankrupt in 1864. #2 (11/12/1869). From 1864, W. Williams & Co. #37 (p.45). In 1865, Williams & Rhys. #37 (p.45). From 1866 to 1870, Powell & Rhys, liquidated in 1871. #37 (p.45). A Mr. James & Son were owners in 1876, with no record after that year.	Graig.	Product : coking coal originally, house-coal by 1861. It was reported that the Graig seam was far superior to any other house-coal seam in Hirwaun. The lineage of ownership of Graig Levels corresponds roughly with that of Gorllwyn Colliery up to 1870. NB - John Bird was also the proprietor of a 'Nine Feet' Colliery on the Common prior to 1861. In 1867, Graig Levels produced 12,007 tons.
137	Graig Vein New Level.	Hirwaun Common, exact location unknown.	Level.	June 1st, 1801 #23 (p.18)		Messrs. A. & T. Bacon of Hirwaun Ironworks. #23 (p.18).		Level contractors were Isaac and Evan Davies of Hirwaun Parish, being paid 18 shillings per yard. Probably part of previous Graig Levels complex.
138	Griffith Shon Levels. [Old Level].	Hirwaun Common. SN 941048. Adjacent to Tower No.3 Old Drift.	Two drifts (Old and New).	1850 W #36 (Map 8)		Probably a Mr. Griffith Shon (John).		Situated near Pantglas Farm. The Old Drift worked the lower measures, and the New was driven to the 9' seam. Also evident on development plan, Old No.3 Drift (Tower).
139	Gutter Level.	Hirwaun Common. SN 965051.	Level.	1840s #36 (Map 6)		Owned at one stage by Hirwaun Iron Co., as it became the main drainage level of the Bute Pit and the River Level Pit. #36 (p.11).	Rosser vein and probably the Knobby vein.	Product : ironstone. Part of the Bute Pit complex, and is in direct line between Bute Pit and River Level.
140	Gwdi - Hw Levels.							See- Bedwlwyn Colliery.

	A	B	C	D	F	G	H	I
141	Gwrhyd Pit.	Abernant, to the NE of Abernant Railway Station.	Shaft was 99' to pit bottom.	Post 1875 #82	1903 W #1 (Parish Returns, 09/12/1903)	Probably Abernant Iron Co. #82. In 1880, James Lewis. (Aberdare Works & Colliery Co.) #3 (08/04/1915). In 1899, Bute Estates. (Aqud.) #3 (08/04/1915). But not worked.	'Gwrhyd' vein, No.1 Yard, 4'.	Product : ironstone, coal later. Production in 1902 - 5,192 tons, in 1903, 4,070 tons. Possible connection with Cigarette Pit. Not listed in 1906
142	High Duffryn Colliery.							See- Ynyscynon Colliery.
143	Hirwaun Bute Pit.							See- Bute Pit.
144	Hirwaun Common Colliery. [Brogden's Graig].	Hirwaun Common. SN 968046.		1890s W #83		Earlier owners unknown. In the 1890s, owned by the Bwllfa & Merthyr Dare Colliery Co. Ltd #47 (pp.76/77).	4', 6', 9'.	Product : at this date, probably steam coal. Brogden was partner to S. Budgett at the time of the Bwllfa ownership.
145	Hirwaun Drifts.							See- Bute Drifts.
146	Hirwaun-Aberdare Steam Coal Colliery. Became Aberdare-Merthyr SC Colliery in 1866. [East Drift], [Dumpy Chain Drift]. [Steam Coal Colliery]	Hirwaun Common, SN 963047, near Grove Farm.	A Drift (East Drift), plus an upcast shaft (135'). The Dumpy Chain Pit was sunk to the west of the main drift, with other airshafts in the vicinity.	1860 W #37 (sec. 1860-1866)	1917 #36 (p.18)	Possibly started by Mr. T. Hopkins. #37 (1860). In 1860, Hirwaun and Aberdare Steam Coal Co. Ltd. (bankrupt in 1866). #37 (1866). From 1867, the Aberdare-Merthyr Steam Coal Co. #2 (21/08/1866). From August 1886, the Aberdare-Merthyr Colliery Co. Ltd. #6 (21/08/1886). By 1900, Bute Estates. #84.	4', 9', 7', Yard and 5'. The 5' seam worked up to 1917.	Product : dry steam coal and house-coal. (For Admiralty, & Patent Fuel.) The colliery was started some time before 1860, as indicated by high output figures at that time (18,513 tons in 1860). The coal was noted for its 'free-burning, smokeless qualities'. There was a direct underground link-up to Tower Colliery, who shared the same management when under Bute Estates control. In 1911, Daniel Jones was Manager, with 200 men employed. There was a link-up also to Pwll-yr-Afon Pit (drainage adit). In 1868, Aberdare-Merthyr SC Co. produced 79,350 tons. A three-year lock-out occurred from 1912 to 1915.
147	Horseway Level.							See- Aberdare Level.
148	Jaci - Daw Pit.							See- Miskin Colliery.
149	James Williams' Level.	Cwmdare. SN 972029, near the Windber complex.	Two Levels.	1934 W #85		James Williams, owner or Manager. (Possibly contractor).	Gorllwyn Fach seam.	Referred to in 'The Story of Cwmdare', by J.F. Mear, also evident on 'Gorllwyn seam' outcrop plan.

	A	B	C	D	F	G	H	I
150	John Bird Colliery. [Nine-Feet Colliery].	Hirwaun Common.		1859 W #37 (1859)	1863 #37 (1864)	In 1859, John Bird. Reference is made to this colliery in cuttings of Graig and Gorllwyn collieries. #2 ((21/12/1861). Bankrupt by 1864. #2 (11/12/1869).	g.	As in the case of Graig and Gorllwyn collieries, probably acquired from Hirwaun Iron Co. (Crawshay). Output in 1861 - 21,704 tons. J. Bird also worked a quarry on the Common.
151	John Bird Levels.							See- Gorllwyn Colliery.
152	John Calvert Colliery.	Hirwaun Common.		1859 W #37 (1859)		John Calvert & Company.		Product and seams unknown. Output figures :- 1859 - 3,829 tons, 1860 - 7,263 tons. The mine was probably worked in the early 1860's. John Calvert was a prominent coal owner in the Rhondda Valley by 1854.
153	Johnson's Level.	Cwmdare. SN 970034	Level.			Probably a Mr. Johnson. #47 (p.65).	Gorllwyn.	
154	Kirkhouse Drift.							See- Bryngwyn Levels.
155	Knobby Drift. [Cnapiog Drift]	Hirwaun Common. SN 956049. 250 yds. S/East of Bute Pit.	Level and airshaft.	1847 W #36 (Map 8)	1865 W #22		Black Pins, Llyfrau, Knobby, Rosser, Black & Blue ironstone veins.	An ironstone mine, and in 1865 was mining the veins shown. The drift was later mining the 5' coal seam, and was directly connected to Tower Colliery airshaft. 'Knobby' vein was also referred to as 'Cnapiog'.
156	'Kyber'.							See- Penrikyber Colliery.
157	L.L. Morgan's Level.	Hirwaun Common. SN 945048.	Level.	1850 W #65				Evident on a plan as being in the vicinity of the later Coronation Drift.
158	Ladder Pit. [Red Pit]	Hirwaun Common. SN 943049.	Shaft est. 9' x 14' diameter.	1876 W #54		Owned at one stage by Bute Estates (Duffryn-Aberdare Co.).	Red Vein seam	At one stage it served as an airshaft for Tower Colliery (West Area), and was connected to Tower No.1 Drift. (Ab.Plan- SWA 1155)

#	A	B	C	D	F	G	H	I
159	Lady Windsor Colliery. (There were various small levels worked above the colliery at different times, but not associated with this pit.)	Ynysybwl. SO.0629-9426 (480yds. east of Ynysybwl church.)	No.1 Shaft, 2057ft. deep, 19ft. diameter. No.2 shaft. 2058ft. deep, 20ft. diameter.	1884, (Sinking commenced) #61.	1986. #61.	1. Scott, Davies & Co. #61. By 1888, Ocean Coal Co. Ltd. 3. 1947, N.C.B. 2. #61	2'9" @ 1597, 4' @ 1629, 6' @ 1683, 9' @ 1803, Bute @ 1830', Yard @ 1869', 7' @ 1890', Gellideg @ 1950'	Product: Steam coal. In 1898, the longwall system was being worked, with safety lamps in use. The first manager was William Bevan, and the colliery was known briefly as the 'Black Rock' pit. Pithead baths were opened on 28.1.1931. At this time the manager was a Mr. M.J.John, who employed 1,116 men. The colliery was linked up to Abercynon colliery in 1973. Output in 1887 was 88,526 tons. Horizon mining system of working was used following link-up. Won safety award in 1977, top position in South Wales.
160	Lan Wood Levels.	SO. 07279150 Near Ynysybwl.	At least 7 adits.	W.1952 #61	By 1969 #61	In 1952, D Adams & Sons. 1957, T Wallace. By #61		
161	Lanky Pit							See- Cwmneol Colliery.
162	Lefel Ceffyl Gwyn.							See- Tirfounder Level.
163	Lefel 'Racks'.							See- Pontcynon Colliery.
164	Level Fach. (1)	Blaengwawr. SN 003019.	A level and an airshaft.	1869 W #87	1914 (about) #61	David Davis & Sons, at some stage. #87	Gorlwyn.	The tramway from the level was linked into Blaengwawr incline and to the main colliery screens. In 1914, 56 men employed underground and 6 on the surface. Product; House coal & Steam coal.
165	Level Fach.(2) [Little Pit].	Mountain Ash (Miskin), near Tyrarlwydd Farm.	Level, and upcast shaft 198' deep.	1857 W #13 (p.46)	By 1880 #2 (06/04/1880)	Early proprietors unknown. Acquired by Fothergill (Aberdare Iron Co.) in 1872. #2 (01/06/1872) Aberdare Plymouth Co. by 1875. #2 (06/03/1880).		Product : bituminous coal. Abandoned before 1872, but held by the Aberdare Plymouth Co. leased from Thomas Charles, (Tyrarlwydd).

	A	B	C	D	F	G	H	I
166	Level Fawr. (And Level Fawr Balance Pit.)	Hirwaun Common. SN 983041.	Level. The first 400 yds. of level was arched. The Balance Pit was 616 yds. to N/West of Level Fawr mouth, and was 120 feet in depth to the 9' seam.	1786 #8 (p.46)	1847.W #117	In 1786, Messrs. Maybery, Overton & Wilkins, Hirwaun Ironworks. #36 (p.12) By 1790, Anthony Bacon, ironmaster of Hirwaun Ironworks. #23 (p.11). In 1803, Homfray & Overton. #23 (p.11). In 1818, Hirwaun Ironworks Co. (Crawshay). #23 (p.11). In 1859, reverted to Bute Estates. #36 (p.12).	4', 9', & 6', 'dirty vein' (Bute).	Product : ironstone and coking coal. Reputed the first level in the Valley to use horses below ground, hence the name 'Fawr'. (A level that a horse can enter). Explosion on 05/04/1803, 2 killed (naked flame lamps). Linked to 'Old Bryngwyn' shaft. Also to 'Thomas Davies' soap vein level. Water was controlled by the use of two horse drawn 'gin' pumps, below ground.
167	Level Francis Phillips. [Blaennant-y-Groes Level].	Cwmbach 'Tunnel' area, opposite 'Pant-y-Blodau' House.	Level.	1870s #89 (1868)	1877 W #2 (02/06/1877)	Francis Phillips & Jones. #90. Later, Francis Phillips. #2 (02/06/1877)	Probably Graig.	A coal level (spoil indicated on Geological Survey Map 1895-7) driven into the crop of the Graig seam.
168	Level Rhys.							See- Merthyr Dare Colliery.
169	Level Siencyn.	Cwmbach, near Llettysiencyn Colliery (Upper).	Level.	1830 W #88 (p.2)				Explosion recorded on 31/01/1830, with 2 men killed and 2 gassed (afterdamp).
170	Level-yr-Afon.							See- River Level Colliery (Abernant).
171	Little Pit.							See- Level Fach (Mountain Ash).
172	Llanwonno Level.	Near Llanwonno Church, & Llanwonno Fault.			Abandoned by 1905. #61			
173	Liesty Levels.	Cwmaman. ST 011987. Near Bedwlwyn Colliery.	Two cross-measure drifts.	1873 #92			Brithdir (2' thickness).	Drift entrance and spoil tip still evident in 1999.

	A	B	C	D	F	G	H	I
174	Lletty Shenkin Colliery (Upper and Lower Pit).	Cwmbach. SO 029013 & SO 025011.	Two main shafts and two ventilation shafts later. Initially, water-balance winding and furnace ventilation. Upper Pit 888' deep and 15' dia. Lower Pit 450' deep to lower seams. In 1891 a ventilation shaft was 504' deep, with a Waddell fan (40' Diameter), producing 60,000 C.F.M.	1843 (Lower Pit) #57 (p.126) 1850 (Upper Pit).	1922 #1 (01.07/1922)	William Thomas (Waunwyllt) #57 (p.126). From 1865, Lletty Shenkin Colliery Co. Ltd. (Lewis & Co.) #2 (13/05/1865). In 1872, Burnyeat, Brown & Co. Ltd. #1 (23/06/1906). In 1900, PDSCC Ltd. #21 ((p.10).	2'9", 4', Yard, 6', 9', Bute, 7' and Gellideg. The 4' & 6' seams were abandoned in 1913.	Product : steam coal. Explosions :- 14/08/1849 - 53 killed (naked flame lamps). 16/09/1853 - 3 killed and 15 burned. 09/08/1862 - 5 killed (naked flame lamps). 01/08/1897 - 3 badly burned. 27/01/1906 - 2 burned. A boy of 10 was killed in 1852. 386 men underground and 95 on the surface in 1891. 113,731 tons were produced in 1863. The 'Longwall' face system was in use in 1862, at the time of an explosion. The Upper Pit was reopened in 1954 by the NCB. as a ventilation & materials shaft for Aberaman Colliery (East Level).
175	Llewellyn's Level.	Hirwaun Common, near Bryngwyn Level. SN 972046.	Level.	1850s W #65				
176	Lluestai-Llwydion Levels.	Cwmdare. SN 973932, near Nantmelin Farm.	Three levels, two of which were driven from the Hirwaun Common side of the spur.	1847 W #91	1929 W #10 (p.104)	In 1847, Richard Thomas, farmer. Later than 1929, it was owned by Bwlch Colliery Co, Ltd., probably acquired from W Humphreys & Co. Ltd. #10 (p.104). Acquired by D.R. Llewellyn & Buxton between 1905 & 1914 (Bwlch) #10. (P.104).	Gorllwyn Fach.	Product : probably house-coal. Shown on the plan of Gorllwyn Fach seam crop (Hirwaun Common).
177	Llwydcoed Colliery.							See- Dyllas Drifts.
178	Llwynhelig Colliery. (New & Old Drifts).	Cwmdare. Green Meadow Riding School.	Four Drifts. (Shown on workings plan.)	1906 #47 (p.63)	1939 #47 (p.65)	Rees Llewellyn of Bwllfa. #47 (pp. 64-65). In 1912, Llwynhelig Colliery Co. In 1915, in sole possession of D.R. Llewellyn. #47 (pp.64-65). From 1920, D.R. Llewellyn & Sons.(Co.) #47 (pp.64-65). In 1930, WAC. #47 (pp.64-65). In 1935, PDACC Ltd. #47 (pp.64-65).	Gorllwyn, Gorllwyn Fach, No.2 Rhondda and Graig.	Product : steam and house-coal. Worked the area to the north-west of and adjacent to Graig (Gadlys) Colliery. Explosion - 2 killed on 06/11/1929. The Inspectorate was not informed until 8 days after the explosion. The output generally was 65,000 Tons/Annum. 290 men working in 1928.

	A	B	C	D	F	G	H	I
179	London & Merthyr Colliery (New Level). Part of Bryngwyn complex (Upper). See 'Bryngwyn Levels'.	Hirwaun Common. SN 964041.	Level.	1866 W #4 (30.11.1866)	By 1883 #2 (12-4-1883).	By 1866, London & Merthyr Steam Coal Co. In 1870, Cefn Merthyr Coal Co. (Lockett & Judkins). In 1872, Bryngwyn Coal Co. (Bwllfa). Advertised for sale or lease in 1883.	2'9", Gorllwyn, fireclay and Blackband Driver vein.	No evidence of working after 1883. Product; Steam Coal.
180	Long Range Level. [New Level]. (With upcast air shaft).	Hirwaun Common. SN 962043.	Level driven in the 9' seam. Shaft - 135ft. deep, 10ft. diameter.	1850 W #36 (fig.8, map)	1895 W #88 (p.33)	Aberdare-Merthyr Steam Coal Co. at one stage (1895) #88 (p.33). Bute Estates in 1900. #36.	4',9' and Yard.	Product : steam coal. There were seven minor explosions from 1885 to 1895 resulting in four deaths and seven badly burned. Level connected to Tower Colliery via the 9' seam to No.1 Drift. Naked lights in 1891, in yard seam, with safety lamps in the 9ft. seam.
181	Lower Duffryn Colliery & Drift. [Lower Pit], [Cwmpennar Pit], [Cefn Cwsg Drift].	Mountain Ash. SO 041002.	Two shafts. Lower Pit 16' dia x 1035' deep. Upper Pit 16' dia x 1128' deep. Furnace ventilation and water-balance winding initially. Also a drift started in 1843, connected later to the pit.	By 1850 #13 (p.37)	1927 #13 (p.109)	Thomas Powell & Sons. #13 (p.37) In 1864, PDSCC Ltd. #21 (p.7).	Graig, 2'9", 4', 6', 9, 7 and Gellideg.	Product : steam coal. Lower (winding) shaft deepened to lower steam coal measures in 1888. Explosions :- 25/02/1858 - 19 killed. 06/11/1860 - 12 killed. 01/12/1860 - 2 killed. 02/05/1867 - 3 killed. 575 employed in 1891. The pit was used for pumping purposes until 1970. A boy of 9 years was killed in April 1861.
182	Meadow Pit. [Ynys Pit].	Aberaman, a quarter of a mile from Blaengwawr Colliery. SO 010021. Alongside river Cynon.	1 shaft, 50' deep in 1864. The actual final depth unknown.	1864 #2 (06/08/1864)	By 1910 #93 (p.57)	Aberdare Iron Co. (No.9 Coll.) Reverted to M. of Bute in 1900. #93 (p.57). In 1915, PDSCC Ltd. (not worked).	6, 9', Bute and No.2 Yard.	Product : steam coal. It was linked underground to No.9 Colliery in the 6' seam, and later was worked from No.9 Colliery. A youth fell down the shaft during sinking (1864). It was later used mainly for pumping.
183	Mercy Level.							See Forest Level (Upper).

	A	B	C	D	F	G	H	I
184	Merthyr Dare Colliery, & Level Rhys. [Penriwllech Colliery]. [Rhys & Richards Pit]. [Pwll Rhys]	Cwmdare. SN 982026.	Two shafts and one airshaft. No.1 shaft - 600'. No.2 shaft - 120'. Furnace ventilated and water balance winding initially. Waddle Fan later. 1 level alongside the Taff Vale Railway in the Dare Valley. (Level Rhys.)	1851 #47 (p.52)	1884 #47 (p.79)	In 1853, David Williams (Alaw Goch). #47 (p.52). By 1861, Rhys & Co. #2 (10/08/1861). In 1864, Rhys & Richards #2 (04/06/1864). Prior to 1876, J. Brogden & Sons. #47 (p.77). In 1876, Bwllfa & Merthyr Dare Colliery Co. Ltd. #47 (p.76).	6', 9' and Bute.	Product : steam coal. The colliery was abandoned for some years from 1876. After final closure, the shafts were used for ventilation of the Llewellyn collieries. In 1869, 44,111 tons were produced. A Level Rhys was working during the 1930's, in the area.
185	Middle Duffryn Colliery.	Cwmbach. SO 031003.	Two shafts. No.1 shaft (downcast), 495' in 1850, and 879' to Gellideg later. 13'6" dia. No.2 shaft (upcast), 504' in 1850. Initially, furnace ventilation.	1843 #45 (p.181)	Coal prodn. ceased 1893 #21 (p.23) Final closure 1927. #26.	In 1843, T. Powell Esq. #45 (p.181) In 1864, PDSCC Ltd. #21 (p.18).	29", 4', 6', 9', 7' and Gellideg.	Product; Steam Coal. Ceased production in 1893, and by 1903 was the main pumping station, washery and electrical power station for the Powell Duffryn Group in the southern end of the valley. The washery was the first in Sth. Wales for the purpose of sizing small coals. Explosions :- 12/12/1850 - 13 deaths. 15/05/1852 - 65 deaths. (18 boys under 16; youngest, 10) Linked to 6 Powell Duffryn collieries by 1903. 489,558 tons produced in 1863. No.1 shaft deepened to 895' in 1890 - 1893. (For pumping.)
186	Miskin Colliery. [Jaci-Daw Pit].	Mountain Ash. ST 052983. Alongside and to the west of the Taff Vale Railway, opp. Jones Street.	Two shafts : upcast 94', downcast 948". Furnace ventilation initially.	1871 #1 (30/05/1903)	1914 #22 (pub.1930)	Jackson & Dawson. #61. From 1903, Prosser & Thornwood. #1 (30/05/1903). From 1913, Penrikyber Navigation Colliery Co. Ltd. #46 (1914), p.130.	No.3 Rhondda.	Product : house-coal. 115 employed in 1909. 30 employed in 1914.
187	Morris's Pit.							
188	Mountain Balance Pit.							See- Cwmneol Colliery. See- Dyllas Colliery.
189	Mountain Drift & Pit (part of Ysgubowen complex).	Llwydcoed.	Shaft and drift, plus a horseway level.	1867 W #2 (22/06/1867)		Prior to 1867,Thomas & Joseph. #2 (22/06/1867). In 1867, S. Thomas & Co. #57 (p.142). From 1879, J.H. Thomas. #1 (23/10/1909). In 1909, PDSCC Ltd. #21 (p.13).	9' and Gellideg.	Product : steam coal. Naked flame lamps in use in 1869. Explosion 17/06/1867, 3 men killed.

227

	A	B	C	D	F	G	H	I
190	Mountain Pit (Abernant).	Abernant. SO 017051.	One shaft evident on plan. Linked later as an upcast shaft for Blaennant Colliery. 456' to 6' seam.	1866 W #2 20/10/1866)	1927 (about) #46 (1928 - not listed)	Aberdare Iron Co. #3 (08/08/1915). In 1875, Aberdare & Plymouth Co. #3 (08/08/1915). In 1882, James Lewis (Aberdare Works & Colliery Co.) #3 (08/08/1915). By 1889, Bute Estates (lease term). #3 (08/08/1915). In 1909, PDSCC Ltd #3 (08/08/1915).	4', 6', 9', Bute, 7', No.1 Yard, 29" and 5'.	Product unknown, probably steam coal.
191	Mynachdy Level.	SO. 0475-9453. Ynysybwl.	Level & 1 airshaft, (6' Dia. x 90' deep) Furnace ventilated, providing 9120 c.f.m.	W.1891. Listed abandoned 1896, reopened later. #46	W.1914.	Mynachdy Coal Co.Ltd.	Darren Ddu seam.	Product: house coal. Longwall method of mining, with naked flame lighting. In 1914, 290 men below ground, & 31 on surface. Output in 1887 was 3,292 tons.
192	Nant Colliery.							See- Nantmelin Colliery.
193	Nantmelin Colliery. (Nant Colliery) (Bwllfa No.2 Colliery)	Cwmdare. SN 975028.	Two shafts & two levels, plus an airshaft (furnace) 60' deep. Main shaft was 520' to 5' seams. A second (upcast) shaft was sunk in 1866, and was 600' to Gellideg. Furnace ventilation and water-balance winding initially.	1860 #57 (p.205)	1957 #58 (1957)	From 1860, Mordecai Jones. #57 (p.205). From 1883, Nantmelin Coll. Co. #47 (p.56). From 1893, Aberdare-Merthyr Steam C. Co. Ltd. #2 (10/04/1897). (Cost - £5,000). From 1897, Bwllfa & Merthyr Dare (1891) Coll. Co. Ltd. #2 (10/04/1897). From 1928, Bwllfa & Cwmaman C.Co. Ltd. #47 (p.72). From 1930, WAC Ltd. #6. From 1935, PDAssCC Ltd #47 (p.72). In 1947, NCB.	4', 6', Bute, Yard, Gellideg. Gorllwyn seam in level.	Product ; steam coal, (large & small), house-coal & manufacturing. Explosion occurred 04/04/1893 - 9 men badly burned. By 1891, longwall method of coal extraction was in use. 716 workmen employed at this time. In 1955, manpower was 385, and annual output was 30,000 tons. In 1934, manpower was 760, and output was 170,000 tons. Mr. G. Kirkhouse, Manager in 1867, discontinued the use of safety lamps.
194	Nantmelin Drift. [Bwllfa New Drift].[Four Feet Drift} [Bwllfa No.4 Drift]	Cwmdare. SN 974029 Adjacent to the upper reservoir.	1 drift 517 yards in length to the 9' seam.	1910 #47 (p.65)	1945 #58	Bwllfa & Merthyr Dare SCC (1891) Ltd. #47 (p.72). In 1928, Bwllfa & Cwmaman CC Ltd. #58. From 1930, WAC Ltd. #47. From 1935, PDAssCC Ltd. #47.	9' and Bute mainly. The 4', but little.	Product: steam coal. The drift was linked underground to the Bwllfa complex, and also to the Dare Inn Level (the latter for drainage and ventilation). In 1921, 150 men were employed, producing 150 tons per day.

	A	B	C	D	F	G	H	I
195	Nantmelin Graig Levels.	Cwmdare, near the Windber complex. SN 965030.	Two levels plus an elliptical airshaft (6 x 4'). Furnace ventilated, producing 7000 C.F.M.	1888 W #47 (p.65)	1929 W #1 (advert. in 1929)	In 1888, William Humphreys & Co. #47 (p.65). By 1892, Humphreys & Griffiths. Later, W.J. Parrish. #47 (p.65). In 1929, Bwlch Colliery Co. Ltd. (D.R. Llewellyn). #1(04/12/1929)	Graig.	Product : house-coal, and fireclay for brick-making. 60 men employed in 1891, with naked flame lamps in use. 8'191 tons produced in 1897, with pillar & stall method in use.
196	Nantyfedw Level. [Tynte Level]	Ynysyboeth. ST.071960	Four Levels.	1912 W #78 (p.28)	1972 #78 (p.28)	In 1912, Nantyfedw CC Ltd. #26 (Nantfedw). Later, D.R. Jones. #61 (H.R.). Last owners, Blacker Bros. #60 (H.R.).	Cefn Glas. (Darren No.2 seam.)	Products : Coke, house-coal, manufacturing and steam coal. 20 men employed in 1932. The levels were not nationalised in 1947.
197	Navigation Colliery and Level. [The 'Navi'].	Mountain Ash ST 051989.	No.1 Pit depth 1350' to 7 seam. North Shaft 1333' to 7 seam (upcast), ventilated by a Waddle fan 40' dia. No.1 shaft was 18' dia.	1855 #13 (p.109). Coal first raised in 1861.	1940 #13 (p.109).	John Nixon. #13 (p.109). By 1861, Nixon, Taylor & Cory Co. Ltd. #2 (23/11/1861). From 1888, Nixon Navigation Co. Ltd. #46 (1928, p.263). In 1929, acquired by W.M. Llewellyn (Llewellyn Nixon Ltd.). #1. (11/05/1929). By 1930, WAC. #1 (29/06/1935). By 1935, PDACC Ltd.	2'9", 4', 6', 9', Yard and 7'.	Products : steam coal, with coking coal from a level.(Little Level) which was worked in 1880. The level was being worked by the 1880s. Explosion on 07/02/1863 - 2 killed. (Sinkers). The colliery was closed from 1931 to 1936. 741 men employed in 1913. Connected below ground to Cwmcynon and Abergorki pits. The winding engine had originally been used in a steam boat.
198	New Level.							See- Long Range Level.
199	New No.3 Drift.							See- Tower Colliery.
200	Newtown Level.							See- Lower Forest Level.
201	Nici-Naci Colliery.							See- Treaman Colliery.
202	No.10 Level.	Cwmbach, 100 yards (est.) to the west of No.9 Pit.	Level.	Later than 1840 (No.9) #97		Probably Aberdare Iron Co. #97. James Lewis later (Aberdare Works & Collieries Co. Ltd.) (lease held by Aberdare Iron Co.). #97.	Known seam - 4' (outcropping near mouth of level).	Product; Steam Coal. Continuation of sequence of Aberdare Iron Co.'s No.9 Pit, and adjacent to it, and worked the area to the N/West of it.
203	No.11 Level.	As No.10 Level.	Level.	As No.10 Level.		As above.	Known seam worked - 4'.	These levels would be producing steam coal from the 4' seam.
204	No.5 Furnace Pit.	Llwydcoed SO 011048.	Airshaft 124' deep x 5' diameter.	1907 W				Shaft opencasted by Bryn Pica opencast site. Probably a shaft from a larger colliery.

	A	B	C	D	F	G	H	I
205	No.8 Level.	Abernant, Near Colliers' Row. SO 015033.	Identified on plans as a level with an airshaft.	1850 W	1910.AB. #22.	In 1850, Aberdare Ironworks Co. who held the leases. By 1889, J.Lewis (Aberdare Works & Colliery Co.) Reverted to Bute Estates later.	No.1 Yard and 6' & 7.	Product : probably coking coal initially, Steam Coal later.
206	No.9 Colliery and Level. [Abernant Colliery].	Cwmbach, near Ynyscynon House. SO 017024.	Two shafts and one level. Main shaft bottom in the 5' seam at 357'. Furnace ventilation initially.	1840 #17 (No.53)	1910 #17 (No.53)	In 1840, R. Fothergill (Aberdare Iron Co. Ltd.) - bankrupt in 1875. From 1875, Aberdare & Plymouth Co. #3 (08/04/1915). About 1882, James Lewis. (Aberdare Works & Colliery Co.) #3 (08/04/1915). By 1899, reverted to Bute Estates. In 1916, acquired by PDSCC Ltd., but not reopened. #3 (08/02/1915).	29", 6', 9', 7' and 5'. The 4 crops at the top of the pit, and was worked by the level.	Product : steam coal. Explosions :- 03/11/1856 - 1 killed (flueman). In 1863, a total of 4 deaths in 3 different explosions. 10/08/1864 - 3 killed, 1 burned. 26/04/1888 - 3 burned. 17/05/1890 - 2 killed, 1 burned. The pit was closed from 1897 to 1899. Following final closure, coal reserves were worked from River Level Colliery, Abernant. No.9 Colliery was then used as a pumping shaft.
207	Old Balance Pit.							See- Blaenant Colliery.
208	Old Duffryn Colliery. [Tirfounder Colliery] [Powell's Pit, No.1.].	Cwmbach SO 025012, near the Crown Inn, and alongside the Canal.	Three shafts 387' to 9' seam, 516 to 7' seam. Upcast was 6' dia. Furnace ventilated and water-balance winding initially. The shafts were later used by Powell Duffryn as upcasts for Aberaman and Llettysiencyn Collieries. (By 1905)	1840 #57 (p.127)	1901 #22 (Vol IV)	In 1840, Thomas Powell. #28 (p.1146). Later, Messrs. Powell & Sons. #21 (p.18). In 1864, following T. Powell's death in 1863, PDSCC Ltd. was formed, which acquired Tirfounder and 15 other pits. #21 (p.18).	2' 9", 4', 6', 9' and 7.	Product : steam coal. There was one major explosion on 13/10/1858. 20 fatalities were recorded. 11 more men were killed in 8 minor explosions between 1848 and 1900. In 1845, Tom Powell was selling coal from Tirfounder for use in Brunel's ship "Great Britain". Output in 1869 was 32,615 tons. A Mr. T. Frame was the manager in 1883.
209	Old Gorllwn.							See- Gorllwyn Colliery.
210	Old Graig Colliery.	Rhigos Common. SN 936047.	Two levels.	1858 W #36 (Map 8)	Before 1870	Hirwaun Ironworks Co. (Crawshay).#23 (p.3). In 1864, Hirwaun Coal & Iron Co. (T.C. Hinde) #37 (1864).	No.2 Rhondda and Graig.	Product : initially, probably coking coal. Later, house-coal.
211	Old Lime Kiln Level.	Hirwaun Common.	Level.	1813 W #77		In 1813, Hirwaun Ironworks Co. #77.	4' and 9'.	Product : coking coal for ironworks.
212	Old No.3 Drift.							See Tower Collieries.
213	Oliver's New Drift.							See- Bute Drifts (Hirwaun).

	A	B	C	D	F	G	H	I
214	Padall-y-Bwlch Colliery.	Hirwaun SN 948036.	Level.	1902 W #1 (07/03/1903).	1906 W #1 (06/01/1906)	R. Buxton & Co. #1 (07/03/1903).		Product: house-coal. Level was closed 1903 - 1904, working by 1905, and also in the 1920's.
215	Pandy Colliery.							See- Rhigos Collieries.
216	Pant Glas Drift.							See- Tower Colliery (Old No.3 Drift).
217	Pant Level.	Hirwaun Common, near Bute Pit. SN 941053.	Level.	1850 W #65 (map)			'Black' vein and 'Rosser' vein.	Ironstone mine. Level sited on the crop of the Rosser vein. The level was used later as a furnace ventilation drift for Bute Pit.
218	Park Little Pit.							See- De Winton Colliery.
219	Park Newydd Levels.							See- Carne Park Colliery.
220	Park Pit. (No. 1.) [Parc Newydd Colliery.]	Robertstown SO 004035. Below Moss Row, Abernant.	Two shafts 399' to Gellideg seam. Upcast shaft 103" dia. Probably linked to Cwmdu-Uchaf Levels later. Furnace ventilated.	1860 #25	1897 #22	In 1860, Aberdare Iron Co. #25. In 1875, Aberdare & Plymouth Co. #2 (07/01/1888). By 1882, James Lewis. (Aberdare Works & Collieries Co. Ltd.) #3 (08/04/1915). In 1915, PDSCC Ltd. #3 (08/04/1915).	9', Bute, No.2 Yard, 7, 5' and Gellideg. The 9' seam crops out at the pit top.	Product: Rosser vein - ironstone. Later, steam coal. Explosion 10/02/1885 - 3 men badly burned, (naked flame lamps.) Seams later worked by PDSCC Ltd. from River Level Colliery. In 1891, manpower was 230, working the Longwall system of mining in 1891.
221	Park Pit. (No. 2.) [Pwll Als]. [Godre-Hirwaun Pit].	Cwmdare (Broncynon Terrace), SN 988033.	Two shafts and airshafts. Initially, furnace ventilation and water-balance winding.	1847 W #47 (p.43).	1876 #47 (p.43).	Hirwaun Iron Co. (Crawshay). #2 (06/05/1865). In 1864, Hirwaun Coal & Iron Co. (T.C. Hinde) - bankrupt in 1871. #2 (04/02/1871). In 1872, Aberdare-Rhondda Coal Co. Ltd. #37 (pp. 44-45). By 1919, Bwlfa & Merthyr Dare SCC (1891) Ltd. #46 (1920 - 21).	6', 9' and Driver, Red Vein Bute. Seams later worked from Nantmelin colliery.	Products: coke and steam coal. In 1866, the pit was refitted at great expense for the working of the Upper 4' seam. At this time the pit was connected to 'Pond Flash' Pits at Glan Road. In 1869, produced 20,323 tons. (N.B. T. Cullinder-Hinde acquired 3 collieries, plus Hirwaun Ironworks in 1864, and was bankrupt by 1871.)
222	Park View Level.	Abernant, location unknown.	Level and airshaft (upcast).		Pre-1921 #1 (04/06/1921).	In 1921, PDSCC Ltd, who had abandoned it earlier. #1 (04/06/1921).		Assumed location near Park View Terrace.
223	Patch Level.	Abernant, 400 yards to the west of Werfa Colliery... SO 019029.	Level.	1891 W #100	1894 W #100	Location suggests James Lewis, into the Bute period. (Aberdare Works & Colliery Co.)	29" and 4'.	Probably so-called due to the proximity of fireclay patch working nearby.

	A	B	C	D	F	G	H	I
224	Patch Levels.	Llwydcoed, Adjacent to Tyrergeyd Patch, & interspersed with Tyrergeyd levels. #113	Two Levels		By 1902. #113	Abernant Coal Co. #113	Gellideg. Seam dipping to south, 1 in 18. Seam section 2' 10" stone, & 2' 8" coal beneath.	Driven prior to Tyrergyd levels, & abandoned. Later used as drains for Tyrergyd levels. Product unknown.
225	Peacock Drift.							See- Rhigos Colliery.
226	Penrhiwllech Colliery.							See- Merthyr Dare Colliery.
227	Penrikyber Colliery. [Kyber].	Penrhiwceiber ST 061971.	Three shafts - No.1 - 1758' deep, No.2 - 1955' deep, No.3 - 554' deep, was sunk in 1912 and later used for pumping. Wooden headgear & single rope for early winding method.	1872 #58 Coal raised by 1879.	1985 #101	Penrikyber Navigation CC Ltd. (Glasbrook). #58. By 1890, Penrikyber Navigation CC Ltd., (Cory Bros.). #46 (1915, p.130). In 1943, PDACC Ltd. #58. In 1947, NCB. #26.	2'9", 4', No.1 Yard, 6', 9', Bute, No.2 Yard, 7, 5' and Gellideg.	Product - steam coal (for power station and smokeless fuels). Explosion in No.3 Pit on 30/03/1921, 1 man killed and 1 injured. Manpower in 1915 - 1,944 men; in 1973 - 800 men. Saleable output in 1973 was 176,324 tonnes. Workable coal reserves in 1973 was 4.6 million tonnes.
228	Pentwyn Merthyr Colliery.	Ynysyboeth ST 065965.	Levels.	1916 #112	1949 W #61	Pentwyn Merthyr CC Ltd. (D.R. Jones). Nantyfedw CC later.	Darren.	Product : house-coal, coking, manufacturing & steam coal. The levels were not nationalised in 1947.
229	Ping-Pong Colliery.							See- Duffryn Dare Colliery.
230	Pistyll-Y-Gorau Level.	Mountain Ash. #62	Level.			Edmunds & Herbert. #62		
231	Plasdraw Level.	Cwmbach Road, in the grounds of Plasdraw House. SO 011027.	Level.	1850 W #92	1870 #93	Aberdare Ironworks (Fothergill). #102. Reverted to Bute Estates by 1882.	6' seam.	Product; steam coal.
232	Plough Pit.							See- Abergwawr Colliery.

	A	B	C	D	F	G	H	I
233	Pond Flash Pits [Glandare Mine Pit].	Gadlys, Upper Glan Road, Glandare bend.	Three shafts. The depth of one shaft was 189'. Probably water-balance winding.	1865 W #2 (02/12/1865)	By 1870 #2 (10/03/1870)	In 1865, Hirwaun Coal & Iron Co. (Crawshay). #2 (2-12-1865) By 1866, Hirwaun Coal & Iron Co. (Hinde). #2 (17-3-1870). In 1872, Aberdare Rhondda CC Ltd. #37 (1872). Later linked to Gadlys Colliery, and acquired by PDSCC Ltd, as airshafts. #35.		Product : ironstone in 1865. A miner was killed by a descending cage at pit-bottom in December 1865. Probably linked to Aberdare Level via the 6' seam (Working Plan, 6' seam). (NB - 'Pond Flash' was a feeder pond for Gadlys Dare Mine, situated to the west of Oxford Street, and shown on the Tithe Map of 1847).
234	Pond Level.							See- Forge Pit.
235	Pontcynon Levels. [Lefel 'Racks'].	Near Abercynon, alongside the canal opp. to Ynysyboeth Isaf.	Two levels.	1850 W #61	1868 #61	Rhys Williams #61. In 1850, owner was J.H. Allen. (worked on lease by W.D.I. Llewellyn). #61. In 1864, R. Williams. #61. By 1868, Philip Davies & Son. #61.	Darren No.2.	Product : house-coal mainly. In 1950, a section of the New Cardiff Road collapsed into the level.
236	Powell's Pit (No.3) [Pwll Troedrhiwllech], [Cwmdare Colliery]. [Bwllfa No.3]	Cwmdare. Sunk where now stands the Country Park Centre.	Two shafts, 570 to 7' seam. Water-balance winding and furnace ventilation initially. A below-ground shaft (staple) sunk from 4' to 9' seam, complete with winding gear and using small 'Lanky' 10 cwt. trams, at one stage.	1851 #47 (p.45)	1936 #47 (p.89)	1846, Thomas Powell. #47 (p.45). From 1864, PDSCC Ltd., who abandoned the pit in 1891. #21 (p.18). From 1907, Bwllfa & Merthyr Dare SCC (1891) Ltd. #29 (p.35). From 1928, Bwllfa & Cwmaman Coal Co. Ltd. #47 (p.89). From 1930, WAC Ltd. #47 (p.72). From 1935, PDAsSCC Ltd. #47 (p.72).	29", 4', 6', 9', Bute, Yard, 7', Gellideg and Gorllwyn.	Product : steam coal and house-coal. Following PD abandonment in 1891, the pit was pumped for three years to enable mining to continue. 3 explosions from 1860 to 1871, with a total of 3 fatalities. About 1865, a boy of 8 years was killed whilst working on the surface, and three men were killed by noxious fumes in 1879. In 1910, 480 men were employed. The pit was stopped also from 1875 to 1879. In 1881, 11 horses were killed in an underground stable fire.
237	Powell's Pit No.1							See- Old Duffryn Colliery.
238	Powell's Pit No.2.							See- Abergwawr Colliery.
239	Prosper Level.	Hirwaun Common SN 938051.	Two levels & three air shafts. One being upcast for Tower Drifts, 1 & 2, at one stage.	1870 W #54 (SWR 2469)	W1897 #54 (SWR2469)	In the 1870s, Rhys Powell & John Rhys Roberts. #36 (p.17). In 1878 - Owned by W. Williams #19. Later, Bute Estates (Duffryn Aberdare SCC Ltd.). #36 (p.21).	Gorllwyn and Graig. Driver seam. (1' 9" of coal in driver).	Product : unknown, probably steam coal. Connection underground with Tower No.1 Drift. Driver seam worked Oct.1882 to 1890. The boundary was alongside Hirwaun No.2 fault. This shows a displacement of 135ft.

	A	B	C	D	F	G	H	I
240	Pwll Als.							See- Park Pit (Cwmdare).
241	Pwll Bach. [Cwmbach Little Pit].	Cwmbach, 220 yards south of Ynyscynon Colliery SO 020017.	Two shafts and a level. 441' to 7' seam. Furnace ventilation initially. Water-balance winding. Horseway level to 4' seam.	W1866 #26	By 1908 #93.(p.55)	In 1860, Abernant Iron Co. #98. In 1875, Aberdare & Pymouth Co. #3 (08/04/1915). By 1888, James Lewis. (Aberdare Works & Colliery Co.) #3 (08/04/1915). By 1915, acquired by PDSCC Ltd. but not worked. #26.	4', 6', 9' and 7'. These seams were worked in 1865. #90.	Product : initially unknown, steam coal later. Following closure, coal worked from Aberaman Colliery. Explosion on 05/04/1876 - 3 men seriously burned. Shafts re-filled in 1997.
242	Pwll Bara Menyn							See- Treaman Colliery.
243	Pwll Blaenant-y-Groes							See- Cwmbach New Pit.
244	Pwll Mwyn.							See- Gadlys Dare Mine Pit.
245	Pwll Rhys							See- Merthyr Dare Colliery.
246	Pwll Spite.							See- De Winton Colliery.
247	Pwll Troedrhiwllech							See- Powell's Pit. No.3.
248	Pwll-y-Graig.							See- Graig Colliery.
249	Pwll-yr-Afon, plus adit, including River Level Balance Pit.	Hirwaun Common (shaft level and level still evident near Pentwyn Farm on the River Cynon in 1998). SO 967048.	One shaft and one adit. The shaft was using water-balance winding and furnace ventilation.	Pre-1840 #36 (Map 3)	Pre-1916 #22 (Vol IV)	By 1850, Hirwaun Ironworks Co. (Crawshay) - probability. Acquired in the 1880s by Aberdare-Merthyr (Steam Coal) Co. Ltd. #36 (p.13). Bute Estates.	Earlier, Black Pins, Blue Vein, Llyfrau, Knobby and Rosser ironstone veins, all abandoned by 1865. Coal seams worked were Yard and 7.	Product : ironstone earlier. The mine was used as a main watercourse from Tower Drifts, Bute Pits etc., and still drains the area. (1999). Explosion on 03/01/1863 - 3 burned.
250	Red Pit.							See- Ladder Pit.
251	Rees Llewellyn Drift.							See- Tirherbert Colliery.
252	Rees's Level.	Llwydcoed SO 010057.	Level.	1907 W #75 (XI-NE-1907)				
253	Rhigos Colliery, including Graig Levels. [Pandy], [Peacock Drift], [British Rhondda Colliery].	Rhigos (Ystrady-fodwg) SN 898050. Near 'Bailey-Glas' Farm.	Total of 7 drifts at different working periods. Drifts 1, 6, and 7 working in 1955. Three airshafts.	1832 #52 (p.218)	1964 #24 (p.510)	Bute Estates. #52 (p.510). In 1842, David Davis (Blaengwawr). #52 (p.219) By 1847, C.L. Clay & Co. #28 (D. Davis', p.1115). By 1890, British Rhondda Colliery Co. In 1935, New British Rhondda C.C. Ltd. #26. In 1947, NCB. (Area 4.)	No.2 Rhondda, 4', 6' and 9'. Ironstone (earlier); Blackband, Little Blue, Rosser, Rhyd. All abandoned by 1865.	Product : Anthracite (stone coal), & Ironstone, earlier. Explosions :- 24/04/1890 - 1 burned 28/09/1892 - 2 burned 10/07/1941 - 16 killed. (Naked flame lamps in use.) 705 men were employed in 1955, producing 223,000 tons. In 1846, production was 5,033 tons/annum.
254	Rhigos Level.	Rhigos.	Level.		1865	Unknown.		Ironstone Mine.
255	Rhydywaun Colliery.							See- Aberdare Navigation Colliery.
256	Rhys & Richards Pit.							See- Merthyr Dare Colliery.

	A	B	C	D	F	G	H	I
257	River Level Colliery [Lefel yr Afon], including Furnace Level.	Abernant SO 009034.	Two shafts. Downcast - 17' x 11' dia., 327 deep in 1891. Furnace ventilation and water-balance winding initially. Three other 9' dia. shafts later. The colliery was later linked up underground to Gadlys Colliery by PDSCC Ltd.	1840 #10 (p.102)	1939 #86 (p.189)	Aberdare Iron Company #3 (08/03/1915). From 1875, Aberdare & Plymouth Co. #3 (08/03/1915). In 1882, James Lewis. (Aberdare Works & Colliery Co.) #3 (08/03/1915). In 1899, reverted to Bute Estates, #3 (08/03/1915). From 1915, PDSCC Ltd. #3 (08/03/1915).	No.1 Yard, 6, 9, Bute, No.2 Yard, 7, Gellideg, also fireclay. Ironstone veins unknown.	Products : Ironstone, coking coal; later, steam coal. On 09/12/1896, an inrush of water killed 6 men and closed the colliery. The colliery was reopened in 1915 by PDSCC Ltd., who sunk two shafts to the 9' seam. 934 men employed in 1932. Explosions :- Between 1836 and 1919, 5 killed and 16 burned, one a boy of 12, killed in 1886. In 1891, 'Pillar & Stall' system was in use, with naked lights.
258	Rosser Drift.							See- Bryngwyn Levels, (Lower).
259	Scales Pit.							See- Ynyscynon Colliery.
260	Screens Level.	SO. 0533-9527 Ynysybwl.		By 1893. #121.			Darren Ddu seam	It was sited about 120yds. from the rear of 'Abernant House', and the school.
261	Shepherd's Pit.							See- Cwmaman Colliery.
262	Soap Vein Level (Coleman's).	Hirwaun Common SN 969040. 170yds. West of Level Fawr.	Level.	1840 W #36 (Map 6)	1847. #117	A Mr. J. Coleman later became a coal proprietor at Mountain Ash - a possibility ? #117.	Soap vein ironstone.	Ironstone mine. Vein adjacent to the Gorllwyn coal seam. These were sometimes worked together.
263	St. Gwynno Level. [Brithdir Level].	Cwmaman, overlooking Cwmneol Colliery from the east.	One level.	1953 #41	1956 #41	E. R. Samuels and B. Samuels (brothers).	No.2 Rhondda - a seam of varying thickness.	A licensed Mine. Closed due to inferior coal quality
264	Steam Coal Colliery.							See- Hirwaun-Aberdare Colliery.
265	T. Hopkins' Level.	Hirwaun Common.	Level.	1875 W #37 (1875-1878)	1878 W #37 (1875-1878)	Thomas Hopkins #37 (1875-1878)		Produced 6,500 tons in 1877.
266	Tan-y-Bryn Level.	Llwydcoed SN 994043.	Levels, plus an airshaft.	1870, possibly earlier #75	1916 #22	First owner unknown. By 1906, Tan-y-Bryn Colliery & Brickworks Co. Ltd #1 (10/03/1906). New company with same title by March 1906. Chairman was Henry Davies, Aberaman. Closed in 1912. #3 (23/09/1912). (Bankrupt.) D.R. Llewellyn in 1914. #8 (Vol 2, p.100).	Garw, & Iron veins earlier.	Products : ironstone, coking coal and fireclay. In 1906, total output of coal was 107 tons. (First year of re-opening.) Garw section abandoned in 1916.
267	Tanygraig Colliery.	Rhigos.	Level.	1880 W #2 (21/02/1880)		William Williams Esq. (Broncynon), Hirwaun.	Graig.	Six horses killed in a stable fire in 1880.

	A	B	C	D	F	G	H	I
268	The 'Navi'.							See- Navigation Colliery.
269	Thomas Davies Soap Vein Dip.	Hirwaun Common. 790yds. N/West of 'Level Fawr'.	One level and two air-shafts. #117	1847W. #117		Thomas Davies. (Probably). #117	Soap Vein ironstone, and possibly Gorllwn coal. (Adjacent).	Products: Ironstone.
270	Tirfounder Colliery.							See- Old Duffryn.
271	Tirfounder Level [Lefel Ceffyl Gwyn], [White Horse Level].	Cwmbach, 200 yards west of Tirfounder Colliery. Near "Sion Terrace"	Level and 2 airshafts.	1884 #26 (SW Div.)	Closed 1901. #116	Opened by Mr. David Jones, landlord of the "White Horse" public house. #2 (16/04/1898). By 1905, PDSCC Ltd., but not worked. #26 (SW Div.).	Gorllwyn. Abandoned by 1901.	Product : house-coal. Produced 5,120 tons in 1897.
272	Tirherbert Colliery [Will Rhys' Level], [Drift Rees Llewellyn].	One drift on Hirwaun Common, plus two other drifts on the Rhigos side of Carn-y-Moesau mountain. SN 931048.	Four drifts. The 'return' drift was sited near to where Tower No 4 shaft would later be sunk. This drift was driven in 1925. (D.R.Llewellyn).	1914 #29 (p.85)	1968 #24 (p.510)	In 1914, D.R. Llewellyn & Sons. #3 (06/11/1914). In 1930, WAC Ltd. #1(11/01/1930). In 1947, NCB.	Graig, Gorllwyn Fach and Gorllwyn.	Product : house-coal, steam coal in 1932. First drift was started but delayed due to First World War. In 1955, production was 160,000 tons with a manpower of 414. There was a 'stay-in' strike lasting two weeks in 1956, led by W. Addiscott, Lodge Chairman. Explosions :- 1933 - 2 men badly burned. 06/09/1938 - 4 men killed. Workforce transferred to Tower Colliery following closure.
273	Tir-y-Lluest Level.	Cwmbach.	Level.	1793 #108 (p.484)		Edward T. Edwards. #108 (p.484).		The coal was transported inside the level in a small boat, as the level was partially flooded. The boat was constructed by a Mr. W.E. Rees of Aberdare, and carried two and a half hundredweight. Possibly the first canal in Cynon Valley ?

	A	B	C	D	F	G	H	I
274	Tower Colliery (No.1 Drift) [Four Foot Drift], and Tower/Bute upcast shaft.	Hirwaun Common. SN 948048.W This drift was started from the surface of 'Goitre Machine' Colliery (Crawshay's).	A drift, plus a return drift. An upcast shaft was sunk by 1870, also used by Bute Pit. It was 265' deep, and 15' in dia., and was furnace ventilated up to 1891. (Furnace, 8' x 7'). Producing 39,892 C.F.M. Fan in use by the 1940's.	1864 #103 (1:1, intro)	1969 #36 (p.33)	Bute Estates (Duffryn Aberdare SCC). #36 (p.16). In 1919, D.R. Llewellyn & Sons Ltd. #46 (1920/21, p.32). In 1930, WAC Ltd. #1 (01/02/1930). In 1935, PDACC Ltd. #1 (29/06/1935). In 1947, NCB. #26.	4', No.1 Yard, Red Vein, Bute, 9', 7, 5, 6'. In 1932, Tower sold Large, washed peas, beans and small, at this stage.	Products : house-coal, steam coal. Underground link-up to Aberdare-Merthyr Steam Coal Ltd., sharing the same management in the Bute period. Pillar & Stall, and 'Longwall' system, were being worked, with naked flame lighting, in 1891. In 1954, a journey 'runaway' killed an official and seriously injured 9 trainees in the 'Libya' district. In 1932, manpower was 700; the Manager was W. Pugh. In 1952, manpower was 1,100, Manager Donald Davies, who was later to sit on the National Coal Board in the 1970's.
275	Tower Colliery (No.2 Drift) [9' Drift.]	Adjacent to, and driven to the west of, Tower No.1 Drift.	Drift to exploit the 9' & 4' seams. Between and to the East of, Hirwaun 1 and 2 faults.	1894 #36 (sect.3, p.18)	1969 #103 (p.33)	Proprietors as in Tower No.1.	Upper 4', Red Vein. Bute, 9', 7, 5' and No.1 Yard.	Product : steam coal only. Linked underground to Tower No.4 in the 1950s. In 1896, two men fatally gassed ('blackdamp'). 2 minor explosions in 1893 and 1902, 3 men burned. Naked flame lighting in 1891.
276	Tower Colliery (Old No.3 Drift). [Pant-Glas Drift.]	Hirwaun Common SN 940048.	Drift. Downcast drift for Tower No.4 by 1944. Originally driven through to Tower No.2 link-up.	1919 #36 (p.22)	1960 #51	In 1919, D.R. Llewellyn & Sons. #36 (p.22). By 1930, WAC. #36 (p.23). By 1935, PDACC Ltd. #1 (29/06/1935). In 1947, NCB.	9', 4', red vein at one stage. Pillar & stall system worked until 1960 in Tower No.4.	Used as a haulage plane drift for the '9 West' coal reserves (35 years of production from this area). Linked underground to Bute Drifts in the 9' seam. Pumping drift later for some years.

	A	B	C	D	F	G	H	I
277	Tower Colliery. (New No.3 Drift.) (Included as part of Goitre Tower Colliery "Buy-Out").	Hirwaun Common SN 941047.	Drift sunk to the 9' seam (intake ventilation for Tower 4 area). It was connected for some years to 6' & Bute coal-faces in the old Tower Drifts area. (In the 1960's).	1968 #103 (1:1, intro. hist.)	Still working at NCB, later 'British Coal'. time of writing. (Year 2000)	In 1995, Goitre Tower Anthracite Ltd. (workforce buy-out following 20 months closure).		Driven as main line conveyor system for Tower No.4, and also for conveying of coal from Fernhill Colliery in the 1970s and from Mardy Colliery in 1986. Tower Colliery was linked up, at different times, to the following mines :- 1. Aberdare-Merthyr Steam Coal Colliery (Pre-1917). 2. Blaenhirwaun Colliery to Tower No.1. 3. Bute (Hirwaun) Drift. 4. Prosper Level to Tower No.1 Drift. 5. Ladder Pit to Tower No.1 & 2 Drifts. 6 Rhigos Colliery (inadvertently) due to inrush of water in 1982, in the 9' seam. 7. Long Range Level in 9' seam. 8. Bute Pit (ironstone) in 1870 to the same airshaft. 9 Knobby Drift (ironstone) connected to airshaft in 5' seam workings. 10. Fernhill Colliery (Rhondda) in Bute seam 1964. (Link-up & conveyance of coal). 11. Mardy Colliery (Rhondda Fach) in 5' seam. 1986. (Link-up for conveyance of coal).

	A	B	C	D	F	G	H	I
278	Tower Colliery. No.4 Pit. [Goitre Tower Colliery].	Rhigos area. SN 926042.	Upcast shaft. 518' to 9' seam. By October 1999, the V40 coalface was estimated as being more than 3¼ miles from pit-bottom, and beneath Glyncorrwg "Take". The shaft was sunk to exploit the immense reserves of 9' coal, and later the 5' & 7' seams.	1941/1942 #103 (1:1, intro. hist.)	Still working in 2000	In 1941, PDACC Ltd. In 1947, NCB. (Closed 01/04/1994) Reopened by 1995, Goitre Tower Anthracite Ltd. (workforce buy-out). Still working. In the year 2000, Tower Colliery will have been open for 136 years.	Bute seam worked in early 1960s. 6' worked in 1963, stopped due to friable roof conditions. 5', up to 1990's.	Product : mainly beans, grains, large coal,& small, house-coal & industrial purposes. "Duff is sold to the Aberthaw power station. The 9' section used the Pillar & Stall method from 1944 to 1962, due to good roof conditions, and 120 horses were working in Tower in the early 1950's. Due to loss of reserves, the 9' seam was abandoned in 1982, and the 6' seam by 1986. From that time to the present, the combined 7/5 seams are the sole operating seams at Tower, and the product is now classified as anthracite. An explosion occurred on 12/04/1962, with 9 fatalities and numerous injuries, some serious. A serious flooding occurred due to an incursion into Rhigos Colliery workings in June 1982, which resulted in the loss of the remaining 9' seam reserves at Tower Colliery. The average annual output from 1995 to 1998, was 532,000 Tonnes. (Anthracite). Production ceased from 22.10.1999 to Jan. 2000, due to gas extraction damage caused by a recorded earth tremor. The Tower 'Buy-Out' was, and is, a complete success. (2000 A.D.)
279	Tower Graig Colliery. (Not associated with 'Tower' Colliery.)	Hirwaun Common.	Two levels.	1870 W #36 (Map 9)	1886 W #2 (02/01/1886)	In 1870, Welsh Iron Co. #25. By 1886, W. Williams. #2 (16/09/1882).	Graig seam.	Product : house-coal. Tower Graig Level was later used as a fan drift for Coronation Colliery. (D.R.Llewellyn).
280	Tower, Gwrangon Shaft.	Rhigos SN 924050, alongside the Gwrangon Brook.	One shaft sunk to the 9' seam (downcast). Tower No.4 intake shaft.	1948 (est.) #103	By 1990 #103	NCB.	9' seam.	No winder system, ladder for inspections. Ventilation shaft (intake). Destroyed by opencasting in the late 1980s. The shaft was the emergency exit from the 9' West district, and was the last shaft to be sunk for coal mining purposes in the Cynon Valley, and probably Wales.

	A	B	C	D	F	G	H	I
281	Treaman Colliery [Nici-Naci], [Williams' Pit], [Pwll Bara Menyn].	Aberaman SO 017012. To the west of the old gasworks.	Two shafts 231' to 4' seam. The upcast shaft was 264' by 1891. Furnace ventilated initially. Three other 'Black Band' shafts were also sunk.(Ironstone) A Guibal fan (10' x 30') was installed by 1891.	1846/1850 #88 (item 239, p.8)	1912 #21 (p.29.)	David Williams of Ynyscynon. #105 (p.193). Before1866, Crawshay Bailey. #21 (p.19). By 1867, PDSCC Ltd. #21 (pp.18/19).	29", 4', 6', 9', Bute, 7, Yard, Black Band ironstone. (4', 6, 7 & 9' abandoned in 1893). Longwall face method in 1891.	Products : ironstone and steam coal. Lower coal seams worked from Aberaman Colliery later. Explosions :- 29/07/1851 - 1 killed. 10/04/1855 - 6 killed. 26/03/1858 - 1 killed. 15/08/1883 - 2 killed. Treaman Colliery was called 'Nici-Naci' due to the noisy rattling of the pit rope over the headgear sheave, heard all over the village. Naked flame lamps in use with some safety lamps, in 1891.180 men employed in 1912. Mr. Ben Lewis the manager. A 'Mackworth' report (1860) stated that; "The pit was dangerous and defective, with no qualified manager - the man in charge was a heavy drinker"
282	Trewen Pit.							See- Cwmaman Colliery.
283	Troedrhiwllech Colliery.							See- Powell's Pit. No.3
284	Tunnel Colliery.	Cwmbach, near Merthyr tunnel entrance. SO 025027.	Two shafts :- No.1 - 481' to pit bottom in 9' seam. No.2 - upcast, 510'. In 1891, ventilated by a Schiele fan 13½' in diameter, producing 61,410 C.F.M.	Pre-1865 #2 (19/08/1865)	By 1904 #61 (1904)	Aberdare Iron Co. (bankrupt in 1875) #2 (13/08/1865). In 1875, Aberdare & Plymouth CC. #2 (01/02/1879). By 1882, James Lewis. (Aberdare Works & Colliery Co.) #3 (08/04/1915). By 1901, Bute Estates. #3 08/04/1915). In 1915, PDSCC Ltd., but not worked. #3 (08/04/1915).	29", 4', No.1 Yard, 9', 7, Bute and No.2 Yard. Longwall extraction in 29", 6', and 4' in 1891.	Product : steam coal. Production ceased in 1904. The shafts were used for ventilation of Windsor and Werfa Collieries (Nixon's), after this time. Explosions :- 2 killed and 6 burned in a total of 6 explosions. By 1891, coal was being transported via No.9 Colliery surface by a tramway across Pant Farm fields. In 1891, labour was 405 below ground, 59, including women, on the surface. Naked flame lamps were used in the 'Bute' seam in 1891. In 1897, tonnage royalties were being paid to Merthyr Parish, for coal ascending Tunnel Pit. (12,117 tons.)
285	Tynte Level.							See- Nantfedw Levels.

	A	B	C	D	F	G	H	I
286	Tyr Ergyd Colliery and Balance Pit. [Wilkin's Level].	Llwydcoed SO 003049, SO 000047.	3 levels & airshaft.	1900 W #113	By 1908 #22 (1908)	In 1900, John Wilkins. #1 (09/05/1903).	Gellideg. Abandoned by 28/03/1908.	Products : ironstone and steam coal. In August of 1904, the colliery office and weighing machine were blown up, 'probably due to the employment of non-union labour during a dispute'. Output in 1903 was 5,720 tons. Mined by longwall method There was an old balance pit alongside the levels. (Ironstone)
287	Ty-Rhos Big Vein.	Llwydcoed. #62.	Level.			Possibly: Gadlys Iron Co.	Probably Ironstone.	
288	Upper Duffryn Colliery.	Cwmbach SO 022015, near to the present 'Remploy' factory (1998).	Two shafts, 372' to the 9' seam. Furnace ventilation.	1844 #26	1875 #29 (p.22)	T. Powell & Sons. #29 (p.22). In 1864, PDSCC Ltd. #29 (p.22).	2'9", 4', 6' and 9'.	Product : steam coal. The pit was badly damaged in an explosion in 1844, with no fatalities. In an explosion in July 1845, 29 workers were killed, 5 of whom were boys - 1 aged 14; 1 aged 12; 1 aged 10; and 2 aged 9. On 07/02/1863, two boys aged 12 and 13 were killed in an explosion. The coal seams were later worked from Aberaman Colliery. In 1863, Upper Duffryn produced 62.126 tons. Colliery manager in 1866 was James Williams.
289	Victoria Pit.							See- Gadlys Colliery.
290	Waun Fawr Level.	Llwydcoed SN 999054. Sit: Above Grey's Place.	Level.	1898 W #47 (p.61)	1922 W #106	Llwydcoed CC Ltd. #47 (p.61). In 1914, acquired by D.R. Llewellyn (Dyllas Collieries) #3 (18/06/1918).	Bute seam in 1915.	Product : Steam coal & housecoal. Reopened in 1914 (Dyllas) and worked two seams of coal. Part of the Dyllas complex. James Evans, manager in 1922.

	A	B	C	D	F	G	H	I
291	Werfa Colliery No.1 Pit.	Abernant SO 019032.	No.1 shaft (main winding shaft) depth 357' to the 9' seam, 13'6" diameter. Furnace ventilation and water-balance winding initially. By 1891, No. 1 shaft was a downcast shaft fitted with a Schiele fan, 7' dia., which must have been a forcing fan. At this time, shaft depth was 502'. The fan produced 50,373 C.F.M.	1846 #4 (Disaster Report 13/09/1851)	1910 #1 (21/05/1910, p.5)	1846, J.Nixon. #4 (19/05/1849). In 1851, Nixon, J. Evens, T. Heath & Williams. #104 (notes). By 1858, Heath, J. Evens & Co. #104 (notes). From 1884, J. Evens & Co. #104 (notes). By 1903, worked by M. of Bute (leased from Thomas of Court, Merthyr.) #1 (21/05/1910).	2'9", 4', Yard, 6', Red Vein, 9', Bute, Brass, 7, 5' and Gellideg.	Product : steam coal. The colliery was linked to Tunnel Pit after 1903. Explosions :- 1847 - 2 killed, 8 injured. 14/05/1849 - 5 killed, 14 injured. 17/03/1856 - 2 killed. 26/03/1886 - 4 killed. Plus 8 other explosions with no fatalities. A boy of 9 years was killed in September 1851, and a boy of 11 in 1864, resulting in a court case. (under age.) Shaft disaster - in May 1851, a snapped chain on the shaft cage sent 11 men and 3 boys aged 11, 13, and 16 years to their deaths. Production in 1869 - 55,629 tons. 350 men employed in 1886.. By 1891. 'Longwall' system of mining was in use, with naked flame lighting.
292	Werfa Colliery No.2 Pit (New Pit).	Abernant SO 019032.	No.2 shaft was sunk to 7' seam and was 335' in depth. An airshaft was sunk before 1868 to the red vein seam. It was 9ft. diameter, and 175ft. deep. (Near 'Nant-Gwyn' House.)	1879 #2 (05/07/1879)	1910 #1 (21/05/1910)	As for Werfa Colliery No.1 Pit. (From 1879)	As for Werfa Colliery No.1 Pit.	As for Werfa Colliery No.1 Pit.
293	Werfa Dare Colliery.	Abernant SO 020034.	Two drifts.	1914 #3 (15/10/1914)	1949 #24 (App. IV, 1949)	Werfa Dare CC Ltd. (Messrs. Williams Bros of Werfa). #1 (28/11/1914). In 1947, NCB.	2'9", 4', Yard, 6', Red Vein, 9' and Bute.	Products : house-coal and steam coal. Two men burned by an explosion in 1918. In 1935, produced 100'000 tons, with 279 men employed. Most of workforce transferred to Tower Colliery in 1949.
294	Werfa Graig Colliery.	Abernant SO 023038.	Two levels.	1908 #104 #115	1914 #104 #6396	Werfa Graig Co. closed by Werfa Dare CC Ltd. in 1914. The Williams family possessed both collieries. #115.	Graig (abandoned in 1914) and No.2 Rhondda. Seam 2'1" thick	Product : house-coal. 222 men employed in 1914. Severe water problems. Closed due to high costs & poor roof conditions. An older trial shaft was used as an upcast for the levels.
295	White Horse Level.							See-Tirfounder Levels.
296	Wigley's Level.							See-Ysguborwen Colliery.

	A	B	C	D	F	G	H	I
297	Wilkin's Level.							See- Tyr Ergyd Colliery.
298	William Ball Level.	Hirwaun Common SN 949044.	Level 260 yards to the west of Tower No.1 Drift.	1850s #65			Probably worked the Gorllwyn, on the crop.	Product : probably coking coal, and ironstone.
299	William Rees' Level.	Cwmdare SN 970032,	Level.	1906 #10 (p.104)		D.R. Llewellyn. #10 (p.104).		Part of Windber Colliery complex.
300	Williams' Pit. (1.)							See- Ynyscynon Colliery.
301	Williams' Pit. (2.)							See- Treaman Colliery.
302	Windber Colliery including Buxton's Level.	Cwmdare SN 972029.	Levels driven in the Gorllwyn-Fach seam.	1903 #47 (p.61)	1934 #47 (p.61)	Rees Llewellyn (Bwllfa & Merthyr Dare SCC Ltd., 1891) #47 (p.61). In 1906, D.R. Llewellyn. #47 (p.61). From 1920, D.R. Llewellyn & Sons Ltd. #47 (p.61). In 1934, WAC Ltd. #47 (p.61). N.B. Rees Llewellyn opened the drift, and was about to close it, (due to a decrease in coal section) when D.R.Llewellyn took over, later, with success.	Gorllwyn and Graig.	Products : house-coal and steam coal. The name "Windber' originated from Berwind, an American coal town. Reputed to be the first colliery in South Wales to use electrical coal-cutters. 220 men employed in 1932, with Mr.G. Barling as manager, selling washed small, peas, and beans, at the time. The colliery was D.R.Llewellyn's first venture.
303	Windber Dare Levels.	Cwmdare, 300 yards to the east of Windber Colliery.	3 levels, 2 of which were reopened disused levels, one of which reads 'Graig Level', on a working plan.	1956 #42 (17/05/1956).	1959 W #107	Lambert Bros. #42 (17/05/1956). Acquired in 1958 by unknown owners.	Graig. The coal section was about 4'.	Product : steam coal, exported via Barry Dock. Mine licenced by NCB.
304	Windsor Level.	Cwmbach, near Crimea Level. SO.017027	Level driven to the north-east.	1890 W #60	1910 #8 (p.98)	By 1892, James Lewis Co. (Aberdare Works & Colliery Co.) #2 (23/01/1892). By 1899, Bute Estates. #3 (08/04/1915). In 1915, PDACC Ltd., but not worked. #3 (08/04/1915).	29" and 4'.	Product : unknown. (4' seam suggests steam coal.) 251 men employed in 1891. Ventilated by Tunnel Colliery fan in 1891, fan producing 7,000 C.F.M.; linked underground to Abernant Patch Level by 1893.
305	Wretched Level.							See- Forest Level (Lower).
306	Ynys Pit.							See- Meadow Pit.

	A	B	C	D	F	G	H	I
307	Ynyscynon Colliery. [Williams' Pit], [Scales' Pit], later, [High Duffryn], when owned by PDACC Ltd.	Cwmbach, Between the Canal, and the Aberdare Railway. (1845 - 46.) N/West of 'Scales' Houses'	Two shafts sunk to 396', in the 7' seam. Initially furnace ventilation and water-balance winding. A third shaft was used as a pumping shaft.	1843 #57 (p.142)	1875 #29 (p.22)	David Williams #57 (p.142). In 1866, acquired by PDSCC Ltd. #29 (p.22). Production ceased in 1875. Seams finally abandoned in 1893.	4', 6', 9', 7', Lower Yard and Bute. (Abandoned, before 1893).	Product : steam coal. On 13/10/1858, 4 men were suffocated by 'black-damp' gas. Coal was worked later from Aberaman Colliery. A shaft was used for pumping until the 1960s. Output for 1863 was 66,220 tons. David Williams (bardic name 'Alaw Goch') later opened Deep Duffryn Colliery, Treaman Colliery, and Merthyr Dare Pit, later still, he sunk pits in Trealaw, (Rhondda Valley).
308	Ynyscynon Level.	Cwmbach, near Ynyscynon Farm.	A drift which struck the 4' seam.	1843 #1 (16/08/1924)		David Williams (Alaw Goch) and Lewis Lewis. #1 (16/08/1924).	4'.	The level became part of Ynyscynon Colliery. Lewis retired before the seam was struck.
309	Ysguborwen Colliery (including numerous levels, Balance Pit, Drain and Mine Pit). [Mountain Pit], [Horseway Level], [Wigley's Level].	Llwydcoed SN 997040, and near Cable Works, SN 999040.	4 shafts in colliery complex, 3 of which were flue vent shafts. Main shaft was 258' deep to Graig seam, and 1 level to Gellideg seam. Levels up to 21 in number.	1849 #109 (p.27)	1919 #22 (Vol IV, Wales & Salop)	S. Thomas & Joseph. #57 (p.142). By 1867, S. Thomas & Co. (died 1879). #57 (p.142). From 1879, D.H. Thomas. #110 (death of S. Thomas). Prior to 1909, a part of the colliery was owned by Mr. George Rake. #1 (23/10/1909). After 1855, S. Thomas took Mr. E. Lewis of Bwllfa as partner for a short time. In 1905, the lease was acquired by P.D.S.C.Co.Ltd.	29", 4', Yard, 9', Nos.1 & 2 Brass veins, 7, Gellideg and Gorllwyn. Ironstone worked from Rosser vein.	Products : ironstone and steam coal. Coal output in 1903 was 7,887 tons. The coal was later worked from River Level Colliery. From 1856 to 1892, 10 explosions recorded, resulting in a total of 15 killed and 12 badly burned. 200 men employed in 1913. Mr. Herbert Kirkhouse was agent for the colliery prior to 1864. The Abandoned Mines Plan (Vol.4.), shows that a total of 18 levels or shafts were abandoned in 1895. Mr.D.H.Thomas (Prop.) was later to become Viscount Rhondda.

Appendix B

List of Sources referred to in Appendix A

1 "Aberdare Leader".
2 "Aberdare Times".
3 "Mountain Ash Weekly Post".
4 "Cardiff & Merthyr Guardian".
5 "Glamorgan, Monmouth & Brecon Gazette".
6 "Western Mail".
7 "Old Aberdare" Vol 1 (CVHS).
8 "Old Aberdare" Vol 2 (CVHS).
9 "Works Diary – Llwydcoed Collieries" – John Price, Sur. Foreman.
10 "Old Aberdare" Vol 4 (CVHS).
11 "Old Aberdare" Vol 5 (CVHS).
12 "Review of the Coal Industry, Mid Glamorgan" – P. Davies (Pontypridd Pub. Lib.).
13 "History of Mountain Ash" – W. Bevan (Trans. A. V. Jones).
14 "Old Aberdare" Vol 8 (CVHS).
15 "Children of the Mines" – D.L.Davies (CVHS).
16 "Aberdare Steam Collieries Ass." – Proportions (Year 1863). (Doc) W. G. Dalziell.
17 "Pictures from the Past" – Vol 1 (CVHS) pub. 1986.
18 "Pictures from the Past" – Vol 2 (CVHS) pub. 1992.
19 "S.W. Coalfield Directory" 1992 (Cardiff Cent. Lib.).
20 Mr. D. Bowen (Former Colliery Surveyor).
21 "PDSCC Ltd.-1864 to 1914" – W. W. Price.
22 Catalogue of Plans of Abandonment, etc., Vol IV – Coal Commission.
23 "South Wales Ironworks, 1700 to 1840" – J. Lloyd.
24 "The Fed" – H. Francis & Dai Smith.
25 "Welsh Coal Mines" (Notes) – (Aberdare) – Dr. G. Thomas.
26 NCB, Vesting Day List of Pits (SW Div., Area 4).
27 "Colliery Year Book, 1935 (Direct)" – Cardiff Cent. Lib.
28 "Dictionary of Welsh Biography" – Aberdare Pub. Lib.
29 "South Wales Coalfield" – Barnett & Willson-Lloyd.
30 "South Wales Coalfield (Geology & Mines)" – H.Davies pub. 1901.
31 "Dedication Booklet of Abercynon Colliery" – (H.Rogers inf.).
32 NCB Booklet (Nat. Rec.).
33 Map – Sheet (Glam.) XI.15.3.
34 Plan – 6′ seam crop (Hirwaun to Aberdare). (Possession of writer).
35 "Table of Acquisitions " – (P.D.S.C.C.Ltd.) – Mr. Douglas Bowen (Area Surveyor).
36 "A History of Ironstone & Coal Mining (Hirwaun Common), 1757 to 1989" – M. L. Evans, Surveyor, NCB. (Unpublished MS.)
37 "Hanes Hirwaun" – Rev. R. M. Rees.
38 "Galloway's Report on Aberdare Mines" (1882) – Cardiff Pub. Lib.
39 NCB (Aberdare Valley Mines in the 20th Century).
40 "History of Powell Duffryn (Aberdare Valley)" – Journal – W. W. Price.
41 Verbal information from proprietor.
42 NCB Licence Document.
43 "History of Cwmaman Institute" – D.L. Davies.
44 "History of Cwmaman" – D. Lloyd. (Trans.).
45 "The Coal Industry, 1750 to 1814" – John Williams.
46 "S.Wales Coal Annual" (index, Aberdare Pub. Lib.).
47 "The Story of Cwmdare" – John F. Mear.
48 Public Record Office, Wales ref. 4(612)1.
49 "Industry Before the Industrial Revolution" Vol.1. – W. Rees.
50 "Cynon Valley in the Age of Iron" – Dr. R.Grant.

51 Writer's personal records and plans.
52 "Cardiff and the Marquess of Bute" – John Davies.
53 Geological Survey Map sheet SO 00 NW, Brecknock & Glamorgan.
54 Abandonment Plans SWR 2469 (Tower Colliery records).
55 "The Crawshay Dynasty; the Triumph of Conservatism". (Aberdare Pub. Lib.).
56 "S. Wales Coal Analysis, 1920" – Ll. J. Davies.
57 "History of the Pioneers of the Welsh Coalfield" – Elizabeth Phillips.
58 NCB Documents (Collieries Year Details). (1973.Pub.)
59 "Aberdare Mines in the 20th Century" (NCB Paper).
60 HM Inspector's Report (Working Methods). (1891). – H. Rogers collection.
61 HM Inspector's Report. – H. Rogers coll.
62 "Listed Mines" – Inspector's report in H. Rogers coll.
63 T. J. Evans BSc notes.
64 The late Mr. William Jones, Gadlys.
65 Map – "Lordship of Hirwaun etc" (Ironstone veins crop, 1850) SWR 2466.1.
66 Lineage of Llewellyn Co.
67 "Port of Cardiff & Aberdare Steam Coalfield" – A. Bassett, paper published in 1864, p.105.
68 Photograph of datestone on drift.
69 Working Plans of Crimea Level in possession of the writer.
70 Plan – Sheet SO. S/W Glam. – Geology Survey.
71 "South Wales News".
72 "An Autobiographical History of Cwmaman" – W. Rhys Jones.
73 Information from Mr.T. Jenkins, Cwmdare (Overman).
74 Working Plan, 5' seam outcrops, Bwllfa 'Take' in possession of writer.
75 Map – Glamorgan Sheet XI.S.E. (1867-75).
76 Mr. Mel Godsall – family involvement.
77 Hirwaun Ironworks sale document.
78 "Old Mountain Ash in Pictures" – H. Rogers & B. Baldwin.
79 Mines Rescue plan, Coronation Level, 1938.
80 "The Changing Character of Coal" – paper by T. Joseph, 1860's.
81 Not evident – Ordnance Survey map 1875.
82 Site leased to Aberdare Iron Co.
83 "S.W. Coal & Iron Statistics" (Hunt's).
84 "Gordon's Map" 1901.
85 Working Plan, Gorllwyn seam outcrops, 1934.
86 "Environmental Studies in Cynon Valley" pub. Mid Glamorgan C.C.
87 Ordnance Survey map 1865 – 1868 Aberdare Pub. Lib.
88 "Catalogue of Colliery Explosions (S. Wales) – H. Rogers Collection.
89 Not Evident – Ordnance Survey map
90 Mr. Walter Rees (documents).
91 Aberdare Rate Books 1847 – Glamorgan Record Office.
92 Geological Sheet 248 (Glam.XVIII N.E., revised 1914).
93 "A History of Aberdare" – E.Greening. (1875 – 1901)
94 Map – Glamorgan Sheet XI – Six Foot seam crops etc.
95 "The Rhondda Valleys" – E. D. Lewis.
96 "Mountain Ash Remembered." – B. Baldwin.
97 Glamorgan Sheet XI – 4' seam
98 W. W. Price Collection, Aberdare Public Library. (Colliery List.)
99 "The Crawshay Dynasty, the Triumph of Conservatism", p.142.
100 Working Plan, 2'9" seam, Hirwaun Common to Cwmbach.
101 Mr. C. Willis, Overman at Penrikyber in 1985.
102 Area of Leasehold to Aberdare Iron Co.
103 "Sale of Tower Colliery" document, 1994 (History, etc.) NCB Survey.
104 Mr. Edward G. Williams, Chepstow, Werfa Collieries historian and descendant of proprietors.
105 "South Wales Coal Industry, 1841-1875" (Mackworth Report).
106 Diary of Mr. John Price, Foreman, Dyllas Colliery, working 1903-1922.
107 Mr. Colin Lambert (son of proprietor).

108 "History of the Rise, Progress, & Prospects of the Coal Trade (S. Wales & Mon.)" 1883. D. Edwards.
109 "Life of Viscount Rhondda" by J. Vyrnwy Morgan.
110 Inheritance of Works.
111 Working Plan, Driver Seam (Hirwaun Common Area). In Writers Possession.
112 Working Plan -- H. Rogers' Collection.
113 Working Plan (abandonment). No.5210. Tyrergyd. (In writers possession.)
114 Working Plan (abandonment). No.3857. Gadlys Graig. (In writers possession.)
115 Working Plan (abandonment). No.6396. Werfa Graig. Ditto.
116 Working Plan (abandonment). No.40740. Tirfounder Level. Ditto.
117 Working Plan of Lefel Fawr Coll. SWR.2467B. Ditto.
118 Working Plan (abandonment). No.2284. Cwm Level. Ditto.
119 Working Plan (abandonment) No.4249. De Winton Coll. Ditto
120 Working Plan Hir/Common. SWR.2467. Ditto.
121 Geological Plan. Glamorgan, Sheet X1X.SW. Ditto.
122 Working Plan No.358867. Ditto.
123 Digest of Welsh Statistics. L. J. Williams. Vol.1 1985.
124 Second Industrial Survey of South Wales. 3 Vols. H. A. Marquand 1937.
125 History of Wales. John Dower 1993.
126 Rebirth of a Nation Wales 1880-1980. K. O. Morgan 1981.
127 Wales Between the Wars: ed. Herbert Jones 1988.
128 A Collier Boy in the 1926 Lock-out. Edwin Greening, Old Aberdare Vol. 8.
129 Census Report.
130 Glamorgan 1921-1931.
131 Census of Occupations 1921 and 1931.

Appendix C

Glossary of Mining Terms

A

ADIT A near-horizontal entrance to a mine, usually acting as a drain from it. It could also be used for ventilation or transport purposes.

ADVANCE HEADING A small exploratory drivage, driven to assess the condition or distance of, for example, a fault or old workings.

AFTERDAMP The deadly mixture of gases following an explosion in a colliery. Mainly composed of carbon monoxide, It could kill more miners than the explosion itself.

AIR BRIDGE Also called 'Air-Crossing'. Where intake and return airways cross, they are kept separate by taking one, usually the intake, over the other.

AIR COMPRESSOR Designed to compress air into a piped system for the purposes of driving tools and machinery for boring holes, pumping, haulage, etc.

AIR DOOR Normally in a series of doors in an airway, to be opened and closed one at a time, to prevent a short circuit of ventilation flow, from another part of the pit.

AIR-STREAM HELMET (Modern) A helmet designed to eliminate the hazard of coal dust in a mine, by using the enclosed fan, filters and airflow to direct dust from a miner's face.

AIRWAY A term used in mining for any underground roadway etc., through which air is directed, whether to faces in use or to abandoned workings, as part of the ventilation plan.

ALLOWANCES Extra payments made to a miner for extreme working conditions (e.g. weak roof; wet conditions, etc.)

ARM See 'Pair of timber'.

ANTICLINE A geological term applicable to strata which are higher in the centre than at their periphery. Opposite – syncline (q.v.)

B

BACK-RIPPING Work being done to renew supports. e.g. distortion or lowering of steel arches in 'crush' areas, outbye of coal-face.

BACK-SHIFT Afternoon or night shift. Intended for repairs to roof and sides, machine maintenance and repairs generally. (Not normally for production of coal).

BAG A flexible hose or pipe, in much use in modern coal-faces, e.g. for compressed air or water.

BALANCE PIT (Water-Balance Pit) An early method of powering the cages in a shaft. Each cage was fitted with a tank which could be filled with water when it was at the pit top. A rope or chain from the top of one cage was taken over a large pulley (or sheave) and then similarly connected to the other cage, the rope being of such a length that when one cage was at the top of the pit the other was at the bottom, and vice versa. The pulley was usually fitted with a brake. When it was necessary to raise a tram of coal to the surface it was placed in the cage at pit bottom and the tank of the topmost cage was filled until it was heavy enough to counter-balance the weight of the loaded tram at the pit bottom and raise it to pit top. The water in the descending cage was let out at the pit bottom and had to be pumped back to the surface unless it could drain from the pit by gravity.

BALL OF MINE Nodule of ironstone, normally in roof of seam. "Mine" was the old word for ironstone. So a "miner" was originally a man who dug for ironstone, not coal.

BANK The surface of a shaft, and at a level from which the pit cages are loaded or unloaded.

BANK The area around the surface of a pit-shaft, where cage stops. ("Brought to Bank".)

BANKSMAN The man in charge of the "Bank" area at pit-top and of the cage upon raising, or lowering, at pit-top. He operates the signals to the winding engine-man and to pit-bottom, from the surface.

BAR-HOOK (W. = "Ci") In the event of a journey rope breaking on a slope, the bar-hook attached behind the last tram, digs into the floor, and throws the runaway journey off the rails, and prevents a potential disaster.

BARRY The 'Barry' system is a method of complete extraction from a finished "Pillar & Stall" district. As many of the pillars as possible are mined, before the roof falls in. (Tower 4 9E. West District, in the 1950's.) B.D.

BAR-SUPPORT Normally a steel bar used for supporting the roof, held in place by posts or "props"

BASIN A geological term applicable to the South Wales Coalfield where the strata form a kind of basin. A syncline.

BAST Mudstone.

BASTARD (Clift) A strong mudstone, but not sandy enough to be called rock. Also called 'Bastard Rock'.

BILLY FAIRPLAY A machine for weighing the amount of small and large coal in a tram, pleasing most colliers, adopted by all collieries eventually (also known as "Billy Catch"). According to his biographer, it was invented by John Nixon, but it has been said that the inventor was a local man, and that "Billy" was in use locally long before Nixon came on the scene.

BLACK BAND Ironstone, with an amount of carbonaceous matter.

BLACK DAMP A gas consisting mainly of Carbon Dioxide (CO_2.) and Nitrogen (N_2), normally found in sumps and at floor level. It would extinguish a lamp flame. Also known as "Choke-Damp", or "Stythe". It is colourless and odourless, and will not support life.

BLACKLEG Strikers' term for a strike-breaker.

BLACK PAN A weak friable roof that collapses immediately it is exposed. Roof supports have to be very close together in order to prevent a bigger fall, eg. Tower no 2—Wembley District, 1953's—9' seam.

BLAST Compressed air, used for boring rock or coal, movement of coal cutters and other machines and pumps. The word is almost certainly derived from the compressed air used in the blast furnaces.

BLOCK (1) A wooden shaped device used in haulage systems; normally to hold trams against a gradient; (2) An offcut of pitwood taken home by a miner for firewood.

BLOCK-LAYER A man skilled in laying rail-track in a pit. (He could well be called in a mining community as "Dai Blocks") It seems likely that this derives from the man who put in place the stone blocks which supported the plates of the earliest tramroads.

BLOWER An outburst of gas, usually methane, which issues from a crack in floor, sides or roof. Dangerous but usually can be controlled by localised fan or brattice hurdle. Blowers are likely near a fault plane.

BODGER "Podger" in South Wales. Also called 'Tommy-Bar'. A lever or lifter bar.

BOMBY An improved tram, with no holes etc. thereby preventing the dropping of fine coal-dust underground. (an explosion hazard). Slightly larger than a normal tram. A local name. Worked in Dyllas drifts in 1920s. Tower in 1950s.

BOND When a cage ascends a shaft the actual journey made is called a bond, e.g. "The manager went up in the last bond".

BORD The main cleat (q.v.) in a coal seam. Coal that separates or splits along that line of cleavage.

BORD & PILLAR A northern name for the "pillar and stall" method of mining a seam.

BOWC (Welsh) A bucket or vessel used when shaft-sinking, for transporting of men and materials.

BRASS (also "Brasses") Iron pyrites, a brass like, hard metal, occurring in, or adjacent to, coal seams. (A possible danger of sparking when struck by a cutter-pick; hard bands or nodules, rich in pyrite.

BRATTICE CLOTH A kind of plastic sheet for covering ventilation doors; also for directing air-flow into places of working. Formerly made of tarred hessian. (In the Cynon Valley pronounced "Braddish").

BRATTICE-MAN An older workman, who erects brattice in a district.

BRIG (Welsh) Locally pronounced 'breeg'. The last stubborn piece of a "slip" of coal. An experienced collier would "go for the brig", making it easier to extract the next "face-slip". (Pre machine mining, hand-got).

BWGI (Welsh) A small tram used for the repairs of restricted airways, originated in Blaencwm colliery, Treherbert, with much usage in the Cynon Valley.

BUTTY Mate; partner; friend; collier's helper or boy.

C

CA-CANNY A form of industrial action, possibly of Scottish origin, and means 'going slow' in a dispute.

CAGE The pit carriage, for the descending or ascending of a shaft.

CANCH The face of a ripping; a breaking into overhead strata; also called "a rippings".

CARTER A boy or girl, wearing a chain and girdle, to draw (pull) the small carts of coal underground. This method used in low seams (19th century).

CAP See 'Gas Cap'.

CARLLUSG (Welsh) (or Cartllusg) An early means of transporting coal, or ore, in or from a level consisting of two shafts for a horse, joined at one end by a platform, i.e. a drag-cart.

CHARGE-HAND (Beltman). A man employed in maintaining and extending conveyor belts, or armoured face conveyors.

CHECK (Lamp-check). A brass token used to prove a miners presence in the pit. Also called a tally. Normally hung in the lamp room, until his lamp is returned.

CHECK-WEIGHER A man appointed to check weight of coal in a tram, and to record that tonnage for the collier who cut that coal. (He would also assess the weight of small coal, and possibly crop the collier, i.e. deduct a sum from his wages.

CHOCK Also known as a cog. A roof support constructed of interlaced horizontal wooden pieces, laid from floor to roof.

CHOCK (Hydraulic) These are steel cogs, fitted with hydraulic supports, made to be pumped against roof. Attached to face conveyor, they are lowered and advanced as the conveyor advances. Cycle repeated every cut of the coal-face. They provide end to end cover in a modern coal-face.

CHOKE-DAMP See 'Black-Damp'.

CLEAT Also known as 'cleavage'. Plane, found at different angles between floor and roof in a seam, along which the coal tends to split readily.

CLIFT-(TOP) The roof of a seam that is composed of very solid, strong strata. Favourable for 'Pillar & Stall' method of mining. ('Blocky' mudstone).

CLOD Thin layers of mudstone directly above a seam of coal, normally it falls with the coal during mining.

COG (Welsh: cogyn) (see "chock"). Filled with rubble if permanent.

COLLIER A hewer; a capable skilled man who cuts the coal from the coal-face, fills it into trams or conveyor, supports the roof, and carries out other numerous tasks. Highest paid workman. (See "cycle of coaling").

COLLIER'S ASTHMA Mining community's name for the dust related diseases of the lungs, e.g. Emphysema, pneumoconiosis, silicosis.

COMET (Early). A naked light used to illuminate main roadways below ground.

COMPRESSOR A machine used for pressurising air (called "blast"), which is used as a power source for the driving of machinery, boring holes, fans, lighting etc. Compressed air is stored in a sealed tank until required.

COPYN (Welsh) A hard cloth cap worn by miners.

CRAMP A square section nail (or pin), which firmly secures a rail to wooden sleepers.

CREEP Gradual, imperceptible movement of lift of floor or roof when friable or damp in nature, (see "pwcins").

CREEPER An endless chain type of conveyor, with lugs, fitted to engage a tram's wheel-shafts and haul it, normally up a gradient. Common usage: screens, washeries etc.

CROP (OUTCROP) When a coal-seam or ironstone vein emerges on the surface.

CROPPING Excess of coal or rock left sticking to roof of seam, which needs to be removed manually, after being undercut by coal-cutter.

CROSS-CUT A wood-saw. A link-up roadway connecting two other parallel drivages, usually for ventilation or supply purposes.

CROSS-MEASURE DRIFT An underground tunnel (not from surface), which is driven through strata from one seam to another required seam.

CRUSH Pressure from weakened roof causing the crumbling of pillars of coal or the sides of the roads. (Extra roof supports and cogs erected quickly might halt a crush).

CURLING-BOX (Welsh: bocs cwrlo) A three-sided metal box with a base and holes cut for handles, used for dragging loose coal from coal-face to a dram and emptying directly into dram, (used from 1800s. A hard start for young boys).

CUT The space left after coal-cutting machine has passed—whether early jib-cutter or modern disc-type cutting machine).

CYCLE The sequence of all operations in coal-face, whether "hand-got" (manually), or "power-loading" with machine cutting and loading. (24 hour cycle normally).

CYCLE (OF COALING) (Period 1930s to 1960s).

1. In a mechanised coal-face, the jib type coal cutter undercuts the seam from end to end—(night-shift operation by two cuttermen).
2. The coal is then cleared by shovel (hand got) by colliers on the following dayshift, leaving a supported vacant track through the face ready for the next cut.
3. The "shifters" and "packers" arrive on afternoon shift. They dismantle the armoured conveyor and re-assemble it in the vacant track. The packers then erect safety packs of rubble through the face.
   The cycle is then resumed the following night-shift.

D

DAMP A term applied to a dangerous gas, e.g. fire-damp.

DAVY Safety lamp invented by Sir Humphrey Davy in 1815. His gauze principle was the fore-runner of the modern safety lamp.

DAY-WAGE MAN A worker paid the same rates daily or weekly. Not on contract work.

DEAD WORK Work that is non-productive, e.g. repairing weak roof, cutting bottom "squeeze", laying of tramways, etc. A collier would receive extra payment for such work.

DECK The floor of a pit cage. Single deck originally, now double or triple-decks are common.

DEPUTY A qualified official (also called of fireman) who is legally in charge of, and responsible for, his district, and all its activities, including production, safety, supplies, ventilation, etc., under the regulations and the "Mines and Quarries" Acts.

DEPUTY'S PROBE Similar to a walking stick, this is used for taking an air sample from the roof cavities, with the aid of a rubber injector bulb. The sample is injected into the official's lamp. He then estimates the percentage of methane present in the cavity from the height of the gas "cap" above the flame.

DINT The cutting of floor in headings, for increasing the height following floor "squeeze", (see "pwccins")

DIP Working a seam to the "dip" means working down-hill, as opposed to working the "rise", uphill.

DIRT Any layer of clay, stone, etc, other than coal, within a seam.

DISC-CUTTER Revolving, spiral drum machine which traverses modern coal-faces from end-to-end, giving continuous output as and when required. (Not hand filled).

DISTRICT The area in a colliery that is legally under the supervision of a mine deputy.

DRWSWR (Welsh) A door-boy. A boy whose job underground was to open and close ventilation doors, to allow the passage of horses and trams, etc. (No boy under the age of twelve was allowed underground after 1862).

"DOSCO" (Firm name). A tunnelling, advancing cutter machine with in-built conveyor mounting.

DOUBLER Working an extra shift following a normal shift.

DOUBLE-PARTING (Welsh: partin dwpwl) A roadway containing one tramway enters a section of a wider roadway containing two sets of tramway. It is a transfer area where a full "journey" of coal is deposited and another "journey" of empty trams is ready to be taken to the coal-face.

DOWNCAST A ventilation shaft, drift or level, where fresh air is drawn (or forced) into the workings, (see fan).

DRAM (Welsh) A soft mutation of "tram"—common usage in Cynon Valley mines. Early drams, wooden on iron frame, designed for a ton of coal when "raced". (See "race").

DRIFT An entrance tunnel into a mine, which is driven through strata and seams into the required seam. Normally at a downward inclination.

DRILL (Welsh: dril) Various types.

1. Early: sharpened, pointed iron bar turned by one man, while another strikes it.

2. Later:- A "breaster" type—manual again. One man only with an iron "cross" against his chest and a handle between the cross and the iron drill. Body pressure applied whilst turning the handle (from 1850s to 1960s).

3. Compressed air ("blast"). Type of boring machine (percussive or rotary).

4. Electrical boring machine.

DRIVAGE An advancing heading (tunnel) in a mine. It could be exploratory or for development.

DUFF Fine coal fragments left in a layer on the floor of a machine cut coal-face, following the completion of a "cut". To "duff-out" the collier has to shovel the duff from the track space between conveyor and the cut face of a seam. He then has to shovel from the cut itself. (This is about 4 inches high at the base of seam). This then allows coal to collapse and be filled out.

DUMB DRIFT In this alternative method of furnace ventilation, a drift is made from a place a suitable distance from the bottom of the upcast shaft. This drift is inclined and joins the upcast shaft. The furnace is placed at the lower end of this "dumb drift" and is fed with "clean" air from the downcast shaft or by any other suitable method. The hot air rising from the dumb drift passes into the upcast shaft and draws to the surface the foul air from the vicinity of the pit bottom.

DUMP An underground transfer point, outbye of faces, where coal is transferred from conveyor to a journey of trams or a larger conveyor.

DUST SUPPRESSION In about 1872 French mining engineers and chemists formed the view that coal dust might be the chief source of damage in a colliery explosion. Tests subsequently proved that this was the case and the attention of mining engineers was then directed to the means of suppressing the coal dust which was formed in the getting of coal. The spraying of water either before, during or after coal cutting and after shot-firing (known as "wet cutting") was found to be a useful expedient, as was "chemical damping". Perhaps the most successful method was the use of stone-dust which was spread on shelves which were upset by the disturbance of the air generated by an explosion. The stone-dust was chemically inert, and when mixed with the coal-dust it acts as a barrier between the particles of coal and prevents the almost instantaneous progression of the originating flame through the workings.

E

EXPLOSIONS An explosion is caused by the ignition of combustible firedamp gas, [a mixture of methane (predominant), carbon monoxide, nitrogen, ethane, carbon dioxide] and air. Firedamp and air mixtures can only be exploded within a definite range. The lower limit of the range is 5.4% and ends at the upper limit of 14.8%. There is a greater chance of an explosion when the percentage is about 9% methane, and air. A more serious type of explosion is the coal-dust explosion, which is caused by very fine dust particles being ignited in dry workings. This could be caused by shotfiring or by the spreading of a minor explosion blast wave, creating a dust-cloud which is then ignited by the initial flame of the explosion. (See also "Dust Suppression").

F

FACE The part of a mine where coal is actually mined from.

FALL A fall of roof, in a coal-face or roadway, to be secured and made safe.

FAN DRIFT A short passage or airway, connecting an upcast shaft and the main colliery fan.

FANS (Forcing). Machinery installed at the top of a downcast shaft to force fresh air through the workings. (Exhausting). A fan near the top of an upcast shaft (return), installed to extract air from a mine. (Most popular method). Small localised fans are used in districts to clear gas in a coal heading, or at the source of a "blower" of methane, (see "venturi"). "Booster Fans" are sometimes installed in an airway, in order to increase the volume of air in a particular section of a mine.

FARRIER An official and chief supervisor of stables and all horses in a colliery (surface and underground). He inspects horses on their daily return to the stable following a shift, ensuring their health and welfare.

FAULT A fracture of the strata caused by earth movement. An "upthrow" fault—where the seam continues at a higher level. A "downthrow" fault—where the seam continues at a lower level.

FIRE-CLAY A band of clay normally found adjacent to a coal-seam and sometimes worked in addition to the coal. It becomes the main constituent of brickmaking. Also used for the "stemming" of shot-holes in a mine.

FIREDAMP Inflammable gas seeping from the coal seams, the chief constituent being methane. It is lighter than air and tends to accumulate in roof cavities if the poor ventilation system is inefficient. It is colourless, tasteless, odourless and invisible. (See explosions).

FIREMAN Local name for a deputy. In the mid 1800s, the man who looked after the ventilation flue was also known as a fireman.

FIRST-AID CONTAINER A large canister hanging up in each district containing stretcher, splints, dressings, morphia injection containers etc. (Only the district deputy is allowed to carry a morphia key and has the qualifications to administer morphia).

FLAT A wooden post, cut lengthways, placed beneath roof in a coal-face and secured there by two posts, supporting that area of the face. (Set at measured distances, as stated by the support rules of the district).

FLOPMAN A percussive compressed-air ("blast") boring machine used for the drilling of shot-holes in stone, normally used in hard-headings or rippings.

FLUEMAN The man appointed to maintain a fire in the flue, (sometimes called "fireman"—early).

FOLD A geological term for complete distortion of seam or strata.

FORE-POLE Modern method of securing a weak roof area in a coal-face. The method involved boring holes beneath roof level and in advance of seam face. Steel bars were then inserted and linked together, providing false floor and support for the bed above and securing same before next cut of cutting machine.

FURNACE VENTILATION An obsolete method of ventilation in which a fire is kept burning near the bottom of the upcast shaft, to draw air into the mine workings. Also called "flue". (For alternative see "dumb drift").

G

GAFFAR HALIAR (Welsh) A master haulier. One who directs hauliers as to their task and place of work. He would also keep records as to the condition and health of horses.

GAS A term normally used for fire-damp (methane), but it could be any gas found in the mine.

GAS-CAP The blue flame found above the lowered wick of an oil-lamp. The height of this blue flame indicates the percentage of fire-damp in the area.

GATE-ROAD In a longwall face, usually on the air intake side, it is a heading for the transporting of coal from the coal-face, normally by conveyor belt. It also provides width for a haulage transport system, for the supplying of steel arches etc., for the advancing of the conveyor head. Most electrical equipment is in the gate road in a district.

GATES (Welsh clwyti) The gates at the top of a shaft, which are automatically opened and closed with the rising and descending of the cage.

GELLIDEG Practically the lowest workable coal seam in the Cynon Valley.

GIN See "whim-gin".

GOB ("Goaf" in Northern England). The waste area left behind the advancing coal-face. Sometimes packs are erected but usually gobs are unsupported to collapse behind the current line of supports. If coal would be left behind in the gob there would be a possibility of a gob fire later. (Rare in South Wales).

GRUB-BOX A tin box, pocket size, to contain food for the miner to eat during the shift, in his "grub-time", (20 minutes). In other coalfields—"snap", "bait" and "tommy".

GUIDES Rods or ropes running vertically down a pit shaft to hold the cage steady in the shaft. They are changed by the pitman on a regular basis. (Compulsory for shafts deeper than 45 feet).

GURNI (Welsh) A small plaited thong of leather used as a whip by a haulier. Normally used in the "breaking-in" of a horse to an underground situation.

GUTTERING So-called when a weak roof in a face collapses for a certain length and leaves a cavity in the roof. This requires extra timbering above normal supports.

H

HADE The angle or inclination of a fault plane. Its deviation from the fault plane.

HAND-GOT Hand filled with shovels. System of mining a coal-face, as opposed to machine cutting and loading directly on to a conveyor, which is called "power loading".

HAULIER Pronounced "halier" in Cynon Valley. A miner who "drives" a horse to the coal-face or stall with an empty tram and returns to the "double-parting" with a full tram of coal, (pillar and stall method). In a conveyor face system he would be transporting supplies to the tail road or supply road, (up to 1970s). He is in sole charge of his horse.

HAULAGE ENGINE A steam, compressed air, or electrical type of fixed engine, surface or below ground. Used for the taking into a district, supplies for the face and returning with a full journey of coal. (For transporting of miners, see "spake").

HAULAGE PLANE The actual "run" of a journey into a particular district, its gradients, turns, etc., details that are familiar to the haulage-engine driver.

HEADGEAR The steel frame with wheels suspended over the pit-shaft, erected to raise or lower the cages. Originally timber in first half of the 19th Century, e.g. De Winton Colliery.

HEADING (Welsh: hedin) A drivage in advance of any coal-face, driven to determine mining conditions ahead; or possibly a "hard heading", driven through rock and coal at an angle to contact a seam for future production.

HEWER See "collier".

HITCHER A man at pit-bottom who operates shaft signals, (earlier pushed full trams of coal into the cage). The signals are heard by the winder and the banksman. He can also be called an "onsetter" (midlands).

HITCHING-PLATE A central strut in the floor of a base of a tram, which projects out from both ends of a tram. A hole in the plates is connected, with a "big pin" bolt, to the shaft which fits around the horse.

HOLING OUT Extracting the "duff" from beneath the coal slip in a machine cut face, (see "duff").

HOLT (Welsh: gavel) The ripping away of the roof of a previously mined underground roadway, then securing it. This increases the height of the roadway, for the passing of a tram.

HOOTER (Welsh: hwtar) Siren blowing from the colliery in the village, informing the relevant shift coming on of the time.

HORIZON MINING In a colliery, undulations, pitching and folding of coal seams may result in transport headings varying in gradient which incur extra expenditure on the underground transport of coal. This extra cost may be avoided by 'Horizon Mining' in which headings are driven (normally at a gradient of 1/500 to facilitate drainage) to intersect the coal seams or appropriate 'horizons'. Horizon cross-measures drifts were then set out through the line of dip of all seams to be worked, which were then cleared topmost first, and so on. Staple shafts (q.v.) were sunk to connect the uppermost horizon tunnel with those beneath it, and these shafts, fitted with spiral chutes, were used to fill the trams waiting at the lowest level. Horizon mining was adopted when making the underground connection between Abercynon and Lady Windsor pits and also the connection between Bwllfa and Maerdy. Horizon mining is inappropriate in a flat-seam area.

HORSE-HEADS system of angled steel bars, set to support a ripping-lip, beneath which the face workers have to pass in safety to the coal-face.

I

INBYE A word to describe the relative position of anyone in a mine e.g. "he has gone in-bye", means he has gone towards the coal-face.

INCLINE Properly 'inclined plane' meaning: (1) On the surface, a tramroad from a colliery to a spoil heap (or tip) on the mountain-side or a tramroad running from a mountain side colliery bringing coal down to a parent colliery on the valley floor with screening and transport facilities; (2) any inclined tramroad underground, usually provided with a haulage engine taking men, stores, etc., inbye and coal or rubbish outbye.

INTAKE The route taken by fresh air from the downcast shaft to the workings.

J

JACK A tin bottle with a cork, used for drinking-water.

JACK (lifting-jack) Used mainly by fitters or chargemen for the lifting of conveyors etc. A hand winch.

JIM CROW A heavy iron device—(letter "C" shaped), used by a "block-layer" for the straightening or bending of rails below ground.

JOURNEY (Welsh: shwrna) A number of coal trams linked together.

JUMP A small geological fault which does not extend beyond the full seam section.

K

KEPS Large steel catches, upon which the cage rests at the pit-top. When the cage is about to descend, the banksman releases the keps. (Known as "fans" in the 19th century).

KNOCKING WIRES A pair of signal wires, hung for the whole length of a haulage road and into the engine-house. A "rider" would signal to the engine-man to move or stop a journey of trams, on these low-current wires.

L

LAGGING Timber "slats" erected above and around the sides of wooden "pair of timber", (or steel arches in a modern mine). These would ensure no stones could fall on a man passing by.

LAMP-STATION In earlier times, it would be a place at the start of an underground district where a lamp could be re-lit on a re-lighting device, and all lamps checked by a deputy. At present there is no re-lighter, but lamps are checked and instructions issued to the workmen of the district.

LAYERING Fire-damp gas forms a layer near the roof of a roadway. Found usually, if the ventilating air-current is weak in that vicinity.

LEVEL A level is a drivage tunnel which follows the seam of coal from the surface. Other factors, such as water and roof conditions, would decide the actual pitch of the level's initial gradient.

LID A wooden block or wedge, placed above a roof support and tightened by the miner with a sledgehammer.

LINESMAN Surveyor's assistant. Main job is to ensure headings and main roads are kept straight and at the correct gradient.

LOCK-OUT An electrical safety trip that, in the event of a potential emergency, isolates the power of a conveyor or cutter. Set at intervals in a coal-face. An earlier meaning would refer to a colliery being closed by an owner during a dispute in an attempt to get the miners back to work on his terms.

LONGWALL (Welsh: "wal hir") A method of mining coal with all the colliers of that district manning one lengthy coal-face. It would have been "hand-got" earlier, and machine cut later. No "pillars" are left behind in a longwall face and roof allowed to "cave-in" behind the line of supports. Some faces would need intermediate packs if roof conditions were inferior. (Also called "longwork", earlier).

LOOSE-END A working place that has been previously worked on one side.

M

MAGAZINE A regulated building, set at a safe distance from other buildings, and used for the safe storing and distribution of explosives and detonators, which are recorded.

MAIN The main roadway (tunnel), leading to each mining district or coal-face, from pit-bottom.

MANAGEMENT OF MINES In recent years the changes in mining methods in the remaining pits has been great, and was based on the change from 'hand getting' to machine cutting. It would be surprising if this change was not accompanied by changes in the number of miners required, and a change in the number of 'officials' required. 'Official' was the generic term for all levels of management, from agent down to shot-firer (also called shotsman). Formerly, in large coal companies one or more 'Agent' would have been in charge of a group of mines. Each mine would have had a manager who was required to be properly qualified and answerable to the Inspector of Mines. The under-manager was generally responsible for the underground activities at the mine and, like the managers, was legally required to be properly qualified in respect of his duties. Each 'district' of a mine was controlled by a 'deputy' (q.v.) who was responsible for the immediate supervision of operations in his district. Up to about 1985 in the Tower Colliery there were still 'overmen' employed, one for each shift, responsible for the provision of supplies when needed, including timber for supporting the roof. The overmen of yore also had responsibility for calculating the wages due to each collier. Today at Tower, the main duties formerly carried out by the overman are carried out by a 'supervisor' and the deputy bears the name of 'inspector'.

MANDRIL (Welsh: mandral) A miner's pick, for the hewing of coal.

MANHOLE Refuge holes made in a roadway for the shelter of a person from shotfiring, or safety from a passing journey. In a haulage-place, manholes are set every ten yards. (M & Q Act).

MASTER-HAULIER An official in the stables, who organises the tasks of hauliers and checks the shifts of the horses in his care. He would also "share the turn" of the sequence of trams to the colliers. (Also called "gaffer haulier", q.v.).

MEASURING BOY A lad who measures up daily the width and height of a collier's stent, and other details of his shift's work for payment purposes.

METHANOMETER A modern device for the detection of methane gas in a mine, carried by officials.

MINE Underground mineral workings. Also, the name given to iron ore.

MINE GASES Firedamp; stink-damp; black-damp; after-damp. For "stythe" and "chokedamp" see black-damp.

MOIL To physically drag and lever a heavy object without the aid of machinery.

O

ONSETTER See "hitcher".

ON WORK An expression used when a "crush" has started on a coal-face. This is evident by noise from cracking timber supports, small stones falling from the roof, coal spilling from the sides of roadways and dusty conditions. Extra supports needed quickly or evacuation from the area of the crush.

OPENCAST As in patch working, but on a massive scale. Removal of top-soil and strata down to required coal seams, which are then shotfired and removed by immense machines. Not proven popular with local population, workforce also small as compared with deep mining.

ORE The mineral or rock containing a metal, e.g. iron ore.

OSTLER A horse attendant, works in underground stables.

OUTBYE Towards the shaft or to the mouth of a level.

OUTCROP The surfacing of a seam of coal or vein of ore, at a particular place.

OVERMAN See 'Management of mines'.

OVERVIEWER Early term for under-manager.

OVERWINDING When a pit cage is drawn up too high. (See "Cwmneol Colliery Disaster" 1855).

P

PACKS In long-wall faces, a wall of loose, available stones would be erected, and then packed tightly with loose debris. This would support roadways at the ends of the face and also direct ventilation efficiently. (At Tower Colliery, in 1950s, packs were also erected at intervals through the face). "Packer", a man employed regularly at this work. Not performed on coaling shift. (See "cycle of coaling").

PAIR OF TIMBER (Welsh: par o go'd) Wooden roof support, consisting of two arms (wooden posts), and a "collar", (to be notched with a hatchet). When erected the collar would be firmly tightened against the roof with wooden wedges.

PAN (Welsh: padell) A round mass of ore, found in the roof, which falls without warning.

PANEL-WORKING The working of a seam in an organised, planned method, and working within the rigid lines of the plan. Is also applied, loosely, to a "longwall" coal-face.

PATCH An early system of working out-cropping coal seams and iron veins. In Cynon Valley, patches were worked extensively on Hirwaun common, Llwydcoed, Abernant mountains and Rhigos area, (e.g. Bryngwyn patch).

PATCHMAN Term for a miner working a patch.

PATENT FUEL A fuel produced from colliery small mixed with other ingredients, and pitch, for binding qualities. The fuel produced in South Wales contains mostly dry steam coal mixed with a small amount of anthracite duff. Production of the renowned "Phurnacite" began at Abercwmboi in about 1942). Patent fuel was produced in Cwmbach in the 1860s by Mr. W Williams (Pantycerdin).

PIECE WORK Contract work. (Tunnelling etc.).

PILLAR AND STALL A system of mining a seam, by mining the coal in parallel "stalls" advancing onwards. (The stalls would be about 22 yards apart, depending on roof conditions and height of seam). "Cross-cuts" would be driven at right-angles every 25 yards to link up all stalls, thus leaving "pillars" of coal to support roof of district. (Could be wasteful method). (N.B. also called "pillar and bord", England). Each stall would be manned by two workmen.

PISIYN TIN (Welsh) A square of leather which fits onto a haulier's leather belt and worn over the buttocks. This protected the lower back during the lifting of a tram which had "jumped the rails", (de-railed).

PITCH The angle of slope of a seam, or of a drivage heading through strata.

PITMAN A man employed to inspect, check and repair the pit shafts of a colliery, also responsible for cage, cage ropes, guides, etc.

PIT-PILLAR An area of solid coal and rock which is not allowed to be worked. This is around every pit shaft and applies to all the seams around and below the shaft. The influence of the coalmaster could sometimes resist the introduction of pit-pillars in a lease. However, in Aberdare for the High Level Station and Abernant House (afterwards the General Hospital) were among the places supported by pit-pillars.

PLACE The portion of a coal-face allotted to a collier, also called "stent"; "stint". (e.g. "Done my stint", completed clearing coal from stent).

POUNCE A sudden loud thud in the workings, sometimes a vibration accompanying it. Caused by a settling or a splitting of roof strata which could be a long way above one. It might also create dustiness in the air.

POWDER Explosives used in a mine. ("Powder monkey"—man employed to carry explosives around a mine— expression not used in every local mine). A powder canister is a leather container for carrying explosives—not more than 5 lbs.—into a pit.

PROP (Early) Also called "post". The erection of wooden roof supports or "slip" supports. (verb: "to post" or "to prop"). By 1960s, hydraulic props were being manually pumped against roof bars of steel, with a "key". (A lever type of tool). It was also a safer, easier method of extraction.

PWCCINS (Welsh) The effect of "squeeze" (pressure) upon the floor of a district causes it to pucker up, which has to be re-cut by a miner to a new level, and the rail-track to be re-laid. ("torri pwccins" means cutting bottom).

R

RACE When a collier hand-filled a tram at the coal face, he would then 'race' the tram, by selecting large lumps of coal and erecting these on a tram as an extra wall on the rim, and filling more coal behind. This could increase his paid weight by half.

RASHING (Welsh: Rashin) A soft friable layer of stone, found in or above a seam of coal.

REGULATOR A wooden shutter in an air door which controls the flow of air inbye to a district.

RE-LIGHTER (Early). This would be kept in a district, below ground, at the "lamp-station". In the event of a miners oil lamp being extinguished, he could have it safely re-lit by an official, without opening the lamp himself. (There was one, unused, in 'Wembley' district, Tower Colliery in 1953. Bollard-shaped, made of iron.).

REPAIRER A workman employed on outbye work, repairing and replacing damaged roof supports, and generally ensuring a good state of airways, etc. (Usually an older collier).

RE-RAILER A metal device designed for the easy lifting of a tram back onto the tram-rails, following derailment. (The original type, of aluminium, was condemned by the 1950s due to a spark from it causing an ignition of gas.)

RESCUE STATION A room on the surface of a mine, kept equipped for the use of rescue teams and officers, in the event of a fire, explosion etc.

RESCUE TEAM Every colliery (N.C.B.), had a trained and qualified team from its own workforce, who were familiar with their mine.

RETURN A ventilation term. The area of a mine through which travels the foul air and gases from the workings and coal faces, on the way to the upcast shaft.

RIB A rib is the solid pillar of coal that is left alongside a coal face, in order to support the roof.

RIDDLINGS The smaller size of coal which has passed through the screens. Left after cobbles, nuts, peas and beans have been extracted. (known as "billy duff" in the anthracite area.

RIDER

1. A coal seam, usually unworkable and thin, usually taking the name of the seam upon which it lies, e.g. No.1 Rhondda rider.

2. A "journey" attendant responsible for the safe movement of a journey.

RING (local) A steel H-section arch, joined to form a permanent roof support outbye of the coal face.

ROAD A local name for a length of rail-track in a colliery. (Usage: "The tram is off the road"). Never called "off the rails". Also an alternative name for a heading, such as "supply road".

RIPPING LIP Removal of stone from above the seam, in headings, in order to create a higher heading. (At entry to coal-face.)

ROCK Hard massive sandstone.

ROOF CONTROL A department of the N.C.B., (from area level down), to advise colliery management and officials how to cope with adverse roof conditions in coal-faces.

ROYALTY A percentage of profits per ton, normally paid as a rent to the land-owner for the right to mine and take his coal.

RUBBISH A general term for any sort of debris, stone, dirt, etc. to be disposed of.

S

SAFETY LAMP See "Davy".

SAFETY POINTS A small hinged portion of rail-track, opened by the journey attendant, when his journey of trams has passed this area. (In case of a "runaway" incident.)

SCOTCH A wedge shaped block of wood placed behind and under a tram on a slope, to prevent a "runaway".

SCRAPER A bar with a disc-shaped end, used for the scraping of coal-dust out of a shot-hole, before the insertion of explosives and detonator.

SCRAPER-CHAIN CONVEYOR A heavy-duty armoured type of face or outbye moving conveyor.

SCREEN (Welsh: scrin) A housed mechanical system consisting of a number of plates each of which is perforated with holes of a size different from all the other plates. When the plates are mechanically shaken, each fragment of coal falls through a hole which it fits. In this way the coal is separated into the sizes required by the market.

SEAM One of a number of beds of coal, normally found throughout a coalfield. e.g. the nine-feet. seam. ("Rhas-las" in other valleys.)

SECONDARY ROCKS Strata that are newer than the primary, and older than the tertiary.

SHACKLE A connecting chain between two trams.

SHAFT The vertical sinking of a colliery to a required seam. Most shafts are circular in section, some being elliptical. The latter was designed to contain large pumping columns, as well as a cage, (or two cages). (See "staple shaft".)

SHALE A normally thin friable band of stone above or below a coal seam.

SHONI-DWY-GORN (Welsh) A large dark grey insect, imported into valley mines via French timber bark. About two and a half inches long, it was attracted by light, and would spring towards a miner's lamp, sometimes dropping from high timber onto a miner's neck or shoulders. Common in old workings of pillar and stall mines.

SHOTSMAN A qualified official who fires shot-holes in a district.

SINKER A specialist miner, employed for the sinking of a pit-shaft (or staple shaft). In some areas also called "sumpers", e.g. Abercynon colliery.

"SKIPPING" THE SIDES (Also termed as "scarging" or "skonging" the sides). The filling into trams of loose coal that has fallen, or is likely to fall, from the sides of a roadway underground. (Not regarded as piecework.)

SKONGE Minerals that are easy to mine due to their proximity to a coal-seam being worked, e.g. iron vein adjacent to a coal-seam. A word also used loosely by a collier while throwing loose lump coal into his tram from an area outbye of his face.

SLACK TIMES The period when collieries would close due to a market slump. (It could signify "haulage ropes are slack and not working".

SLAG Properly, the waste material produced in iron making, consisting of limestone combined with the impurities in the ore, such as sand, clay, etc. The term is used loosely for the shales, etc., which the miner discards and which are brought out of the mine and heaped up in "tips" on the surface, known to the miners as "spoil heaps", "rubbish tips" and, incorrectly, "coal tips".

SLANT A mine roadway turned at an angle from the main roadway, probably to the "dip" of a seam.

SLEEPER Wooden rail supports between rails and floor. The rails are firmly secured to these with a steel "cramp". Steel sleepers have been used in the last 40 years.

SLIDING SCALE A method of providing for wages of miners to vary automatically in line with the selling price of coal. (Commenced late 1800s.)

SLIP See "cleat".

SLUSHER A drag shovel or bucket type of container using a "main and tail" rope system which drags coal or rubble from a heading face, to be unloaded onto a conveyor or tram.

SMALL A generalised term for smaller sized coal, as used in coal-fired power stations, etc.

SNORE When a pump has completely cleared a body of water, it is commonly said "to be on snore". (The suction end of the column emits a snoring noise, which confirms this.)

SPAKE A journey of man-riding trams with seating facilities, used to carry men into and out from, their working districts.

SPELL (Welsh: spel) Having a short rest from the hard work one is performing.

SPLIT A division of the air current.

SPOIL TIP See "slag".

SPOUT HOLE A small cutting through the seam from one "stall" to the next, for ventilation or exploratory purposes.

SPRAG A piece of wood (4"x12"), tapered at each end and inserted between the spokes of a tram wheel to stop the tram or to prevent it running away when on an incline. Used frequently with horse and tram system, on steep tram roads and sharp turns. Also refers to a temporary prop, erected to support a ripping lip until a permanent steel arch is stood.

SQUEEZE The increasing pressure of a weak roof in mine workings, detected by the crushing of timber supports and the bending of steel arches—sometimes accompanied by audible cracking of roof strata. Normally a slow process.

STABLE A regulated area of roadway for the safe keeping of horses below ground. White-washed, drained, clean, and ventilated with a fresh water availability, and ostlers for the general care of the horses.

STABLES Are situated at the "gate-end" and "tail-end" of a longwall coal-face, large enough to contain machinery and conveyors, and also for the turning around of a mechanical coal cutter. It is an area which advances with the coal-face.

STALL See "pillar and stall".

STAPLE SHAFT An underground shaft that connects from one seam to another seam below. Usually vertical, it can be used to transport coal by chute or trams, to an existing transporting system in the lower seam.

STEAM COAL Produced primarily as the most efficient fuel for the steam engine. Aberdare steam coal was famous for its slow burning qualities, smokelessness, low ash content with less "clinkering" (binding) of the residue ashes, and efficient calorific value. It was classed, especially from lower Cynon Valley, as "first admiralty coal".

STEAM VENTILATION Early method of assisting the ventilation of a colliery, by the blowing of steam up a shaft (1850s), e.g. at Middle Duffryn Colliery, Cwmbach.

STEMMING Clay or other inert material, used to pack behind the explosives in a shot-hole.

STENT The amount of yardage of coal expected to be produced by a collier in any one shift. The word stent was normally applied to longwall face system of work. (20th century.)

STINK DAMP A gas, mainly composed of sulphuric hydrogen, (could be fatal).

STINKING VEIN A local term for the No. 2 Rhondda seam, so-called because of the smell from the sulphurous nature of the seam, especially so in lower Cynon Valley and parts of Rhondda.

STONE DUST An inert, ground stone dust, (produced in Penderyn). This would be scattered throughout mine workings, in order to reduce the possibility of a coal dust explosion, which could occur following a gas explosion. A man (sampler) is employed in collecting samples of floor dust, which would be analysed in a laboratory regularly.

STONE-DUST BARRIER A series of shelves with planks heaped with dry stone-dust, lightly resting on them. The blast wave of a gas explosion would travel in advance of the flame, scattering the shelves and stone-dust, thus preventing the spread of the explosion, by its neutralising, cooling, qualities.(The barriers would be about 15 yards long, placed at specified distances in the intake.)

STRIKE (Surveying.) The straight line in which the plane of a seam cuts the plane of the horizon.

STYTHE Poisonous atmosphere, generally carbonic acid. (Term not generally used in the Cynon Valley.)

SUBSIDENCE The process of strata sinking above worked-out seams. (Sometimes as far as the surface strata, which affects surface buildings' foundations.)

SUMP An extension downwards at the bottom of a pit-shaft to contain the water that seeps down the shaft. It would then be pumped to the surface.

SUMPER See "sinker".

SUPPORT RULES Rules as laid down by a manager for the systematic roof supporting of a coal-face or heading. A copy is given to the district deputy and is on display at the lamp-station of the district.

SWAMP A syncline area of an underground heading or face. Water normally collects in a swamp which, if long-term, would be pumped periodically.

SYLVESTER A ratchet type of pulling appliance for the dragging of heavy equipment in a colliery. It was totally banned from use by 1987, being regarded as unsafe, after about 50 years of common usage in all coalmines. (Also known as a "faker" and sometimes a "buller", it had a long history of accidents).

SYNCLINE see Basin.

T

TAIL ROPE A haulage rope attached to an empty 'journey' of trams, used for the pulling inbye of the 'journey', when the gradient is unsuitable for the free running of it towards the coal face. (A terminal sheave would control the tail rope.)

TASH (To 'Tash') To drag machinery or heavy equipment where there are no transport facilities. This could be achieved by use of a 'sylvester' or 'tirfor' device, or a horse, and is usually done in the more remote parts of the mine.

THROW The measurement of the vertical displacement of a seam in a 'fault' situation.

TIMBERMAN A workman who would 'notch' and prepare wooden posts for the securing of the roof. (Early).
A man employed for the re-timbering of the supports of an old roadway.

TIMEKEEPER A surface official who calculates the wages and stoppages of all workmen in a colliery. (Also called a 'cashier'.)

TIP The build up of pit spoil (rubble, shale, etc.) near the surface of a colliery or iron mine.

TIPPLER A mechanical device used to tip trams of coal on to the screens of a colliery.

TON Imperial term of weight of coal etc. (20 hundredweights [cwts.] 2,240lbs. to a ton). Prior to metrication.

TOP Commonly used in mines to describe the roof of a seam or vein, e.g. "The top needs extra supports"

TORRI (Welsh) To cut. (As in "pwccins", or 'coal'.)

TRAM (Welsh = dram) A small wheeled truck, used for the transporting of coal or other materials from the face to the surface or vice versa.

TRAMMER Two boys or girls, who pushed trams, filled with seven hundredweights of coal (19th century).

TROLLEY A specially shaped tram, used for carrying supplies or machinery.

TRUCKSHOP An early method of a master paying his miners and iron workers by 'tokens', to be exchanged for food and supplies in his shop only.

TUBBING The lining of a shaft during sinking, used primarily in friable, wet, or unstable strata conditions. (e.g. used at Deep Duffryn pits, Abercynon colliery etc.)

TUMBLE "To tumble an empty tram", meaning to tip the tram on its side, in order for the full tram of coal to pass it towards outbye. A "tumble-up" is a few thin posts laid down to ease the re-railing of the empty tram.

TUNNEL A subterranean passage with an entrance at each end.

TURFOR A mechanical device used for dragging machinery or switchgear into position underground.

TURN (Welsh = Tyrn) A shift at work in a colliery. (e.g. "losing a turn" means missing work for that day.)

TWLL (Welsh) A hole. Often used in a derogatory sense. ("What a twll!" meaning a bad place of work.)

TRAFFIC A name for an afternoon shift in a mine. So called originally because the shift was used for the movement of full journeys of coal from the workings to the surface and for the return of empty trams to the coal faces in preparation for the oncoming coaling shift.

U

UNDERCAST An air crossing where the intake ventilation current is bridged *over* the return road. (i.e. the 'return' airway is undercast.)

UNDER-MANAGER The qualified person in charge of the mine in the absence of the manager. (Known as 'under-viewer' in the 19th. Century.)

UPCAST SHAFT A secondary shaft that returns stale air to the surface. It normally contains an "exhausting" fan to extract this air. (Earlier—a furnace fire at shaft bottom.)

UPTHROW An upthrow is the name given to the strata which were forced upwards by the forces creating the fault.

V

VENTILATION The requirement to draw air through the workings of a colliery so as to remove the noxious or flammable gases emitted by the coal-bearing strata. Ventilation today is usually carried out by electric fans.

W

WET CUTTING The application of a spray of water under pressure from the cutter picks or otherwise when cutting coal so as to render the dust non-explosible and less susceptible to inhalation by the coal miner.

WHIM GIN A drum and rope used in early collieries mainly for winding in the shaft. The axis of the drum is vertical and the drum is set at a height which leaves room for the horse to walk a circular track around the drum, rotating it by means of a projecting beam to which the horse is attached.

Y

YORKS The name given to the (usually) leather straps which the miner used to tie around each trouser-leg below the knee. Curiously, no two miners seem to agree on what they were supposed to do. Some say they were intended to keep the bottom of each trouser leg dry or to prevent particles of coal on or in the miners' clothing from ending up in his boots, thereby causing discomfort. Others believe they were supposed to prevent rats running up the trousers, a suggestion which never fails to provoke a hilarious discussion.

Appendix D

Bibliography

V. Evans, 'What did you do in the War Daddy?' Old Aberdare, Vol. 5 (1988).

Rev. R. I. Parry, Early Industrial relations in Aberdare. Old Aberdare, Vol. 3(1984).

Ibid., History of Aberdare, compiled by Mr. Dafydd Roberts.

Hywel Francis, 'Society and Trade Unions in Glamorgan 1800-1987, Glamorgan County History.

Raymond Grant, Parliamentary History of Glamorgan 1542-1976, Swansea, 1978.

Henry Pelling, The History of British Trade Unionism, Penguin, 1992.

G. A. Williams, When was Wales? Penguin, 1985.

John Davies, A History of Wales, Penguin, 1993.

Ibid, Cardiff and the Marquesses of Bute.

K. O. Morgan, Rebirth of a Nation: Wales 1880-1980, U.W.P 1990.

Ibid, Wales in British Politics 868-1922, U.W.P. 1991.

David Williams, A History of Modern Wales, London, 1951.

Phillip Jenkins, Modern Wales 1536-1990, Longman, 1992.

E. P. Thompson, The Making of the English Working Class, Penguin, 1991.

G. D. H. Cole & R.Postgate, The Common People 1746-1946, Routledge, 1987.

M. Stephens, The New Companion to the Literature of Wales, Cardiff, 1998.

G. E. Jones & Dai Smith (eds), The People of Wales, Gomer, 1999.

A. H. John, The Industrial Development of South Wales.

B. Baldwin, Mountain Ash Remembered.

Ibid, Mountain Ash and Penrhiwceiber remembered in Pictures.

J. B. Lowe, Welsh Industrial Workers housing, 1775-1875.

Thomas Evans, The Story of Abercynon.

A. Trystan Edwards, Merthyr, Rhondda and "The Valleys".

A. P Barnett & D. Willson-Lloyd, The South Wales Coalfield.

Philip N. Jones, The Glamorgan Coalfield between 1881 and 1911: Some Aspects of Immigration.

Raymond Grant, Water and sanitation, The struggle for Public Health in Merthyr Tydfil.

Ibid, Cynon Valley in the Age of Iron.

Glamorgan County History Vol 5.

J. H. Morris and L. J. Williams, The South Wales Coal Industry 1841-1875.

Canon E. T. Davies, Religion in the Industrial Revolution in South Wales (1966).

D. B. Rees, Chapels in the Valley.

Brinley Thomas, The Industrial Revolution and the Welsh Language.

Edwin Greening, A History of Aberdare for Slow Learners.

Ivor Astle, History of Aberdare.

CVHS, Old Aberdare, vols 1-8.

Ibid, Aberdare, Pictures from the Past Vols 1 & 2.

Tydfil Thomas, Poor relief in Merthyr Tydfil Union in Victorian Times.

Nansi Selwood, The Story of Penderyn.

Ibid, A History of the villages of Hirwaun and Rhigos.

Thomas Evans, History of Miskin Higher.

Mid-Glam C C. Environmental Studies in the Cynon Valley.

Anthony Môr O'Brien (ed), The autobiography of Edmond Stonelake.

William Bevan, History of Mountain Ash 1896.

The Rev. J. K. Lloyd Williams, Jottings on the History of Mountain Ash.

Successively John Williams and W. G. Thomas, Surveyor's Reports to the Mountain Ash Council (1893-1940).

D. L .Davies, Children of the Mines in the Cynon Valley.

J. F. Mear, The story of Cwmdare.

Ibid,   Aberdare, the Railways and Tramroads.

W. H. Mills, Electricity in the Aberdare Valley over the last Fifty Years (Script of a lecture).

Anon, Aberdare UDC minute books (1895-1903).

Anon, Aberdare Board of Health (committee) minute book 1866-1881.

Ivor Morgan, Saint Elvan, Parish History and Churches.

The Rev Roger L. Brown, "Ruined by the Living", (To be included in a forthcoming publication "The Diocese of Llandaff in the Nineteenth Century").

Ceinwen Thomas, Tafodiaeth Nantgarw.

Charles Preece, Woman of the Valleys.

A. C .Davies, Aberdare 1750-1850.

W. W. Price, Collection.

Anon, Aberdare Almanacs, 1891-1896, 1901-1908, 1913-1919, 1922 (ACL).

John Evans, Report of the Inspector of Nuisances to the Aberdare Board of Health 1877-1883.

Anon, Aberdare's Big Week, 1930.

Father John Cahalane, St Joseph's Church Aberdare (booklet).

Ibid, Roman Catholicism in Aberdare.

Richard Arnold, Water supply in the Urban District of Aberdare.

Appendix E

Brief Histories of Main Coal Masters

The mining industry was not the result of a natural growth process but grew from the unshakeable belief in the value of the coal deposits by the early pioneers and their preparedness to take risks and sacrifices in its development. The Aberdare steam coal industry owes its existence to the courage and entrepreneurial spirit of those businessmen who were prepared to back their coal-mining ideas with the money to realise their ambitions.

The early sale coal was bituminous coal and anthracite but by 1824, the Swansea and Llanelly coal masters opened a London market for steam coal. In Merthyr, Robert and Lucy Thomas of Waunwyllt obtained a foothold in the same market for their steam coal but the subsequent sales expansion was slow and confined to the output of Waunwyllt coal. However, this changed dramatically when the steam coal industry in Aberdare received an impetus unparalleled in the history of the coal trade when the benefits of smokeless steam coal were brought to the attention of the world. This provided the opportunity for those with entrepreneurial spirit to move into a rapidly expanding industry that would provide great rewards for those who chose to invest in this field.

The following coal proprietors, with their foresight and entrepreneurial spirit, were among the leaders of the steam coal industry and in so doing placed the Cynon Valley firmly at the top of the South Wales coal industry.

Thomas Wayne

Thomas Wayne, 1810-1867, was the second son of Mathew Wayne, c.1780-1853, ironmaster and coal master of Merthyr. He gained prominence as furnace manager of Cyfarthfa, owned by Richard Crawshay who so highly thought of Wayne that he left him £800 in his will. By 1827, Wayne had established the Gadlys Ironworks and by 1837, due to his increasing age, his sons came to assist in the management of the works.

Thomas Wayne, following the example of Lucy Thomas of Waunwyllt, persuaded his father and elder brother to sink a shaft to reach the Four-Foot-Seam of steam coal. In this venture, they were assisted by the David family of Abernant-y-Groes, Cwmbach and formed the Wayne's Merthyr-Aberdare Steam Coal Co. On land owned by the David family at Abernant-y-Groes, the sinking of the colliery began in June 1837 and by December they had sunk the shaft 60 yards and reached the steam coal seam they were seeking. By December 1837, coal from the colliery was being exhibited in London.

From now on both father and son were busily employed, not only with the Gadlys Ironworks and the associated coal pits, but with the new colliery at Cwmbach. By 1839, 3370 tons of coal were sent from Cwmbach by canal to Cardiff, increasing in 1840 to 48,000 tons.

On the death of his father in 1853, Thomas Wayne became the manager of the Gadlys Ironworks which he enlarged and improved, building new forges and mills. He died 19th March 1867.

There can be little doubt that Thomas Wayne was the first to realise the importance of Aberdare steam coal and must be recognised as its pioneer.

David Williams (Alaw Goch) 1809-1863

David Williams was born in 1809 at Llwyn Drain, Ystrad Owen, two miles north of Cowbridge. In 1821 the family moved to Aberdare where he initially found work as a sawyer at the Abernant Ironworks, but soon left this for coal-mining where he started work as a haulier. With marked ability, grit and determination, coupled with a degree of luck, David Williams soon established for himself a prominent position in the South Wales coal-mining industry. In partnership with Lewis Lewis of Cefn Coed he began to sink a shaft at Ynyscynon, Cwmbach in 1842 and when Lewis gave up, he continued the project alone with the pit opening in 1843. The success led him to obtain a lease from Crawshay Bailey, Aberaman, enabling him to open another pit at Treaman (which became known as Williams's pit).

His next project, Deep Duffryn pit, Mountain Ash, although successful, proved costly, and in 1852, he sold the pit to John Nixon for £42,000. He then sank another pit at Cwmdare in 1853 which he again sold at a good profit, investing his money in land across South Wales in such places as Meidrim and Kidwelly in Carmarthenshire and Llanwonno, Trealaw in the Rhondda (Williamstown and Trealaw were named after him) and Miskin Manor.

This acquisition of wealth was carried out without infringing the rights of others and with kindness to his employees. David Wiliams did not lose touch with the working class, in fact he enjoyed close contacts with all classes of Welsh society fostered by his keen interest in Welsh literature—he was fond of composing Welsh poetry. He became a popular figure in Welsh literary circles, often presiding and adjudicating at local eisteddfodau, and tried to infuse some vitality into the National Eisteddfod. He became treasurer of the national Council for a short time, spending considerable sums of money in trying to establish the National Eisteddfod alternately in North and South Wales.

As well as supporting the Eisteddfod, he served the community in a variety of ways including being a Poor Law Guardian, a member of the Highways Board and of the Local Board of Health. He was a prominent member of the Welsh Calvinistic Methodist Church at Aberdare.

David Williams was a promoter and supporter of the first daily newspaper in Wales, the Cambrian Daily Leader, and Y Gwladgarwr, the Welsh language newspaper published in Aberdare, was established with the help of David Williams.

On 3rd August 1837 he married Ann Morgan and their early home at Ynyscynon House, Cwmbach was the resort of poets, musicians and writers.

He branched out into the Rhondda Valley and finally settled at Miskin Manor in the Vale of Glamorgan.

David Wiliams died on 28th February 1863 at Bridgend and was buried at Aberdare Cemetery.

There can be little doubt that David Williams, Alaw Goch of Ynyscynon, is a fine example of the indigenous Welsh coal master who earned the respect of his fellow countrymen for all the good work he had carried out.

David Davis, sen., of Blaengwawr (1797-1866)

David Davis was born at Llanddeusant, Carms., in 1797 and following an apprenticeship with his maternal uncle, he opened his own grocery shop at Hirwaun. He married Mary Lewis, with whom he raised ten children. As his family grew up, he was able to leave the shop in their care and moved into the coal business by leasing in 1842 a small Rhigos level from Lord Bute; With its wharf at Briton Ferry, this was sold in 1847.

Prior to this Davis had leased valuable steam-coal seams on the Blaengwawr estate, Aberaman and in 1843 he began sinking the Blaengwawr colliery which started production in 1845. He initially used the Aberdare canal for transporting his coal to Cardiff but the business was transferred to the new Aberdare Railway in 1847. His Hirwaun shop was run by his second son Lewis, and the Trecynon shop by his elder son, David. By 1851 he started sinking a new pit at Abercwmboi and moved into a newly-built house at Blaengwawr and his son David now joined him in the running of the collieries, moving into Maesyffynon House, Aberaman. Soon the Hirwaun shop was sold and Lewis Davis became the Sales Agent for the company at Cardiff.

This allowed Davis to move into the previously unexploited Rhondda Fach valley leaving his sons to control his Aberdare interests.

In protest at the high charges being levied at the Bute (Cardiff) Docks, Davis, with other coalowners, opened a new Docks at Penarth in 1865.

He died on 9th May 1866 and was buried in St. John's Churchyard, Aberdare.

David Davis, jun., (1821-1884)

Davis, jun., was a more public minded figure than his father and was deeply involved in the political life of the town. He was considered a good employer keeping the Davis collieries open throughout the 'lock-out' of 1875, and subsequently becoming a member of the Conciliation Board.

At Aberdare he took a leading part in local affairs, especially education, and was a generous supporter of the University Colleges at Cardiff and Aberystwyth.

The family were conscientious Nonconformists (Wesleyans and later Congregationalists) and patriotic Welsh-speaking Welshmen and Davis, jun., built a 'Reformers' chapel at Aberdare which eventually became Congregationalist.

Lewis Davis (1829-1888)

Although originally intended for the law, he was soon involved in his father's concerns. He was a deeply religious man and a pillar of Wesleyanism at Ferndale, to which place he moved in 1867.

He died at Mumbles on 1st January 1888.

Sir William Thomas Lewis (1837-1914), the first Baron Merthyr

W.T. Lewis was born 5th August 1837 at Merthyr. After being articled to his father, an engineer, he obtained work in the office of W.S. Clark, Chief mineral agent of the Marquess of Bute and eventually became his Chief Assistant. When Clark died in 1864, he was chosen to succeed him. The post carried a salary of £10000 per annum and an offical residence at Mardy House, Aberdare. (Now demolished and the Beeches Nursing Home erected on the site).

In 1864, he married Anne Rees, daughter of William Rees owner of Lletty-shenkin Colliery. In 1828, her grandfather Robert Thomas had opened at Waunwyllt, Abercanaid what appears to have been the first level for marketing household (as opposed to smelting) coal, and his widow, Lucy Thomas carried on the work after his death and was instrumental in opening up the Welsh steam coal trade in London.

Lewis developed a large practice as a Mining Engineer and in 1867 became a colliery proprietor, with interests at Pontypridd and Rhondda. In addition to managing the Bute pits at Treherbert, W.T. Lewis now launched out on his own account with control of the Lewis Merthyr pits in the lower Rhondda. He had further interests in the Rhymney valley, including the infamous Universal Colliery at Senghenydd.

In 1872, Lewis was instrumental in forming the South Wales and Monmouthshire Coalowners Association, whereby all the interests of the coal-owners, as well as the iron and steel industry, were combined. This organisation was set up in response to the growth of trade unionism and the increasing strikes that were affecting the industries. After playing a leading part on behalf of the employers in the 1873 strike, which saw the workers defeated, he is said to have played a major role in formulating the Sliding Scale, whereby miners' wages were determined by the selling price of coal.

In 1855, he was knighted and eleven years later he was rewarded for his service to the community with a Baronetcy. In 1911, he was created a Baron of the United Kingdom and took the title of "Baron Merthyr of Senghenydd". A statue to his honour was erected in Merthyr, near the former Merthyr Hospital. He died in 1914.

John Nixon (1815-1898)

John Nixon was born in Barlow, Durham. Following formal education he was apprenticed to John Gray, a noted mining engineer and chief mining agent to the Marquess of Bute (presumbly, this refers to mines owned by Bute in the North Country). After holding various positions, by 1839, he was commissioned to report on Lord Bute's Dowlais property and while thus engaged, he was impressed by the qualities of Welsh steam coal. In 1840 he moved to France to work for a short time before returning home. Convinced of the quality of Welsh steam coal, he exported some to France at his own expense and was able to gain several large orders.

His next step was to own his own colliery to produce coal for the French market. To this end, he obtained the lease of the Werfa property gaining access to the famous Four Foot Seam.

With William Cory as his partner, he sunk the Navigation colliery, which, with its elaborate ventilation system and up-to-date equipment, became the most important colliery yet opened in Wales.

In addition, he purchased Deep Duffryn colliery from David Williams of Ynyscynon.

Although he was energetically developing his own mining interests, whilst so doing he was largely responsible for finding and developing markets for Welsh coal, thereby creating the opportunity for the great development of the South Wales coal trade. John Nixon stands second to none in that great company of coal pioneers.

He died at Brighton in 1899 and was buried in Aberffrwd cemetery, Mountain Ash.

Thomas Powell (1780-1863)

Thomas Powell of The Gaer, Newport, Mon. was one of the first great coal-masters of South Wales. He began as a timber merchant but moved into the coal trade with collieries in the Rhymney valley.

In 1840 he moved into the Aberdare valley to exploit the steam coal with his first pit at Tirfounder striking the famous "Four-foot Seam".

His collieries in the Aberdare valley included Tirfounder, or Old Duffryn (1840), Abergwawr, also known as "Powell's Pit" or "Plough Pit" (1845); Upper, Middle Duffryn, Lower Duffryn or Cefnpennar Pit (all three were alongside the Aberdare canal), and Powell's Pit at Cwmdare, also known as Cwmdare Colliery and Bwllfa No. 3.

The increasing use of steam propulsion over wind-powered sailing ships proved vital for the South Wales smokeless steam coal trade and provided Powell with a rapidly expanding market. He quickly appreciated the value of the railways for transporting his product and was one of the leading promoters of the Taff Vale and Monmouthshire railways but not of the Aberdare railway. At a time when it was rare for a coal-master to own more than one pit, Powell stands out by the sheer scale of his business enterprise. However, not content with this great success, he moved into the Aberdare valley where he sought to gain a monopoly in the steam coal trade. In 1862, when he exported over 700,000 tons of coal, he was probably the greatest exporter of coal in the world.

At his death in March 1863, he is said to have owned sixteen collieries and employed 6,000 people and in 1864 his colliery interests in the Aberdare and Rhymney valleys, were purchased by a business consortium for £365,000. The business was renamed the Powell Duffryn Steam Coal Company Ltd., whose enterprises became world-wide and by its name perpetuated the memory of a pioneer of the South Wales coal trade.

George Elliot (1809-1893)

George Elliot was born in Gateshead and spent his early working life as a door-boy and later a collier. Successful studies enabled him to return to the colliery as overman, with further promotion following until, at the age of 29, he was manager of the deepest pit colliery in England.

By 1864, being convinced that the Powell collieries could be a paying proposition, he persuaded others to combine with him to purchase them. Thus was born the Powell Duffryn Steam Coal Company Ltd.

However, financial problems and costly litigation took place before the full legal ownership was granted to George Elliot and his partners on 10th November 1873.

He was chairman of the company from 1886 to 1889 and a director for three years before his death.

In 1874 he was created a Baronet, being thereafter referred to as Sir George Elliot, Bart. He made his home at Aberaman House but maintained seats at Durham where he had colliery interests. He was Conservative M.P. for North Durham from 1868 to 1885 and for Newport from 1886 to 1892.

A man of great energy and enterprise, he founded a wire-rope making business ; was the principal promoter of the North Alexandra Dock at Newport and, in the face of fierce opposition from the Bute estate, constructed the Pontypridd, Caerphilly and Newport railway, which opened in 1883.

The George pit, on the mountain above Cefnpennar, was named after him (opened 1881 and closed 1905) and in Aberaman, there are two street named after him and his wife—George Street and Margaret Street. St. Margaret's Church, Aberaman was built at his own expense in memory of his wife and it was opened on 30th September 1883.

Sir George Elliot died on 23rd December 1897 and is buried in Kensal Green cemetery.

The Llewellyn family

Rees Llewellyn (1851 – 1919) was the founder of the Cwmdare coal-owing family. He was born in the Rhondda and after completing his education at Bridgend Grammar School, he became an articled Surveyor at Hirwaun. In 1869 he became a Surveyor at the Ocean Colliery, Cwmparc but by 1872. he was Surveyor and Under-manager at Bwllfa. In 1877 or 1878, he became Manager and by this time was an M.E.

From his new home in the old Bwllfa House, he married Elizabeth Llewellyn of Goitre Farm, Ystradfellte on 15th May 1878. From the children born to the couple, five boys and one girl survived into their adulthood.

Among these children were David Richard Llewellyn and Wiliam Morgan Llewellyn, known respectively as D.R. and W.M. respectively.

The role played by Rees Llewellyn in the early days of the Bwllfa and Merthyr Dare Steam Collieries (1891) Ltd., is not clear but it is a fact that in due course, he became the Chairman of the company. The build-up of the company was accompanied by Rees Llewellyn's own personal move into public and professional affairs. He became a member of the South Wales Institute of Engineers, President in 1897 of the Colliery Managers Association and a member of the South Wales and Monmouthshire Coal Owners Association.

At a local level he was, at different periods, a member of the Aberdare School Board, the Aberdare Board of Health, the Aberdare Urban District Council and the Glamorgan County Council -of which he became Alderman. He was High Sheriff of Breconshire and High Constable of Miskin and in 1909 was made a J.P.

He retired in 1918 and died at Bwllfa House on 21st August 1919 and was buried at Aberdare cemetery.

The many tributes paid to him after his death are clear testimony to the many qualities of Rees Llewellyn who it was claimed, " changed the history of the Bwllfa Colliery and incidentally the upper portion of the Aberdare district from one of repeated failure and hardship to success and prosperity".

David Richard Llewellyn (1879-1940)

D.R. Llewellyn, following early education locally, qualified as M.E. at Cardiff University College in 1903. In 1919, following his father's death, D.R. became Chairman of his father's company. From then on, he amalgamated companies to gain profitability.

He was involved in many colliery and shipping enterprises and was director of several large undertakings including G.K.N. Ltd.

In 1930 he formed the Welsh Associated Collieries Ltd., with the object of obtaining majority holdings in twelve mining and associated companies including Bwllfa and Cwmaman Coal Company Ltd., and D.R. Llewellyn and Sons Ltd.

He lived in Goytre, Llewellyn Street, Trecynon and afterwards at Fairfield, Aberdare before moving to Cardiff. Following his father, he was a member of Aberdare U.D.C., (including being Chairman), a J.P. and High Constable and was a generous contributor to many worthy causes.

In 1922, he was created a Baronet, with great local celebrations being held. He died on 15th December 1940 at Tynewydd, Penderyn and his ashes were scattered over the Darran, Cwmdare.

William Morgan Llewellyn (1887-1943)

Born in 1887, W.M. Llewellyn became agent to the Bwllfa Collieries in 1913, after receiving his Colliery Managers Certificate from Christ College, Brecon.

On his father's retirement in 1918, he became general manager of the collieries in his place. In the early thirties he rebuilt Nantmelin Farm and lived there until the Powell Duffryn take-over occurred, when he moved to the re-built Tynewydd at Penderyn where he concentrated on farming pursuits.

He followed his father and brother in local politics serving at one time or another as High Constable of Miskin, High Sheriff of Brecon, President of Aberdare Hospital, President of the Aberdare Horse Show, J.P., Alderman of the County of Brecon, County and District Council member and a member variety of other professional bodies.

He was well liked and popular and it is not difficult to find evidence of this - even amongst trade union and political leaders.

He died on 19th September 1943 in London, after a short illness.

Thomas Joseph

Thomas Joseph, the son of Morgan Joseph of Cyfarthfa, was born in Merthyr Tydfil. He started in the coal industry in 1842, by working in a level at Dan-y-Deri, Merthyr Vale with Samuel Thomas, a Merthyr grocer.

The partnership flourished and in 1842 they sank the Ysgugorwen Pit at Aberdare to be followed with Bwllfa Colliery (Bwllfa No 1) at Cwmdare, but soon the partnership split up with each partner going his own way. By 1851, Thomas Joseph who had lived in Hirwaun, was now to be found living in Mill Street, Trecynon with his wife, Louisa, herself born in Hirwaun and their infant son, David. During the 1850s, Samuel Joseph developed the Dunraven collieries in the Rhondda, which he eventually sold to a new company, the Dunraven United Collieries Company, although he remained as managing director.

In 1854, while still living at Trecynon, Thomas Joseph was elected to the first Board of Health in Aberdare, polling 937 votes and coming second to David Davies, Blaengwawr.

It appears that sometime after this, Joseph moved his family out of Aberdare and they established themselves at Barry, Treherbert and Pontypridd where Joseph died at his residence in Court-House Street. His death and burial (at Cefn Cemetery, Merthyr) took place in early July 1890. Thomas Joseph was involved in many industrial enterprises (not all of them successful). He was regarded as an authority on the South Wales coalfield and wrote many valuable papers on the mining of coal and ironstone. Little further knowledge concerning him and his family has come to light.

Samuel Thomas (1800-1879)

Samuel Thomas, born 1800, was the eldest son of John Thomas of Magor, who had moved to Merthyr about 1790 and who became haulage-contractor to the Crawshays. Samuel was educated at Cowbridge and became a shop-keeper at Merthyr before turning to the coal industry in 1842. He married as his second wife, Rachel, daughter of Morgan Joseph of Merthyr Tydfil and by her had seventeen children. The fifteenth was D.A. Thomas, born at Ysguborwen in 1856, who was to become the first viscount Rhondda.

Samuel Thomas in partnership with his brother-in-law, Thomas Joseph, was responsible for the sinking of many pits in Aberdare. See paragraph above on Thomas Joseph.

Samuel Thomas followed Joseph to the Rhondda valley, sinking pits in Clydach Vale in 1878 which was to form the basis for the of the Cambrian Combine that was later further developed by his son, D.A. Thomas, M.P.

In 1858, he was elected to the Aberdare Board of Health, following in the footsteps of his brother-in-law.

Samuel Thomas died in 1879.

David Alfred Thomas (1856-1918)

D.A. Thomas was born at Ysguborwen, Aberdare on the 26th March 1856.

He was educated at Dr. Hudson's School, Clifton, Bristol going on to Gonville and Caius College, Cambridge where he gained a B.A. in 1880, an M.A. in 1883 and a Hon. Fellow in 1918. He started work at Clydach Vale at 23 years of age to study coal mining at first hand at his father's colliery.

In June 1882, he married Sybil Mgt. Haig of Pen Ithon, Radnorshire—they had one daughter.

Up to 1906, his real interest was in politics, topping the poll four times as Liberal Member of Parliament for Merthyr Tydfil. However, success at Westminster was to elude him and in 1906, after the Liberal 'landslide' victory, when Cambell-Bannerman did not give him an office, he turned away from politics, concentrating all his energy on the Cambrian collieries.

The amassing of a fortune was to prove the substitute for political success and in a few years a series of shrewd deals led to the establishment of the Cambrian Combine with a capital of £2,000,000.

His capitalist appetite and his taste for sharp polemics brought him frequent clashes with the militant leaders of the South Wales Miners' Federation.

Plans for Anglo-American industrial combination and the opening up of the remote north-west of Canada were included in the wide scope of his plans as a captain of industry. However, empire building in the business world was not to be his chief claim to fame. After an important mission to America in 1915, Lloyd George made him a peer—Viscount Rhondda; in December 1916, he was appointed President of the Local Government Board and in June 1917 he became Food Controller.

Thus we see him back to his first love, politics and he proved to be an outstanding success as the architect of a great socialist experiment—food rationing.

Viscount Rhondda had a boyish zest for life and a remarkable capacity for man-management. However, apart from his towering influence on the development of the South Wales coalfield, he was not involved in any way with the national life of Wales.

He was a true Victorian individualist who believed that life was a tournament offering glittering prizes to the enterprising. D.A.Thomas had little direct contact with Aberdare, apart from having been born there but he played an important part in the building of the South Wales coal industry. This, it can be argued, directly contributed to the success of the industry in the Cynon Valley. He will chiefly be remembered for his masterly administration of the food supply in Great Britain during the dark years of World War 1.

On the 3rd July 1915, he died of heart failure at his home at Llan-wern, Mon.

Crawshay Bailey (1789-1872)

Crawshay Bailey (1789-1872) of Nantyglo and Aberaman was an iron-master and M.P. He was the younger son of Joseph Bailey of Wakefield and Susannah, sister of Richard Crawshay, iron-master, of Cyfarthfa. At about twelve years of age, he left Yorkshire to join his older brother, Joseph, at Cyfarthfa and to assist at his uncle's iron-works. Following the death of his uncle in 1809, he was bequeathed the sum of £1,000. Little is known of his next few years, but it is likely that he remained for some time in Merthyr and he may have accompanied his brother when he commenced work at Nantyglo in partnership with Mathew Wayne in 1811.

It is certain though that he took over Wayne's partnership, when he departed in 1820. From then on the two brothers co-operated in developing the Nantyglo works and, later the Beaufort works.

A tradition existed for some years in the Rhymney area that he was also the owner of the iron-works there until about 1825 and this appears to be corroborated by the Crawshay papers, now in the National Library of Wales. It seems that his cousin William Crawshay 1 of London who was then proprietor of Cyfarthfa, for reasons not known, prevented Crawshay Bailey from continuing in possession.

Crawshay Bailey constructed the tramway from Rhymney to Bassaleg, which appears to confirm that he was in fact connected with the Rhymney iron-works.

During 1835 when the Calvinistic Methodists Association of South Wales held its quarterly meeting at Salem, Nantyglo, Crawshay Bailey, who was an Anglican, provided hospitality for the Moderator and five leading ministers. This was possibly in gratitude to the denomination which had decided in its Association at Tredegar on 19th October 1831, the year of the famous Merthyr Riots, that no trade unionist could be admitted to church membership.

Although generally accepted as a great iron-master, Crawshay Bailey distinguished himself from the others by his forward-looking attitude to the future of the coal industry. He realised quite early, the wealth that could be generated from the development of the South Wales coal basin, many large areas of land at their agricultural value, including land at Mountain Ash, Aberaman and the Rhondda.

The Aberaman estate had been the home of generations of the Mathews family and had been used as a summer resort by the descendants of Anthony Bacon. It was from the executors of Anthony Bacon 11 (died 1827) that Crawshay Bailey bought the estate in 1836, conveyed to him by indenture dated 17th February 1837.

Lying beneath the land were some of the finest seams of coal in the world, and also iron, but nothing had been done to develop them. Another nine years would pass before he appeared to make use of his purchase and during this time he continued to live at Nantyglo.

Meanwhile, collieries had been at sunk at Cwmbach, alongside the Aberdare canal, but Crawshay Bailey waited until the valley seemed ripe for a railway. Then in 1845, together with Sir Josiah Guest, he obtained a Parliamentary Act to build the Aberdare Railway to connect with the Taff Vale Railway at Abercynon (then known as Navigation). Leaving his nephew in charge of the Nantyglo works, he moved to Aberaman and work started in earnest with the sinking of the Aberaman colliery and the construction of blast furnaces and all the necessary other buildings for an iron-works.

By 1st August 1846, the railway was opened and leased to the Taff Vale Railway from 1st January 1847. By the first week in May 1847, a quantity of iron was puddled for the first time at Aberaman.

Crawshay Bailey had by now become involved with his adopted community and was appointed High Sheriff of Brecknock in 1837 and of Monmouthshire in 1851.

In 1846, he promoted the formation of the Aberaman and Aberdare Gas Company and in 1854 he became a member of the Aberdare Board of Health on its foundation. He contested and won five Parliamentary elections for Monmouth boroughs, which included Newport, being its M.P. from 1852 to 1868.

He continued to be a great promoter of railways, which also helped him financially by creating a demand for iron rails. Besides the Rhymney to Bassaleg tramway and the Aberdare Railway, he made a new tramway from Beaufort and Nantyglo down the Clydach Valley to Llanfoist where it joined the Brecon and Abergavenny canal. In 1852, he promoted a railway from the Forest of Dean, by Coleford, Monmouth and Usk to Pontypool.

He conveyed by indenture dated 2nd February 1867, the Aberaman estate with its collieries, iron-works, brick-works, private railway etc., to the Powell Duffryn Steam Coal Co., at an aggregate price of £123,500. By 1869-70, the Nantyglo works had been disposed of and Crawshay Bailey retired to Llanfoist House, Monmouthshire.

He died 9th January 1872, leaving an only son as his heir, Crawshay Bailey 11 of Maindiff Court.

William Crawshay II (1788-1867)

Richard Crawshay (1739–1810) a very successful and resourceful entrepreneur, under whom the Cyfarthfa ironworks prospered and became the largest of their kind in the world. Although his son, William Crawshay I did not follow in his father's footsteps, William Crawshay II, his grandson certainly did. He became the very epitome of an Iron Master.

In about 1813, his father placed him in charge of the Cyfarthfa Ironworks rather than managing the works himself, preferring to remain in London. Under his control the works prospered and rapid and significant expansions were undertaken. When he took over control there were six blast furnaces in operation, each having an average yield of sixty-five tons: by 1845 there were eleven furnaces in blast each now having an average yield of eighty tons.

He was given to flamboyant radicalism and the Merthyr Rising of 1831 proved to be an embarrassment to him.

Although he expanded Cyfarthfa works, his nearby rivals, Dowlais works were proving to be more flexible in adapting to technological changes taking place in the industry. But he was among the first of the Iron-masters to see the advantages in the growing coal trade. He also took an interest in the family's Hirwaun Iron-works where improvements and developments took place under his guidance. In 1825 he sank the first balance pit in South Wales at Winchfawr, near Heolygerrig on the outskirts of Merthyr.

By the time of his death in 1867, the total annual iron yield had reached some sixty thousand tons, with a workforce of five thousand people with an average wages bill of £30,000. In addition, the company also owned ten iron ore mines, eight collieries and land containing six miles of railways.

During his early years he lived at Cyfarthfa House within the works complex and at Gwaelod-y-Garth, but in 1825 he ordered the building of Cyfarthfa Castle, the mock-Gothic house on the outskirts of Merthyr. This still stands as a memorial to the family.

William II married three times. Firstly to Elizabeth Homfray by whom he had three children. Secondly in 1815 at Chepstow, he married Isabel, eldest daughter of James Thompson of Kendal who died in 1827 after bearing two sons and seven daughters; and thirdly to Isabella, sister of Richard Thompson of the Rhymney Ironworks, who bore him one daughter.

William Crawshay II died in 1867.

Appendix F

Cynon Valley Coal Output Figures from 1844 to 1988

Preliminary Note

Despite intensive searching and personal enquiries, it has proved very difficult to obtain accurate coal output statistics for the Cynon Valley, separate from the remainder of the coal-field. Therefore, the following notes are provided for the reader to ensure that the figures given are to be read and examined with some care.

From 1844 to 1860 inclusive, the figures have been taken from the Mineral Statistics of 1860. The statistics from 1860 to 1897 have been taken from the following publications: R. Hunt, Minerals Statistics 1857-1882 (Parish Returns); 1882-1897, Cardiff and Channel Tide Tables and Almanack; and 1883-1898 (Valley Statistics).

In both cases the figures given should be regarded as an accurate record of the coal output for the Cynon Valley.

In the absence of detailed statistics relating particularly to Cynon Valley coal output from 1898 to 1987/88, the amounts given are estimated figures only.

The estimated figures have been calculated on the following basis:

1. Using detailed figures from the above publications, it has been calculated that between the years 1856 and 1897, the average yearly percentage output of Cynon Valley coal compared with the total output of the Glamorgan coal-field was approximately 12 per cent.

2. Using total output figures for the South Wales Coal-field, as supplied by British Coal, Llanishen, Cardiff (dated October 1988), the estimated output for the Cynon Valley has been determined.

It is hoped that the reader is provided with a continuous picture of the level of output that will at least reflect the general trends in the coal production of the Cynon Valley over the period covered in the book.

Year	Output (tons)	Year	Output (tons)	Year	Output (tons)	Year	Output (tons)	Year	Output (tons)
1884	176,953	1874	2,187,146	1903	5,058,480	1933	4,122,600	1960	2,344,440
1845	192,950	1875	1,780,518	1904	5,247,600	1934	4,220,700	1961	2,207,820
1846	223,934	1876	2,150,000	1905	5,184,360	1935	4,203,000	1962	2,321,960
1847	269,116	1877	2,004,915	1906	5,646,720	1936	4,066,320	1963	2,324,060
1848	396,378	1878	2,041,604	1907	5,997,760	1937	4,532,760	1964-65	2,359,240
1849	434,207	1879	2,057,561	1908	6,027,240	1938	4,235,160	1965-66	2,012,530
1850	477,208	1880	2,354,889	1909	6,043,680	1939	4,232,280	1966-67	1,966,140
1851	555,708	1881	2,377,607	1910	5,844,000	1940	3,882,240	1967-68	1,889,520
1852	680,259	1882	2,547,993	1911	6,024,120	1941	3,291,120	1968-69	1,740,600
1853	832,274	1883	2,825,089	1912	6,013,920	1942	3,206,760	1969-70	1,534,580
1854	1,008,807	1884	2,935,951	1913	6,819,600	1943	3,015,920	1970-71	1,402,250
1855	1,203,807	1885	2,997,780	1914	6,465,600	1944	3,689,160	1971-72	1,159,830
1856	1,450,955	1886	2,722,430	1915	6,054,360	1945	2,456,400	1972-73	1,297,080
1857	1,447,277	1887	2,997,732	1916	6,249,720	1946	2,514,000	1973-74	889,640
1858	1,408,388	1888	3,140,896	1917	5,820,960	Coal industry was		1974-75	1,035,800
1859	1,632,782	1889	3,490,695	1918	5,606,040	nationalised on 1st		1975-76	1,012,460
1860	1,754,813	1890	3,635,077	1919	5,702,640	January 1947		1976-77	934,200
1861	1,790,771	1891	3,748,204	1920	5,549,880	1947	2,725,440	1977-78	893,460
1862	2,214,455	1892	3,828,564	1921	3,668,640	1948	2,869,560	1978-79	917,600
1863	2,148,969	1893	4,072,784	1922	6,039,000	1949	2,905,000	1979-80	901,440
1864	2,048,472	1894	4,443,086	1923	6,510,240	1950	2,917,400	1980-81	943,330
1865	1,976,364	1895	No return	1924	6,130,200	1951	2,960,280	1981-82	931,380
1866	2,368,157		available	1925	5,355,600	1952	3,001,440	1982-83	859,536
1867	2,221,992	1896	4,428,154	1926	2,432,760	1953	2,996,560	1983-84	787,440
1868	2,253,225	1897	4,849,995	1927	5,550,720	1954	3,007,000	1984-85	This was
1869	2,347,278	1898	3,206,880	1928	6,397,440	1955	2,907,240		the year of the
1870	2,309,678	1899	4,784,400	1929	5,778,000	1956	2,896,800		Miners' Strike
1871	1,987,635	1900	4,719,380	1930	5,412,960	1957	2,912,280	1985-86	784,200
1872	2,247,163	1901	4,705,080	1931	4,450,200	1958	2,738,640	1986-87	777,500
1873	2,291,979	1902	4,956,720	1932	4,184,880	1959	2,543,040	1987-88	597,040

Index

CYFANSODDIADAU BUDDUGOL

Eisteddfod y Cross Inn,

TRECYNON, ABERDAR,

MAWRTH 22AIN, 1875.

PRIS TAIR CEINIOG.

ABERDAR:

ARGRAFFWYD GAN MILLS, LYNCH A DAVIES.

1875.